SAP NetWeaver®

Process Integration:

A Developer's Guide

James Wood

Bowdark
PRESS

Disclaimer

Contents

Introduction

These days, there's a wealth of information out there about SAP NetWeaver® Process Integration (SAP NetWeaver PI). Indeed, at the time this book was written, a random Google search on the term *SAP NetWeaver PI* yielded approximately 275,000 results. Of course, there's a fundamental difference between information and *knowledge*.

As we set out to write this book, we wanted to develop a holistic curriculum that provides you with the knowledge you need to become a successful PI developer and consultant. In order to achieve this, we endeavored to strike a balance between theoretical concepts, nitty-gritty details, and hands-on access using real-live examples.

We hope that you'll find the structure and organization of the material conducive to learning. So, whether you are new to PI, looking to broaden your PI development skills, or simply interested in becoming an SAP-certified PI development consultant[1], we think this book can provide you with the tools you need to be successful. Ultimately, our goal is to adequately prepare you to hit the ground running on an integration project using SAP NetWeaver PI.

Target Group and Prerequisites

In many ways, determining the target audience for this book was a difficult challenge. In over 7 years of experience working with SAP NetWeaver PI technology, we have encountered developers from all walks of life:

> ➢ ABAP™ developers who do not have much (if any) experience with Internet-based technologies such as XML, HTTP, etc.

> ➢ Experienced middleware developers looking to transition their skills into the world of SAP.

---

[1] Specifically, it will prepare you to sit for the *SAP Certified Development Associate - Process Integration with SAP NetWeaver (PI 7.1)* exam. See *http://www.sap.com/services/education/certification/certroles/certificationrole.epx?context=[[ROLE_C_TBIT44_71|]]|* for more details.

> ➢ Novice developers just getting started in their careers.

Given the diverse backgrounds of those interested in learning more about SAP NetWeaver PI, we decided to approach the writing of this book under the premise that the reader has little to no experience working with SAP NetWeaver PI and its surrounding technologies. This is especially evident in Part 1 of this book as we explore basic concepts and set the foundation for more advanced topics later on in the book.

The potential downside to this approach is that you run the risk of boring experienced developers who are already familiar with basic concepts. To guard against this, we have organized the content into distinct sections such that you can safely skip over the concepts that you are already familiar with. An added benefit of this approach is that it makes it easier to refer back to sections of the book as needed without having to dig and dig looking for answers to specific questions.

Despite our best efforts, there are certain sections of the book that require some background knowledge in order to firmly grasp the concepts being presented. For example, in our discussion on message mappings, you'll have an easier time understanding how Java™ or ABAP-based mapping programs work if you have some experience working with these languages. Where appropriate, we will supplement this content with links to relevant reference materials. In many cases, we will also point out alternative techniques which may be easier to understand based upon your skill sets.

While this book is chock full of screenshots and examples that should help guide you through the learning process, we cannot stress enough the importance of getting hands on with the development tools. Therefore, if you have access to an SAP NetWeaver PI development system[2], we recommend that you use it to follow along with the book's examples. Alternatively, you might want to look at hosting services such as *http://www.sapaccess.com*.

---

[2] Unfortunately, unlike other SAP NetWeaver products, SAP NetWeaver PI is not available for trial download on the SAP Developer Network (SDN).

Tour of the Book

One of our goals in writing this book was not to simply compile a bunch of loosely related information together into a reference manual. While this book can certainly be used as a reference in your day-to-day work, we also hope that you'll find each chapter to be an interesting read in and of itself. Though each of the chapters are designed to be self-contained, we think you'll get the most out of your experience by reading the book in order as each chapter builds upon previous concepts. The chapters are organized as follows:

➢ **Chapter 1: Foundations**
In this first chapter, we attempt to lay some groundwork by describing what SAP NetWeaver PI is, where it came from, and what value it brings to the table in the world of enterprise software development. As such, this chapter is a microcosm for the entire book.

➢ **Chapter 2: Working with XML**
For developers new to the world of interfacing in the Internet age, this chapter will introduce you to the *eXtensible Markup Language* (XML) and some of its surrounding technologies such as XML Schema.

➢ **Chapter 3: The Web Services Technology Stack**
If you're not familiar with Web service technologies such as SOAP, WSDL, and UDDI, then this chapter will provide you with a gentle overview to bring you up to speed. Having an understanding of these concepts is important for being able to comprehend how interfaces are defined and processed within the SAP NetWeaver PI runtime environment.

➢ **Chapter 4: Getting Started with the ESR**
In this chapter, we begin getting our hands dirty with the PI design time environment. Here, you will learn how to organize and manipulate SOA assets within the *Enterprise Services Repository* (ESR).

➢ **Chapter 5: Service Design Concepts**
This chapter sets the stage for service interface development by introducing you to some SAP and industry-best practices for designing and modeling business processes in the SOA context. Along the way, you will become familiar with some SOA modeling tools that can be

used to visualize various aspects of a business process at different levels of abstraction.

> **Chapter 6: Service Interface Development**
  In this chapter, you learn about the various approaches to service development supported by SAP NetWeaver PI. Here, you'll learn how to develop custom services from scratch, or leverage pre-existing services.

> **Chapter 7: Mapping Development**
  This chapter introduces you to some of the basics of mapping development in SAP NetWeaver PI. In particular, we will show you how to implement graphical message mappings and import custom mapping programs written in Java and XSLT.

> **Chapter 8: Advanced Mapping Development**
  This chapter picks up where Chapter 7 left off by showing you some advanced mapping development concepts. Here, you will learn how to define and configure operation mappings, perform value mappings and mapping lookups, and much more.

> **Chapter 9: Integration Processes**
  In this chapter, we will show you how to implement sophisticated message processing requirements using integration processes. As you'll see, these workflow-like components can be used to implement stateful processing, conditional logic, and much more.

> **Chapter 10: Working with the Integration Builder**
  This chapter introduces the Integration Builder tool which is used to define configuration objects within the Integration Directory.

> **Chapter 11: Collaboration Profiles**
  In this chapter, you will learn how collaboration profiles are used to model the endpoint systems that will participate in collaborative business processes.

> **Chapter 12: Integration Server Configuration**
  This chapter shows you how to configure collaborative business processes for execution within the Integration Server, which is an ABAP-based runtime component of SAP NetWeaver PI. Here, you will learn how to define logical routing rules and some of the other configuration-time objects used to influence the behavior of the messaging components at runtime.

- ➢ **Chapter 13: Advanced Configuration Concepts**
  In this chapter, we will introduce you to some advanced communication variants that are supported in version 7.1 of SAP NetWeaver PI. Here, you will learn how to configure local processing within the Advanced Adapter Engine (AAE) as well as point-to-point scenarios between SAP-based Web service runtime environments.

- ➢ **Chapter 14: Process Integration Monitoring**
  This final chapter presents some of the various monitoring tools provided with SAP NetWeaver PI. Here, we'll show you how these tools can be used to monitor the flow of messages, the health of messaging components, and so on.

- ➢ **Appendix A: Proxy Programming Concepts**
  In this appendix, you'll learn about proxy programming concepts. Specifically, we'll show you how to develop proxy objects in ABAP that can communicate with the PI Integration Server using the native XI protocol.

- ➢ **Appendix B: Enhancing Enterprise Services Provided by SAP**
  This appendix demonstrates techniques for enhancing enterprise services provided by SAP.

- ➢ **Appendix C: Collecting Mapping Requirements**
  In this appendix, we'll provide you with some tips for collecting mapping requirements from the various stakeholders involved in a collaborative business process.

Conventions

This book contains many examples demonstrating programming language syntax, etc. Therefore, to distinguish these sections, we use a monospaced font type similar to the one used in many integrated development environments to improve code readability:

```
public class MyMappingProgram
  extends AbstractTransformation
{
  ...
}
```

As new syntax concepts are introduced, these statements will be highlighted using a bold face font like the code snippet shown above.

How to Contact Us

If you have questions, comments, (or even complaints!) about this book, we'd love to receive your feedback. You can e-mail the author directly at *james.wood@bowdarkconsulting.com*.

We will post errata, updates, and any additional information out on the book's companion site at *http://www.bowdark.com/books/pibook*.

Acknowledgments

This project has been in incubation for the better part of two years. During that time, I would have never gotten to this point without the help of some very special people:

> First, I would like to thank Shelly Adamie, Mike Trinka, John Worley, Brande Sanson, Shaan Parvaze, and Chris Smith for their useful and informative feedback concerning various topics within the book.

> To my wife, Andrea, thank you for your tremendous support throughout the entire publication process. I would have never gotten through this without you.

> And finally, to the people who take the time out of their busy lives to contribute to the SAP Developer Network (SDN), a hearty thanks. Whenever we needed clarification or insight into different topics, we were always able to find what we needed on the SDN. It is truly amazing how far this community has come in the past several years.

Foundations 1

SAP NetWeaver® Process Integration (SAP NetWeaver PI) is a middleware platform that provides the foundation for implementing a service-oriented architecture (SOA) for business applications. As such, it has emerged as a key enabler for developing cross-system business processes both within the SAP landscape and beyond.

In this chapter, we will introduce you to SAP NetWeaver PI and show you how it is used to develop cross-system business processes. After completing this chapter, you will be able to:

- ❖ Understand the positioning of SAP NetWeaver PI as a SOA middleware platform.

- ❖ Detail the key capabilities and benefits of SAP NetWeaver PI.

- ❖ Describe the basic architecture of SAP NetWeaver PI.

1.1 Introducing SAP NetWeaver PI

Once upon a time, in the not-so-distant past when large monolithic ERP systems like SAP® R/3® reigned supreme, SAP developers were blissfully unconcerned with the complexities of distributed computing. However, over the course of the past decade or so, the landscape has changed considerably. Nowadays, with ever-increasing demands for complex business processes that span multiple systems and corporate boundaries, the need for integration is everywhere. This is where tools like SAP NetWeaver PI come in.

SAP defines SAP NetWeaver PI as "...an open integration and application platform that provides tools that enable you to create a service-oriented architecture for business applications." (SAP). The verbal imagery inspired by this definition provides you with a pretty clear overview of what SAP NetWeaver PI is all about. In particular, there is an emphasis on:

> ➢ Process-oriented and service-based integration

> ➢ Open communication based on established industry standards

> ➢ Flexible tool support for a wide range of integration scenarios

Throughout the course of this book, we'll see these core principles on display at every turn. However, before we embark on our journey into the world of SAP NetWeaver PI, it is important to first understand how SAP NetWeaver PI fits into the overall IT landscape and the SAP NetWeaver technology stack in particular.

1.1.1 The NetWeaver in SAP NetWeaver PI

From a software logistics perspective, SAP NetWeaver PI is just one of many components that can be deployed on the SAP NetWeaver technology platform. In the SAP parlance, the term "Process Integration" refers to a specific *usage type* of the SAP NetWeaver technology stack. Here, other examples of NetWeaver usage types include *Business Intelligence* (BI), *Enterprise Portal* (EP), and the *Mobile Infrastructure* (MI).

Figure 1.1 illustrates the positioning of the PI usage type within the overall SAP NetWeaver technology stack. As you can see, the PI usage type sits on top of the core NetWeaver application platform which is made up of two distinct application server types: the AS ABAP and the AS Java. Each of these application server types offer similar capabilities in terms of a development and runtime environment, enabling you to develop solutions using either SAP's proprietary ABAP™ programming language or the Java™ 2 Platform, Enterprise Edition (J2EE™). Unlike most other NetWeaver usage types, PI is implemented using components from both the AS ABAP and AS Java stacks. We'll look at some of the architectural implications of this in Section 1.3.1.

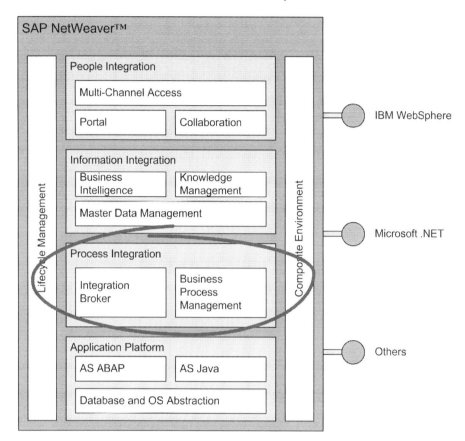

Figure 1.1: The SAP NetWeaver Technology Platform © Copyright 2010. SAP AG. All rights reserved

Looking closely at the diagram from Figure 1.1, you can see that the PI usage type brings two main pieces of functionality to the table:

> ➢ An *integration broker* that enables disparate applications/platforms to communicate with one another in a reliable fashion.

> ➢ A robust *business process management* (BPM) framework that allows you to model cross-component business processes.

The core functionality of the PI usage type is complemented by other usage types within the NetWeaver platform. For example, you can develop Web applications on the Enterprise Portal that leverage Web services deployed on the SAP NetWeaver PI platform. Similarly, there is significant synergy between the capabilities of SAP NetWeaver PI and the SAP NetWeaver Composition Environment (CE) used to develop composite applications (i.e. SAP® XApps™).

The key take-away from all this is that SAP NetWeaver PI is one of many possible usage types of the SAP NetWeaver technology platform. Here, you can mix-and-match usage types to meet the specific needs of your organization. Some IT shops run the entire SAP NetWeaver technology suite, others just SAP NetWeaver PI, and the rest are somewhere in the middle in terms of their SAP NetWeaver portfolio.

1.1.2   SAP NetWeaver PI's Position in the Marketplace

Now that you understand the role SAP NetWeaver PI plays in the SAP NetWeaver technology platform, let's take a look outside the SAP landscape and see how SAP NetWeaver PI stacks up against the competition. As an integration platform, SAP NetWeaver PI is classified as an *enterprise application integration* (or EAI) tool. Therefore, it competes with other leading integration products such as IBM WebSphere® Business Integration, TIBCO ActiveMatrix BusinessWorks™, Oracle® Fusion Middleware, and Microsoft® BizTalk®.

So how well does SAP NetWeaver PI measure up against its competitors? Well, the answer depends on who you talk to. Each tool has their strengths, so it is hard to declare a clear cut winner without a certain amount of subjectivity. However, in its relatively short lifespan, SAP NetWeaver PI has acquitted itself quite well for many SAP customers – especially when it comes to integrating SAP systems. It has also picked up quite a bit of market share in an already competitive market. Over time, SAP NetWeaver PI is likely to continue to snatch up additional market share as customers see the benefits it has to offer for integrating both SAP and 3rd-party systems together.

As a developer, you'll find that SAP NetWeaver PI compares quite favorably with other industry leaders in the most important category: *functionality*. SAP has already committed quite a bit of research and development resources towards the long-term growth of SAP NetWeaver PI, and that investment continues to grow. Indeed, in a recent address to the SAP Mentors Initiative, Udo Paltzer, the SAP Solution Manager for NetWeaver Middleware, declared that "SAP remains committed to SAP NetWeaver PI. We continue to invest in it and are planning to deliver continuous improvements through both enhancement packs and new releases." Suffice it to say that the future of SAP NetWeaver PI looks to be very bright indeed.

1.1.3   Some Historical Perspective

Surprisingly enough for many, SAP NetWeaver PI has been around for quite a while. When it was initially released in early 2002, SAP NetWeaver PI was known as *SAP Exchange Infrastructure* (or XI). At first, XI's integration capabilities were somewhat limited as SAP continued to develop the product in conjunction with some early adopting customers who provided useful feedback. This feedback proved to be quite influential towards the shape of version 3.0, which was the first fully-functional productive release of XI.

The release of SAP XI 3.0 coincided with the initial release of the SAP NetWeaver platform in 2004. This milestone proved to be a huge turning point for the product as many customers began to sit up and take notice of all the features XI had to offer. Indeed, within a year or so, there had been so much innovation with XI and NetWeaver that customers were having a hard time keeping pace with it all. Therefore, in early 2005, SAP decided to rearrange the NetWeaver technology stack to bring product version numbers into alignment and organize the constituent products into the aforementioned *usage types*. Consequently, the product formerly known as XI was effectively rebranded as SAP NetWeaver Process Integration (SAP NetWeaver PI) in Release 7.0 of NetWeaver. In this book, we will always use the product name SAP NetWeaver PI when referring to the PI usage type of SAP NetWeaver.

At the time of this writing, the current release of SAP NetWeaver PI is version 7.1, Enhancement Pack 1. Version 7.11 offers quite a few improvements in the areas of developer productivity and performance when compared with previous versions. Therefore, for the purposes of this book, we will focus our discussion on this latest release of SAP NetWeaver PI.

1.2   A Platform for SOA

Over the past several years, SAP has been working furiously to transform the SAP® Business Suite from a set of tightly bound stovepipe systems into a modular and dynamic *business process platform*. Here, the emphasis is on organizing the system(s) in such a way that businesses can mix-and-match functionality to meet their needs. In this way, customers can get more out of their investment with SAP by leveraging areas of the system that they might not have considered before due to functionality gaps, etc. Of course, the glue that binds all this together is an integration platform like SAP NetWeaver PI.

In this section, we'll look at how SAP NetWeaver PI is positioned as an integration backbone for SOA. However, rather than simply enumerating all of the features that SAP NetWeaver PI has to offer, we'll attempt a more descriptive approach. First off, we'll take a look at some prior approaches to integration and reflect on some important lessons that were learned along the way. From there, we'll segue into a discussion about the origins of SOA. When compared side-by-side, you'll see that modern SOA didn't simply appear out of thin air; instead, it blends best practices and principles discovered over the course of several decades. With these concepts in mind, we'll wrap up our discussion by examining how SAP NetWeaver PI follows this path by drawing the best traits from prior approaches and current trends to provide a holistic platform for implementing an SOA.

1.2.1 The Evolution of Middleware

In his book *Enterprise Service Bus*, David Chappell asserts that "Information is locked up in applications within different departments and organizations, and it is both time-consuming and costly to pry that data loose. *In short, the enterprise is far from integrated.*" (Chappell, 2004). A curious irony of this assessment is the fact that a large percentage of annual IT budgets are allocated towards integration projects. This begs the question: Why aren't these projects more successful? And furthermore: How do we achieve success in integration? Rather than attempting to answer these questions head on, let's see if we can gather any insight by looking at some of the more popular techniques for implementing integration scenarios over the years. Then, in Section 1.2.3, we'll look at how a modern architectural approach promises to address these shortcomings by drawing from the best traits of prior integration methods.

1.2.1.1 File Transfer with ETL

Despite the many advances in modern middleware technology, the most common method of integration today is the so-called *Extract, Transform, and Load* (ETL) technique. As the name suggests, the ETL process *extracts* data from a source system, *transforms* it into a (typically proprietary) file format that can be accepted by a target system, and then *loads* it into a target system. Since almost all systems support file processing, the ETL technique often represents a least common denominator approach to integration. However, despite its low technological barriers, the ETL method is not very flexible. For example, adding or changing a field in the data extract can introduce quite a bit of rework on both sides of the exchange. What is more, the complexity of this rework effort increases exponentially if additional systems leverage the same file-based interface.

Another consequence of the ETL technique is the fact that it may take a considerable amount of system resources to process the files in the sender/receiver systems. Frequently, ETL files are quite large since it is difficult to isolate the changes made to data between transmissions. Here, developers are forced to choose between implementing a complicated selection/filtration algorithm for identifying change records and simply dumping the entire data source each time (sometimes referred to as "kill-and-fill"). In either case, the performance implications are substantial – especially when you consider the fact that multiple jobs might be contending for the same system resources within a tight batch schedule.

Perhaps the biggest issue with ETL solutions is the fact that it is easy for the sender/receiver systems to get out of sync with one other. This could be because a job fails to run, a connection error occurs during an FTP transmission, and so on. Since ETL jobs frequently only run once a day, such failures could result in a 24-hour turnaround time, or worse. The error resolution process becomes even more complex if there are data issues associated with some of the individual records in the file. Here, imagine searching for a needle in a haystack – it's not a pretty thought.

1.2.1.2 Point-to-Point Integration with RPC

As client-server architectures became popular in the late 1980s/early 1990s, another integration approach that evolved was the *Remote Procedure Call* (RPC) model. In a nutshell, RPC allows you to call a function on another system in such a way that it is transparent to the calling system. For example, using SAP's proprietary Remote Function Call (RFC) protocol, two SAP systems can directly communicate with one another by calling a remote-enabled function module. Other RPC-style architecture examples include Java™ Remote Method Invocation (Java™ RMI), Microsoft's .NET Remoting, and CORBA.

In its most basic form, RPC implies a *synchronous* call between the sender and receiver systems. Here, the sending application stops what it is doing (i.e. it *blocks*) while it waits on the function to finish. Only after the call is completed can the program then move on to perform other tasks. This has several important implications:

> ➢ The speed of the exchange is often subject to network performance/latency issues.

> ➢ Careful attention must be paid to error handling as the target system could be down, the network unavailable, etc.

> ➢ The solution creates a tight coupling between the participating systems. Over time, this can lead to what is commonly referred to as "integration spaghetti" (see Figure 1.2).

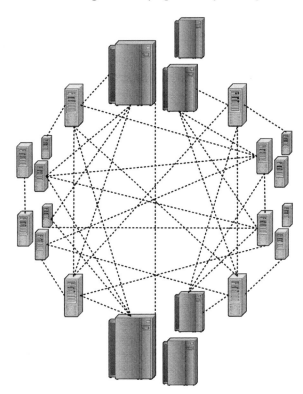

Figure 1.2: The Complexity of Point-to-Point Integration

Aside from the issues described above, another problem with the RPC approach is the so-called *symmetrical requirement* (Papazoglou, 2008). Whenever a message is sent from a sender to a receiver using RPC, the contents of that message must be *serialized* into a sequence of bits that can be transmitted across a network link. On the other end of the exchange, it is up to the receiver to reassemble the message into a format that can be processed. Typically, such low-level details are delegated to protocol libraries; which are then usually further abstracted by *proxy objects* as demonstrated in Figure 1.3.

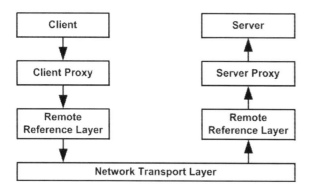

Figure 1.3: RPC Programming with Proxies

As you can see in Figure 1.3, the RPC model comes with quite a bit of baggage. For example, imagine that you want to connect a legacy system to an SAP system by calling an RFC-enabled BAPI® function. In this case, you would have to install an RFC library on the legacy system in order to communicate with the SAP system using the RFC protocol. If the legacy system happens to be written on a platform in which SAP provides an RFC SDK, then that's great. But what if an RFC SDK is not available for a particular platform? Not so great.

If you've had some exposure to Web services, then you can probably imagine where we're going with some of this. Web services address many of the limitations of RPCs through the use of ubiquitous technologies like XML and HTTP. These open technologies make it possible for just about any platform to consume and/or provide Web services. However, despite of all the good things they have to offer, keep in mind that Web services are in many respects just another incarnation of the RPC model. We'll explore the implications of this further in the upcoming sections.

1.2.1.3 Message-Oriented Middleware (MOM)

As you learned in Section 1.2.1.1, the ETL technique is primarily concerned with moving data from point A to point B. However, one thing that gets lost in the shuffle is *context*. In other words, the events that lead up the creation of a piece of data are lost in the translation. Consequently, it is up to the sender/receiver systems to pick up the pieces; an oftentimes non-trivial task.

One common approach for addressing the context problem is to migrate towards a *message-oriented* solution in which system events are broadcast in (near) real time to other systems as self-contained *messages*. These messages contain important information about a transaction as well as the events that led up to it (e.g. references to linked transactions, etc.). In general, you have two basic options for implementing message-oriented solutions:

1. You can develop a point-to-point messaging solution between a sender and receiver system using RPCs as demonstrated in Section 1.2.1.2.

2. You can use a message-oriented middleware (MOM) to broker communications between the two systems.

As we have seen, the point-to-point approach is messy since it can be difficult for systems to agree on messaging protocols, etc. The MOM approach on the other hand offers quite a bit of flexibility:

➤ Rather than having to implement a slew of protocols, communicating systems only need to be able to communicate with a centralized *message broker*.

➤ Once a message is delivered to the message broker, it becomes the responsibility of the broker to deliver the message on to its intended recipients.

➤ Since the message broker is a separate piece of middleware, it can have its own persistence store/database for storing messages. Using a "store-and-forward" approach, the integration broker can queue up messages for systems that are unavailable and deliver them later when they come back online.

> ➢ It decouples the sender from the receiver such that messages can be processed *asynchronously*. This frees the sender up to go perform other tasks and potentially enables the receiver to process incoming messages at times that are most convenient.

MOM supports two different kinds of messaging models: *publish-and-subscribe* (or pub/sub) and *point-to-point* (P2P) queuing. In the pub/sub model, a message is broadcast to one or more interested consumers via a *topic*. Consumers can then choose to subscribe to this topic and receive messages on demand. Conversely, the point-to-point queuing model supports a direct connection between a sender and a receiver using a queue. Figure 1.4 illustrates these two messaging models.

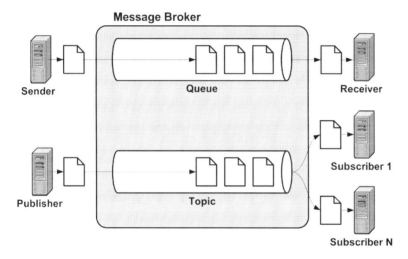

Figure 1.4: Event-Based Messaging with a Message Broker

1.2.1.4 Integration Brokers and the Hub-and-Spoke Model
Although the MOM-based approach delegates many of the integration responsibilities onto a separate platform (i.e., the message broker), it does not completely decouple a sender from a receiver. Indeed, no matter how well you design the solution, you'll always end up with a certain amount of integration logic co-mingled within the application logic.

Ideally, we would like to shift as much of the integration logic as we can onto the middleware layer so that we don't have to maintain it separately on each of the endpoint systems within the landscape. Such centralization makes the integration landscape much more transparent. Furthermore, it also offers the opportunity for value-add operations that would not be feasible to implement in each of the endpoint systems. For example, wouldn't it be great if we could inspect the contents of a message at runtime and then figure out what to do with it based on some configuration rules?

Recognizing the need for enhanced message processing capabilities, MOM vendors began bolstering their message brokers to offer more sophisticated messaging services such as dynamic and rule-based message routing, message transformation, etc. Taking a cue from the airline industry, integration architects began to utilize these enhanced message brokers to develop a *hub-and-spoke architecture* (see Figure 1.5). In this scenario, the entry point to integration is the connection of an endpoint system with a centralized *integration broker*. Once this connection is established, messages can be routed just about anywhere. This is analogous to the way airlines develop flight itineraries by connecting small airports through a centralized hub. Here, if you can get to the hub, then you can get anywhere.

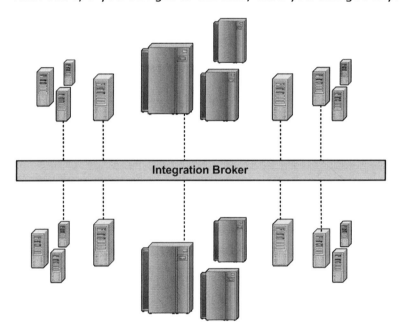

Figure 1.5: Integration Using a Hub-and-Spoke Architecture

Another advantage integration brokers have over traditional MOM solutions is the fact that they support a wide variety of *communication channels*. With MOM, the entry point for any system is the ability to communicate with the MOM's API, which is often proprietary. While the Java™ Message Service

(JMS) API has eliminated many of these barriers for Java-based solutions, the issue still remains that non-Java environments may not be able to easily communicate with the message broker. Integration brokers get around this limitation through the use of various lightweight protocol adapters. These adapters support a wide range of communication protocols such as FTP, SOAP, and even proprietary protocols like SAP's RFC protocol. From the endpoint system's perspective, this is all transparent; they simply connect to the adapter and it takes care of forwarding the message on to the integration broker. From there, the message is processed just like any other message, and is thus subject to all of the value-add features afforded by the integration broker.

1.2.2   The Origins of SOA

By the late 1990s/early 2000s, many companies had transitioned towards hub-and-spoke integration broker solutions. However, despite the many benefits these solutions had to offer, companies were experiencing mixed results with their integration projects. This paradox caused many to wonder whether or not this was a technical problem or a functional problem. In other words, were the failures due to limitations of the technology, or was there something fundamentally wrong with the integration process?

Around this same time, many software architects started to talk about a new architectural approach to integration called *service-oriented architecture* (SOA). This methodology promised to put an end to a lot of the problems that plagued integration projects. However, while the promises were clear, the how was a little more fuzzy. With that in mind, let's investigate the principles of SOA.

These days, there is a lot of misinformation out there about what SOA is and what it has to offer. Despite what you might read in various product whitepapers, SOA is an *ideal*, not a product. In essence, it is a frame of mind in which you attempt to develop applications in a modular fashion by weaving together a series of *callable services*. These services need not exist on a single platform; you can integrate services from anywhere within the enterprise and beyond.

In order to achieve this kind of reuse, careful consideration must be placed on the service design process. In particular, services should embody the characteristics outlined in Table 1.1.

Characteristic	Description
Accessibility	Services should be easy to access and use in a wide variety of environments.
Autonomy	Ideally, a service should be able to stand on its own without having a lot of external dependencies.
Intuitiveness	A service should have a clearly defined purpose and provide a solution for predefined tasks. The interface of the service should be clear and easy to understand.
Abstraction and Encapsulation	The interface of a service should serve as a *contract* between the service provider and a service consumer. As long as a service provider adheres to the terms of the contract, they are free to make changes to the service behind the scenes.
Reliability	The behavior of the service should be predictable across invocations. Similarly, a client should be able to depend on a stable service interface.

Table 1.1: Desired Characteristics of Reusable Services

Looking back at the progression of integration solutions described in Section 1.2.1, you can begin to see traces of a movement towards service-orientation all along. As middleware technology evolved, did you notice how more and more integration logic was shifted away from endpoint systems and onto the middleware layer? Once this transition process is complete, all that is left on the endpoint systems are a series of service interfaces that are focused on performing application-level tasks like creating a sales order, etc. Such decoupling is often referred to as a *separation of concerns*.

What does it mean to "separate concerns"?

In computer science, the phrase *separation of concerns* is used to describe an architectural approach in which programs are broken down into separate modules that overlap in functionality as little as possible. In terms of integration, we're interested in separating application-level concerns from integration concerns. In the end, this eliminates the barriers to integration, which in turn reduces cost.

One final thing we should point out here is that there is a fundamental difference between services in the SOA context and *Web services*. Conceptually speaking, Web services represent one of many ways to implement services in an SOA. However, "Web-servicifying" a handful of software modules is not the same thing as implementing an SOA. The danger here is a fall back into the mindset of point-to-point integration as described in Section 1.2.1.2. This is not to say that Web services are bad, or that they shouldn't be used to implement an SOA; indeed, one could argue that they are the most natural solution for implementing services. The point is that the requirements for implementing an SOA in the enterprise demand a robust integration solution that extends well beyond the scope of a Web services toolkit.

1.2.3   Migrating Towards the Enterprise Service Bus

When Web services exploded onto the scene in the early 2000s, many IT pundits began to loudly proclaim that middleware was dead. However, despite all the great things Web services have to offer, this short-sighted view fails to take into account certain shortcomings of the Web services technology stack. In particular, there is still a need for reliable messaging, transactional integrity, process orchestration, and so on. In essence, enterprise SOA needs a robust and flexible implementation platform to stand on. It is out of this spirit that the *Enterprise Service Bus* (ESB) was born.

The ESB is the next evolution in integration technology. Conceptually, it expands upon the hub-and-spoke integration broker model to provide additional flexibility in the design and deployment of integration scenarios. In the canonical reference on the subject, David Chappell describes an ESB as having the following characteristics (Chappell, 2004):

> ➢ Adaptability for a wide variety of integration requirements
>
> ➢ A flexible and distributed architecture as opposed to a monolithic architecture based upon a single integration broker.
>
> ➢ Selective deployment and usage of integration components on an as-needed basis
>
> ➢ Security and reliability in message exchange
>
> ➢ Orchestration and process flow for messages flowing through the bus
>
> ➢ XML-centric messaging instead of proprietary message formats
>
> ➢ Support for *Business Activity Monitoring* (BAM)
>
> ➢ Distributed system management capabilities

When you put all this together, you arrive at a flexible framework for deploying integration scenarios based on SOA principles. In this light, middleware is not a competing technology with SOA and Web services, but rather a complementary platform that helps you get the most out of your SOA investment. Throughout the remainder of this book, we'll see how SAP NetWeaver PI embodies these characteristics in its tools and services.

1.3   SAP NetWeaver PI: The Dime Tour

Having now briefly considered the origins and positioning of SAP NetWeaver PI, let us now shift our attention towards more practical matters. In this section, we'll take you on a tour of the features and architecture of SAP NetWeaver PI. To guide this tour, we'll consider three phases of integration development as they relate to SAP NetWeaver PI:

- Design time
- Configuration time
- Operation and Maintenance

This perspective will help you to see how SAP NetWeaver PI supports you in all phases of the interface development lifecycle.

1.3.1   Architectural Overview

Before we look at the tools and services PI offers at the different phases of integration development, it is first beneficial to observe the basic architecture of SAP NetWeaver PI. Having an understanding of these concepts will make it easier for you to orient yourself as you progress through the interface development lifecycle. It also helps you get the most out of the various tools and services that PI has to offer.

Figure 1.6 provides an overview of the basic technical components provided with SAP NetWeaver PI. The directed arrows in this diagram demonstrate the relationships between these components as you progress from design time to configuration time to runtime. We'll explore the design and configuration time tools in Sections 1.3.2 and 1.3.3, respectively. However, in the meantime, let's take a closer look at the PI runtime environment.

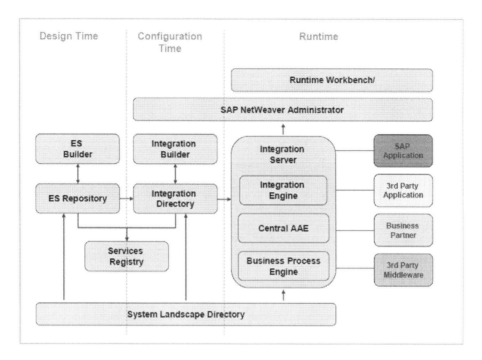

Figure 1.6: PI Technical Component Overview (Gutsche) © Copyright 2010. SAP AG. All rights reserved

1.3.1.1 The SAP NetWeaver PI Runtime Environment

The runtime environment of SAP NetWeaver PI is based on a distributed architecture that leverages components deployed on both the AS ABAP and AS Java stacks of the SAP NetWeaver technology platform. Collectively, these components combine to form what is known as the *Integration Server*. Figure 1.7 depicts the architecture of the Integration Server. In the upcoming sections, we'll examine the functionality of the components that make up the Integration Server.

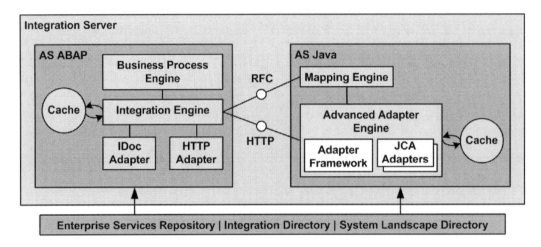

Figure 1.7: The SAP NetWeaver PI Integration Server

Integration Engine (IE)

The primary messaging component within the Integration Server is the *Integration Engine* (IE). The IE plays the role of central integration broker, and its job is to process incoming messages based on configuration settings defined within the Integration Directory. Here, the configuration data is used to determine who the receiver(s) of the inbound message should be, which receiver interfaces to call, which adapters to use, and so on.

Internally, the IE uses an SAP-proprietary protocol called the *XI protocol* to process messages. The XI protocol is essentially an extension of the W3C's *SOAP Messages with Attachments* (SwA) protocol (W3C, 2000) that includes various custom header blocks that document the flow of a message through the IE pipeline. If all that techno-speak just caused your brain to spin into hypnosis, don't worry; the key takeaway here is that the IE deals exclusively with XML-based messages. This approach levels the playing field, allowing you to get the most out of the value-add features that the IE has to offer.

In particular, the IE offers the following features:

> ➤ It can dynamically determine the receiver(s) of an incoming message using information contained within the message header or the message contents.

> ➤ It supports the execution of XML mapping programs that map between different XML schema types.

➢ It can support different quality of service levels for messaging based upon your needs:

  o Best Effort (BE)

  o Exactly One (EO)

  o Exactly Once in Order (EOIO)

➢ It keeps detailed logs that allow you to closely monitor the flow of messages.

➢ It works in conjunction with the Advanced Adapter Engine to forward messages to a wide variety of systems using various protocols.

Advanced Adapter Engine (AAE)

The *Advanced Adapter Engine* (AAE) is new to version 7.1 of SAP NetWeaver PI; though it leverages quite a bit of its functionality from the previous Adapter Engine architecture found in prior releases. As you might expect, the primary function of the AAE is to enable connectivity to various systems through the use of lightweight, pluggable *adapters*. These adapters are based on the *J2EE™ Connector Architecture* (JCA) specification (Sun Microsystems). Essentially, you can think of a JCA adapter as a Java-based protocol adapter that can be loaded into a J2EE server environment like the SAP AS Java.

SAP NetWeaver PI ships with quite a few standard adapters out-of-the-box, including the following:

➢ IDoc Adapter

➢ RFC Adapter

➢ Plain HTTP Adapter

➢ File/FTP Adapter

➢ JDBC Adapter

➢ JMS Adapter

➢ SOAP Adapter

➢ Mail Adapter

➢ XI Adapter (for native communications)

➢ WS Adapter

In addition to the standard adapter types, you can also install adapters developed by 3rd-party software vendors as well as custom adapter types that you develop yourself. You can find a list of supported 3rd-party adapters by logging onto the SAP Developer Network (SDN) available online at *http://www.sdn.sap.com*. From the home page, select the menu path *SOA Middleware → Service Bus → Third-Party Adapter*.

Adapters in the AAE are supported by a surrounding *Adapter Framework* that takes care of message queuing, monitoring, and so on. The Adapter Framework is customizable, allowing you to enhance the functionality of adapters using custom *Adapter Modules* that act like user exits in the adapter process flow. We'll learn more about adapters and the Adapter Framework in Chapter 11.

The "advanced" portion of the AAE moniker refers to some additional features that were added to the Adapter Engine in version 7.1 of SAP NetWeaver PI. Here, the AAE was enhanced to support local message processing without having to involve the IE. In certain scenarios, this offers significant opportunities for performance improvement as messages don't have to "hop stacks". We'll see how this works in Chapter 13.

Business Process Engine (BPE)

Most of the time, the IE acts as a pass-through; routing incoming messages on to their final destination. Occasionally, you may come across a requirement that calls for more sophisticated processing. To address these requirements, you can develop *integration processes*.

Integration processes are workflow-like components that are deployed on the *Business Process Engine* (BPE). From a technical perspective, the BPE is implemented using the same WebFlow Engine used to process workflow tasks defined using SAP Business Workflow. However, the BPE supports a handful of additional task types that enable integration processes to access features of the IE (e.g. dynamic receiver determination, data transformation, etc.).

Besides its support for implementing custom integration logic, the BPE adds another key capability to the mix: *stateful processing*. In other words, the BPE keeps track of the *state* of an integration process over potentially long periods of time. Furthermore, it enables integration processes to have an event-based process flow instead of a sequential process flow. This makes it easier to model business processes that involve the asynchronous exchange of a series of messages across multiple systems. We'll learn more about integration processes in Chapter 9.

1.3.2 Service Development in the ESR

Now that you're familiar with the basic architecture of SAP NetWeaver PI, let's take a step back and look at how integration scenarios are developed. This process begins with the modeling and specification of service interfaces and their supporting objects. In SAP NetWeaver PI, these objects are stored in a central repository called the *Enterprise Services Repository* (ESR). To maintain these objects, you use a tool called the *Enterprise Services Builder* (ES Builder). In this section, we'll introduce you to the ESR and show you how it is used to develop design time SOA assets.

1.3.2.1 Getting Started with the ES Builder

Before we begin looking at specific development objects within the ESR, we first need to show you how to logon to the ES Builder tool so that you can follow along in your own local environment. You can access the ES Builder tool in one of two ways:

> ➢ By logging onto the PI ABAP stack and executing transaction SXMB_IFR.
> ➢ By opening up a Web browser and navigating to *http(s)://{AS Java Host}:{AS Java HTTP(s) port}/dir/start/index.jsp*.

In either case, you will end up at a Web screen like the one shown in Figure 1.8.

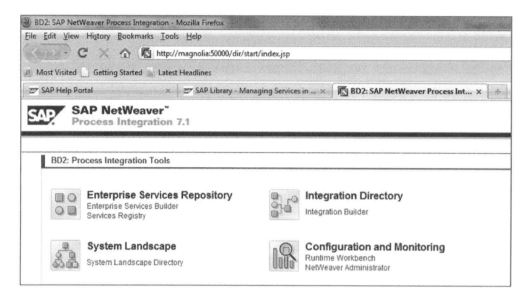

Figure 1.8: Accessing the Enterprise Services Builder © Copyright 2010. SAP AG. All rights reserved

The ES Builder is implemented as a Java™ Web Start rich client application that can be downloaded and run on most any workstation that has a Java™ Runtime Environment (JRE) installed on it[3]. Once you have the JRE installed, you can access the ES Builder tool by clicking on the *Enterprise Services Builder* link on the screen shown in Figure 1.8. This will open up the application using Java Web Start tool.

After the application is loaded, you will be prompted to log on via the logon screen shown in Figure 1.9. Here, you will log on using the same user account you used to log onto the PI ABAP stack. If you're not sure which account to use, check with your system administrator.

---

[3] If you do not have the JRE installed on your machine, you can download it for free by logging onto the Java™ SE Downloads page at *http://www.oracle.com/technetwork/java/javase/downloads/index.html*.

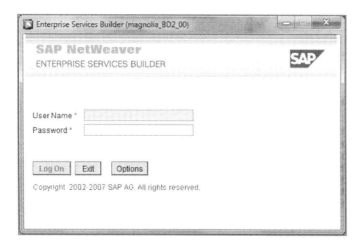

Figure 1.9: Logging onto the Enterprise Services Builder © Copyright 2010. SAP AG. All rights reserved

The first time you log on, you will be prompted to select an *application profile*. Here, you'll want to select the *Process Integration* application profile. Ultimately, you'll arrive at a screen like the one shown in Figure 1.10.

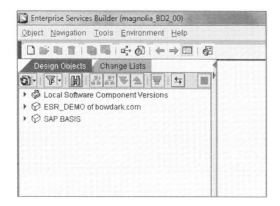

Figure 1.10: Working with the Enterprise Services Builder © Copyright 2010. SAP AG. All rights reserved

1.3.2.2 Service Interfaces

In the landmark software design book *Design Patterns: Elements of Reusable Software*, the authors emphasize that one of the primary ways of achieving reusability in software development is to "program to an interface, not an implementation" (Gamma, Helm, Johnson, & Vlissides, 1995). In essence, this principle is all about removing unwanted dependencies between software components. If we extend this concept to interface development, then you can see a distinction between a service's *interface* and its underlying *implementation*. For instance, there are certain aspects of an interface that are independent of the technology used to implement it. Such facets include the interface's communication mode (i.e. synchronous vs. asynchronous), the structure and format of the message types being exchanged, and so on.

Rather than commingling such design-level concerns with implementation details, SAP elected to define a separate design-time artifact within the ESR called a *service interface* to capture these details up front[4]. As you'll see throughout the course of this book, this design decision provides you with tremendous flexibility at implementation time.

The ES Builder provides several tools to support you in the creation of service interfaces. Which one(s) you use depends primarily on whether or not the service already exists in a system. Table 1.2 describes the service development approaches supported in the ES Builder tool.

Development Approach	Description
Inside-Out Approach	If a service exists already in a system, then you can use tools in the ES Builder to import the service's definition into the ESR.
Outside-In Approach	When starting from scratch, you use ES Builder tools to graphically define a service interface and its supporting object types (e.g. *message types* and *data types*). Once the service interface definition is created, the implementing systems can then use it to generate the development objects (e.g. proxies) necessary to consume or provide the service.

Table 1.2: Service Development Approaches in Enterprise Services Builder

In order to survey the interface development tools provided by the ES Builder, select the *Object* → *New* menu option from the top-level menu bar. This will bring up the *Create Object* dialog box shown in Figure 1.11. Here, if you expand the *Interface Objects* submenu, you can see all of the types of interface objects that you can create with the ES Builder.

---

[4] As you'll see a little bit later on, service interfaces are based on the industry-standard *Web Services Description Language* (WSDL). We'll learn more about WSDL in Chapter 3.

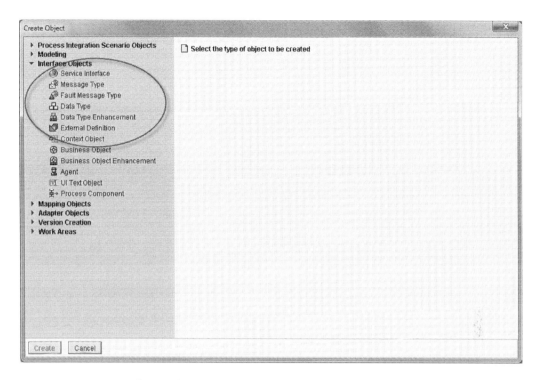

Figure 1.11: Interface Objects in the Enterprise Services Builder © Copyright 2010. SAP AG. All rights reserved

Table 1.3 contains descriptions for the main interface objects you will be interacting with during the service design process. In Chapter 6, we'll examine each of these objects in much more detail.

Interface Object	Description
Service Interfaces	According to SAP, a service interface "enables you to describe - independently of a platform or programming language - operations that you require later for an implementation in the application system at a later stage" (SAP AG). Each (service) operation defined within a service interface can have a request message type, and optional response and fault message types. The underlying service description is encoded using the WSDL standard.
Message Type	Message types are used to define the *signature* of service operations (e.g. the operation's request and response messages). A message type is based on a *data type*.
Fault Message Type	Similar to a message type; used to represent application-specific errors in a service operation.
Data Type	Data types define the structure of message types. Data types can be simple or complex. Behind the scenes, a data type is constructed using the XML Schema language. We'll learn more about XML Schema in Chapter 2.
Data Type Enhancement	Data type enhancements (DTEs) provide a mechanism for enhancing SAP-delivered standard types in a safe and portable way. See Appendix B for more details about DTEs.
External Definition	An external definition allows you to upload pre-existing XML definitions (e.g. XML Schema files, WSDL files, and so on) into the ESR. These external definitions can be used to specify the message types exchanged by service interface operations, etc.

Table 1.3: Interface Objects in the Enterprise Services Builder

1.3.2.3 Mediated Collaboration Objects

As you learned in Section 1.2.1.4, integration brokers offer the possibility of interjecting certain value-add operations during message processing. For example, in order to enable system A to talk to system B, we might need to map the source data from system A into a format that system B will accept. Similarly, we might want to develop some kind of workflow process to orchestrate more complex message flows. In the vernacular of SAP

NetWeaver PI, these value-add operations are implemented using *mediated collaboration objects*.

Mediated collaboration objects are created independently of a physical environment at design time. That way, they can be mixed-and-matched and reused in one or more integration scenarios at configuration time. The following subsections highlight the types of mediated collaboration objects provided by SAP NetWeaver PI.

Data Transformation

If you look back at the hub-and-spoke architecture diagram depicted in Figure 1.5, you can see that an integration scenario between two systems requires two separate interfaces:

> - One between the sending system and the SAP NetWeaver PI Integration Server.

> - One between the SAP NetWeaver PI Integration Server and the receiving system.

Frequently, the formats of the messages defined for the service interfaces in the sender and receiver systems differ. Therefore, a *data transformation* step is usually required to bind everything together. From a development perspective, this implies that we develop an XML mapping program that can translate between a source and target schema type.

There are several ways of developing mapping programs in SAP NetWeaver PI. In particular, you can:

> - Interactively create a Java-based mapping program using a graphical message mapping tool.

> - Develop and import a Java-based mapping program from scratch using your preferred Java API for XML processing.

> - Create and import a mapping program using the *eXtensible Stylesheet Language for Transformations* (XSLT) language.

> - Build an XML mapping program in the ABAP Workbench using ABAP Objects.

We'll explore each of these mapping techniques in Chapters 7 and 8.

Service Orchestration

Besides the typical data transformation requirements, many integration scenarios also need to have some measure of *service orchestration* that coordinates message traffic in more sophisticated ways. For example, we might have a requirement to batch a series of messages together and send them to some receiver system in a specific format. Here, we would need to interject some custom logic into the message processing. In SAP NetWeaver PI, you can implement this kind of logic by creating an *integration process*.

You can think of an integration process as a kind of workflow process that you can install on the Integration Server. Indeed, from a runtime perspective, that is exactly what is happening behind the scenes. As a result, integration processes enjoy many of the same benefits you have come to expect from workflow tools including:

> ➤ Graphical modeling of program logic with conditionals, loops, etc.

> ➤ The capability for *stateful* processing. Here, the integration process can keep track of a long-running integration scenario involving multiple messages from different systems.

> ➤ The ability to react to error situations and handle them in more elegant ways.

Figure 1.12 illustrates a sample integration process that ships by default with every SAP NetWeaver PI installation. As you can see, the graphical editor contains a palette of step types that help you model complex integration scenarios. Internally, the integration process is represented using the *Web Services Business Process Execution Language* (WS-BPEL), version 2.0. We'll consider integration processes in much more detail in Chapter 9.

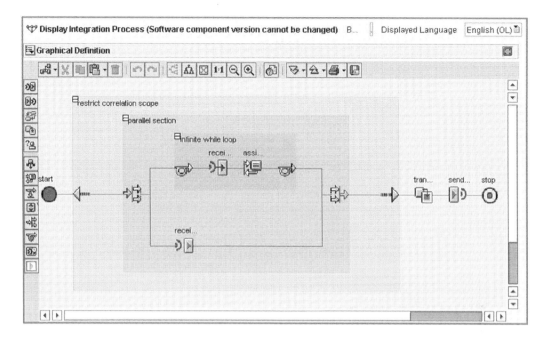

Figure 1.12: A Sample Integration Process in the ES Builder © Copyright 2010. SAP AG. All rights reserved

1.3.2.4 Shared Collaboration Knowledge

One of the primary benefits of a having a centralized repository like the ESR is the fact that it promotes *shared collaboration knowledge*. In other words, instead of having to dig through multiple systems to see how a message is mapped, you can simply log onto the ESR and everything's right there for everyone to see. Of course, in order to find what you're looking for, you have to know where to look.

In Chapter 4, we'll see how to arrange some of this content using folders, namespaces, etc. However, another effective way of organizing this content is to use the modeling tools provided with release 7.1 of SAP NetWeaver PI. These tools allow you to model integration scenarios at varying levels of granularity, providing the ability to drill into more detailed objects via context-based navigation. We'll have an opportunity to look at these tools in Chapter 5.

1.3.3 Integration Directory Configuration Concepts

In some respects, you can think of repository objects created in the ESR as nothing more than basic building blocks that can be used to implement integration scenarios. In order to do anything useful with these building blocks, you must combine them to form a logical business process that can be deployed within a specific technical landscape. Within SAP NetWeaver PI, such assembly takes place at configuration time within the Integration Directory. In the upcoming sections, we'll look at some of the configuration options you have to work with inside the Integration Directory.

1.3.3.1 Getting Started with the Integration Builder

Much like the ESR, the Integration Directory is an online repository that you access using a Java Web Start application called the *Integration Builder*. You can access this tool by clicking on the *Integration Builder* link on the *Process Integration Tools* home page (see Figure 1.8). Once the application loads, you'll be prompted to authenticate. Here, you'll use the same PI user account you used to log onto ES Builder tool. After you've logged in, you'll arrive at a screen that looks like the one shown in Figure 1.13.

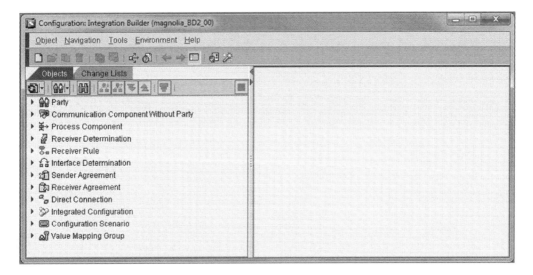

Figure 1.13: Accessing the Integration Builder Tool © Copyright 2010. SAP AG. All rights reserved

As you can see in Figure 1.13, the look-and-feel of the Integration Builder is more or less the same as the ES Builder, which is of course by design.

1.3.3.2 Defining Collaboration Profiles

The first step in configuring an integration scenario is the specification of the endpoints that will be sending and receiving messages to one another. Within the Integration Directory, these endpoints are defined using *collaboration profiles*. Collaboration profiles describe two important aspects of communication:

> ➤ They model the sender/receiver endpoints that exchange messages. In terms of the Integration Directory, these endpoints are represented using *communication parties* and *communication components*.

> ➤ They also contain a set of *communication channels* (or simply channels) that describe the technical communication capabilities of the endpoint systems.

You can configure three different types of communication components in the Integration Directory. Table 1.4 describes each of these component types in turn.

Component Type	Description
Business System	Represents a logical system defined in the *System Landscape Directory* (SLD). You'll learn more about the SLD in later chapters. For now, suffice it to say that business systems would typically be used to represent other SAP-based systems within your landscape (e.g. SAP® ERP, SAP® CRM, and so on).
Business Component	Represents an abstract unit for addressing endpoints that sit outside of your SAP landscape. For example, if you were interfacing with a 3rd-party system using Web services, you would define a business component to model that system.
Integration Process	Enables the direct addressing of an integration process defined in the ESR as a communication component. This is necessary in order to route messages to and from integration processes.

Table 1.4: Communication Component Types

In many respects, a communication component is merely a logical construct used to enable internal routing, etc. The physical communication with an endpoint system is realized via the use of the various adapter types described in Section 1.3.1.1. Therefore, in order to complete the definition of a collaboration profile, you must define a series of communication channels that bind a logical communication component with physical connection media.

To illustrate how this relationship works, imagine that you want to model communication between an internal SAP® ERP system and a 3rd-party supply chain optimization product called AcmeSoft. In this case, you define a business component called AcmeSoft to represent the receiver system (see Figure 1.14). Since AcmeSoft exposes their service interfaces in the form of Web services, you will need to use the PI SOAP adapter to connect to their Web service runtime environment. Figure 1.14 demonstrates a communication channel called SOAPReceiver that defines the connection parameters the SOAP adapter will need to send a SOAP request message to AcmeSoft. Collectively, the AcmeSoft business component and the underlying SOAPReceiver channel define a complete collaboration profile for the receiver system.

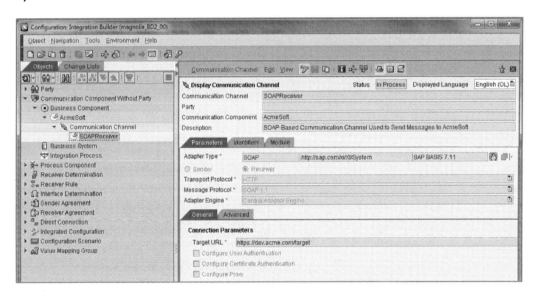

Figure 1.14: Defining a Communication Channel © Copyright 2010. SAP AG. All rights reserved

Once you define the relevant collaboration profiles for your scenario, you're ready to begin configuring logical routing rules, etc. Beginning with release 7.1 of SAP NetWeaver PI, you have several communication variants to choose from. The following sections provide a high-level overview of these communication variants.

1.3.3.3   Integration Server-Based Communication

In order to take advantage of all the features of the SAP NetWeaver PI runtime environment, you must configure *Integration Server-based communication*. In this scenario, messages are brokered through the Integration Engine on the AS ABAP stack. This is not to say that the AS Java stack is not involved in this scenario; it is still used to facilitate communication via the AAE and possibly message mapping via the Java mapping engine. Rather, the point is that the Integration Engine assumes the primary responsibility for orchestrating message processing.

To understand how this works, let's consider an integration example where System A sends a message to System B. For the purposes of our discussion, let's assume that System A communicates using Web services and System B can receive XML files via FTP. Figure 1.15 illustrates this exchange.

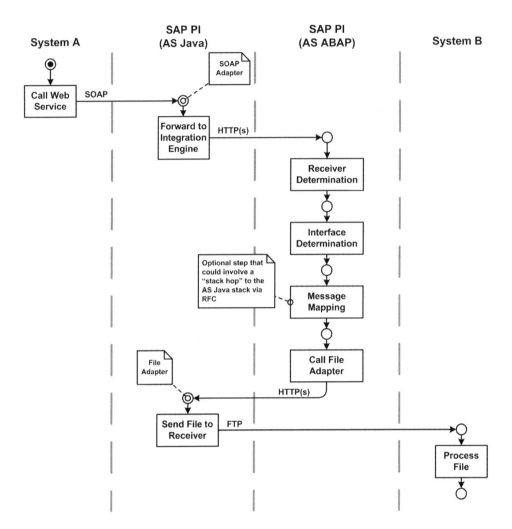

Figure 1.15: Example Message Flow for Integration Server-Based Processing

As you can see in Figure 1.15, System A initiates the flow by calling a Web service hosted on PI. This message is received by the SOAP adapter in the AAE and forwarded on to the Integration Engine. From here, the message is transformed and sent to System B via FTP using the file adapter on the AAE. In between, the Integration Engine is tasked with inspecting the message and performing the following steps:

➢ **Receiver Determination:** Which communication component(s) should receive the message?

➢ **Interface Determination:** Which service interfaces should be called on those receiver components?

➢ **Message Mapping:** Is an XML transformation required to convert the inbound message into a format that the receiver component can accept?

➢ **Call Adapter:** Which adapter types are used to communicate with the receiver components? What are the parameters that should be used to initiate the communication?

As you might expect, the answers to these questions come from configuration objects maintained in the Integration Directory. Table 1.5 describes each of these objects in detail.

Configuration Object	Description
Receiver Determination	This object determines which communication components should receive a message from a particular sender. These bindings can be static or dynamic in nature. For example, instead of hard-coding a receiver component, you can build a logical expression that routes a message to a particular receiver based upon the contents of its payload, etc.
Interface Determination	Once a receiver component is identified via receiver determination, you can specify an interface determination to determine which service interface to call on that receiver. Interface determinations also allow you to plug in an XML mapping program that can convert between the source and target interface schemas.
Sender Agreement	Sender agreements determine which communication channel a sender will use to call a particular service interface. This information is used by the AAE for internal routing purposes.

Configuration Object	Description
Receiver Agreement	Receiver agreements determine which communication channel will be used to call a particular service interface on a receiver component. This information is used by the Integration Engine to determine which adapter to call at runtime.

Table 1.5: Configuration Objects for Integration Server-Based Communication

1.3.3.4 AAE-Based Communication

Looking back at the Integration Server-based communication flow example depicted in Figure 1.15, you might have noticed that there were several *hops* between the AS ABAP and AS Java stacks. From a performance perspective, these stack hops can prove costly in situations where speed is of the essence. Recognizing this, SAP enhanced the Adapter Framework in the AAE to support local message processing as described in Section 1.3.1.1. At runtime, this implies that AAE must assume responsibility for each of the message processing tasks described in Table 1.5.

Unlike Integration Server-based communication, the AAE receives its configuration details from a standalone object called an *integrated configuration*. Figure 1.16 shows an example integrated configuration in the Integration Directory. As you can see, all of the various configuration options are laid out across a series of tabs within the editor screen.

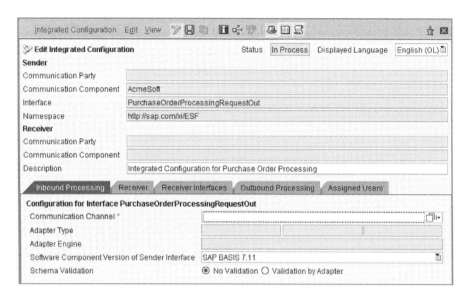

Figure 1.16: Defining an Integrated Configuration © Copyright 2010. SAP AG. All rights reserved

1.3.3.5 Direct Communication

In certain situations, all of the enhanced processing afforded by the Integration Server is overkill. For example, imagine that you have a scenario where a Web service consumer on an SAP® CRM system is called a Web service provided on an SAP® ERP system. Now, technically speaking, you could configure this communication directly between the two systems without involving PI. However, in keeping with the *shared collaboration knowledge* principle, you would prefer to maintain these configuration settings centrally. In this case, you can configure *direct communication*.

Direct communication is a new feature in 7.1 that allows you to configure direct Web service communication between two backend systems based upon the AS ABAP (version 7.10+). Here, you define the communication centrally and effectively push it out to the backend systems. At runtime, the backend systems communicate directly with one another without having to go through the Integration Server.

From a configuration perspective, direct communication is set up via a configuration object called a *direct connection*. In some ways, a direct connection looks kind of like a lightweight integrated configuration that has been stripped down to remove references to logical routings, and so on. The primary difference is the use of the new WS adapter type that is used to configure the Web service endpoints. We'll explore these concepts further in Chapter 13.

1.3.4 Process Integration Monitoring

In a perfect world, every message received by the Integration Server would be forwarded on successfully to its final destination(s). However, in reality, there are many obstacles that can prevent this from happening. For example, we might receive a message that we don't know how to map, or the target system might be unavailable, etc. In any case, it is important to be able to track a message's progress as it flows through the system. In the world of EAI, this kind of analysis is referred to as *Business Activity Monitoring* (BAM).

As it turns out, SAP NetWeaver PI provides a number of BAM tools that can be used to monitor various aspects of the system. Table 1.6 describes each of these tools at a conceptual level.

Monitoring Tool	Description
Integration Engine Monitoring (Transaction SXMB_MONI)	An ABAP-based tool provided on the SAP NetWeaver PI system that can be used to display a detailed audit trail of messages processed within the Integration Engine.
Runtime Workbench (RWB)	A Web-based tool hosted on the PI AS Java stack that supports monitoring of the following types of components: ❖ Adapter Engines/Communication Channels ❖ Message Monitoring ❖ End-to-End/Performance Monitoring ❖ Cache Monitoring In addition, the RWB also enables you to configure alerting based upon various business rules, etc.

Monitoring Tool	Description
SAP NetWeaver Administrator (NWA)	An SAP standard Web-based monitoring tool that allows you to view system/application logs as well as the overall health of the underlying application servers. In addition, in release 7.1, the NWA allows you to monitor PI-based components in much the same way that you would monitor these components in the RWB.
Computing Center Management System (CCMS)	An SAP standard ABAP-based monitoring tool that can be used to monitor technical aspects of the system such as disk space, database health, queue blockages, and so on. CCMS can be configured to implement auto-reaction methods that automatically respond to certain conditions within the system. For example, if a queue gets blocked, you can set up a method to alert key stakeholders of the problem.
PI Monitoring with SAP® Solution Manager	In addition to the PI-centric tools, you can also monitor certain aspects of message processing centrally using dashboards provided with SAP Solution Manager.

Table 1.6: SAP NetWeaver PI Monitoring Tools

1.4 Summary

This concludes our introduction of SAP NetWeaver PI. At this point, you should have a basic understanding of what SAP NetWeaver PI is and what it is used for. Throughout the course of the rest of this book, we will expand upon these concepts and more in greater detail. However, before we embark on this journey, we first need to take a look at some of the core Internet-based technologies that SAP NetWeaver PI uses to enable message processing. We'll begin this discussion by taking a look at the ins-and-outs of XML in Chapter 2.

References

Chappell, D. A. (2004). *Enterprise Service Bus.* Sebastopol: O'Reilly Media, Inc.

Gamma, E., Helm, R., Johnson, R., & Vlissides, J. (1995). *Design Patterns: Elements of Reusable Object-Oriented Software.* Addison-Wesley.

Gutsche, P. (n.d.). *Process Integration Handbook.* Retrieved February 3, 2011, from SAP Developer Network (SDN): http://www.sdn.sap.com/irj/sdn/index?rid=/library/uuid/8078cff3-e045-2c10-9bae-abf0ca5040c5

Papazoglou, M. P. (2008). *Web Services: Principles and Technology.* Pearson Education.

SAP AG. (n.d.). *Service Interface.* Retrieved March 29, 2011, from SAP Help Library: http://help.sap.com/saphelp_nwpi711/helpdata/en/48/5b14cf63424992e100 00000a42189c/frameset.htm

SAP. (n.d.). *SAP NetWeaver Process Integration Library*. Retrieved July 23, 2010, from SAP Library: http://help.sap.com/saphelp_nwpi711/helpdata/en/c0/3930405fa9e801e100 00000a155106/frameset.htm

Sun Microsystems. (n.d.). *J2EE Connector Specification, 1.0.* Retrieved August 2010, from Java Connector Architecture: http://java.sun.com/j2ee/connector/download.html

W3C. (2000, December). *SOAP Messages with Attachments*. Retrieved August 17, 2010, from W3C: http://www.w3.org/TR/SOAP-attachments

Working with XML 2

SAP NetWeaver PI was designed from the ground up to include support for many open Internet standards such as XML and XML Schema. Therefore, given the widespread use of XML-based technologies in SAP NetWeaver PI, it is very important that you understand how to work with XML.

After completing this chapter, you will be able to:

❖ Understand what XML is and how it can be used to create message types.

❖ Recognize basic elements of XML syntax.

❖ Understand how to process XML documents using XML parsers.

❖ Describe the structure and format of XML documents using XML Schema.

2.1   Getting Started with XML

As you learned in Chapter 1, SAP NetWeaver PI uses XML as its medium for message exchange. Unlike prior approaches based on proprietary technologies or fixed-length/delimited formats, XML offers openness and transparency in message exchange on an unprecedented scale. Throughout the course of this book, we'll see how an XML-based approach to messaging simplifies the design and development of cross-system business processes in SAP NetWeaver PI.

In the upcoming sections, we'll take a look at what XML is and see how you can use it to construct messages. We'll also introduce you to XML parsing technologies that simplify the way that you process XML documents. If this is your first foray into the world of XML, don't worry - we'll take it slow. Plus, we'll revisit many of these concepts in greater detail when we get into the hands-on portion of this book in Part 2.

2.1.1   What is XML?

Since the late 1990s, the *eXtensible Markup Language* (or XML) has emerged as the lingua franca for information exchange over the Internet. XML is a standard endorsed by the W3C[5] that can be used to define the format of text-based documents. Like its not-so-distant cousin HTML, XML uses special annotations called *tags* to organize and describe the content within a document. However, unlike HTML, the XML standard does not prescribe any particular kind of markup. Rather, it describes a syntax that can be used to define *other* markup languages such as XHTML, MathML, SVG, and so on.

In order to facilitate the creation of other markup languages, the XML standard was designed to be extremely flexible. This flexibility allows you to customize the format of a class of documents such that *form follows function*. In other words, since the XML standard has very little to say about the elements and content of a document, you don't have to try and bend an application data model to fit within the confines of some ill-fitting standard. Instead, you can define the document format using domain-specific terms that help to make the document *self-describing*. This characteristic of XML makes XML documents much easier to read for both humans and computers alike.

---

[5] W3C stands for *World Wide Web Consortium*. You can find out more about the W3C online at *http://www.w3.org*.

Much of the beauty of XML lies in its simplicity. Indeed, when you get right down to it, XML doesn't really *do anything* in and of itself. However, like any good standard, it has provided a common ground for software developers to develop tools that simplify the process of exchanging data in a structured format. Compared with other document formats such as PDF, XML offers transparency and openness through its use of plain Unicode text. Ultimately, this openness removes barriers for exchanging information between heterogeneous systems. We'll see evidence of this at many points as we progress through this book.

2.1.2   Understanding XML Syntax

Now that you have a feel for XML's background and positioning, let's take a look at the syntax of XML markup. Figure 2.1 depicts a sample XML document containing a purchase order message. As you can see, the contents of this document are fairly easy to understand even if you're not familiar with XML syntax. In the upcoming sections, we'll examine the syntactical elements that give this document its structure.

2.1.2.1   Elements

The content of an XML document is organized into a series of *elements*. An XML document must define a *root element* (sometimes called a *document element*) that is the parent to all other elements within the document. For example, in the purchase order document example from Figure 2.1, the `PurchaseOrder` element is the root element; all of the other elements defined within the document are *child elements* of the `PurchaseOrder` element.

Listing 2.1 demonstrates the basic syntax of an XML element. As you can see, elements are escaped by tags that consist of the element's name surrounded by the angle bracket characters (i.e. the < and > characters). The space between the element tags is referred to as the element's *content area*. Within an element's content area, you can embed child elements, simple text, or both.

```
<element_name>

   <!-- Element content goes here... -->

</element_name>
```

Listing 2.1: Basic Syntax of an XML Element

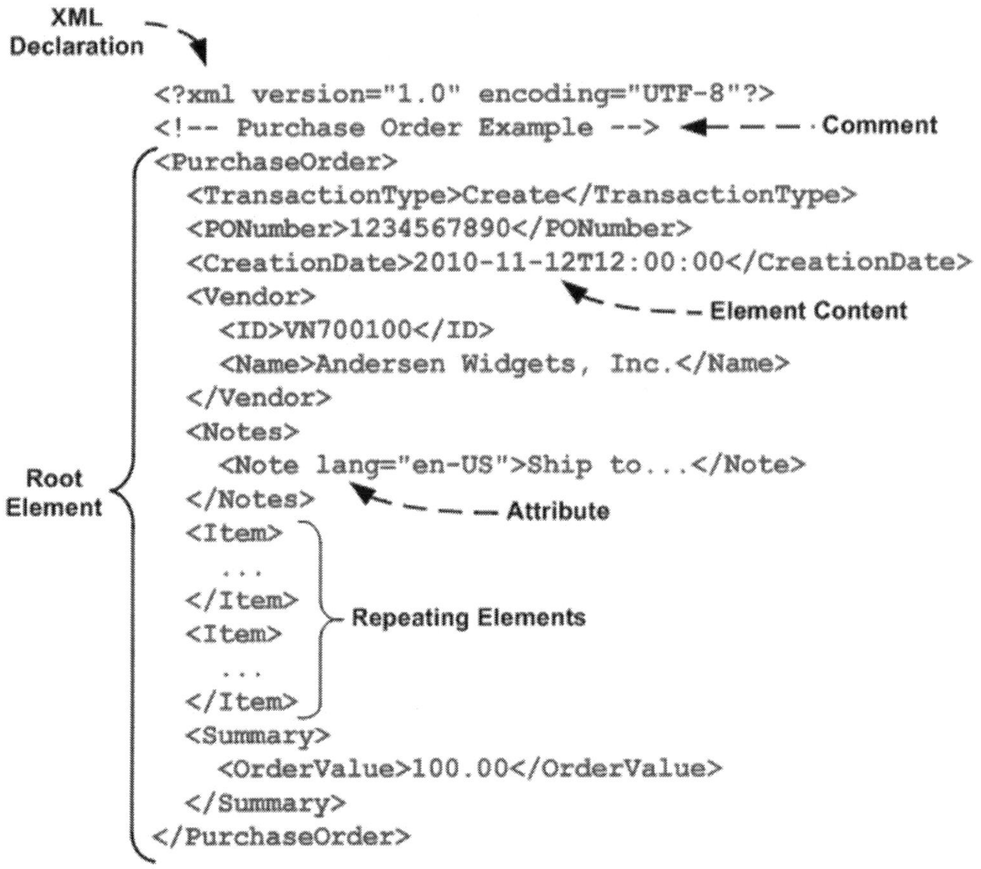

XML
Declaration

```
<?xml version="1.0" encoding="UTF-8"?>
<!-- Purchase Order Example -->   ←  — — · Comment
<PurchaseOrder>
    <TransactionType>Create</TransactionType>
    <PONumber>1234567890</PONumber>
    <CreationDate>2010-11-12T12:00:00</CreationDate>
    <Vendor>
        <ID>VN700100</ID>       ←  — — — Element Content
        <Name>Andersen Widgets, Inc.</Name>
    </Vendor>
    <Notes>
        <Note lang="en-US">Ship to...</Note>
    </Notes>                    ←  — — — Attribute
    <Item>
        ...
    </Item>
    <Item>                     — Repeating Elements
        ...
    </Item>
    <Summary>
        <OrderValue>100.00</OrderValue>
    </Summary>
</PurchaseOrder>
```

Root
Element

Figure 2.1: Anatomy of an XML Document

Every element in XML must have an opening tag and a corresponding closing tag in order to be valid. The lone exception to this rule is the so-called *empty element* whose syntax is shown in Listing 2.2.

```
<element_name />
```

Listing 2.2: Basic Syntax for Defining an Empty Element in XML

Looking at the purchase order document in Figure 2.1, you can see that each of the elements was given a meaningful name. For the most part, the XML standard does not restrict you in defining element names. However, there are a few rules that you need to be aware of:

> ➢ An element name may consist of letters, numbers, and other printable characters.

> ➤ An element name must not contain any spaces.

> ➤ An element name cannot begin with a number or punctuation character.

> ➤ An element name cannot begin with the letters "xml" in any form (e.g. "XML", "Xml", etc.).

Another thing to keep in mind is that XML is case-sensitive, so the element names PURCHASEORDER, purchaseorder, and PurchaseOrder are not the same. Typical convention within the industry is to define element names using *CamelCase notation*. Here, the first letter in each word within a compound word is capitalized such as CreationDate.

2.1.2.2   Attributes

Aside from the information enclosed in an element's content area, elements can be also enhanced to include special name-value pairs known as *attributes*. Attributes supplement an element with additional information that isn't contained within the element's body. Listing 2.3 demonstrates the basic syntax for defining attributes in XML.

```
<element_name attr1="attribute1" attr2="attribute2"...>
```

Listing 2.3: Basic Syntax for Defining Attributes in XML

As you can see in Listing 2.3, an element can include one or more attributes that are defined according to the following set of rules:

> ➤ Each attribute name must be unique within the element.

> ➤ An attribute is assigned a value using the equals (=) sign.

> ➤ The value of an attribute is text string that can be enclosed using either single quotes (') or double quotes ("). Both forms are acceptable, though double quotes are normally used. Of course, if the attribute value string contains a double quote, then single quotes should be used, and vice versa.

> ➤ Each name-value pair must be separated by one or more spaces.

From a technical perspective, the XML standard does not restrict you from defining many attributes to describe a particular element. However, in practice, attributes are used very sparingly. So how do you know when you should use attributes? Well, if you remember that XML is a language that can be used to define a grammar, then you can think of attributes as a type of *adjective*. If you recall from language class in grade school, an adjective is a word that helps describe a noun. For example, consider the noun *car*. When you talk about a car, you might refer to it as "the red car" or "the little car", etc. In this case, the adjectives "red" or "little" represent distinguishing characteristics used to describe a particular car. Similarly, attributes should be used in much the same way: to describe *distinguishing characteristics* of an element.

The `Note` element from Figure 2.1 illustrates an example of an attribute called `lang`. In this case, the `lang` attribute can tell us what language the purchase order note was written in. Of course, we could have just as easily defined a child element called `Language` underneath the `Note` element to serve the same purpose. However, if we define this characteristic as an attribute, it will be easier to search for `Note` elements of a particular language at runtime. This is analogous to defining a primary key or index to make it easier to search for records in a database table.

2.1.2.3 Processing Instructions

Most XML documents begin with an optional XML declaration that specifies the version of XML used to create the document as well as the character encoding scheme of the document. XML declarations are an example of *XML processing instructions*. As the name suggests, processing instructions provide useful information to the applications that will be processing the XML document. As such, they are not part of the actual document content.

Processing instructions begin and end with the character sequences `<?` and `?>`, respectively. Listing 2.4 demonstrates this syntax with an XML declaration.

```
<?xml version="1.0" encoding="UTF-8"?>
```

Listing 2.4: Basic Syntax of XML Processing Instructions

2.1.2.4 Namespaces

The hierarchical, tree-like structure of XML markup lends itself well to grafting in content defined in other markup languages. For example, imagine that someone within your organization has created a markup language to describe a common object like an address. Rather than re-inventing the wheel, it would make sense to reuse this vocabulary in other markup languages that contain addresses (e.g. purchase orders, business partners, etc.). This is analogous to the use of include programs or common data types defined in data dictionaries.

Whenever you mix-and-match markup languages in this fashion, you need to be careful to avoid *naming collisions*. Naming collisions occur whenever two or more elements/attributes in an XML document share the same name, but have different meanings. The XML excerpt in Figure 2.2 demonstrates this phenomenon using a sales order document. Here, the element `Address` is used in two different contexts: the first occurrence refers to the customer's mailing address (albeit using a strange syntax that we'll investigate shortly); the second occurrence refers to the e-mail address of a customer contact person.

```
<?xml version="1.0" encoding="utf-8"?>
<SalesOrder xmlns="http://acme.com/schemas/sales"      ⎫ Namespace
            xmlns:cdt="http://acme.com/schemas/cdts">  ⎬ Declarations
  <Header>                      ⬤ - ─ Namespace Prefix
    <Customer>
      <CustomerId>1234567890</CustomerId>
      <cdt:Address>
        <cdt:Name>Acme Company</gdt:Name>
        <cdt:Street>1234 Some St.</gdt:Street>
        <cdt:City>Albuquerque</gdt:City>
        . . .
      </cdt:Address>
      <ContactPerson>
        <Name>Paige Wood</Name>
        <Phone>
          <Number>866-555-1212</Number>
          <Extension>1212</Extension>
        </Phone>      ─ ─ ─ Default Namespace
        <Email>    ⬤
          <Address>paige.wood@acme.com</Address>
        </Email>
      </ContactPerson>
    </Customer>
    . . .
  </Header>
  . . .
</SalesOrder>
```

cdt Namespace (bracket annotation for the `<cdt:Address>` through `</cdt:Address>` block)

Figure 2.2: Working with XML Namespaces

While the context of each use of the `Address` element in Figure 2.2 might be clear enough for a human being, computers aren't so clairvoyant. One way to get around such ambiguity is to *qualify* each occurrence of the `Address` element so that the meaning is explicit. In XML, such qualifications are specified using *XML namespaces*.

XML namespaces provide qualified names for elements or attributes in an XML document. Such qualification takes a lot of the guesswork out of XML processing, allowing software modules to focus in on particular processing tasks. With that in mind, let's take a look at some syntax and scoping issues with XML namespaces.

Namespace Declarations

Listing 2.5 demonstrates the basic syntax for declaring a namespace in XML. As you can see, namespaces are declared within an element using the reserved XML attribute `xmlns`. The value of this attribute refers to a *Uniform Resource Identifier* (URI).

```
<element_name xmlns="http://someuri">

   . . .

</element_name>
```

Listing 2.5: Example Syntax for a Namespace Declaration

What are URIs?

URIs are used to uniquely identify a name or resource on the Internet. In the case of Listing 2.5, we have specified a *Uniform Resource Locator* (URL), which is a type of URI[6]. The URL `http://someuri` may or may not actually refer to a valid Web address; but that's not the point. The purpose of the URI is to guarantee the *uniqueness* of the namespace. Since Internet domain names are unique worldwide, URLs are commonly used to define namespaces as they guarantee exclusivity.

An alternative syntax for declaring namespaces involves the specification of a *namespace prefix*. Listing 2.6 demonstrates this syntax, assigning a prefix called `pfx` to the namespace name `http://someuri`. Namespace prefixes provide a convenient method for qualifying element names in terms of a particular namespace. For example, in Figure 2.2, the `cdt` prefix is used to bind the `Address` element and its children to the `http://acme.com/schemas/cdts` namespace. Such bindings are achieved by

---

[6] URIs can also be classified as a *Uniform Resource Name* (URN). A URN has a syntax that looks like this: `urn:isbn:9781592292356`.

qualifying the element names using syntax like `cdt:Address`, `cdt:Name`, etc. In XML parlance, the combination of a namespace prefix and an element name such as `cdt:Address` is referred to as a *qualified name* (or *QName*).

```
<pfx:element_name xmlns:pfx="http://someuri">

  ...

</pfx:element_name>
```

Listing 2.6: Declaring Namespace Prefixes

Namespace Scope

Technically speaking, a namespace can be declared within any element in an XML document. In practice though, namespaces are normally declared within the root element of an XML document to avoid clutter. This practice raises an interesting question though: How do we determine which elements belong to which namespace? Here, there are three basic scoping rules to keep in mind:

3. First of all, it pretty much goes without saying that an element that is explicitly qualified with a namespace (either directly or via a namespace prefix) belongs to that namespace.

4. Next, if there is no explicit namespace assignment for an element, then you must look at the element's predecessors to determine if a *default namespace* has been declared for any of those elements. Default namespaces are defined whenever an element specifies a non-prefixed namespace (e.g. the `SalesOrder` element from Listing 2.5). This default namespace applies to the element that declares it and all its children unless one of those children overrides it by explicitly declaring a namespace of its own (e.g. see the `cdt:Address` element and its children in Listing 2.5).

5. Finally, if neither of the previous conditions applies, then the element does not belong to any namespace.

Unlike elements, attributes are only assigned to a namespace whenever they are qualified with a namespace prefix. This is to say that attributes are unaffected by the specification of default namespaces, etc.

2.1.2.5 Comments

Unlike various forms of binary message types, XML documents purely consist of text. This means that XML documents can be read by human beings. Of course, while XML documents are intended to be self-describing, it never hurts to pass along some additional information to the reader. This information can be captured in the form of a *comment*.

Listing 2.7 shows the syntax used to create a comment in XML. The comment text within the `<!--` and `-->` character sequences can span multiple lines as needed. At runtime, comments are ignored by XML processors.

```
<!-- Comment Text -->
```

Listing 2.7: Syntax for Comments in XML

2.1.2.6 Entity References and CDATA Sections

As you have seen, certain characters have a special meaning in XML. For instance, the angle bracket characters (i.e. the `<` and `>` characters) are used to mark the boundaries of an element. In some cases, however, we may need to embed these special characters somewhere inside the text content of the XML document. For example, consider the XML markup used to describe a material in Listing 2.8. In the `LongDescription` element, notice that the left angle bracket character (`<`) is being used to specify certain tolerances for the material. As you might expect, the system will complain whenever you try to process this document because it can't match a closing tag with each opening element tag.

```
<Material id="721004896">
  <Description>Bolt</Description>
  <LongDescription>
    If hole positional tolerance < 0.03...
  </LongDescription>
</Material>
```

Listing 2.8: Dealing with Special Characters in XML

To avoid the kinds of errors shown in Listing 2.8, you can *escape* special characters in XML using *entity references*. For example, to correct the processing error from Listing 2.8, you must replace the `<` character with the `&lt;` entity reference. Table 2.1 shows the predefined entity references in XML.

Special Character	Entity Reference	Description
<	&lt;	Less Than
>	&gt;	Greater Than
&	&amp;	Ampersand
'	&apos;	Apostrophe
"	&quot;	Quotation Mark

Table 2.1: Predefined Entity References in XML

Alternatively, you can wrap up whole sections of text inside of CDATA sections as shown in Listing 2.9. CDATA (or *character data*) sections define areas within the XML markup where the content should only be interpreted as text. Within a CDATA section, you are not required to follow any XML syntax rules; here, text is simply text.

```
<Material id="721004896">
  <Description>Bolt</Description>
  <LongDescription>
    <![CDATA[
      If hole positional tolerance < 0.03...
    ]]>
  </LongDescription>
</Material>
```

Listing 2.9: Defining CDATA Sections in XML

Whenever you compile XML documents using data from external sources, it is a good idea to get into the habit of wrapping text content in CDATA sections or escaping special characters with entity references. This best practice prevents you from having to troubleshoot pesky XML syntax errors down the road.

2.1.3   Processing XML with XML Parsers

From a technical perspective, an XML document is nothing more than a raw sequence of characters. Of course, conceptually, there's a whole lot more to it than that. This begs the question: How can you tap into the richness of XML without having to spend countless hours building a custom processing tool? The answer is to enlist the services of an *XML parser*.

XML parsers analyze an XML document according to its grammatical structure, producing an abstraction that more closely aligns with the semantics of the markup. This frees you as the developer from having to worry about low-level string processing details so that you can focus your attention on the business process at hand.

While the XML specification states that "It shall be easy to write programs which process XML documents" (W3C, 2008), it doesn't have much to say about how this simplicity should be achieved. Therefore, various parser APIs have been developed over the years to address different XML processing requirements. The following sections describe some of the more common processing APIs available today.

2.1.3.1 Working with the SAX API

The *Simple API for XML* (or SAX) enables you to *listen* for parsing events that occur while the parser is analyzing an XML document. Here, for example, the parser will tell you that it has encountered an element with a particular name, an attribute, etc. These events are passed back to registered *callback methods* in which you can develop custom code to process the events.

The SAX API is classified as a stream-based processing API since the content of an XML document is *streamed* to the callback methods in a serial fashion. A useful analogy to describe this would be to imagine that you're drinking from a water hose. Here, lots of water is streaming by, but you only drink what you want. Similarly, SAX allows you to only grab hold of the data that you actually want; everything else is simply discarded. As such, SAX-based processing is highly efficient since the entire XML document does not need to be loaded into memory in order to process it.

2.1.3.2 Working with the DOM API

Another popular way to process XML is to use the *Document Object Model* (or DOM) API. Unlike the SAX API, the DOM API models the contents of an XML document in terms of a tree-like data object. Given the hierarchical nature of XML, this natural abstraction makes it easy to walk up and down an XML document using familiar node traversal functions such as `getChild()` or `getParent()`. In addition, the API also defines operations for creating new XML documents and manipulating an existing document's content (e.g. by grafting and pruning nodes, etc.).

Compared to the lightweight SAX API, DOM can be something of a resource hog since it must bring the contents of an entire XML document into memory. Therefore, while it may be more convenient to work with DOM, it is not always the best tool for the job. This is particularly the case when you know that the XML documents you will be processing are going to be quite large.

2.1.3.3 XML Data Binding

Much like the DOM API, XML data binding represents an XML document as an object in memory. However, rather than building a generic tree-like object, the XML data binding approach constructs an object whose structure mirrors the organization of the XML markup. Such specialization is achieved through code-generation tools that build a model of the XML document using an XML Schema document. We'll learn more about XML Schema in Section 2.2.

In order to understand how XML data binding works, let's consider an example. Imagine that you are using XML data binding to represent the purchase order XML document from Figure 2.1 and you want to access the order's line item data. In a DOM-based approach, you would have to obtain a reference to the root element and traverse your way down to the line item elements using the generic `getChildren()` operation. Conversely, with XML data binding, you would invoke an operation such as `getItems()`. In the latter case, you are hardly aware of the fact that you're processing XML; the generated data object looks and behaves just like any other structured data object.

2.2   Describing Documents with XML Schema

XML documents that adhere to the syntax rules outlined in Section 2.1.2 are considered to be *well-formed*. This is to say that the XML markup doesn't have any hanging elements, etc. However, just because an XML document is well-formed doesn't mean that it is *valid*; after all, it could just be a well-formed piece of gibberish. This begs the question: What makes an XML document valid?

Before we look at any formal definitions for document validity, let's think about what you would need to know in order to be able to process the purchase order example from Figure 2.1:

> ➤ The basic structure of the document (i.e., the `TransactionType` element comes first, then the `PONumber` element, etc.).

> ➤ The data types of the elements and attributes contained within the document.

> ➤ Whether or not certain elements are required or optional.

> ➤ The cardinalities of the elements (e.g. how many items are there?).

In essence, you need to know what the rules are for working with this particular XML markup language. Such rules can be expressed through the use of an *XML schema language*.

The term "schema" is derived from a Greek word that means *shape*. As such, the primary purpose of an XML schema language is to describe the structure and format of XML content. This description is realized in terms of a series of *constraints*. These constraints provide the information necessary to determine whether or not an XML document is valid. In this context, the XML schema document acts like a *contract* that must be upheld by producers of a particular class of XML documents. By extension, XML schema documents also serve as a definitive form of documentation for an XML markup language.

Most XML parser implementations provide native support for XML schema validation, allowing you to validate an XML document as you parse it. From a developer's perspective, this is a very powerful feature since tedious content validations can be handed off to a standard set of tools that are optimized for this purpose. Such delegation frees you from having to implement custom defensive programming logic to guard against severe runtime errors related to malformed content, type mismatches, etc.

Two of the more popular XML schema languages are the *Document Type Definition* (DTD) and *XML Schema Definition Language* (XSDL) languages. However, due to its more advanced capabilities, the W3C's XSDL (or more commonly, *XML Schema*) has surpassed DTD as the de facto standard for defining XML schemas. In the upcoming sections, we'll see how XML Schema can be used to build a rich data dictionary based upon XML.

2.2.1   Syntax Overview

XML Schema documents are defined using an XML-based syntax. Figure 2.3 illustrates this syntax with a schema that describes the purchase order document introduced in Section 2.1.

```
<xsd:schema xmlns:xsd="http://www.w3.org/2001/XMLSchema"
            xmlns:acme="http://acme.com/schemas/purchasing"
            targetNamespace="http://acme.com/schemas/purchasing">
  <!-- Global Element Declaration -->
  <xsd:element name="PurchaseOrder" type="acme:PurchaseOrderType"/>

  <!-- Complex Type Definition -->
  <xsd:complexType name="PurchaseOrderType">
    <xsd:sequence>
      <xsd:element name="TransactionType"
                   type="acme:TransactionType" />
      <xsd:element name="PONumber" type="acme:PONumberType" />
      <xsd:element name="CreationDate" type="xsd:dateTime"/>
      <xsd:element name="Vendor" type="acme:PartnerType" />
      <xsd:element name="Notes" minOccurs="0">
        <xsd:complexType>
          <xsd:sequence>
            <xsd:element name="Note" type="acme:NoteType" />
          </xsd:sequence>
        </xsd:complexType>
      </xsd:element>
      <xsd:element name="Item" type="acme:POItemType"
                   minOccurs="0" maxOccurs="unbounded" />
      <xsd:element name="Summary" minOccurs="0">
        <xsd:complexType>
          <xsd:sequence>
            <xsd:element name="OrderValue" type="acme:CurrencyType"/>
          </xsd:sequence>
        </xsd:complexType>
      </xsd:element>
    </xsd:sequence>
  </xsd:complexType>
  ...
</xsd:schema>
```

Built-in Data Type

Compositor

Custom Data Type

Occurrence Constraints

Figure 2.3: Anatomy of an XML Schema Document

As you can see in Figure 2.3, XML Schema documents begin with a document element named `schema`, which must be bound to the `http://www.w3.org/2001/XMLSchema` namespace. In addition, you can see that the purchase order schema also defines an optional *target namespace* `http://acme.com/schemas/purchasing`, which is the default namespace for XML documents created in reference to this schema. Beneath the root `schema` element, you'll find an assortment of different types of components. In general, these components can be classified into two basic categories: *component declarations* and *type definitions*.

2.2.1.1   Component Declarations and Type Definitions

In order to specify a class of XML documents, you must declare the elements and attributes that may appear in conforming instance documents. As you would expect, this implies much more than just enumerating a set of element and attribute names; you also need to specify the structure and format of these components. Therefore, each component declaration must include a *type assignment*. These type assignments refer to type definitions based upon built-in XML Schema types or custom types defined elsewhere within the XML Schema document.

As you'll learn in Section 2.2.3, XML Schema provides a very flexible type definition system that can be used to characterize just about any kind of content imaginable. This includes the definition of complex structured types as well as simple types such as strings, numbers, dates, and so on.

2.2.1.2   Scoping Issues

Components within an XML Schema document can be declared both *globally* and *locally*. Global components are named components that are declared as immediate descendants of the `schema` element. These components can be referenced anywhere within the schema document or reused in other schemas (Papazoglou, 2008). In addition, global elements can also be referenced by XML instance documents (i.e., documents based upon the XML schema).

Conversely, local component declarations are scoped to the definition or declaration that contains them (Walmsley, 2001). This implies that they cannot be directly addressed outside of the complex type definition. For example, the `Summary` element declaration in Figure 2.3 is a local declaration whose scope is limited to the `PurchaseOrderType` type definition.

So why should you care about declaration scoping issues? Well, once you understand the distinction between these two declaration types, you can start to see how XML schemas are organized. The W3C's XML Schema recommendation does not specify the order in which schema components must appear. Therefore, if you're trying to determine the structure of an XML document, you must first locate the declaration of the root element of the document. From there, you can recursively trace through type definitions to assemble the remaining pieces. If this sounds complex, don't worry - there are many useful schema editor tools to assist you in this process[7]. Nevertheless, it helps to understand the organization conceptually so that you can follow along with the tool.

2.2.2   Component Declarations

Now that you understand how XML Schema documents are organized, let's see how to declare the components that may appear in conforming XML instance documents. In particular, we'll investigate how to declare elements and attributes, which are the basic building blocks of XML documents.

2.2.2.1   Element Declarations

Elements are declared in XML Schema using the `element` element[8]. To see how this works, consider the declaration example contained in Listing 2.10. Here, we have declared an element called `PurchaseOrder` and indicated that it has the type `PurchaseOrderType`. In this particular case, the type `PurchaseOrderType` is a custom type defined elsewhere within the schema (see Figure 2.3). We'll learn more about type declarations in Section 2.2.3.

```
<xsd:element name="PurchaseOrderOrder"
             type="acme:PurchaseOrderType" />
```

Listing 2.10: Declaring Elements in XML Schema

In addition to having a *name* and a *type*, element declarations can also specify the number of occurrences of the element in an instance document using the `minOccurs` and `maxOccurs` occurrence constraints. For example, consider the `Item` element declaration contained in Figure 2.3. The given values of the `minOccurs` and `maxOccurs` attributes indicate that you can have zero or more occurrences of the `Item` element in a conforming instance document. Similarly, the `TransactionType` element can only occur once (which is the default behavior).

---

[7] An excellent tool for this is Progress Software's *Stylus Studio®*. See *http://www.stylusstudio.com* for more details.

[8] You can find out more options for element declarations in the W3C XML Schema recommendation available online at *http://www.w3.org/TR/xmlschema-1/#cElement_Declarations*.

2.2.2.2   Attribute Declarations

As you learned in Section 2.1.2, attributes can be used to describe distinguishing characteristics of an element using name/value pairs. In XML Schema, you declare attributes using the attribute element[9]. This element contains attributes that determine the attribute's name and data type, among other things.

To see how attributes are declared, let's take a closer look at the definition of the Notes element from the PurchaseOrderType definition in Figure 2.3. As you can see, the Notes element contains a child element called Note. This element is designed to contain a short note about the order. Since this note text could be written in many languages, we want to qualify the Note element with an attribute called lang that refers to the language used when the note was written.

Listing 2.11 contains the complete definition for the NoteType type (omitted from Figure 2.3 for brevity's sake). Here, you can see that we are using the attribute element to specify our lang attribute. The type of the lang attribute is the built-in xsd:language type. Though we'll learn more about types in Section 2.2.3, for now, simply note that attributes can only be assigned elementary types that have atomic values.

---

[9] You can find out more options for attribute declarations in the W3C XML Schema recommendation available online at *http://www.w3.org/TR/xmlschema-1/#cAttribute_Declarations*.

```
<xsd:complexType name="NoteType">
  <xsd:simpleContent>
     <xsd:extension base="acme:ShortNoteType">
        <xsd:attribute name="lang"
                       type="xsd:language"
                       default="en-US" />
     </xsd:extension>
  </xsd:simpleContent>
</xsd:complexType>
```

Listing 2.11: Declaring Attributes in XML Schema

By default, the use of attributes is optional. Therefore, if the data an attribute contains is needed for downstream processing, it is often a good idea to provide a default value for the attribute using the `default` attribute shown in Listing 2.11. Alternatively, you can declare required attributes using the `use` attribute shown in Listing 2.12.

```
<xsd:attribute name="lang" type="xsd:language" use="required" />
```

Listing 2.12: Declaring Required Attributes in XML Schema

2.2.3 Working with Data Types

Underneath the hood, XML documents are nothing more than one long string of characters. Therefore, in order to do something useful with them, we must apply a series of abstractions that differentiate between a *lexical space* and a *value space* (van der Vlist, 2002). For example, if you have an element called `CreationDate` that is supposed to contain a date, you would want to make sure that the contents of that element represent a valid date value (e.g. "2010-05-13"). Such semantics are realized in XML Schema through the use of *data types*.

Data types in XML Schema come in two basic flavors: *simple types* and *complex types*. As the name suggests, simple types are basic, elementary types that have atomic values. Examples of basic types include integers, strings, etc. Complex types, on the other hand, are aggregates that combine simple and complex types together in meaningful ways. In the following sections, we'll look at each of these data types in turn.

2.2.3.1 Simple Data Types

Much like programming languages, XML Schema provides many built-in simple data types[10] that form the building blocks for modeling more complex data types. These simple types include string types, numeric types, and date and time types, among others. Looking at Figure 2.3, you can recognize these types by the xsd namespace prefix (e.g. xsd:dateTime).

In addition to the built-in types, XML Schema also allows you to define your own custom simple types through a technique referred to as *restriction*. We'll see how to achieve this in Section 2.2.3.3.

2.2.3.2 Complex Data Types

Complex data types are analogous to structured data types in ABAP or classes in Java; they are aggregates that stack simple data types together like building blocks to model complex entities such as an address or purchase order. To see how this works, let's take a closer look at the sample schema from Figure 2.3, starting with the PurchaseOrderType type definition. As you can see, the PurchaseOrderType is defined as a complex type using the complexType element. Internally, the content of a complex type is arranged using *compositors*. Table 2.2 contains a list of the compositor types supported in XML Schema.

Compositor	Description
sequence	Requires a strict ordering of the elements defined within a complex type.
choice	Forces you to choose between one of several different elements within a complex type.
all	Allows you to include all or none of the elements defined within a complex type in any order.

Table 2.2: XML Schema Compositor Types

Looking back at the PurchaseOrderType definition in Figure 2.3, you can see that it uses the sequence compositor to aggregate its child elements; many of which are defined using additional custom complex types. If you recursively trace through the sample schema from Figure 2.3, you can see

---

[10] You can find a comprehensive list of the provided built-in data types at *http://www.w3.org/TR/xmlschema-2/#built-in-datatypes*.

that eventually you will arrive at a level in which elements are defined in terms of simple types such as `xsd:string` or `xsd:dateTime`. Taken as a whole, these complex type relationships form the structure of an XML document. Once the structure is in place, you can begin to apply further constraints by defining element value ranges, cardinalities, etc.

2.2.3.3 Type Derivation Techniques

Rather than having to reinvent the wheel each time you need to define a custom type, XML Schema allows you to derive new data types from pre-existing types using *restriction* and *extension* techniques. Besides saving on development time, type derivation also offers the possibility of dynamic type substitution in XML instance documents. We'll see how this works a little bit later on.

Type Derivation via Restriction

As the name suggests, restriction *restricts* a type by limiting its value range, length, or even structure in the case of complex types. To see how restriction works, let's look more closely at the `NoteType` type definition contained in Listing 2.11. Here, notice that the content of the `NoteType` type is defined in terms of another custom simple type called `ShortNoteType`.

Listing 2.13 shows the definition of the `ShortNoteType` type. As you can see, custom simple types are defined using the `simpleType` element. Internally, the content model for elements based on the `ShortNoteType` is defined by *restricting* the built-in `xsd:string` type to a maximum length of 100 characters. This restriction is achieved by applying a *facet* to the base `xsd:string` type: namely the `xsd:maxLength` facet.

```
<xsd:simpleType name="ShortNoteType">
  <xsd:restriction base="xsd:string">
    <xsd:maxLength value="100" />
  </xsd:restriction>
</xsd:simpleType>
```

Listing 2.13: Defining Custom Simple Types via Restriction

Facets can constrain the values of simple types in different ways. For example, the `xsd:maxLength` facet shown in Listing 2.13 is restricting the length of the `xsd:string` type. Facets can also be used to define value ranges, precision, enumerations, and even complex patterns through the use of regular expressions[11].

For complex types, restriction involves the removal of elements and/or attributes from the content model. For example, Listing 2.14 shows how we might condense the PurchaseOrderType to remove the Notes element. This is possible since the parent type declared the Notes element to be optional. Here, we're simply taking things a step further and removing the element altogether. While this might seem like an awful lot of work, there are benefits to restricting complex types this way. We'll learn about these benefits shortly.

```xml
<xsd:complexType name="CondensedPurchaseOrderType">
  <xsd:complexContent>
    <xsd:restriction base="acme:PurchaseOrderType">
      <xsd:element name="TransactionType"
                   type="acme:TransactionType" />
      <xsd:element name="PONumber" type="acme:PONumberType" />
      <xsd:element name="CreationDate" type="xsd:dateTime"/>
      <xsd:element name="Vendor" type="acme:PartnerType" />
      <xsd:element name="Notes" minOccurs="0" maxOccurs="0" />
      ...
    </xsd:restriction>
  </xsd:complexContent>
</xsd:complexType>
```

Listing 2.14: Restricting Complex Types

Type Derivation via Extension

Extension allows you to enhance the content model of complex data types with additional elements and attributes. Listing 2.15 contains an example that shows how this works. Here, we have defined a base BusinessPartner type that describes the basic characteristics of a business partner. The Vendor type *extends* the BusinessPartner type by adding an attribute named type and an element called TaxPayerId.

---

[11] You can find a more detailed description of facets online at *http://www.w3.org/TR/xmlschema-2/#facets*.

```xml
<xsd:schema xmlns:xsd="http://www.w3.org/2001/XMLSchema"
            xmlns:cdt="http://acme.com/schemas/cdts"
            targetNamespace="http://acme.com/schemas/cdts">
  <!-- Base BusinessPartner Type -->
  <xsd:complexType name="BusinessPartner">
    <xsd:sequence>
      <xsd:element name="Id" type="xsd:string" />
      <xsd:element name="Name" type="xsd:string" />
      <xsd:element name="Address" type="cdt:Address" />
    </xsd:sequence>
  </xsd:complexType>


  <!-- Extended Vendor Type -->
  <xsd:complexType name="Vendor">
    <xsd:complexContent>
      <xsd:extension base="cdt:BusinessPartner">
        <xsd:attribute name="type" type="cdt:VendorType" />
        <xsd:element name="TaxPayerId" type="xsd:string" />
      </xsd:extension>
    </xsd:complexContent>
  </xsd:complexType>
</xsd:schema>
```

Listing 2.15: Extending Complex Types

Type Substitution

As we mentioned earlier, one of the benefits of deriving types in terms of existing ones is the fact that the base and derived types can be used interchangeably in XML document instances. For example, consider a purchase order schema that contains a content area for specifying business partners based on the BusinessPartner type introduced in Listing 2.15. Since the Vendor type is defined as a sub-type of the BusinessPartner type, instances of the Vendor type can be substituted in purchase order documents without causing validation errors.

If you've ever worked with an object-oriented programming language, these concepts might sound vaguely familiar. In the context of XML Schema, type derivation is analogous to *inheritance*, and type substitution is analogous to *polymorphism*. By extension, many of the same useful design patterns associated with object-oriented programming apply to XML Schema. Ultimately, this provides you with the flexibility necessary to build rich data dictionaries.

2.2.4   Modularization Techniques

So far, all of the schema examples we have considered have been fairly arbitrary in nature. However, as you can imagine, real-world schemas can become quite large very quickly. Therefore, it usually makes sense to break the schema definition out into multiple files[12]. Fortunately, XML Schema makes it easy to modularize schemas using the `include` and `import` elements.

2.2.4.1   Schema Includes

The `include` element is used to break up components that belong to the same target namespace into manageable chunks. For example, we could take the `NoteType` definition from the purchase order schema document depicted in Figure 2.3 and store it in a separate file. Then, we can include it in the purchase order schema using the `include` element as depicted in Listing 2.16.

```
<?xml version="1.0" encoding="utf-8"?>
<xsd:schema xmlns:xsd="http://www.w3.org/2001/XMLSchema"
            xmlns:acme="http://acme.com/schemas/purchasing"
    targetNamespace="http://acme.com/schemas/purchasing">
  <!-- Include the Order Notes schema -->
  <xsd:include schemaLocation="OrderNotes.xsd" />
  ...
</xsd:schema>
```

Listing 2.16: Including Schemas

2.2.4.2   Importing Schemas

The `include` element is useful if you want to separate schema components that belong to the same namespace. However, as your data dictionary grows, you will want to reuse types that belong to other namespaces. For

---

[12] Typically, XML Schema definitions are contained in files ending with the `.xsd` extension. However, this is not a strict requirement in most cases.

this, you must use the `import` element shown in Listing 2.17. Here, we are bringing the components from the `http://acme.com/cdts` namespace defined in the `CoreDataTypes.xsd` file into context so that they can be used just like components defined within the importing schema (with the appropriate namespace qualifiers of course).

```xml
<?xml version="1.0" encoding="utf-8"?>
<xsd:schema xmlns:xsd="http://www.w3.org/2001/XMLSchema"
            xmlns:acme="http://acme.com/schemas/purchasing"
            xmlns:cdt="http://acme.com/cdts"
    targetNamespace="http://acme.com/schemas/purchasing">
  <!-- Import global data type definitions -->
  <xsd:import namespace="http://acme.com/cdts"
            schemaLocation="CoreDataTypes.xsd" />
  ...
</xsd:schema>
```

Listing 2.17: Importing Schemas

2.2.5   XML Schema as Documentation

More often than not, XML Schema documents are considered to be nothing more than technical artifacts used by developers to handle low-level XML processing details. However, this limited view ignores the fact that XML schemas provide an excellent form of documentation for message types.

In addition to the schema components themselves, you can also provide further documentation for schema types using the `annotation` element shown in Listing 2.18. This element allows you to provide a text-based description of a schema component as well as a link to more detailed documentation. Furthermore, it also possible to embed other types of useful information inside the `documentation` element such as HTML markup, images, etc. Such information can be exploited by advanced schema processor tools to depict complex relationships or background details.

```xml
<xsd:complexType name="POItemType">
  <xsd:sequence>
    <xsd:element name="ItemNumber" type="xsd:positiveInteger">
      <xsd:annotation>
        <xsd:documentation xml:lang="en"
```

```
        source="http://acme.com/schemas/ddic/PO#ItemNumber">
        Purchase Order Line Item Number
      </xsd:documentation>
    </xsd:annotation>
  </xsd:element>
 </xsd:sequence>
</xsd:complexType>
```

Listing 2.18: Documenting XML Schema with Annotations

2.3   Summary

This chapter provided a whirlwind tour of XML and XML Schema. While we endeavored to touch on all the high points, there is quite a bit more to learn when working with these technologies. Much of this knowledge comes with experience; something we'll be gathering as we proceed throughout the course of this book. For everything else, we have provided a list of references at the end of this chapter that are better suited to covering more advanced concepts.

In the next chapter, we'll move forward and explore the world of Web services and the surrounding technologies that make them a viable solution for interface development.

References

Monson-Haefel, R. (2004). *J2EE Web Services.* Pearson Education.

Papazoglou, M. P. (2008). *Web Services: Principles and Technology.* Pearson Education Limited.

van der Vlist, E. (2002). *XML Schema.* O'Reilly.

W3C. (2008, November). *Extensible Markup Language (XML) 1.0.* Retrieved May 4, 2010, from World Wide Web Consortium: http://www.w3.org/TR/REC-xml/#sec-origin-goals

Walmsley, P. (2001). *Definitive XML Schema.* Prentice Hall.

The Web Services Technology Stack

3

SAP NetWeaver PI uses Web service technology extensively throughout its solution architecture. From designing service interfaces to executing Web service calls at runtime, you'll find Web service technology on display at every turn. Therefore, as a PI developer, it is very important that you understand some of the core elements that make up the Web service technology stack.

After completing this chapter, you will be able to:

- ❖ Realize how Web services work conceptually.
- ❖ Understand how the SOAP protocol defines the rules for message exchange between Web service consumers and providers.
- ❖ Describe service interfaces using WSDL.
- ❖ Understand the Web service discovery process with UDDI.

3.1 Web Services Overview

Since they exploded onto the IT scene in the early 2000s, Web services have quickly become the de facto standard for implementing new interface solutions. However, despite their popularity, many people have a difficult time pinning down exactly what Web services are and why they're so important. Therefore, before we delve into the technical details of Web services, let's briefly take a look at Web services from a conceptual point-of-view.

The W3C defines a Web service as "...a software system designed to support interoperable machine-to-machine interaction over a network..." (W3C, 2004). This generic definition leaves much to the imagination in terms of implementation details. However, most of the time, whenever people talk about Web services, they are talking about Web services based on the *SOAP protocol*. SOAP defines a mechanism for exchanging XML messages between a Web service *consumer* and a Web service *provider* using common Internet protocols such as HTTP. This exchange is analogous to the kinds of HTTP requests that you send with your browser every day; the only difference is that the exchange is happening behind-the-scenes in an automated fashion.

At first glance, some might look at such simplicity and find themselves underwhelmed. However, it is such simplicity that gives Web services their power. Given the overall ubiquity of XML and HTTP, one can implement a Web service on just about any kind of platform imaginable. Of course, in order for all this to work, a set of rules had to be established to determine how messages are exchanged. With that in mind, let's take a closer look at SOAP.

3.2 SOAP-Based Messaging

With widespread vendor support and an ever-increasing portfolio of Web service implementations, SOAP has emerged as the de facto standard for implementing Web services within the enterprise. Therefore, as an interface developer, it's vitally important that you understand how to work with SOAP. This is particularly the case with SAP NetWeaver PI as it uses its own proprietary flavor of SOAP to route messages internally through its service bus.

In this section, we'll take a look at what SOAP is, and how it is used to facilitate message exchange. Along the way, we'll see how SOAP messages are constructed and processed by SOAP runtime environments. Finally, we'll conclude our analysis with a discussion on SOAP protocol bindings.

3.2.1   What is SOAP?

SOAP is defined by the W3C as "...a lightweight protocol intended for exchanging structured information in a decentralized, distributed environment." (W3C, 2007). More specifically, we're talking about exchanging XML documents using standard Internet protocols such as HTTP[13].

One of the things that sets SOAP apart is the fact that it is truly platform/language-independent. The only things you need to deal with Web services are an XML parser (or heck, even a string library) and an HTTP library. Of course, most modern environments like SAP NetWeaver PI have more sophisticated tools for dealing with Web services. Nevertheless, the point is that SOAP is an extremely flexible protocol that makes it easy for distributed applications to exchange messages with one another.

At the time of this writing, the current version of the SOAP standard is version 1.2. However, you'll still find that many Web service toolkits are still primarily based upon version 1.1. Where appropriate, we will point out differences between these two versions. However, for the most part, you'll find that the concepts we'll describe will apply equally to both versions of SOAP.

3.2.2   Anatomy of a SOAP Message

In many ways, SOAP messages are analogous to letters that you send via the postal service. For example, when you send a letter to someone, you don't just fold up the letter and stick it in the mailbox. Rather, you place it in a stamped *envelope* that contains address information about the intended recipient. This information helps the postal service process the message effectively and reliably. Similarly, when sending SOAP requests, you don't just send raw XML over an HTTP connection; instead, you wrap it up in a *SOAP envelope* as demonstrated in Figure 3.1.

---

[13] Technically speaking, you can exchange SOAP messages with a number of protocols such as SMTP or FTP, but HTTP is by far the most common protocol used.

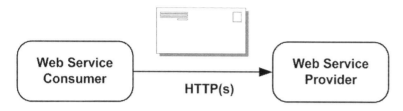

Figure 3.1: Transmitting a SOAP Envelope over HTTP

SOAP messages are comprised of three basic elements: an `Envelope` that is the root element of the message, an optional `Header` element that contains various metadata about the message, and a `Body` element that contains the message payload. Figure 3.2 depicts the basic anatomy of a SOAP message.

```
<?xml version="1.0" encoding="UTF-8"?>
<soap:Envelope xmlns:soap="http://schemas.xmlsoap.org/soap/envelope/"
               xmlns:wsse="http://docs.oasis-open.org/wss/..."
               xmlns:acme="http://acme.com/schemas/sales">
  <soap:Header>
    <wsse:Security>          ◄── SOAP Header Block
       ...
    </wsse:Security>

    <!-- Additional SOAP header blocks can go here... -->
  </soap:Header>

  <soap:Body>
    <sales:SalesOrder>         XML fragment;
       ...               ◄── Could be document-oriented
    </sales:SalesOrder>        or formatted as an RPC call...
  </soap:Body>
</soap:Envelope>
```

SOAP Header

SOAP Body

Figure 3.2: Anatomy of a SOAP Message

As you can see in Figure 3.2, the SOAP message format is not terribly restrictive. However, there are a few rules that you must abide by when working with SOAP:

➢ The root element of the message must be called `Envelope`, and it must belong to a specific namespace[14].

---

[14] For SOAP version 1.1, the namespace is `http://schemas.xmlsoap.org/soap/envelope/`. Version 1.2 uses the `http://www.w3.org/2003/05/soap-envelope` namespace.

- ➤ A SOAP message can optionally contain a `Header` element. However, if the `Header` element is present, it must be the first child of the `Envelope` element.

- ➤ Within the `Header` element, you can define multiple sub-elements referred to as *header blocks*. Each header block must be namespace-qualified.

- ➤ A SOAP message must contain a `Body` element. Inside the `Body` element, you can embed an XML document fragment or an XML representation of an RPC call. We'll explore these concepts further in Section 3.2.2.2.

- ➤ The SOAP `Body` element can also contain a `Fault` element that describes SOAP processing errors in the case of request/reply services.

Now that you have a feel for how SOAP messages are organized, let's take a closer look at some of the internal components that give SOAP messages their meaning.

3.2.2.1 SOAP Header Blocks

SOAP header blocks provide additional metadata about a SOAP message. Getting back to the postal service metaphor from above, you can think of a SOAP header block like a processing stamp or label that describes some aspect of the message. For example, a first class label on a letter implies a specific quality of service for message delivery by the postal service. Similarly, there are standards for defining SOAP header blocks that ensure that messages are processed reliably, in order, and so on.

Listing 3.1 contains an excerpt of a SOAP message that is using a header block defined by the WS-Security specification[15] to provide authentication details to the target Web service provider. Here, notice that the `Security` element is defined using a distinct namespace as outlined in the WS-Security specification (partially omitted for brevity's sake). Within the `Security` element, authentication credentials are provided in the form of a user name and password. Of course, WS-Security also supports additional token formats such as Kerberos, X.509, and so on.

---

[15] You can find out more about the WS-Security specification online at `http://www.oasis-open.org/specs/#wssv1.0`.

```
<soap:Envelope
    xmlns:soap="http://schemas.xmlsoap.org/soap/envelope/"
    xmlns:wsse="http://docs.oasis-open.org/wss/..."
    xmlns:wsu="http://docs.oasis-open.org/wss/...">
  <soap:Header>
    <wsse:Security>
      <wsse:UsernameToken>
        <wsse:Username>andersen</wsse:Username>
        <wsse:Password Type="...">casperp1</wsse:Password>
        <wsu:Created>2010-07-01T21:55:00-0500Z</wsu:Created>
      </wsse:UsernameToken>
    </wsse:Security>
  </soap:Header>
  <soap:Body>
    ...
  </soap:Body>
</soap:Envelope>
```

Listing 3.1: Defining a WS-Security Header Block

In addition to the many Web service standards that make use of header blocks, the SOAP specification also allows you to create as many custom-defined header blocks as you want. We'll see the benefits of this flexibility in Section 3.2.3.

3.2.2.2   SOAP Body

The SOAP `Body` element contains the actual payload of the message being sent. For example, in the SOAP request shown in Figure 3.2, we have embedded a `SalesOrder` document. Alternatively, we could transmit the sales order information in the form of a remote procedure call (RPC) as shown in Listing 3.2. In the latter case, the XML payload models a function call by defining elements that correlate with function parameters (e.g. `documentDate`, `customerId`, and so on).

```
<?xml version="1.0" encoding="UTF-8"?>
<soap:Envelope
    xmlns:soap="http://schemas.xmlsoap.org/soap/envelope/"
    xmlns:sales="http://acme.com/schemas/sales">
```

```
<soap:Body>
  <sales:createSalesOrder>
    <documentDate>2010-07-01</documentDate>
    <customerId>1234567890</customerId>
    ...
  </sales:createSalesOrder>
</soap:Body>
</soap:Envelope>
```

Listing 3.2: A SOAP Message Using the RPC Messaging Style

Generally speaking, you'll find that both document and RPC messaging styles are used quite a bit in Web service implementation projects. As you can imagine, RPC style messaging lends itself well to "Web servicifying" existing application modules such as BAPIs®, Enterprise JavaBeans™, etc. However, in Chapter 5, we'll see how lessons learned from SOA implementations have caused many to shift towards document-oriented service definitions.

3.2.2.3 SOAP Fault Messages

SOAP supports two different kinds of messaging: request/reply messaging and one-way messaging. In the case of request/reply messaging, the SOAP call is a synchronous one in which the client waits to receive a response. Frequently, some kind of error situation may prevent a SOAP provider from responding to a given request. In these circumstances, the SOAP provider can report exceptions back to the client using *SOAP fault messages*.

You can think of SOAP fault messages as being analogous to exceptions triggered in an ABAP function module or Java method. Their purpose is to report an exception situation back to a client so that they can decide what to do next. Like exceptions, SOAP faults are an all-or-nothing kind of proposition; if a SOAP fault message is returned to the client, the Body element of the response must contain a single Fault element and nothing else.

Listing 3.3 contains a sample SOAP fault message used to report an exception that occurred while processing a sales order creation request. Within the Fault element, you can see that the fault message provides the following types of information to the client:

> ➢ A `faultCode` element that contains a type of return code for the operation.

> ➢ A `faultString` element that contains a brief description of the error.

> ➢ An optional `detail` element that contains application-specific details about the exception. Here, the contents of the message are structured according to a customized XML schema type (e.g. the `SalesOrderCreationFault` type in Listing 3.3).

```xml
<?xml version="1.0" encoding="UTF-8"?>
<soap:Envelope
    xmlns:soap="http://schemas.xmlsoap.org/soap/envelope/"
    xmlns:sales="http://acme.com/schemas/sales">
  <soap:Body>
    <soap:Fault>
      <faultCode>soap:Client</faultCode>
      <faultString>Invalid creation request</faultString>
      <detail>
        <sales:SalesOrderCreationFault>
          <ValidationError>
            <Field>CustomerId</Field>
            <Description>
              Customer Id is missing or invalid.
            </Description>
          </ValidationError>
        </sales:SalesOrderCreationFault>
      </detail>
    </soap:Fault>
  </soap:Body>
</soap:Envelope>
```

Listing 3.3: An Example SOAP Fault Message

3.2.3   Processing SOAP Messages

Technically speaking, it would be possible to write a custom HTTP handler routine each time you needed to process a SOAP message. However, from a practical perspective, it's much more convenient to delegate the nitty-gritty details of SOAP processing to a SOAP runtime environment that is optimized for this purpose. Not only does the runtime environment take care of low-level communication issues, it can also abstract the details of the Web service to the point that a Web service looks just like any native function call.

In this section, we'll briefly consider some key aspects of SOAP message processing. This information will help guide more detailed discussions later on in this book. Moreover, having a basic understanding of SOAP message processing will help you to troubleshoot those pesky runtime errors that crop up from time to time.

3.2.3.1 SOAP Messaging Modes

As you have seen previously, SOAP doesn't have much to say about how you structure the contents of the body of a message. However, SOAP runtime environments care about these details quite a bit. In particular, they care about how the messages are *encoded*.

In Section 3.2.2.2, we described the two basic messaging styles employed by SOAP: RPC and document. These messaging styles are further categorized by the *encoding style* used to encode the message. Here, you can choose between two different encoding styles: *literal* and *encoded*. This yields four distinct possibilities for defining SOAP messaging modes:

> ➢ RPC/Literal
>
> ➢ RPC/Encoded
>
> ➢ Document/Literal
>
> ➢ Document/Encoded

As the name suggests, the literal encoding style reflects a *literal* representation of some XML schema type. Conversely, the encoded encoding style describes a type of mapping "...between common RPC semantics and programmatic types on one hand and XML on the other." (Monson-Haefel, 2004). These days, the encoded style is primarily a carry-over from a failed attempt at defining a platform-independent encoding for RPC-style messages in the SOAP 1.1 specification. Indeed, if you've ever heard someone complain about interoperability issues with SOAP, it's a good bet that the problems stem from the use of the encoded encoding style somewhere along the way. Nevertheless, as many legacy environments still use the encoded encoding style, it is important to be aware of its existence.

3.2.3.2 Understanding SOAP Intermediaries

Most of the time, whenever we think about Web services, we tend to think of point-to-point communications between a service consumer and a service provider. However, the SOAP specification defines a mechanism by which a SOAP request can be processed by one or more *intermediaries* along the message path between a service consumer and a service provider as illustrated in Figure 3.3.

Figure 3.3: SOAP Message Path

SOAP intermediaries are designed to provide some sort of value-add operation that enhances the message processing. For example, you might implement a SOAP intermediary to perform customized logging on inbound requests or carry out some kind of specialized authentication procedure. As such, SOAP intermediaries normally operate on SOAP header blocks that contain information pertinent to the value-add operation in question.

While the lower-level details of SOAP message processing are beyond the scope of this book, it is important to be aware of the fact that SOAP intermediaries can be chained together to enhance the processing of a Web service request. We'll see an example of this when we look more closely at the SAP NetWeaver PI Integration Engine pipeline in Chapter 12.

3.2.4 SOAP Protocol Bindings

Up to this point, we've been primarily focused on the semantics of SOAP processing at the conceptual level. Now, let's turn our attention toward some implementation-level concerns by looking at how SOAP is bound to other application protocols via *protocol bindings*.

Generally speaking, the SOAP protocol was designed to sit on top of common Internet protocols including HTTP, SMTP, and FTP. However, most of the time, HTTP is the preferred protocol binding for SOAP messaging. Indeed, it is the only specific binding demonstrated in the official W3C SOAP recommendation. Therefore, for the purposes of this book, we'll focus our attention solely on the HTTP protocol binding.

3.2.4.1 SOAP HTTP Binding

In many respects, Web services were originally conceived as behind-the-scenes extensions of online services accessed interactively via a Web browser. Given these origins, HTTP was an obvious choice for implementing SOAP processing. After all, most companies already had a large infrastructure of Web servers and programmers familiar with HTTP programming.

Another advantage of an HTTP binding is the fact that HTTP is a fairly "firewall-friendly" protocol. This is because most companies have already gone through the exercise of opening up an HTTP port (typically port 80 for plain HTTP and 443 for HTTPS) for various Web applications. Therefore, by *tunneling* SOAP messages through the existing HTTP infrastructure, you reduce many of the typical network/security obstacles associated with standing up a distributed integration scenario. With that in mind, let's consider how SOAP messages are delivered using the HTTP protocol.

Sending a SOAP Request over HTTP

The SOAP HTTP binding uses the HTTP POST method to transmit SOAP messages from a SOAP client to a SOAP provider service. Listing 3.4 demonstrates an example SOAP request to a sales order processing service. As you can see, this request is fairly straightforward: we're simply posting a SOAP message to the SalesOrder service provided by the acme.com host. Aside from the application/soap+xml content type used to transmit the message, this HTTP request looks like just about any other POST request that gets generated by a Web browser – and that's the point.

```
POST /SalesOrder HTTP/1.1
Host: acme.com
Content-Type: application/soap+xml; charset=utf-8
Content-Length: nnn

<soap:Envelope
    xmlns:soap="http://schemas.xmlsoap.org/soap/envelope/"
    xmlns:sales="http://acme.com/schemas/sales">
  <soap:Body>
    <sales:SalesOrder>
       . . .
```

```
      </sales:SalesOrder>
    </soap:Body>
</soap:Envelope>
```

Listing 3.4: Sending a POST Request over HTTP

In the case of synchronous calls, the SOAP response message is embedded in the HTTP response as demonstrated in Listing 3.5. Here, the `Body` element of the response could contain response information or a SOAP fault message in the event of a processing error.

```
HTTP/1.1 200 OK
Content-Type: application/soap+xml; charset=utf-8
Content-Length: nnn

<soap:Envelope
    xmlns:soap="http://www.w3.org/2001/12/soap-envelope">
  <soap:Body>
    ...
  </soap:Body>
</soap:Envelope>
```

Listing 3.5: Receiving a SOAP Response via HTTP

SOAP with Attachments (SwA)

Sometimes SOAP messages need to include data that is not very easy to represent using XML. For example, imagine that you're developing a Web service to process claims for an insurance provider. Here, in addition to the basic data about the claim, you might need to provide access to images, scanned forms, and other types of unstructured binary data that are included in the claim file. To deal with these types of requirements, the W3C came up with an extension to the HTTP binding called *SOAP Messages with Attachments* (W3C, SOAP Messages with Attachments, 2000).

SOAP Messages with Attachments (or SwA) uses the MIME (or *Multipart Internet Mail Extensions*) standard to break an HTTP message up into multiple parts: a SOAP envelope and one or more *attachments*. Listing 3.6 contains an example SwA request based on the insurance claim example described above.

```
POST /claimsService HTTP/1.1
Host: gecko.com
Content-Type: Multipart/Related; boundary=MIME_boundary;
type=text/xml; start="<claim12345.xml@gecko.com>"
Content-Length: XXXX

--MIME_boundary
Content-Type: text/xml; charset=UTF-8
Content-Transfer-Encoding: 8bit
Content-ID: <claim12345.xml@gecko.com>

<soap:Envelope
    xmlns:soap="http://schemas.xmlsoap.org/soap/envelope/"
    xmlns:claims="http://gecko.com/schemas/claims">
  <soap:Body>
    <claims:Claim id="12345">
      <ClaimHeader>
        ...
      <ClaimHeader>

      <Attachments>
        <Attachment type="image/tiff" description="Claim Form"
                    href="cid:claim12345.tiff@gecko.com" />
      </Attachments>
    </claims:Claim>
  </soap:Body>
</soap:Envelope>

--MIME_boundary
Content-Type: image/tiff
Content-Transfer-Encoding: base64
Content-ID: <claim12345.tiff@gecko.com>

...Base64 encoded TIFF image goes here...
```

Listing 3.6: A Sample SOAP with Attachments Message

As you can see in Listing 3.6, the content type for a SwA request is `Multipart/Related` instead of the typical `application/soap+xml` content type used for normal SOAP requests. In addition, the contents of the message are broken up into MIME boundaries that are identified with a specific *content ID*, one of which is designated as the *start* of the message. From the root message, references to other message parts are made through links to a message part's content ID. For example, notice how the `Attachment` element in Listing 3.6 points to the scanned claim form using the `href` attribute. A SOAP processor can trace these references and process the attachments accordingly.

SwA and SAP NetWeaver PI

Even if you don't have plans for working with attachments in your own Web services, it is important as an SAP NetWeaver PI developer to be aware of SwA as it is the foundation for the proprietary XI protocol that SAP uses internally to route messages through the PI service bus. You can think of the XI protocol as an extension of the SwA protocol that includes the definition of several custom SOAP header blocks specific to SAP NetWeaver PI.

The use of SwA enables the service bus to deal with non-XML payloads as necessary. For example, IDoc messages can be routed through the service bus as an attachment with content type `application/x-sap.idoc.bin`. We'll see further examples of the XI protocol as we progress throughout this book.

3.3 Describing Web Services with WSDL

As you learned in Section 3.2, the SOAP protocol makes it pretty easy for Web service consumers to call a Web service. However, despite its simplicity, there are still a few questions that you have to answer before you can call a SOAP-based Web service:

> ➢ What is the format of the message(s) being exchanged?

> ➢ What kind of protocol binding is used for the Web service?

> ➢ Where is the Web service located? What is its network address?

> ➢ What are the security requirements for accessing this service?

While the answers to such questions could be documented many different ways, there are advantages to structuring the documentation in a format that is machine-readable. The *Web Services Description Language* (or WSDL) is an example of one such format. In this section, we'll explore the use of WSDL for describing both SOAP-based Web services and service interfaces in general.

3.3.1   Introduction to WSDL

In a nutshell, WSDL (commonly pronounced "whiz-dul") is a flexible XML-based standard endorsed by the W3C that is used to document Web services. Besides answering basic questions about where a Web service is located and how it is addressed, WSDL can also be used to provide details about non-functional characteristics of Web services such as quality of service (QoS) and so on. Collectively, a WSDL document can provide a Web service consumer with everything it needs to know in order to access a Web service.

Due to its structured format, WSDL is well-suited for use with code generators. Here, the code generator can use the information in the WSDL document to build a proxy object that abstracts the details of the Web service call. We'll show you how to develop proxy objects in ABAP in Appendix A.

Most of the time, you do not have to build a WSDL document yourself. Instead, the Web service toolkit you're working with will usually generate it for you automatically. However, as a Web service consumer, you are oftentimes at the mercy of a Web service provider who may not follow best practices for service interface development. In these situations, it is crucial that you at least know how to read WSDL documents to figure out what's going on.

In the upcoming sections, we'll dissect a WSDL document and see what it looks like under the hood. As you're reading through this, keep in mind that SAP NetWeaver PI uses WSDL extensively to describe its service interfaces – regardless of whether or not they are actually implemented as Web services. In other words, even if you only plan to use SAP NetWeaver PI to process files or IDocs, you still have to describe these service interfaces using WSDL.

3.3.1.1 WSDL Document Organization

The contents of a WSDL document can be organized into two basic parts (Papazoglou, 2008):

> ➢ A *Service Interface Definition* that describes the interface of the service in abstract terms.

> ➢ A *Service Implementation Definition* that binds the abstract interface to a concrete protocol, address, and so on.

Figure 3.4 illustrates how the basic elements of a WSDL definition are related to one another[16]. As you can see, the root element of a WSDL document in version 1.1 of the standard is the `definitions` element. The direct children of the `definitions` element include:

> ➢ An optional `types` element that uses XML Schema to declare the custom types used to define the format of the messages being exchanged.

> ➢ One or more `message` elements that describe the messages being exchanged by service operations. Each `message` element can contain one or more `part` elements that organize the contents of the message. As you might expect, the use of the `part` element will vary based upon the style of messaging used (e.g. RPC or document).

---

[16] The details of these relationships are described in further detail in the provided XML Schema document for the WSDL standard available online at *http://www.w3.org/TR/wsdl#A4*.

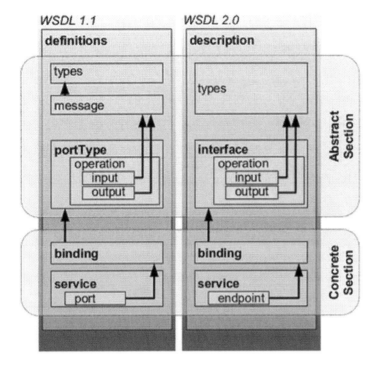

Figure 3.4: Organization of a WSDL Document (Wikipedia)

> ➤ One or more `portType` elements that define an abstract interface for the Web service. From a programming perspective, the `portType` element is roughly analogous to an interface in an object-oriented language such as ABAP or Java. A `portType` consists of one or more `operation` elements that define the operations (or *methods*) provided by the service interface.

> ➤ One or more `binding` elements that binds a `portType` to particular protocol such as HTTP, messaging style, and so on.

> ➤ One or more `service` elements that assign an address to a particular `binding`. The address is realized in the form of a sub-element called `port`.

Now that you are familiar with the basic organization of a WSDL document, let's look more closely at how service interfaces are defined and implemented using WSDL.

3.3.2   Defining Service Interfaces

As we mentioned earlier, WSDL allows you to define a service interface independently from its implementation. This abstraction is realized in the form of a port type definition that describes supported operations in terms of messages. The following sections explore these relationships in detail.

3.3.2.1 Port Type Definitions

The basis of a service interface definition in WSDL is the `portType` element. Listing 3.7 demonstrates how the `portType` element is used to define a service interface called `SalesOrderProcessing_In` and an operation called `SalesOrderCreateRequest_Async`.

```
<wsdl:definitions name="SalesOrderProcessing_In" ...>
  ...
  <wsdl:portType name="SalesOrderProcessing_In">
    <wsdl:operation name="SalesOrderCreateRequest_Async">
      <wsdl:input message="sales:SalesOrder" />
    </wsdl:operation>
  </wsdl:portType>
  ...
</wsdl:definitions>
```

Listing 3.7: Defining a Port Type in WSDL

In the `portType` definition from Listing 3.7, we only defined a single `operation`, but we could have defined additional operations such as `SalesOrderCloseRequest_Async` or `SalesOrderStatusRequest_Sync` if we had wanted to. In Chapter 5, we'll explore ways of organizing services at the right level of granularity.

Each `operation` element in the `portType` definition can contain an `input` element or an `output` element (or both), and zero or more `fault` elements. As you might expect, the `input`, `output`, and `fault` elements describe the *signature* of the service operation. This signature is defined in terms of *messages,* which we'll discuss in Section 3.3.2.2.

Message Exchange Patterns (MEPs)

The WSDL specification allows you to arrange the `input` and `output` elements within an operation to form familiar *messaging exchange patterns* (or MEPs). Table 3.1 describes the four message exchange patterns defined in the WSDL standard. While it is not important to memorize the names of these patterns, it is useful to familiarize yourself with them as they are used extensively within SAP NetWeaver PI to model service interfaces between senders and receivers.

MEP	Description	Operation Grammar

Notification	Represents an asynchronous request from the perspective of the sender.	`<wsdl:operation name="op1">`
		`  <wsdl:output`
		`      message="request" />`
		`</wsdl:operation>`

Solicit/ Response	Represents a synchronous request from the perspective of the sender.	`<wsdl:operation name="op1">`
		`  <wsdl:output`
		`      message="request" />`
		`  <wsdl:input`
		`      message="response" />`
		`</wsdl:operation>`

One-Way	Represents an asynchronous request from the perspective of the service provider.	`<wsdl:operation name="op1">`
		`  <wsdl:input`
		`      message="request" />`
		`</wsdl:operation>`

Request/ Response	Represents a synchronous request from the perspective of the service provider.	`<wsdl:operation name="op1">`
		`  <wsdl:input`
		`      message="request" />`
		`  <wsdl:output`
		`      message="response" />`
		`</wsdl:operation>`

Table 3.1: Message Exchange Patterns in WSDL

3.3.2.2 Message Definitions

WSDL uses XML Schema as its type system. Consequently, the structure and format of the messages defined in a WSDL `portType` definition is specified using XML Schema. The excerpt of the WSDL document contained in Listing 3.8 shows how a `SalesOrder` message is defined in WSDL. Here, notice that we have embedded a `SalesOrder` XML schema document inside the `types` element. This allows us to define the `SalesOrder` message in terms of the `SalesOrder` element declaration.

```
<wsdl:definitions name="SalesOrderProcessing_In" ...>
  ...
  <wsdl:types>
    <xsd:schema xmlns:xsd="http://www.w3.org/2001/XMLSchema">
```

```
    <xsd:element name="SalesOrder"
                 type="sales:SalesOrderType" />
    ...
  </xsd:schema>
</wsdl:types>
<wsdl:message name="SalesOrder">
  <wsdl:part name="SalesOrder" element="sales:SalesOrder" />
</wsdl:message>
...
</wsdl:definitions>
```

Listing 3.8: Defining Messages in WSDL

Technically speaking, it is possible to embed an arbitrarily large XML Schema document inside the `types` element. However, if you prefer to keep things modularized, you can define XML Schemas in separate WSDL documents and import them using the `import` element defined by the WSDL standard.

3.3.3   Creating a Protocol Binding

As you learned in Section 3.3.2, the WSDL `portType` element defines a service interface in terms of a series of abstract service operations. In order to put these operations to use, we need to bind them to a concrete protocol and endpoint address. In WSDL, this is achieved using the `binding` and `service` elements which are described in the following sections.

3.3.3.1   Protocol Bindings

The WSDL `binding` element maps an abstract `portType` definition to a set of concrete service implementation details. In particular, the `binding` element defines the message protocol, messaging style, and encoding style used to access the service operations.

Listing 3.9 contains an excerpt of a WSDL document that defines a possible binding for the `SalesOrderProcessing_In` port type definition from Listing 3.7. Here, we have defined a binding called `SalesOrderProcessingBinding` that references the `SalesOrderProcessing_In` port type. Within the binding, the implementation details are organized as follows:

> ➢ First, we have a SOAP-specific `binding` element that assigns the SOAP/HTTP protocol binding to the service interface via the `transport` attribute.

➢ Next, the SOAP-specific `binding` element also sets the default messaging style for the service interface as `document` using the `style` attribute.

➢ Finally, we realize the implementation details for each `operation` described in the `portType` definition using the familiar WSDL `operation` element. In this case, however, we are focused on determining the encoding style of the messages being changed. For instance, in the excerpt shown in Listing 3.9, we're using the SOAP-specific `body` element to assign a literal encoding to the input message of the `SalesOrderCreateRequest_Async` operation.

```
<wsdl:definitions name="SalesOrderProcessing_In" ...>
  ...
  <wsdl:binding name="SalesOrderProcessingBinding"
                type="SalesOrderProcessing_In">
    <!-- Set the default messaging style and
         transport protocol for the operations -->
    <soap:binding style="document"
        transport="http://schemas.xmlsoap.org/soap/http" />

    <wsdl:operation name="SalesOrderCreateRequest_Async">
      <soap:operation soapAction="" />
      <wsdl:input>
        <soap:body use="literal"
             namespace="http://acme.com/schemas/SalesOrder" />
      </wsdl:input>
    </wsdl:operation>
  </wsdl:binding>
  ...
</wsdl:definitions>
```

Listing 3.9: Defining Implementation Details for a Service Interface in WSDL

The details of the WSDL `binding` element will vary somewhat depending upon the chosen protocol, messaging style, etc. Fortunately, these low-level details are often abstracted by Web service toolkits that have a user-friendly GUI or wizard to guide you through the configuration process.

3.3.3.2 Defining the Service Endpoint(s)

Once you define a binding for a port type, the last thing you need to do to tie everything together is define a *service endpoint*. Listing 3.10 demonstrates how to define a service endpoint in WSDL.

```
<wsdl:definitions name="SalesOrderProcessing_In" ...>
  ...
  <wsdl:service name="SalesOrderProcessingService">
    <wsdl:port name="SalesOrderProcessingServiceDefault"
               binding="SalesOrderProcessingBinding">
      <soap:address
          location="http://acme.com/services/SalesOrder" />
    </wsdl:port>
  </wsdl:service>
  ...
</wsdl:definitions>
```

Listing 3.10: Defining a Service Endpoint in WSDL

As you can see in Listing 3.10, service endpoints are defined using the WSDL service element. Within the service element, you can define one or more *ports* using the port element. The port element is used to assign a physical address (i.e., a URL) to a binding. For example, in Listing 3.10, the SalesOrderProcessingServiceDefault port is assigning an address to the SalesOrderProcessingBinding binding described in Listing 3.9. Since this binding specifies the use of the SOAP/HTTP protocol, the service endpoint address is defined using the SOAP-specific address element. Here, the address is the URL specified using the location attribute.

3.3.4 Uses of WSDL

Most of the time, WSDL is used to describe a Web service from both an interface and implementation perspective. When used in this context, WSDL gives you everything you need to consume a Web service. Indeed, as discussed earlier, most Web service toolkits can consume WSDL documents of this type and generate a proxy object that abstracts and simplifies the process of consuming the Web service.

Looking back at Section 3.3.2, you can see that WSDL is also useful as a tool for documenting service interfaces independently from an underlying implementation. This capability is very useful for tools like SAP NetWeaver PI that implement integration scenarios using a wide array of communication channels (e.g. flat files, IDocs, and so on). In other words, in order to maximize flexibility when designing integration scenarios in SAP NetWeaver PI, it is important to be able to separate the interface from the implementation so that the two can vary independently. We'll see the advantages of this more clearly later on in this book.

3.4 Service Discovery with UDDI

Developing service interfaces is a necessary first step towards implementing an SOA. However, your development efforts are wasted if no one within the organization uses these services in their own developments. Of course, you could try and advertise the existence of these services, but the effectiveness of your campaign is subject to the attention spans of developers that are often narrowly focused on other tasks.

A more effective way to get the word out about Web services is to publish them in a publicly available *service registry*. That way, developers can come along and browse for services on demand. Recognizing the need for this, industry leaders decided to develop a standard for implementing and accessing service registries. That standard is now known as *Universal Description, Discovery, and Integration* (UDDI) (OASIS).

Figure 3.5 shows how a UDDI service registry unites a Web service consumer with a Web service provider. As you can see, the description and discovery process takes place in three steps:

1. First, a Web service provider creates a Web service and publishes the WSDL to the UDDI service registry.

2. Next, a Web service consumer comes along looking for a particular kind of Web service and browses through the UDDI registry looking for a match. After a match is found, the consumer can then download the provider's WSDL file and generate a Web service proxy object.

3. Finally, at runtime, the Web service proxy object is used to broker a SOAP-based Web service call to the Web service provider.

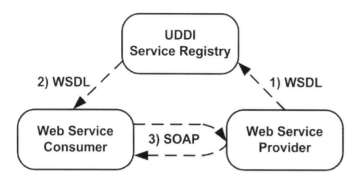

Figure 3.5: Web Service Description and Discovery Cycle

Beginning with SAP NetWeaver 7.1, SAP has delivered a UDDI-compliant registry called the *Enterprise Services Registry*. For an in-depth analysis of this tool and its usage, we highly recommend *Developing Enterprise Services for SAP* (Pohl & Peter, 2010).

3.5   Summary

This chapter provided an overview of Web services and their surrounding technologies. In particular, we examined how the SOAP protocol is used to coordinate the exchange of messages between a Web service consumer and a Web service provider. We also looked at how WSDL can be used to document services independently from their implementation. Finally, we wrapped up our discussion by introducing you to the service discovery process using UDDI.

This concludes the introductory section of this book. In the next chapter, we'll shift gears and turn our attention towards more practical matters starting with service development in the ESR.

References

Monson-Haefel, R. (2004). *J2EE Web Services.* Boston: Pearson Education.

OASIS. (n.d.). *OASIS UDDI Online Community*. Retrieved July 9, 2010, from UDDI Online Community Homepage: http://uddi.xml.org/

Papazoglou, M. P. (2008). *Web Services: Principles and Technology.* Pearson Education.

Pohl, T., & Peter, M. (2010). *Developing Enterprise Services for SAP.* Galileo Press.

W3C. (2000, December). *SOAP Messages with Attachments*. Retrieved July 8, 2010, from W3C Note: SOAP Messages with Attachments: http://www.w3.org/TR/SOAP-attachments

W3C. (2007, April). *SOAP Version 1.2 Part 1: Messaging Framework (Second Edition)*. Retrieved July 1, 2010, from W3C Web Site: http://www.w3.org/TR/2007/REC-soap12-part1-20070427/#intro

W3C. (2004, February). *Web Services Architecture*. Retrieved July 1, 2010, from W3C Web site: http://www.w3.org/TR/ws-arch/#whatis

Wikipedia. (n.d.). *Web Services Description Language.* Retrieved December 2, 2010, from Wikipedia: http://en.wikipedia.org/wiki/Web_Services_Description_Language

Getting Started
with the ESR

The Enterprise Services Repository (ESR) is a defined by SAP as a "central repository where you define, access, and manage SOA assets such as services, data types, and so on" (SAP AG). As such, it houses all of the design-time objects that you create to implement integration scenarios.

In this chapter, we will introduce you to the ESR and its editor, the *Enterprise Services Builder* (ES Builder). After completing this chapter, you will be able to:

- ❖ Understand how content is organized in the ESR.
- ❖ Define products and software components in the SLD software catalog.
- ❖ Work with the ES Builder tool.
- ❖ Understand how to transport content into and out of the ESR.

4.1   ESR Content Organization

During the course of the interface development process, you will accumulate a number of SOA assets. Therefore, before you kick off your development project, it's a good idea to have a software logistics plan in place beforehand. That way, you can group related assets together in a clear and intuitive way that promotes reuse.

In this section, we will present you with an overview of software logistics concepts within the ESR. Once you understand these concepts, we'll then show you how they are applied on a practical level in Sections 4.2 and 4.3.

4.1.1   Software Component Versions

Design objects in the ESR (hereafter referred to as *repository objects*) are grouped together within a shipment unit called a *software component version* (SWCV). If you have experience developing Java objects using the *SAP NetWeaver® Development Infrastructure* (NWDI) usage type, then you are probably already familiar with software components. If not, then for now, suffice it to say that software components are part of a software catalog provided with another SAP NetWeaver product called the *System Landscape Directory* (SLD). We'll have more to say about the SLD in Section 4.2.

Once a SWCV is defined in the SLD, it can be imported into the ESR. From a development perspective, this is analogous to creating a project or package in an IDE to organize your development objects. As such, the importing of a SWCV is a necessary first step to kicking off the development process in the ESR.

Figure 4.1 shows an example of a SWCV called `SAP BASIS 7.11` that is provided by default with every SAP NetWeaver PI installation. This SWCV contains core repository objects as well as some demo objects that you can use as a guide for your own developments.

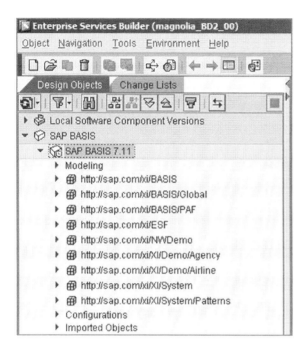

Figure 4.1: SWCVs in the ESR © Copyright 2010. SAP AG. All rights reserved

4.1.2   Namespaces

Within a SWCV, repository objects are further organized by *namespaces*. Syntactically speaking, namespaces in the ESR use the same syntax as namespaces in XML (see Chapter 2 for a refresher on XML namespaces). However, the similarities between these two concepts pretty much stop there. In the ESR, a namespace qualifies a repository object with a unique identifier based on a URI. Collectively, this implies that a repository object is uniquely identified by a 3-tuple within the ESR:

> ➢ SWCV

> ➢ Namespace

> ➢ Repository object name

SWCVs can contain as many namespace definitions as needed. For example, Figure 4.2 shows how namespaces are defined within the `SAP BASIS 7.11` SWCV. As you can see, each of these namespace definitions is defined using URLs. Here, notice how SAP used their own domain name (i.e. `sap.com`) to uniquely define the namespaces. The subsequent resource paths drill in further to demarcate specific functional areas, etc.

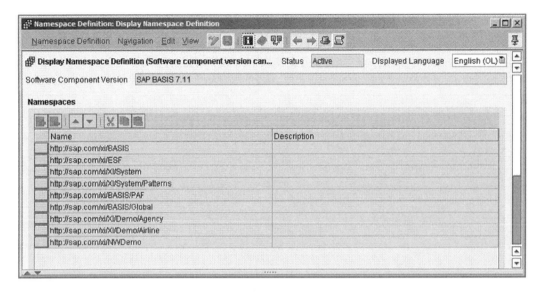

Figure 4.2: Namespace Definitions within a SWCV © Copyright 2010. SAP AG. All rights reserved

4.1.3   Folders

Beginning with Release 7.1 of SAP NetWeaver PI, SAP introduced another organizational object within the ESR: *folders*. Folders in the ESR are used in much the same way that you use folders on your local workstation. As such, they can be organized and nested in order to group repository objects in an intuitive manner (see Figure 4.3).

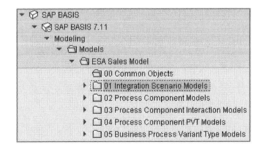

Figure 4.3: Folders in the ESR © Copyright 2010. SAP AG. All rights reserved

Unlike SWCVs and namespaces, folders are not part of the repository object definition. In other words, you can move repository objects between different folders without changing their location within the ESR. The folders just make it easier to find what you're looking for.

4.1.4   Repository Objects

At the bottom of the ESR logistics tree are the repository objects themselves. Here, we're talking about service interfaces, data types, message mappings, and so on.

From a logistics perspective, repository objects are versioned objects defined within the context of a SWCV/namespace. Internally, repository objects are assigned an object ID within the ESR. You can view this object ID by opening up a repository object in the ES Builder and selecting the *Properties* (▣) button. This will bring up the *Object Properties* dialog window shown in Figure 4.4.

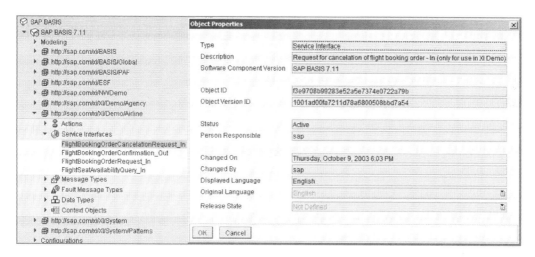

Figure 4.4: Viewing Repository Object Properties in the ESR © Copyright 2010. SAP AG. All rights reserved

If you look closely at Figure 4.4, you'll notice that besides an object ID, repository objects also maintain an object version ID. This identifier points to specific versions of repository objects maintained within the ESR. You can view the version history of a repository object by selecting the *History* menu item in the object editor main menu (see Figure 4.5). Figure 4.6 shows the version history for a particular repository object. To retrieve a prior version, simply select the version that you want and click on the *Open Version* (▣) button.

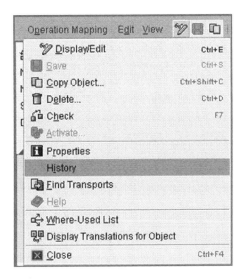

Figure 4.5: Viewing the Version History of Repository Objects – Part 1

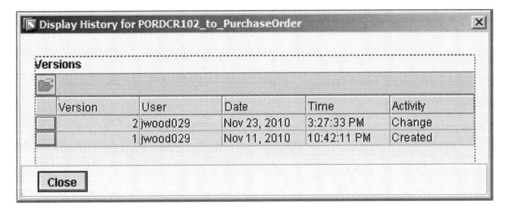

Figure 4.6: Viewing the Version History of Repository Objects - Part 2

4.2 Defining Software Components in the SLD

In the previous section, we made mention of the fact that SWCVs are defined outside of the ESR in a separate SAP software product called the SLD. In this section, we will show you how these components are maintained within the SLD software catalog.

4.2.1 What is the SLD?

Before we delve into specifics of working with the SLD, it is important to first understand exactly what it is. In general, the SLD is positioned as a "central information repository for your system landscape" (SAP AG). As mentioned previously, part of this repository includes a software catalog in which you can define installable software components. Furthermore, the SLD can also maintain information about the technical systems installed within your system landscape.

From a technical perspective, the SLD is part of the AS Java system installation[17]. As such, it has a Java-based Web user interface that allows you to view and configure specific aspects of the system landscape. Figure 4.7 shows the layout of the main page. You can get to this page by executing transaction SXMB_IFR and selecting the *System Landscape Directory* link.

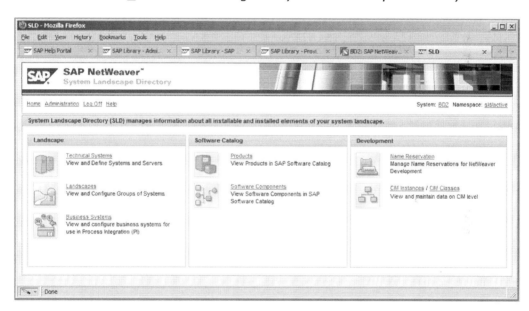

Figure 4.7: System Landscape Directory Main Page © Copyright 2010. SAP AG. All rights reserved

In addition to its Web-based user interface, the SLD also provides an HTTP-based interface that enables peripheral systems to synchronize information

---

[17] Technically speaking, the PI installation wizard gives you the option of installing a new SLD or linking up with an existing one. For more information, see the SAP SDN Weblog entitled *Planning a Strategy for the System Landscape Directory (SLD) of SAP NetWeaver* (Zarske).

with it. In particular, this makes it possible for each SAP system in your landscape *register* itself with the SLD. We'll see the utility of this system metadata in Part 3 of this book.

4.2.2 Understanding the SAP Component Model

The SLD software catalog contains a listing of all of the installable products within your system landscape. This includes products provided by SAP as well as custom products developed in-house. In the context of SAP NetWeaver PI, these products represent the content used to implement integration scenarios within the ESR. To put this into perspective, let's take a closer look at the component model that drives all this.

Figure 4.8 illustrates the component model used within the SLD software catalog. As you can see, this all starts with the definition of a product, which can exist in versions. From SAP's perspective, a product basically represents a piece of shrink-wrapped software that customers purchase from them (e.g. SAP ECC 6.0, SAP NetWeaver PI 7.11, and so on). At the customer site, this distinction gets a little fuzzier. For custom development, we suggest that you define your products in terms of the products that you're integrating with[18].

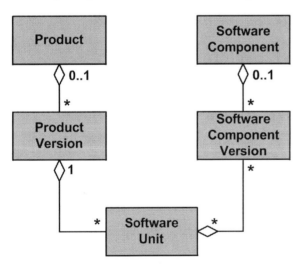

Figure 4.8: Products and Software Components in the SLD Software Catalog

---

[18] The SAP NetWeaver How-To Guide called *PI Best Practices: Naming Conventions* serves as an excellent guide for determining the organization of products and software components within the SLD. See Section 3.1, *System Landscape Directory* of this guide for more details.

As you can see in Figure 4.8, products are aggregates that are comprised of one or more *software units*. According to the SAP help documentation, a software unit is an "aspect of the product function that is always installed as a bundle." (SAP AG). As such, it represents a logical link between a product and its constituent *software components*.

As the name suggests, software components represent reusable components or modules that provide the core functionality for a product. Like products, software components also exist in versions, and can be mixed and matched to implement various product requirements.

To see how all this fits together, let's consider the SAP ECC product model depicted in Figure 4.9. Here, you can see that SAP has defined a product called SAP ECC. At the time of this writing, there are currently two versions of the SAP ECC product: version 5.0 and 6.0. As you can see, the SAP ECC 6.0 product version is split into multiple software units, one of which is called SAP ECC Server 6.0. Internally, the SAP ECC Server 6.0 software unit bundles together familiar software components such as SAP APPL 6.00, SAP BASIS 7.00, and so on.

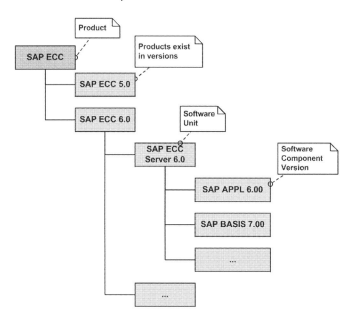

Figure 4.9: Understanding the Relationships between Products and Software Components

4.2.3   Working with the SLD Software Catalog

Now that you understand the relationships between products and software components, let's see how they are maintained in the SLD software catalog. To guide this presentation, we'll consider how we might model some software components used to implement a purchase order interface scenario between an SAP ERP system and a 3rd-party supply chain optimization product produced by a fictitious software vendor called Acme, Inc.

> **Note**
>
> In order to be able to maintain components in the SLD software catalog, you must have the proper role assignments assigned to your user account. You can read more about these roles in the SAP help library documentation in the section entitled *Configuring SLD Security Roles* (SAP AG).

4.2.3.1   Creating Products

A common mistake made by developers new to PI is to simply create a single product/software component and pack all of their repository objects into it. While this might make matters easier up front, it can cause huge problems down the road. Fortunately, SAP has published an SAP NetWeaver How-To Guide called *PI Best Practices: Naming Conventions* (SAP AG) that can help you avoid such pitfalls. Throughout the course of this book, we will develop our component model according to these conventions.

One of the recommendations in the aforementioned How-To Guide is to group products *vertically* rather than *horizontally*. This implies that you do not create a separate product for each integration scenario. Instead, you create a product for each application that you are integrating with, and then supplement those products with *application products* containing the collaboration objects that crosscut both applications. For example, in our PO interface scenario, we are implementing an interface between SAP ERP and a 3rd-party application. Therefore, we will need three products to implement the integration scenario:

> ➢ A product called BOWDARK_I_SAPERP_EXT to group together repository objects specific to the sending SAP ERP system[19].

---

[19] Here, you might be tempted to reuse the SAP ECC product that SAP ships by default with the SLD. However, SAP recommends that you do not use their standard products for custom development.

➢ A product called BOWDARK_I_ACME to group together repository objects specific to the receiving Acme system.

➢ A product called BOWDARK_A_PROCUREMENT to group together repository objects which intersect both systems (e.g. message mappings, integration processes, and so on).

To create these products in the SLD, perform the following steps:

1. Log onto the PI AS ABAP system and execute transaction SXMB_IFR. Then, from the *Process Integration Tools* page, select the *System Landscape Directory* link. This will bring you to the SLD main page shown in Figure 4.7.

2. From the main page, click on the *Products* link in the middle of the page.

3. This will bring you to the *Software Catalog* editor screen shown in Figure 4.10. Click the *New...* button to launch the product creation wizard.

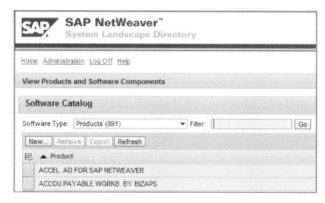

Figure 4.10: Creating a Product in the SLD (Part 1)
© Copyright 2010. SAP AG. All rights reserved

4. The first roadmap step requires you to select the type of maintenance you wish to perform. For new products, you'll want to select the *Create a New Product and Version* radio button. Click the *Next* button to continue.

5. On the *Product* roadmap step, you must specify three things:

   a. In the *Product Name* field, you must give your product a unique name within the catalog. For example, in Figure 4.11,

we have given our SAP ERP-based product the name
`BOWDARK_I_SAPERP_EXT`. See the aforementioned SAP
NetWeaver How-To Guide for details about this naming
convention.

b. In the *Product Vendor* field, you will want to enter your
company's domain name. For example, in Figure 4.11, we
have selected `bowdark.com`.

c. In the *Product Version* field, you specify a version number for
the product. New products usually start out with version 1.0.

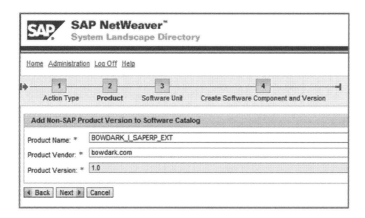

Figure 4.11: Creating a Product in the SLD (Part 2)

6. After you specify the basic product information, you can click the
Next button to move on to the *Software Unit* roadmap step. Here,
you can define an initial software unit to organize your product in
the *Unit Name* field. Once you're satisfied with your selection, click
Next.

7. On the next final roadmap step, you have the option of defining an
initial software component for the product (see Figure 4.12). Here,
you must simply provide the vendor name (which will mirror the
product selection), the software component name, and a version
number. Click the *Finish* button to commit your changes.

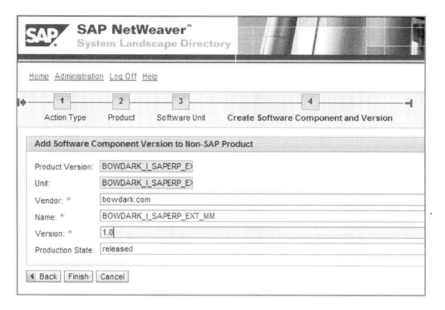

Figure 4.12: Creating a Product in the SLD (Part 3)
© *Copyright 2010. SAP AG. All rights reserved*

4.2.3.2 Creating Software Components

For the most part, the process of creating a software component in the SLD is very similar to the one used to create products, albeit with fewer steps. To create a software component in the SLD, perform the following steps:

1. From the main SLD page, click on the *Software Components* link in the middle of the page.

2. Click on the *New...* button to kick off the software component creation wizard.

3. On the *Action Type* roadmap step, select the radio button *Create a New Software Component and Version* and click on the *Next* button.

4. Then, on the *Create Software Component and Version* roadmap step, you must fill in the following attributes:

    a. In the *Product Version* dropdown list, select the corresponding product version that you want to assign the software component to.

    b. You also have the option of selecting a specific software unit using the *Unit* dropdown list.

   c. In the *Vendor* input field, you will enter your company's domain name (e.g. `bowdark.com`).

   d. You enter the software component name in the *Name* field (see Figure 4.13).

   e. In the *Version* field, select a version number for the software component.

   f. In the *Production State* dropdown list, you can select from various production states for your component. In almost all cases, the default `Released` state is the proper choice.

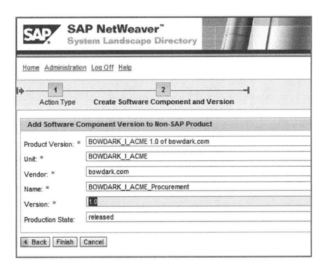

Figure 4.13: Creating a Software Component in the SLD
© Copyright 2010. SAP AG. All rights reserved

2. Once all of the relevant parameters have been filled in, you can click on the *Finish* button to save your changes.

In our PO interface example, we ended up with three software components: `BOWDARK_I_SAPERP_EXT_MM`, `BOWDARK_I_ACME_PROCUREMENT`, and `BOWDARK_A_PROCUREMENT_MAPPING`, respectively.

4.2.4 Software Component Dependencies

Sometimes, one software component might be dependent upon functionality provided by another software component. For example, when developing XML mapping programs, there might be a core library that you want to reuse in a number of different scenarios. In this case, rather than importing this library over and over again, you can import it into a base software component. Then, as you create software components that need to leverage this library, you simply create a *dependency* between them. In this context, the base software component is referred to as an *underlying software component* to the component that defines the usage dependency.

To create a dependency between two components, perform the following steps:

1. Open up the Software Catalog and select the using component. Then, click on the *Dependencies* tab (see Figure 4.14).

2. On the *Dependencies* tab, click on the *Define Prerequisite Software Component Versions* button to create a new dependency[20].

3. This will take you to the *Define Prerequisite Software Components* view in which you can search for your prerequisite software component.

4. Once you locate the target component, select it and click on the *Define as Prerequisite Software Components* button to define the dependency relationship (see Figure 4.15).

---

[20] Within the software catalog, dependencies can be defined in different *contexts*. However, for the purposes of PI development, the default `Installation Time` context is the correct choice.

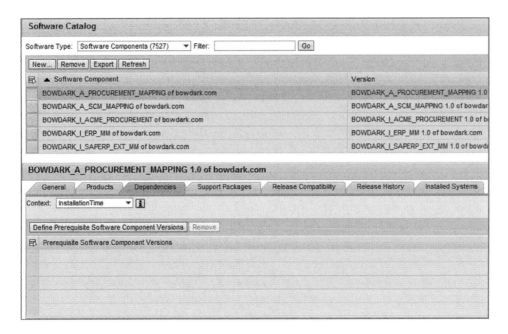

Figure 4.14: Defining Dependencies between Software Components (Part 1)

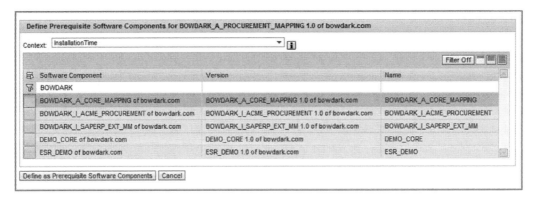

Figure 4.15: Defining Dependencies between Software Components (Part 2)

4.3   Working with the ES Builder

Now that you have a feel for how ESR content is organized, let's take a closer look at the tool you use to create it: the ES Builder. As you may recall from Chapter 1, the ES Builder is a Java Web Start application that you can access by executing transaction SXMB_IFR and selecting the *Enterprise Services Builder* link off of the *Process Integration Tools* page.

In the upcoming sections, we'll show you how to kick start your development projects in the ES Builder. We'll then expand on these concepts in subsequent chapters when we consider specific tools included within the ES Builder.

4.3.1 Importing Software Component Versions

Before you can begin developing content in the ES Builder, you must first import a SWCV from the SLD. Here, you must perform the following steps:

1. Within the ES Builder, select the menu option *Object → New* from the top-level menu bar.

2. In the *Create Object* dialog box, expand the *Work Areas* submenu on the left-hand side of the screen. Then select the *Software Component Version* menu option (see Figure 4.16).

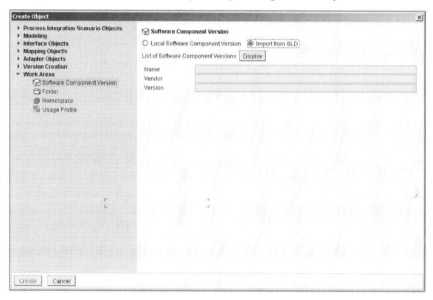

Figure 4.16: Importing a SWCV into the ESR (Part 1)
© Copyright 2010. SAP AG. All rights reserved

3. Next, click on the *Display* button to open up the *Import of Software Component Versions* dialog box shown in Figure 4.17. Here, you can scan through the list and find the target component you wish to import.

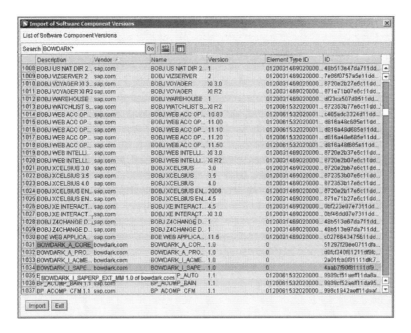

Figure 4.17: Importing a SWCV into the ESR (Part 2)

4. Once you locate your SWCV, select it and then click on the *Import* button (see Figure 4.17). Afterwards, click on the *Create Object* screen from Figure 4.16 to import the SWCV into the ESR.

5. After the import is complete, you can edit the properties of the SWCV in the *Edit Software Component Version* editor shown in Figure 4.18. Table 4.1 provides details about the parameters you can configure on this screen.

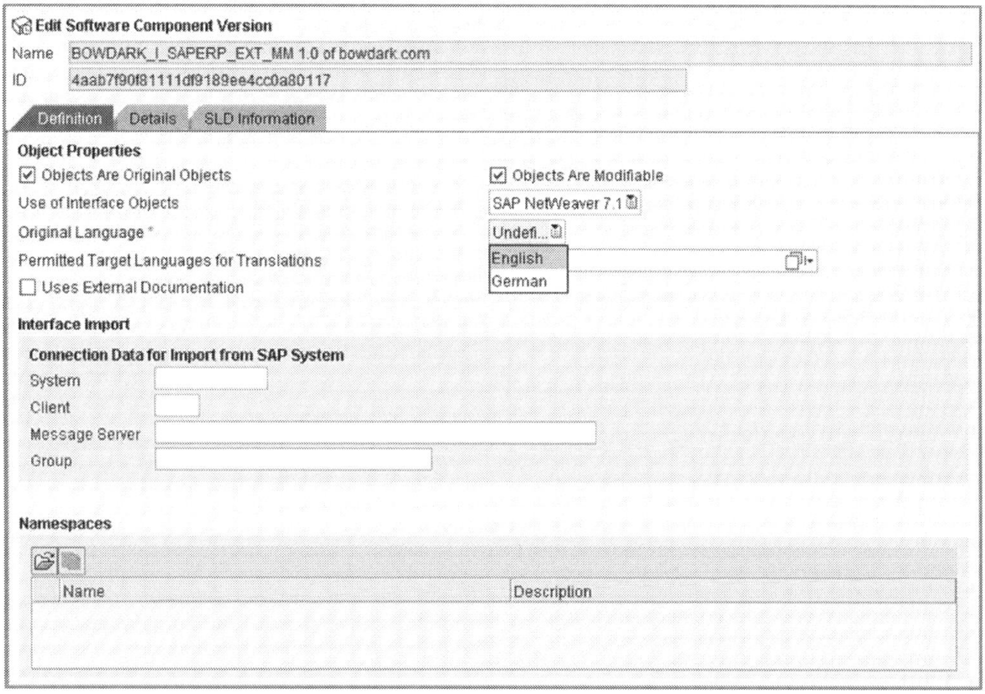

Figure 4.18: Defining SWCV Properties in the ES Builder © Copyright 2010. SAP AG. All rights reserved

Object Property	Description
Objects Are Original Objects	This checkbox determines whether or not the objects created in the SWCV are *original objects* initially defined within the ESR that you are currently connected to. This checkbox is normally only selected in development systems.
Objects are Modifiable	Whenever this checkbox is checked, the objects within the SWCV are modifiable within the ES Builder.
Usage of Interface Objects	This option is primarily related to backwards compatibility with prior versions of SAP NetWeaver PI. We'll learn more about the implications of this setting in Chapter 6.

Object Property	Description
Original Language	Determines the original language used to create the repository objects within the SWCV.
Permitted Target Languages for Translations	This option specifies the supported target languages when translating language-dependent texts.
Uses External Documentation	You use this option to enable links to external documentation about the software component.
Interface Import (Connection Data)	These parameters make it possible to import RFC & IDoc metadata out of an SAP backend system. We'll see how this works in Chapter 6.

Table 4.1: Editing Properties of SWCVs

4.3.1.1 Underlying Software Component Versions

If the SWCV you imported has a usage dependency assigned to it in the SLD software catalog, then you'll notice an additional node within your SWCV called *Basis Objects* (see Figure 4.19). Here, you can see the repository objects that are *inherited* from the underlying SWCV. These repository objects can be used just like the ones created within the inheriting SWCV. We'll consider the ramifications of this further in Section 4.3.5.

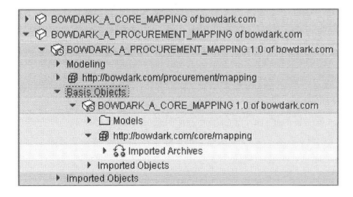

Figure 4.19: Viewing Underlying SWCV Relationships in the ESR © Copyright 2010. SAP AG. All rights reserved

4.3.2   Creating Namespaces

Once a SWCV is imported into the ESR, the next step is to organize it using namespaces. For this task, you must open up the namespace definition editor shown in Figure 4.20. You can get to this screen by clicking on the *Open* ( ) toolbar icon in the *Namespaces* section of the SWCV editor (see Figure 4.18).

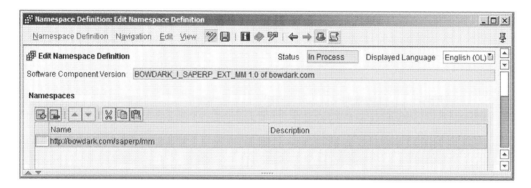

Figure 4.20: Maintaining Namespaces for a SWCV © Copyright 2010. SAP AG. All rights reserved

Within the namespace definition editor, you can use the *Namespaces* table to add/remove namespaces as necessary[21]. Be sure to click on the *Save* button in the top-level toolbar to save your changes.

4.3.3   Creating Folders

For the most part, folders can be created pretty much anywhere within an imported SWCV. To create a new folder, right-click on the desired node level and select the *Create Folder* menu option (see Figure 4.21). A new folder will then appear in the navigation bar with the name attribute highlighted in an editable state. From here, you can key in the folder name and hit the *Enter* key to commit your changes (see Figure 4.22).

As we mentioned in Section 4.1, folders can be nested arbitrarily deep within the ESR. Such nested folder structures can be defined by repeatedly applying the previous steps over and over again.

---

[21] See the aforementioned *PI Best Practices: Naming Conventions* how-to guide for naming conventions.

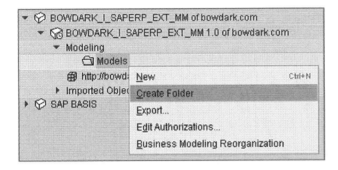

Figure 4.21: Creating Folders within a SWCV (Part 1) © Copyright 2010. SAP
AG. All rights reserved

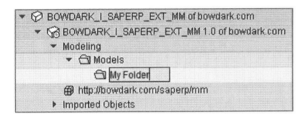

Figure 4.22: Creating Folders within a SWCV (Part 2) © Copyright 2010. SAP
AG. All rights reserved

4.3.4 Creating Repository Objects

Once you have imported your SWCVs and defined their underlying
namespaces, the actual creation of repository objects in the ES Builder is
relatively straightforward. To create new repository objects, perform the
following steps:

1. To begin, simply right-click on a folder or namespace and select the
   New menu option. This will open up the *Create Object* dialog box
   shown in Figure 4.23.

2. Within the *Create Object* dialog box, you can browse through the
   repository object types on the left-hand side of the window to select
   the kind of object you wish to create.

3. As you select object types in the *Create Object* dialog box, you'll
   notice that the right-hand side of the editor will change to reflect
   the type of object you have selected. For example, in Figure 4.23,
   notice how the editor contains input fields for specifying a service
   interface. Here, you can enter a name for the repository object as
   well as an optional description.

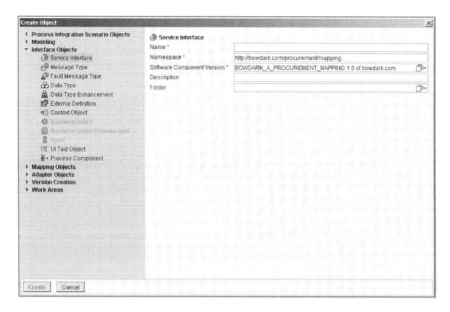

Figure 4.23: Creating Repository Objects in the ES Builder © Copyright 2010. SAP AG. All rights reserved

4. Once you fill in the object name and all of the other required fields, you can click on the *Create* button to create the object. However, keep in mind that the object will not be saved in the ESR until you click on the *Save* button in the corresponding object editor tool.

After the repository object is created, you'll see it show up in the navigation bar on the left-hand side of the ES Builder screen. At this point, you can edit or view the objects in their respective object editor tool by simply double-clicking on them. Also, if you right-click on a repository object, you'll notice menu options that allow you to copy and/or delete the object from the ESR.

4.3.5   Understanding Object References

In some cases, a repository object may reference one or more additional repository objects. For example, an operation mapping references a mapping program as well as multiple service interfaces. From a logistics perspective, these objects need to be defined in close proximity to one another. Otherwise, you might end up in a situation where certain "half-baked" repository objects are transported to an upstream ESR.

For the most part, the rules for defining object references in the ESR are fairly intuitive. Of course, if you're fuzzy on the rules, the validity check within the object editor tool will tell you if you've gone awry. You can also find a detailed description of supported object reference types in the online help documentation under the section entitled *Object References* (SAP AG).

4.3.6   Managing Change Lists

As you create and maintain content within the ESR, the ES Builder keeps track of your changes in the form of a *change list*. You can view your change lists by selecting the *Change Lists* tab in the left-hand navigation area of the ES Builder screen (see Figure 4.24). As you can see in Figure 4.24, a separate change list is maintained for each SWCV in which you edit repository objects.

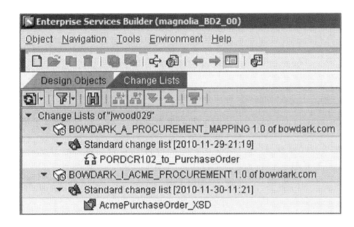

Figure 4.24: Viewing Change Lists in the ES Builder © Copyright 2010. SAP AG. All rights reserved

To commit your changes to the ESR, you must *activate* your change list; otherwise your updates are only visible to your user account. To activate your change list, simply right-click on it and select the *Activate...* menu option (see Figure 4.25). This will open up the *Activate Change List* dialog box shown in Figure 4.26. By default, all of the objects within the change list will be selected. However, if you wish, you can pick and choose the objects you wish to activate by de-selecting objects in the *Objects in Change List* table. In either case, you can activate the change list by clicking on the *Activate* button (see Figure 4.26).

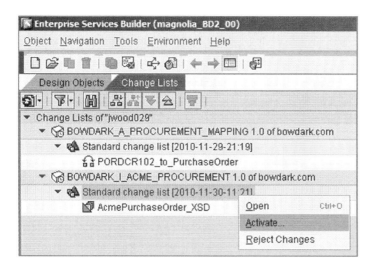

Figure 4.25: Activating a Change List in the ES Builder (Part 1) © Copyright 2010. SAP AG. All rights reserved

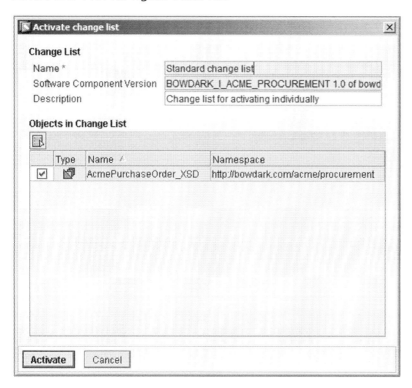

Figure 4.26: Activating a Change List in the ES Builder (Part 2) © Copyright 2010. SAP AG. All rights reserved

4.3.6.1 Dealing with Activation Errors

Sometimes, there may be objects in your change list that contain errors. In this case, if you try and activate the change list the ES Builder will stop the activation process and display a list of errors that you must correct prior to activation. Here, you must either fix the error(s) or de-select the erroneous objects in order to activate the change list.

4.3.6.2 Accessing the Change Lists of Other Users

Since change lists are user-specific, the ES Builder will filter the change list view to only show your personal change lists by default. However, in some cases, you might need to access another user's change list. To do so, select the drop-down list on the *Change Filter Settings* button and choose the *Display Filters* menu option (see Figure 4.27). This will expand the filter view shown in Figure 4.28. This view allows you to filter the change list view by different user names which can be selected using the value help provided with the *User* input field.

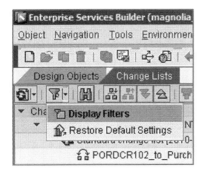

Figure 4.27: Editing Display Filters for Change Lists © Copyright 2010. SAP AG. All rights reserved

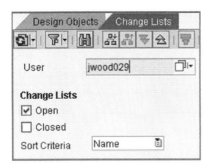

Figure 4.28: Changing Display Filters for Change Lists © Copyright 2010. SAP AG. All rights reserved

4.4   Transporting ESR Content

Typically, ESR content is defined in a development system and then transported to upstream environments. While transports in general are typically performed by system administrator types, it is useful for developers to at least be aware of the process from a conceptual point-of-view. Indeed, since developers typically have a much better understanding of the content being transported than their administrative counterparts, you may sometimes find yourself being called upon to help troubleshoot transport issues, etc.

In this section, we will survey the options you have for transporting content to/from the ESR. Along the way, we'll show you how these features can also be used to import pre-delivered content provided by SAP or other SAP software partners. This content can go a long way towards kick starting your development project in certain cases.

4.4.1   Transport Options

In general, you have three basic options for transporting ESR content to/from the ES Builder:

> ➢ You can perform file-based transports.

> ➢ You can integrate with the *Change Management Service* (CMS) provided with the NWDI.

> ➢ You can integrate with the familiar *Change and Transport System* (CTS) using CTS+.

The following sections describe each of these options in turn.

4.4.1.1 Transporting ESR Content with the File System

With file-based transports, relevant repository objects are packaged up in a special archive file with a `.tpz` extension and downloaded to a directory on the server[22] or client. These archive files can then be uploaded into the target ESR via an import wizard provided with the ES Builder.

---

[22] If you choose the option to transport objects using the server file system, then the file will be exported to the `/usr/sap/{SID}/SYS/global/xi/repository_server/export` **directory on** the PI application server host.

Exporting ESR Content Using the File System

To export ESR content using the file system, log on to the source ESR and perform the following steps:

1. In the main menu bar, select the menu option *Tools → Export Design Objects...*. This will open up the *Export Design Objects* wizard shown in Figure 4.29.

Figure 4.29: Exporting Repository Objects from the ESR (Part 1)

2. The first step in the wizard requires you to select the source SWCV that contains the repository objects you wish to transport. In the *Software Component Version* field, you can use the provided value help to lookup the proper SWCV.

3. Next, you must also select the *mode* of the transport. In the *Mode* dropdown list, you'll want to select the *Transport Using File System* option. Here, you also must specify whether or not you want to download the file to the client or server using the *Download File to Client* checkbox (see Figure 4.29). Click the *Continue* button to proceed.

4. At the *Select Objects* step, you can filter the set of repository objects you want to export using the *Object Set* dropdown list (see Figure 4.30). You also have the option to include deleted objects using the *Include Deleted Objects* checkbox. Click the *Continue* button to proceed.

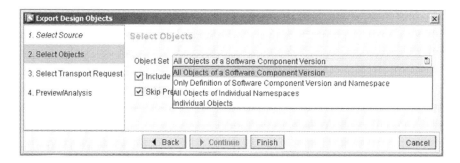

Figure 4.30: Exporting Repository Objects from the ESR (Part 2)

5. Finally, at the *Preview/Analysis* step, you will see an overview of the objects to be exported, the target file name, and so on. Click on the *Finish* button to complete the export.

Importing ESR Content Using the File System

To import content into the ESR using the file system, perform the following steps:

1. In the main menu bar, select the menu option *Tools → Import Design Objects…*. This will open up the *Select Import Source* dialog box shown in Figure 4.31. Here, you can choose whether or not you want to upload an ESR content package from the client or the server[23].

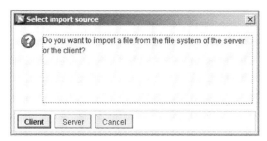

Figure 4.31: Importing Repository Objects into the ESR (Part 1)

---

[23] If you choose the option to transport objects using the server file system, then the file will be imported from the `/usr/sap/{SID}/SYS/global/xi/repository_server/import` directory on the PI application server host.

2. In the next step, you will be provided with a dialog box in which you can select the file that you want to upload. Once you select the file, the import will begin.

3. If the repository objects in question exist already within the target ESR, the system will prompt you to ensure that you want to overwrite the target objects (see Figure 4.32). If you're sure that you want to import the changes, click on the *Import* button to proceed.

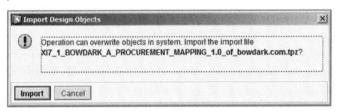

Figure 4.32: Importing Repository Objects into the ESR (Part 2)

4.4.1.2 Transporting ESR Content with CMS

As mentioned previously, the CMS is part of the NWDI usage type. Though it is typically used to transport Java development objects, you can also define an *XI track* that is used to transport content defined within the ESR and Integration Directory. If you have an NWDI in place already, then using the CMS to manage your transports may be preferable to moving files around by hand.

Realistically, a detailed description of the steps required to set up CMS is beyond the scope of this book. However, if you're interested in setting up CMS in your landscape, a good guide to get you started is Praveen Mayalur's blog on the SAP SDN entitled *Configuration of CMS in Central NWDI & SLD to Transport XI Objects* (Mayalur).

4.4.1.3 Transporting ESR Content with CTS+

If you've been around the ABAP world for a while, then you're no doubt familiar with the CTS system used to transport ABAP development objects. For years, this tool has been used by SAP system administrators to transport ABAP source code, dictionary objects, etc.

Beginning with Support Pack 14 of the SAP NetWeaver 7.0 release, CTS was enhanced to include support for Java-based transports, PI content, and more. This enhanced version of CTS is called *CTS+*. To learn more about how CTS+ integrates with SAP NetWeaver PI, consult the online help documentation under the section entitled *Transporting Objects using CTS* (SAP AG). SAP has also published a SAP NetWeaver How-To Guide entitled *How to Configure Enhanced CTS for SAP NetWeaver Exchange Infrastructure 7.0* that has some useful information in it.

There are several advantages to using CTS+ to manage your ESR transports:

> ➤ Since it also supports ABAP and Java-based transports, you can define a single package to transport all of the relevant development objects created to support an integration scenario.

> ➤ It provides a user interface that most SAP system administrator types are accustomed to working with.

> ➤ It integrates nicely with the *SAP Solution Manager Change Request Management* (ChaRM) framework that supports more complex change management scenarios (e.g. workflows, etc.).

4.4.2   Performing Release Transfers

As you learned in Section 4.1.4, repository objects are maintained in versions within the ESR. In this case, a new version is generated each time a repository object change is activated via a change list. This version history can be used to go back in time and retrieve specific versions of a repository object.

However, you may reach a point in your project in which it makes sense to define a new version of a product, and by extension, its underlying software components. For example, imagine that you're developing an interface for a project that is being rolled out using a phased approach. Here, it might make sense to have a separate SWCV for each phase of the project. That way, you have multiple tracks for development: e.g. the latest SWCV for new development, the previous version for defect work, and so on.

Technically speaking, you could import a new SWCV and copy-and-paste the repository objects from the prior version into the new version one-by-one. Fortunately, the ES Builder provides an easier way through a function called *release transfer*.

To perform a release transfer in the ESR, perform the following steps:

1. First, create the new SWCV in the SLD and import it into the ESR.

2. Once the SWCV is imported, you must define identical namespaces to those defined in the prior version.

3. Then, in the main menu bar, select *Tools → Transfer Design Objects…*. This will open up the *Transfer Design Objects* wizard.

4. The first step in the wizard describes how the transfer function works and what it is used for. Click the *Continue* button to move to the next step.

5. On the next screen, you must select the source/target SWCVs that you wish to transfer between (see Figure 4.33). Click on the *Continue* button to proceed.

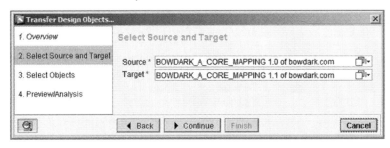

Figure 4.33: Transferring Design Objects in the ESR

6. At the *Select Objects* step, you can select the repository objects that you wish to transfer. Here, you can select all objects within the source SWCV, or pick-and-choose the ones that you want to bring over.

7. Once you have identified the objects you wish to transfer, you can click on the *Finish* button to perform the migration.

As you may recall from Section 4.1.2, a repository object is uniquely qualified by its SWCV, namespace, and object name. Therefore, all of the objects copied over into the new SWCV are completely independent from their predecessors. At configuration time, this means that you can use both sets of repository objects to define old and new versions of an interface in parallel. This feature can come in handy during migrations, etc.

4.4.3   Importing Pre-Delivered Content

Most of the time, whenever people think about transports in the ESR, they focus on the transport of custom repository objects created in-house. However, these days, there's a wealth of pre-delivered content available online for SAP customers. Therefore, before you set off to reinvent the wheel, it's not a bad idea to take a peek at what's available and see if it applies for your use cases. In the worst case scenario, you can at least use this content as a springboard for initiating your own custom development.

You can find a comprehensive list of pre-delivered content on the SAP Developer Network which is available online at *http://www.sdn.sap.com*. From the main page, select the menu path *SOA Middleware → Modeling and Design* on the left-hand navigation area. Then, under the section entitled *Integration Content*, you'll find links to content provided by SAP as well as 3rd-party vendors.

As you look around, you'll find content to help you integrate different products within the SAP Business Suite, implement EDI scenarios, and so on. The pre-delivered content comes bundled as a `.tpz` file which you can download and install using the steps outlined in Section 4.4.1.1.

4.5   Summary

This chapter introduced you to some fundamental concepts for working with the ESR and its editor, the ES Builder. You also learned about the SLD software catalog and its underlying component model. Collectively, the concepts you learned should help you to organize your development projects in such a way that you are the most productive.

In the next chapter, we'll take a look at some service design concepts and explore the SOA modeling tools provided with the ES Builder.

References

Mayalur, P. (n.d.). *Configuration of CMS in Central NWDI & SLD to Transport XI Objects.* Retrieved November 30, 2010, from SAP Community Network Blogs: http://www.sdn.sap.com/irj/scn/weblogs?blog=/pub/wlg/6639

SAP AG. (n.d.). *Configuring SLD Security Roles.* Retrieved November 23, 2010, from SAP Help Library: http://help.sap.com/saphelp_nwpi71/helpdata/en/48/b7b38fecf26745e1000 0000a421937/frameset.htm

SAP AG. (n.d.). *Managing Services in the Enterprise Services Repository.* Retrieved November 23, 2010, from SAP Help Library: http://help.sap.com/saphelp_nwpi711/helpdata/en/61/fec608bc27654daadb 20c1e6da7dd1/frameset.htm

SAP AG. (n.d.). *Object References.* Retrieved November 30, 2010, from SAP Help Library: http://help.sap.com/saphelp_nwpi711/helpdata/en/08/cf69e8b2376c4da833 0eaa1566b14d/frameset.htm

SAP AG. (n.d.). *PI Best Practices: Naming Conventions.* Retrieved April 1, 2011, from SAP Developer Network (SDN): http://www.sdn.sap.com/irj/scn/index?rid=/library/uuid/40a66d0e-fe5e-2c10-8a85-e418b59ab36a

SAP AG. (n.d.). *Products and Software Components.* Retrieved November 24, 2010, from SAP Help Library: http://help.sap.com/saphelp_nwpi711/helpdata/en/48/b682cd96655295e10 000000a42189b/frameset.htm

SAP AG. (n.d.). *System Landscape Directory.* Retrieved November 23, 2010, from SAP Help Library: http://help.sap.com/saphelp_nwpi711/helpdata/en/48/c46505095735b6e10 000000a42189d/frameset.htm

SAP AG. (n.d.). *Transporting Objects Using CTS.* Retrieved November 30, 2010, from SAP Help Library: http://help.sap.com/saphelp_nwpi711/helpdata/en/9a/775de286874bc78dcb 1470bc80f0f9/frameset.htm

Zarske, B. (n.d.). *Planning a Strategy for the System Landscape Directory (SLD) of SAP NetWeaver.* Retrieved November 23, 2010, from SAP Community Network:

http://www.sdn.sap.com/irj/scn/weblogs?blog=/pub/wlg/6711

Service Design Concepts

5

As the saying goes, failure to plan is planning to fail. Therefore, before you begin the service development process, it is imperative that you spend some time modeling the business process up front. In this chapter, we will consider some SOA design and modeling techniques that you can use to get started off on the right foot.

After completing this chapter, you will be able to:

❖ Understand how to develop enterprise services using SOA design concepts.

❖ Apply SAP's model for enterprise service development.

❖ Realize how business processes can be modeled using tools provided with the ES Builder.

5.1 SOA Explained

Some years ago, the United Parcel Service® (UPS) started an ad campaign focused around the tag line "Moving at the Speed of Business". Whether they want to or not, most IT departments can probably relate with this slogan. Indeed, in a world of tight project deadlines, limited budgets, and ever-changing functional requirements, many IT departments find themselves struggling just to tread water. It is through this chaos that the service-oriented architecture (SOA) emerged as a vehicle for driving innovation and reducing costs.

In this section, we will introduce you to some basic SOA concepts and attempt to dispel some of the myths associated with SOA. Having a basic understanding of these concepts is important as interface development involves more than just the provision of a bunch of ad hoc point-to-point interfaces. When designed properly, interfaces can become investments with the potential for many returns.

5.1.1 Why SOA?

It has been said that "necessity is the mother of invention". Such a statement surely applies to the origins of SOA. To see why, let's rewind the clock back a bit and look at some of the difficult requirements IT departments were facing when SOAs were first conceived:

> ➢ Numerous requests to integrate disparate systems both within the enterprise and beyond.

> ➢ Requests for new "cross-applications" (or xApps™) that combined new features with existing functionality provided in legacy systems.

> ➢ Mandates to shorten development cycles and reduce development costs.

In other words, businesses wanted the world in a box, and they wanted it yesterday. Such difficult demands called for more than just a shiny new technical solution to an age-old problem. What was needed was a paradigm shift towards some pragmatic ideals that could change the culture of IT departments for the better.

At the forefront of these ideals was a *rededication* towards the reuse of existing software assets. We emphasize the term "rededication" here since that goal had been there all along. The problem was, very few enterprises ever succeeded in actually pulling it off. Nevertheless, if IT organizations were to ever achieve the productivity levels mandated by the business, they had to figure out a way to combine and reorganize existing software assets into new and innovative solutions. These are the kinds of problems that SOAs were designed to solve.

5.1.2 What are the Benefits of SOA?

SOA is all about eliminating the barriers that prevent IT organizations from reusing existing software assets. Such barriers include:

> ➤ The presence of so-called "stovepipe" applications and systems that contain useful functionality that is closed off from the rest of the enterprise.

> ➤ Proprietary APIs that make it difficult or impossible for different applications to communicate with one another.

> ➤ An overall lack of standards compliance at all levels of development.

So how does SOA confront such obstacles? Well, it starts with a shift in mindset towards the bigger picture. As the name suggests, SOA is focused on *service-orientation*. In this context, software is divided into components whose functionality is provided via a series of *services*. Each service has a well-defined interface and provides a solution to a particular problem. Therefore, when developed properly, services become more than just a one-time investment for a particular application; they become reusable assets that can be recombined elsewhere in ways that might not have been anticipated at the time of development.

Services vs. Web Services

Looking over the description above, you'll notice that we are using the generic term *service* rather than *Web service*. Though Web services do represent a fairly natural approach to service development in the SOA context, they are not the only game in town. Therefore, if you're thinking that all those tried-and-true legacy or mainframe assets cannot be used to implement an SOA...think again. While it is certainly easier to implement an SOA from scratch, an incremental approach is definitely possible[24]. After all, one of the main goals of SOA is to achieve as much reuse of software assets

---

[24] Especially when you have a SOA middleware platform like SAP NetWeaver PI at your disposal.

as possible. If you're looking for an example of this kind of *SOA by Evolution*, look no further than the SAP Business Suite (Pohl & Peter, 2010).

5.2   Evolving Towards Enterprise Services

In Chapter 1, we touched on some of the desirable characteristics that SOA-based services should possess. Looking back on those traits, you'll notice a common theme: most of them are realized through *design decisions* rather than sophisticated technological capabilities. Therefore, in order to achieve these qualities in your own services, you must adjust your mindset from the outset of the design process. In this section, we'll explore this thought process and show you how to transform ordinary services into *enterprise services*.

5.2.1   The Semantic Interoperability Problem

When developing services in a SOA context, there are several important functional questions that need to be addressed:

1. How do you convey the meaning of a service interface and its operations to potential consumers? For example, depending on the service, the terms "business partner", "vendor", and "supplier" could mean the same thing, or something different.

2. What should the signature of the service operations look like?

3. At what level of granularity should the services be scoped?

4. What is the behavior of a service at runtime? Is such behavior consistent with user expectations?

In the book *Developing Enterprise Services for SAP*, the authors consider these questions to be part of a larger *semantic interoperability problem* (Pohl & Peter, 2010). This is to say that, even if you remove all technical barriers for communication, there are still many functional obstacles that must be cleared in order to maximize reuse. To put this into perspective, imagine a Web service with an obscurely defined service interface. In this case, though it should be relatively easy to access the service on a technical level, it may take considerable time to figure out how to call the service from a functional perspective. Such time might be spent figuring out the meaning of particular parameters, testing out the behavior of the service, etc.

As you might expect, such problems are not easily solved. Indeed, if you were to perform a postmortem on most failed SOA projects, you would find this semantic interoperability problem to be at the center of what went wrong in a lot of cases. So, the question becomes: How do you address these kinds of issues during the service development process?

5.2.2 Predicable Results through SOA Governance

Unfortunately, given the human element involved in designing service interfaces, there is no way to completely eliminate the semantic interoperability problem. However, you can take measured steps to avoid many of these pain points by adopting a *SOA governance process*.

A SOA governance process defines standards for service development. Here, we're talking about much more than just a set of naming conventions. Rather, SOA governance is about defining a holistic process that guides developers in the modeling, design, and implementation of components and services. Ancillary topics of interest include the specification of message exchange patterns, error handling and quality of service, runtime behavior, and much more.

Clearly, many aspects of the SOA modeling process are subject to interpretation. Therefore, it is important to remove as many ambiguities from the process as possible. This starts with the definition of a *common language* that is well understood by business analysts, service consumers, and service providers alike. Short of discovering the mythical *universal language*, the most obvious choice here is to use the language of the business world. This design decision, coupled with the expressiveness of XML, helps to make services much more intuitive and easy to use. Of course, you don't always have to start from scratch. Frequently, you'll find that there are many XML-based standards that can be used to develop your service interfaces. For example, the OAGIS standard defines a common business language for many common business documents such as purchase orders, accounting journal entries, material master records, and so on (OAGi).

Once everyone is on the same page language-wise, the next step is to work towards the definition of a *harmonized business model* (Pohl & Peter, 2010). This model describes the structure of an enterprise in terms of real-world concepts such as departments rather than vendor/software-specific interpretations. This approach avoids overlaps and/or gaps in functionality and helps you to conceptualize services in terms of real-life services provided by human beings within the various departments. We'll explore these concepts further in Section 5.3.

After the business model is in place, the individual services and their interfaces should derive fairly naturally. Here, you can apply a combination of object-oriented analysis and interface/communication patterns to define the service cuts. From there, the last step is to model the message types being exchanged. We'll evaluate this process flow in further detail in Section 5.3.

Ultimately, the goal of a SOA governance process is to produce *consistent results* when developing services. This implies that best practices and standards are followed to the fullest extent possible during the development cycle. Disciplined adherence to a SOA governance process should help you develop services that are easy to understand and use in a wide variety of use cases.

5.2.3　Enterprise Services: Defined

Put simply, an enterprise service is a service that has been developed using SOA best practices. In particular, SAP attributes some of the following characteristics to enterprise services (Pohl & Peter, 2010):

> ➢ A software service that provides functionality relevant for business processes.

> ➢ Guaranteed quality and stability.

> ➢ Structured by means of a harmonized enterprise model.

> ➢ Good documentation.

> ➢ Based on open standards and the use of standardized data types.

Of course, measuring the quality of such characteristics is highly subjective. Consequently, you'll find that some enterprise services will be better-rounded than others. Nevertheless, the point is that enterprise services should be developed with a close eye on (re)usability. In particular, quite a bit of attention should be paid to getting the interface right.

As a service provider, you have to think of a service interface as a type of contract or agreement between you and the consumers of your service. Like any sort of business arrangement, you want to make sure that you get the terms of the deal right. For instance, you want to make sure that you don't lock yourself into terms that you can't fulfill. On the other hand, you don't want to make the contract so restrictive that no one will want to use your service. There is a balance, and it can usually be discovered if you spend some time modeling up front.

5.3 SAP's Model for Service Development

In order to maximize reuse with your service interfaces, it is very important that you model them beforehand. Indeed, even the most informal of modeling processes can help flesh out many of the common obstacles that prevent reuse. Of course, an even better approach is to adopt a formalized modeling process that leaves behind a series of artifacts that document the business process at different levels of abstraction. Such artifacts make it easier for important stakeholders to visualize the process and oftentimes become the springboard for further innovation.

In Section 5.4, we will take a look at the modeling environment provided with SAP NetWeaver PI. However, in order to work with these tools, you must first understand the underlying metamodel. Therefore, in this section, we will explore the *SAP Enterprise Services Metamodel*. Understanding these concepts will help you get the most out of the provided modeling tools and should also make it easier to browse through the catalog of enterprise services provided with the SAP Business Suite[25].

5.3.1 The SAP Enterprise Services Metamodel

In Chapter 3, you learned about the WSDL metamodel that defines concepts such as services, service interfaces, service operations, and so on. While this metamodel is useful in documenting and describing technical details of services, it is not sufficient in and of itself to model the overarching business processes. Here, we're looking for answers to questions such as:

> How should a system/application be split up into components?

> Which services are required to implement the process?

> How detailed should the service interfaces be?

Since services are somewhat analogous to functions in programming languages, some developers attempt to address these questions by applying *functional decomposition* techniques. However, as we have learned with procedural programming over the years, this approach can severely limit the

---

[25] This catalog is provided with the *Enterprise Services Workplace* online at *http://esworkplace.sap.com*. Here, you will find comprehensive resources on all of the enterprise services delivered by SAP.

amount of reusability you can get out of a service. This is primarily due to the fact that functional decomposition techniques tend to place too little emphasis on the underlying business objects. As a result, the message types used to define the service operations are usually too heavily customized around the original use case to be of much reuse.

Another approach to service design is to start with the modeling of the business objects and then work your way outward. This is the approach adopted by SAP. If you have experience with object-oriented programming, then you can think of business objects as a type of domain or entity class that models some aspect of the business process at hand. This abstraction lends itself well for integrating with the WSDL metamodel (e.g. methods are analogous to service operations, interfaces are analogous to service interfaces, and so on).

Figure 5.1 illustrates how the business object model aligns with the WSDL metamodel to comprise the *SAP Enterprise Services Metamodel*. In the following sections, we'll analyze each of the related modeling entities in turn. For further details, including best practices and naming conventions, refer to the SAP How-To Guide entitled *PI Best Practices: Modeling* (SAP AG, 2009). Another excellent resource is *Developing Enterprise Services for SAP* (Pohl & Peter, 2010).

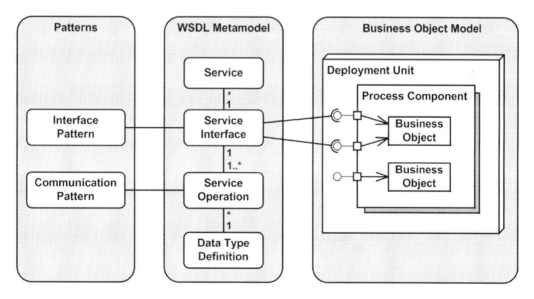

Figure 5.1: The SAP Enterprise Services Metamodel

5.3.2   Business Objects

SAP defines a business object as "...a specific view of data of a well-defined and outlined business area. Business objects are identified in such a way that there are no overlaps." (SAP AG). In other words, they are the objects that make up the business domain that you are working in. In the metamodel notation, business objects are depicted using rectangular boxes.

A general rule of thumb is that business objects model real-world concepts that are described using *nouns* (i.e. a person, place, thing or idea). For example, if you are working in the production planning business area, then you might model a bill of material (BOM) business object like the one shown in Figure 5.2. Of course, you can also model transactional data such as planned orders or production orders using business objects.

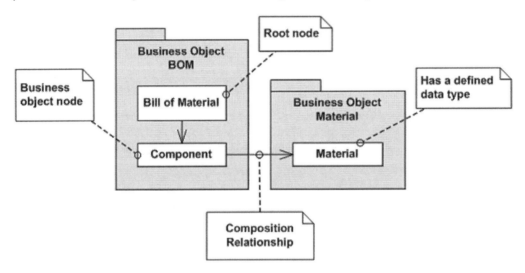

Figure 5.2: A Business Object Example

As you can see in Figure 5.2, business objects are structured internally using *business object nodes*. Each business object node describes a particular aspect of the business object and has a defined data type. At first glance, you might be wondering what the difference is between a business object and a business object node. After all, in a pure object-oriented context, these nodes would also be implemented as standalone classes in most cases. However, with business objects, the general rule of thumb is that an object node must be *independent* from a business standpoint in order to be classified as a business object. For example, the Component object node can only exist within the context of a BOM object; without the BOM object, the Component object doesn't have any meaning.

Business objects can have relationships with other business objects. For example, as you can see in Figure 5.2, each Component object node within the BOM object is linked to a Material object. In some cases, these relationships can get pretty complex. For instance, a Sales Order business object would likely have relationships with business partners, products, and so on.

5.3.3   Process Components

One of the most difficult aspects of SOA design is determining how to break a complex system or application down into individual components. In general, components need to be *modular* and *cohesive*. This is to say that components should be self-contained and each of their exposed service operations ought to be closely related.

While there are many ways to achieve componentization, SAP chose to define component boundaries in terms of *departments* within the enterprise. In the SAP Enterprise Services Metamodel, such components are referred to as *process components*. According to the online help documentation, a process component is a "*...part of a value chain that is normally (in large companies) performed in a department*" (SAP AG).

The core functionality of a process component is realized in terms of one or more embedded business objects[26]. Figure 5.3 demonstrates this relationship with some process components that encapsulate functionality normally performed by the production operations department within the enterprise. Other examples of process components within the enterprise might include Sales Order Processing, Business Partner Data Management, and so on.

---

[26] The relationship between a process component and a business object is exclusive; a business object can belong to exactly one process component (SAP AG).

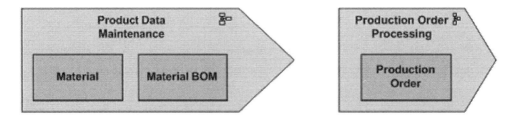

Figure 5.3: Process Component Examples

> **Note**
>
> Process components are intended to be designed generically in terms of the harmonized business model. Therefore, you'll want to avoid trying to define your process components specifically in terms of pre-existing SAP software logistics concepts (e.g. using software components or modules within the SAP Application Hierarchy). This practice ensures that you avoid vendor lock-in with your components.

5.3.4   Service Interfaces

By default, all of the functionality provided by process components (and their underlying business objects) is hidden from the outside world. In order to expose this functionality, you must define one or more *service interfaces*.

Getting back to the object-oriented programming metaphor, you can think of service interfaces as an *interface* that is implemented by a business object. Much like object-oriented interfaces, service interfaces group together a series of related service operations. However, in this context, the semantic meaning of the service interface varies based upon the *direction* of the interface (e.g. inbound vs. outbound interfaces). Service interfaces are depicted in the SAP Enterprise Services Metamodel using a notation similar to class diagrams in UML (see Figure 5.4).

From an accessibility standpoint, service consumers program to these interfaces instead of the underlying business object implementation. Such indirection frees service providers to vary the implementation of the business objects behind the scenes without affecting the integrity of the interface.

5.3.4.1 Interface Patterns

Looking back at the schematic of the SAP Enterprise Services Metamodel in Figure 5.1, you can see that service interfaces are complemented by a series of *interface patterns*. These patterns help you to model your service interfaces in a consistent manner.

For the most part, you can derive interface patterns intuitively by thinking about the positioning of your service interface and the types of service operations you want to expose[27]. For example, service operations for A2A and B2B service interfaces are usually coarse-grained and asynchronous in terms of their process mode. Conversely, service interfaces provided in the xApp/UI context (sometimes called A2X services) will likely be much more granular in nature than A2A or B2B services.

Figure 5.4 provides an example of a common A2X interface pattern: the Manage <Business Object> pattern. Here, the service interface Manage Production Order In defines an inbound service interface that provides service operations that can be used to maintain production orders.

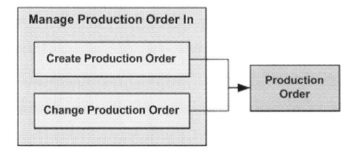

Figure 5.4: A Manage Business Object Interface Pattern Example

5.3.5   Service Operations

If you think of business objects as a type of entity class within the SAP Enterprise Services Metamodel, then you can consider service operations to be the methods provided by those classes. As such, service operations perform specific tasks on a business object (e.g. creation, updates, queries, etc.). For example, in Figure 5.4 the Create Production Order and Change Production Order service operations both manipulate the Production Order business object.

---

[27] You can find detailed descriptions of common interface patterns in the aforementioned SAP How-To Guide: *PI Best Practices: Modeling*.

5.3.5.1 Communication Patterns

The signature of a service operation is defined in terms of XML-based *message types*. Here, you can define an input message type as well as optional output and fault message types. As you may recall from Chapter 3, the arrangement of these message types and the direction of the interface (i.e. inbound or outbound) combine to form *message exchange patterns* (MEPs).

Within the SAP Enterprise Services Metamodel, MEPs are described in terms of *communication patterns*. In this context, the MEPs are further characterized by the roles being played by the service consumers/providers. Figure 5.5 illustrates the four basic communication patterns (Pohl & Peter, 2010).

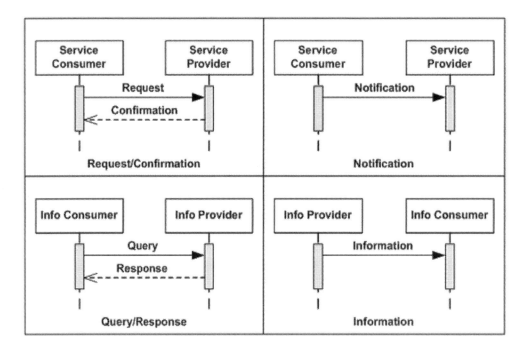

Figure 5.5: Communication Patterns for Service Interfaces

5.3.6 Data Type Definitions

As you proceed through the service modeling process, you'll find that each step focuses in more closely on particular aspects of the business process. Indeed, by the time you get down into the nitty-gritty details of the service operations, you must begin modeling the format of the messages being exchanged. These formats are described using XML-based *data type definitions*.

The crafting of the messages exchanged with enterprise services is a subtle art. However, it helps if you think of the messages as business documents or forms that might be exchanged via mail. Such documents should be well-organized, and only contain data that is pertinent to the job at hand. Furthermore, you'll want to avoid use of proprietary or in-house terms that obscure the meaning of the service. After all, you wouldn't send a form out to a customer and expect them to fill in two-digit match codes, etc. Instead, you would define such elements in generic terms so that their meaning is well understood.

RPC vs. Document Messaging Styles: Revisited

As you may recall from Chapter 3, there are two basic styles used in service-based messaging: *RPC* and *document*. In the former case, messages are usually defined in terms of some pre-existing software module (e.g. a BAPI or EJB). Conversely, the document messaging style encodes the message as a full-fledged XML document.

Many developers prefer the RPC messaging style because it makes it easier to generate service interfaces on top of pre-existing software modules. The problem with this approach is that it limits the utility of the service to a finite set of use cases. For example, imagine wrapping a Web service around a BAPI used to create a purchase order in SAP ERP (i.e. `BAPI_PO_CREATE1`). In this case, the signature of the interface is chock full of elements whose meaning is only understood within the context of the underlying SAP ERP system and its configuration. While you might use this service internally within your organization, you would most certainly not want to expose it to business partners.

Realistically, spending the time up front to model the message types being exchanged can be tedious at times. Nevertheless, if your goal is to develop reusable enterprise services, then this is a worthwhile effort. In general, we recommend that you use the document messaging style when developing your service interfaces.

One thing to keep in mind as you develop your message types is that you should not model every attribute defined within the business object that provides the service operations. Rather, your message types should be a *projection* or *view* of that business object; taking only a subset of the elements that are relevant to the processing of the service operation. Indeed, each data type definition should be pared down to include only the essentials.

Depending upon the nature of the service interface, you may find that there are existing data type definitions that you can leverage to define your message types. These days, there are many organizations that define standards for message exchanges in particular business sectors. Examples include RosettaNet, xCBL, and the aforementioned OAGIS standard, among others. Wherever possible, you should strive to use these standards rather than defining custom data types. Not only is this design choice economical, it also improves the usability of your service in a wider variety of contexts.

5.3.7   Deployment Units

Ideally, process components are autonomous in nature. However, this is not to say that they exist in isolation; process components frequently need to exchange messages with other process components to implement task flow. Therefore, whenever you look at your business process models on a macroscopic level, it is helpful to be able to visualize the relationships between process components that are logically related. In the SAP Enterprise Services Metamodel, these groups are defined using *deployment units*.

Figure 5.6 shows how deployment units group process components together. The process components within this deployment unit will be installed together on a logical system. However, deployment units should not be confused with actual software logistics artifacts such as software components, etc. Instead, they are merely logical constructs that help you visualize boundaries between groups of related process components.

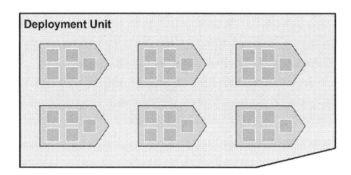

Figure 5.6: Deployment Unit Fxample

5.4   Modeling Tools in the ES Builder

Now that you are familiar with the SAP Enterprise Services Metamodel, let's take a look at how you can use it to model business process flows. In this section, we will introduce you to some of the modeling tools that are provided with the ES Builder. Realistically, these tools are complex enough that they could take up the better part of a book on modeling. Therefore, we will not provide a thorough step-by-step analysis of the tools here[28]. Rather, we will consider some existing models that are provided by default with SAP NetWeaver PI. Then, once you have a general idea for how these models work, you can begin to extend these concepts towards your own modeling efforts.

You can follow along with these models on your local instance of PI by logging onto the ES Builder and selecting the `SAP BASIS 7.11` SWCV. From here, you can expand the underlying folder structure *Modeling → Models → ESA Sales Model* to find some of the various model types. These model types are organized by folders (e.g. *01 Integration Scenario Models*, and so on).

5.4.1   Integration Scenario Models

The first model type we will consider is the *integration scenario* model. This model type provides a macroscopic view of the business process from start to finish. Figure 5.7 demonstrates an integration scenario model called `Sell From Stock (ESM)` that depicts the processing of a sales order. As you can see, this process flow utilizes multiple process components (which are grouped by their surrounding deployment units). The interactions are depicted using directed arrows that represent service calls.

---

[28] If you are looking for this kind of thorough treatment, you can find it in *Developing Enterprise Services for SAP* (Pohl & Peter, 2010).

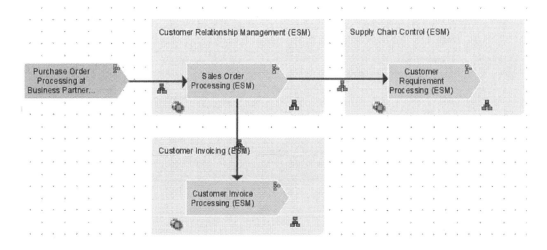

Figure 5.7: An Integration Scenario Model Depicting the Sales Order Process Flow © Copyright 2010. SAP AG. All rights reserved

As you build these models, keep in mind that you don't have to constrain the model to components within your landscape. For example, in Figure 5.7, notice the shaded process component on the far left-hand side. This component encapsulates purchase order processing at an external business partner. These placeholders can be useful at times to model B2B communication or simply to visualize the process on a broader scale. You can also include placeholders for other process components that are indirectly affected by the process flow (e.g. accounting components, etc.).

5.4.2   Process Component Models

Integration scenario models are nice if you want to see the big picture. However, if you want to drill in and see what's going on in the individual process components, you'll want to develop a *process component* (or SAP ProComp) model. Figure 5.8 contains a ProComp model called `Customer Invoice Processing (ESM)` that illustrates the structure of the `Customer Invoice Processing (ESM)` process component shown in Figure 5.7.

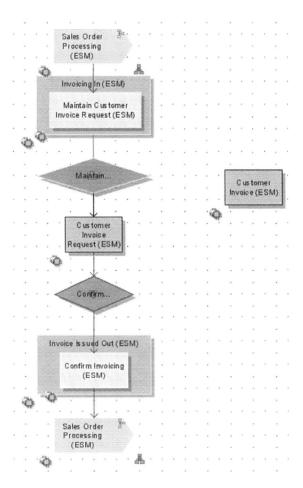

Figure 5.8: A ProComp Model Depicting Customer Invoice Processing

Looking at the ProComp model in Figure 5.8, you can see some of the service interfaces and business objects used to fulfill the processing of a customer invoice. In general, these model elements are organized such that asynchronous communication runs top-to-bottom and synchronous communication from left-to-right. This flow gives you a perspective of the process component from the provider view.

When designed properly, ProComp models should make it easy to determine which services are needed/used to implement a specific business process flow. In particular, you see the flow of the data in and out of the component juxtaposed with the implementing business objects. This should help you conceptualize the structure of the documents that are passed between the components.

5.4.3   Process Component Interaction Models

If your goal is to focus in on the interactions between individual process components, then you can use the *process component interaction* model type. Figure 5.9 demonstrates this model, illustrating the interactions between a `Purchase Order Processing` process component and a `Sales Order Processing` process component.

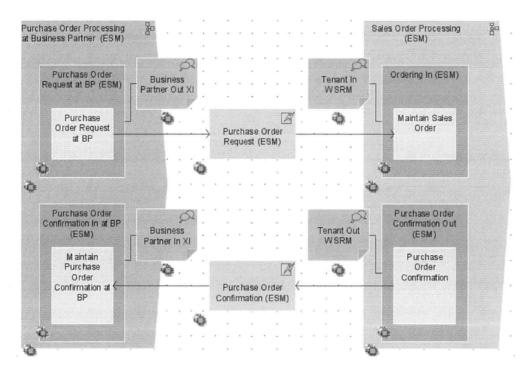

Figure 5.9: A Process Component Interaction Model Depicting PO/Sales Order Processing © Copyright 2010. SAP AG. All rights reserved

As you can see in Figure 5.9, the process component interaction model illustrates the interactions between service interfaces by attaching directed arrows between service operations. These arrows are bisected by the *message types* being exchanged (e.g. `Purchase Order Request` or `Purchase Order Confirmation`).

You can get a feel for the sequence of the events by following the interactions from top to bottom. For example, in Figure 5.9, the flow begins with a call to the `Maintain Sales Order` operation from the `Ordering In` service interface. From there, a sales order is either created or updated and a confirmation message is forwarded back to the customer via the `Purchase Order Confirmation` operation of the `Purchase Order Confirmation Out` service interface.

5.4.4   Process Integration Scenarios

So far, each of the model types that we have considered has been defined in terms of the SAP Enterprise Services Metamodel. In addition to these generic model types, you also have the option of working with a more PI-centric model type: the so-called *process integration scenario*.

Figure 5.10 depicts a sample process integration scenario called `SingleFlightBooking`[29]. This model illustrates a flight booking scenario between a travel agency and an airline. If you are familiar with the UML, then you'll see some likenesses to activity diagrams that are used to model business process flows. As you can see, the participating components are arranged from left-to-right and the process flow from top-to-bottom. In the upcoming sections, we'll see how all these pieces fit together from a bird's eye view. You can find a more detailed description of process integration scenarios in the online help documentation underneath the section entitled *Defining Process Integration Scenarios* (SAP AG).

---

[29] This process integration scenario is provided with the core `SAP BASIS 7.11` SWCV underneath the `http://sap.com/xi/XI/Demo/Agency` namespace.

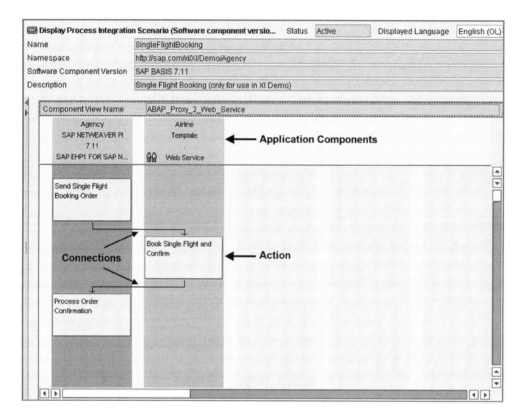

Figure 5.10: An Example Process Integration Scenario © Copyright 2010. SAP AG. All rights reserved

5.4.4.1 Application Components

The participants in a process integration scenario are represented using application components[30]. Each application component is assigned a *role* that determines the component's positioning within the process. For example, in the sample scenario contained in Figure 5.10, you have two application components playing the role of *travel agency* and *airline*, respectively. Similarly, if you were to model a B2B scenario, you might define application components to represent a *customer* and *vendor*, etc.

---

[30] From a technical perspective, application components are normally defined in terms of products and software components maintained within the SLD. However, it is also possible to define an application component in terms of an integration process. In either case, these application components are mapped to technical components at configuration time within the Integration Directory.

5.4.4.2 Actions

Conceptually speaking, process integration scenarios model the business process flow in terms of a series of abstract *actions* (or functions) provided by the participating application components. Though used exclusively within the context of process integration scenarios, actions are defined as standalone objects within the ESR.

Figure 5.11 depicts the `SendSingleFlightBookingOrder` action referenced within the `SingleFlightBooking` process integration scenario shown in Figure 5.10. As you can see, there are three basic attributes that you can configure for an action:

> **Type of Usage**
> Actions can have an *internal* or *external* usage type. See the online help documentation underneath the section entitled *Defining Process Integration Scenarios* (SAP AG) for more details about how this attribute is used.

> **Outbound Interfaces**
> The set of outbound service interfaces which represent the interfaces that can be triggered by the action.

> **Inbound Interfaces**
> The set of inbound service interfaces which represent interfaces that trigger the action.

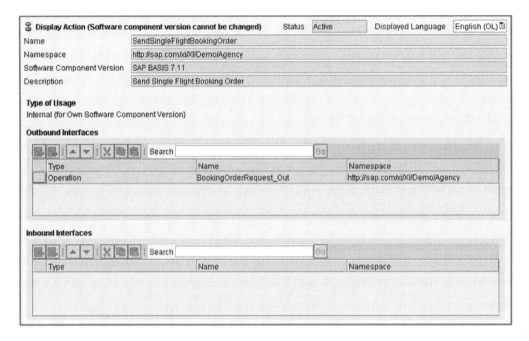

Figure 5.11: Actions within a Process Integration Scenario © Copyright 2010. SAP AG. All rights reserved

5.4.4.3 Connections

The flow of a process integration scenario is defined in terms of a series of *connections* that link a pair of related actions together. These connections are represented graphically via directed arrows. For example, in the SingleFlightBooking scenario depicted in Figure 5.10, notice the arrow that links the Send Single Flight Booking Order and Book Single Flight and Confirm actions together. In this case, the connection illustrates the interface that a travel agency uses to book a flight with an airline.

Whenever you define a connection between actions, you have the option of annotating that connection with various attributes about the interface. As you can see in Figure 5.12, you can use these attributes to identify the sender/receiver interfaces involved in the message exchange as well as other PI-centric items such as mapping programs and communication channel templates. Besides providing traceability to design-time repository objects, these attributes also come in handy at configuration time as you can use them to automagically configure an integration scenario using a tool called the *model configurator*.

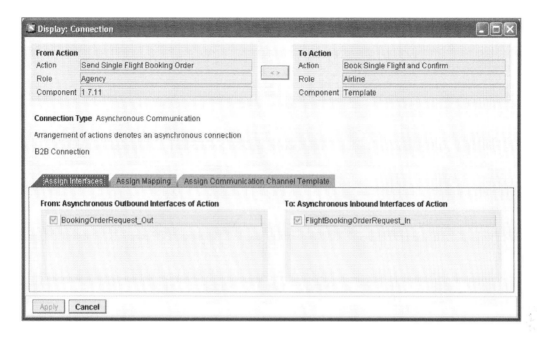

Figure 5.12: Viewing a Connection between Related Actions © Copyright 2010. SAP AG. All rights reserved

5.5　　Summary

In this chapter, we observed some best practices for service design that should serve you well in your service development as you go forward. Of course, you'll pick up many other tricks along the way. At this point though, you should be ready to dig in and get your hands dirty with service development. Therefore, in the next chapter, we'll pick up where this chapter leaves off and explore some of the different options you have for developing service interfaces in SAP NetWeaver PI.

References

OAGi. (n.d.). *Open Applications Group Home Page*. Retrieved July 13, 2010, from Open Applications Group Web site: http://www.oagi.org/dnn2/Home.aspx

Pohl, T., & Peter, M. (2010). *Developing Enterprise Services for SAP.* Boston: Galileo Press.

RosettaNet. (n.d.). *RosettaNet*. Retrieved from RosettaNet: http://www.rosettanet.org

SAP AG. (n.d.). *Basics of Process Component Architecture Models*. Retrieved July 15, 2010, from SAP Help Library: http://help.sap.com/saphelp_nwpi711/helpdata/en/0c/499f0fc9f048c5a9800 e2d736e4e9b/frameset.htm

SAP AG. (n.d.). *Defining Process Integration Scenarios.* Retrieved February 2, 2011, from SAP Help Library: http://help.sap.com/saphelp_nwpi711/helpdata/en/88/7adb7a030b424b8ef2 9b99461e52a8/frameset.htm

SAP AG. (2009, May 1). *PI Best Practices: Modeling.* Retrieved November 16, 2010, from SAP Community Network: http://www.sdn.sap.com/irj/scn/go/portal/prtroot/docs/library/uuid/303856c d-c81a-2c10-66bf-a4af539b8a3e

xCBL. (n.d.). *xCBL*. Retrieved from xCBL: http://www.xcbl.org/

Service Interface

Development 6

When it comes to the development of service interfaces, SAP NetWeaver PI covers a wide range of development scenarios. You can import pre-existing service definitions, or you can create new ones from scratch. In this chapter, we will explore these options.

After completing this chapter, you will be able to:

❖ Understand what a service interface is and how it is used to describe enterprise services independently of a particular platform, programming language, or protocol.

❖ Develop service interfaces using the inside-out and outside-in approaches.

❖ Import pre-existing service descriptions and message schema types into the ESR.

❖ Import IDoc and RFC definitions from backend SAP systems.

6.1 Service Interface Overview

Throughout the course of this book, we have described the benefits of separating a service's interface from its implementation. However, to this point, we've expressed these concepts using abstract terms. Now, it is appropriate to segue into a more practical discussion focused on the development of service interfaces within the ESR. Therefore, in this section, we'll begin our journey by taking a closer look at what service interfaces are and some of the different approaches you can take to develop them.

6.1.1 What are Service Interfaces?

SAP defines a service interface as an object that "enables you to describe – independently of a platform or programming language – operations that you require later for an implementation in an application system at a later stage" (SAP AG). Behind the scenes, service interfaces are specified using the *Web Services Description Language* (WSDL) which was described in Chapter 3.

From a PI perspective, service interfaces are design-time objects that you create within the ESR. At design time, you're interested in modeling an abstract service interface from the perspective of a *logical system*. Here, the logical system can play the role of the service provider or service consumer. In either case, the functionality of the service interface is defined in terms of a series of *service operations*. For each service operation that you define, you must specify the communication mode of the operation (i.e. synchronous vs. asynchronous), the message types being exchanged, and so on.

To put all this in context, consider the diagram contained in Figure 6.1. As you learned in Chapter 4, ESR objects such as service interfaces are defined within a software component. At configuration time, you can imagine that this software component is installed (virtually) on a particular business system in your landscape through configuration settings in the Integration Directory. These settings bind logical service operations with concrete implementations made available on the consumer/provider systems. As you'll soon see, such clear separation gives you tremendous flexibility at configuration time.

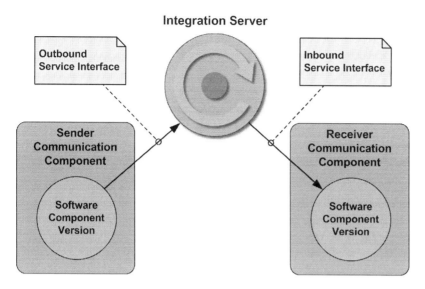

Figure 6.1: Understanding the Positioning of Service Interfaces

6.1.2   Development Approaches

Before you begin the development of a service interface, there are a number of questions that you need to answer:

> Where is a particular service needed?

> How will the service be used? For example, will it be used as an internal A2A service or a cross-company B2B service? Or will the service be used to facilitate real-time lookups for an xApp?

> Is there a pre-existing service that you can leverage from?

To a large extent, the answers to these questions will determine the method you use to develop your service interface. In general, there are two basic methods for defining service interfaces within the ESR:

> You can use the tools provided in the ES Builder to develop a new service interface from scratch.

> Or, you can define your service interface in terms of pre-existing service descriptions (based upon industry-standard technologies such as WSDL or XML Schema) that you import into the ESR.

SAP refers to these interface development methods as an *outside-in approach* and *inside-out approach*, respectively. Here, the use of the directional terms helps you to orient yourself from the perspective of the endpoint systems. For example, in the outside-in approach, the service interface definition is defined *externally* (i.e. in the ESR) and then imported into an endpoint system where it is used to generate proxy objects. Conversely, the inside-out approach leverages service descriptions that already exist in an endpoint system (e.g. WSDLs or even IDocs/RFCs). These descriptions are then imported into the ESR and used as the basis for defining service interfaces. We'll consider both of these approaches to service interface development in Sections 6.2 and 6.3, respectively.

6.1.3 Characteristics of Service Interfaces

Having now considered the basics of service interfaces, let's take a closer look at the attributes that given them their meaning. If you are familiar with the WSDL metamodel described in Chapter 3, then most of these characteristics of service interfaces should seem familiar to you. However, there are certain aspects of service interfaces that are SAP-specific.

Figure 6.2 depicts a service interface in the service interface editor of the ES Builder tool. As you can see, this editor is broken up into two sections: *Attributes* and *Operations*. In the top-level *Attributes* section, you define basic attributes of the interface. Table 6.1 describes each of these attributes in detail.

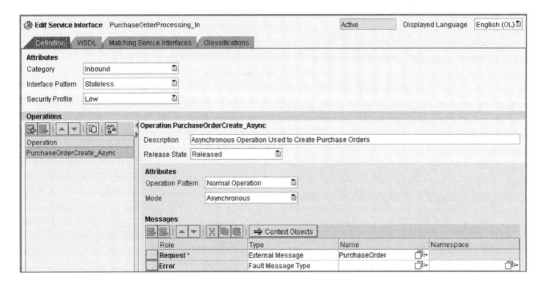

Figure 6.2: Editing a Service Interface in the ESR © Copyright 2010. SAP AG. All rights reserved

Attribute	Possible Values	Description
Category	Outbound Inbound Abstract	You can think of a service interface's category as a type of *role assignment*. By specifying this attribute, you determine whether or not the interface plays the role of service consumer (Outbound) or service provider (Inbound). The Abstract category is used to model the interfaces brokered by integration processes. We'll examine this category of service interfaces further in Chapter 9.
Interface Pattern	Stateful Stateless Stateless (XI30) TU&C/C	The interface pattern attribute determines whether or not the service is *stateless* or *stateful*. Conceptually, this comes down to whether or not the message server keeps track of the *transactional context* for service calls. In keeping with best SOA practices, you'll want to prefer the use of stateless interfaces over stateful interfaces wherever possible. Here, you must also determine whether or not the service interface should be XI 3.0-compatible[31]. If you do choose to use the Stateful and TU&C/C patterns, keep in mind that they require enhanced functionality on the backend systems (e.g. the Web Service Runtime provided in modern SAP backend systems). In the latter case, the term TU&C/C stands for *Tentative Update & Confirm/Compensate*, a protocol devised by SAP to define a logical transaction context around synchronous service calls.

---

[31] If you never worked with prior versions of SAP NetWeaver PI, then this distinction requires further clarification. In previous versions of PI, a service interface did not support the specification of multiple operations as defined in

Attribute	Possible Values	Description
Security Profile	No Low Medium High	As you would expect, the security profile attribute describes the baseline security level for a service interface. This attribute can be used to influence the way that a service is implemented at implementation time[32].

Table 6.1: Attributes of Service Interfaces

In the *Operations* table of the service interface editor, you can define each of the operations provided by your service interface (see Figure 6.2). Table 6.2 describes the attributes that you can use to specify a service operation.

Attribute	Possible Values	Description
Description	N/A	In this field, you can provide a brief description about what the operation is used for.
Release State	Not Defined Not Released Rel. w/Restrictions Released Deprecated Revoked	The release state attribute is similar to annotations used in programming languages such as Java to advise that a method has been deprecated, etc. In keeping with the shared collaboration knowledge principle, you should use this attribute to notify service consumers of updates in an operation's lifecycle. For example, the status of an operation could move from Not Defined → Released → Deprecated → Revoked.

---

the WSDL metamodel. Thus, if you select the XI 3.0-compatible pattern, you cannot define multiple operations in your service interface.

[32] For the most part, you'll find that this attribute has nothing to do with SAP NetWeaver PI. However, as the ESR is a shared tool used by both the SAP NetWeaver PI and SAP NetWeaver CE usage types, you'll find a certain amount of overlap in some object definitions. We'll endeavor to point out these situations where appropriate.

Attribute	Possible Values	Description
Pattern	Commit Operation Compensate Operation Confirm Operation Normal Operation Rollback Operation Tentative Update Oper.	Depending upon the interface pattern selected for the service interface, you may find different options for specifying the pattern of the individual operations. However, from a PI perspective, you'll almost always choose the default Normal Operation pattern.
Mode	Asynchronous Synchronous	This attribute specifies the mode of communication.
Messages	Request Response Error	In this table, you can define the messages are exchanged by the operation. These messages can be defined in terms of custom message types defined in the ESR, or pre-existing types imported from an external XML Schema or WSDL document.

Table 6.2: Attributes of Service Operations

In the upcoming sections, we'll have an opportunity to see many of these attributes on display as we show you ways of developing service interfaces. You can also gain insight into how specific attributes work by toggling between the *Definition* and *WSDL* tabs. Here, you can compare and contrast the generated WSDL with a wide variety of WSDL examples available online.

6.2   Development Using the Outside-In Approach

With the outside-in approach to service interface development, you have the opportunity to design and develop a service interface from scratch. Ideally, this process begins with the application of the SOA design concepts described in Chapter 5. Then, once you've modeled the business process, you can begin to specify your service interface using the attributes described in Section 6.1.3.

In the upcoming sections, we'll show you how to define a service interface using the built-in tools provided with the ES Builder. Here, in addition to the service interface editor that you've already seen, we'll introduce you to the message and data type editors that are used to model the messages exchanged by the individual service operations. Collectively, you'll see how these tools can be used to rapidly develop service interfaces.

6.2.1 Defining Data Types

As the name suggests, a service interface provides an *interface* (or boundary) between a software component/system and the outside world. At this point of interaction, data passes into or out of a software component in the form of messages provided via service operation calls. Ideally, these messages should be self-contained; providing all of the pertinent information needed to perform the task at hand.

As described in Chapter 5, defining the messages exchanged via service interfaces is a non-trivial task. However, the process will go a lot more smoothly if you spend some time modeling up front. In particular, it helps if you decompose a message down into smaller building blocks that can be reused in other scenarios. Not only does this improve productivity, it also lends consistency to your interface definitions.

In the ESR, you can define the structure and format of message types by creating reusable *data types*. Under the hood, these data types are defined using XML Schema. In the upcoming sections, we'll show you how to develop data types using the XSD editor included in the ES Builder tool. Along the way, we'll introduce you to some new innovations for data types introduced by SAP in version 7.1 of SAP NetWeaver PI.

6.2.1.1 Freely-Modeled Data Types

The first class of data types that we'll look at is the so-called *freely-modeled data types*. The idiom "freely-modeled" in this context implies that you are free to define these data types in pretty much any way you choose. Of course, you still have to obey the rules of XML Schema. However, as you'll soon see, the XSD editor simplifies this task a great deal.

To create a freely-modeled data type, perform the following steps:

1. Log onto the ES Builder and expand the SWCV that you wish to define the data type in. Then, right-click on the target namespace and select the *New* menu option.

2. In the ensuing *Create Object* dialog window, expand the *Interface Objects* submenu in the left-hand navigation area and choose the

Data Type menu option. This will adjust the view to include input fields that are specific to data types (see Figure 6.3).

3. In the *Data Type* edit mask shown in Figure 6.3, you must enter the name[33] of the data type as well as an optional description. Also, for freely-modeled data types, you must select the (default) classification `Free-Style Data Type` in the *Classification* field.

4. Finally, click the *Create* button to open up the data type in the XSD editor tool.

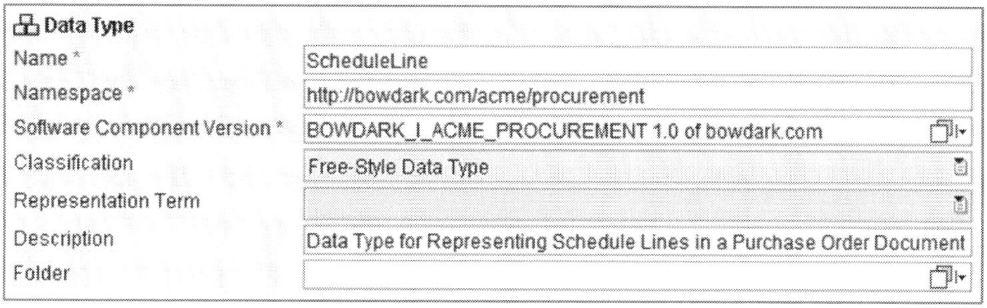

🔲 Data Type	
Name *	ScheduleLine
Namespace *	http://bowdark.com/acme/procurement
Software Component Version *	BOWDARK_I_ACME_PROCUREMENT 1.0 of bowdark.com
Classification	Free-Style Data Type
Representation Term	
Description	Data Type for Representing Schedule Lines in a Purchase Order Document
Folder	

Figure 6.3: Creating a Free-Style Data Type in the ES Builder © Copyright 2010. SAP AG. All rights reserved

Figure 6.4 contains a view of the XSD editor tool that you use to edit data types. By default, the editor will open up on the *Type Definition* tab that contains a table that you can use to specify the data type's components (i.e. its elements and attributes). To add new components to your type definition, simply highlight a row and click on the *Insert New Lines* 🔳 button. Here, you can use the button drop-down list to add multiple lines, define an attribute, and so on. Similarly, to remove a line item, simply select it and click on the *Delete Selected Line* 🔳 button.

---

[33] See the SAP NetWeaver How-To Guide *PI Best Practices: Naming Conventions* (SAP AG) for naming conventions.

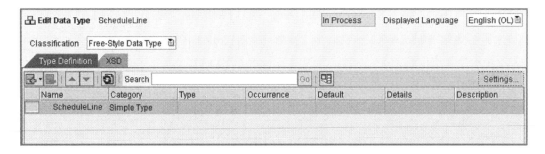

Figure 6.4: Editing a Data Type in the XSD Editor © Copyright 2010. SAP AG. All rights reserved

The columns in the table contained within the *Type Definition* tab shown in Figure 6.4 are used to specify attributes of the individual component declarations contained within the data type. Table 6.3 provides a detailed description of these attributes.

Column Name	Description
Name	Refers to the name of a component (i.e., an element or attribute) being modeled in the data type definition. These names must conform with XML syntax rules. In the case of nested types, the editor will indent the component names to match the layout of the data type.
Category	This column defaults to the value `Simple Type`. However, if child components are added to the data type, then the value will automatically be updated with the value `Complex Type`. The XSD editor will not allow you to edit this field directly.
Type	In this column, you specify the data type of the component being modeled. Here, you can choose between built-in XSD types or other data types defined within the ESR. In the latter case, you can use custom data types you define or leverage pre-existing types provided by SAP or a 3rd-party vendor[34].
Occurrence	This column allows you to specify occurrence constraints for a given component using the familiar XSD `minOccurs` and `maxOccurs` attributes.

---

[34] Here, a usage dependency must first be established between your SWCV and the SWCV in which the leveraged data types are defined.

Column Name	Description
Default	For simple component types, you can use this column to specify a default value.
Details	You can use this column to extend built-in XSD types via *restriction*. Here, the popup editor provides you with an input mask for specifying facets relevant to the selected built-in type. Refer to Chapter 2 for more information about type derivation through restriction.
Description	In this column, you can provide an optional description for the component.

Table 6.3: Attributes of Data Types in the XSD Editor

Case Study: Constructing a Purchase Order Message

To see how data type definitions work, let's consider an example based upon a purchase order message. Here, the PO message needs to be structured hierarchically to include header-level data, item data, and schedule line data. To begin, we'll start at the bottom and work our way up by examining the creation of the ScheduleLine data type.

Initially, the XSD editor starts us off with a clean slate, defining a simple data type matching the name we provided in the creation wizard. To model complex types, we'll need to add new rows to represent each of the constituent component declarations. In the case of the ScheduleLine type, we'll want to add three rows to represent the child elements LineNumber, Quantity, and DeliveryDate, respectively. For this, we will select the drop-down menu on the *Insert New Lines* button and choose the *Insert Rows...* menu option (see Figure 6.5). Then, in the *Insert Rows* popup, we can enter the number of lines we want to add and click the *OK* button (see Figure 6.6).

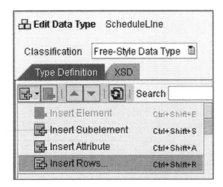

Figure 6.5: Declaring Components in a Data Type Definition (Part 1)

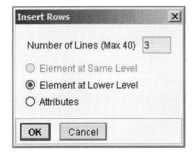

Figure 6.6: Declaring Components in a Data Type Definition (Part 2)

Once the rows are created, we can begin defining the component declarations within the table editor. For example, in Figure 6.7, you can see how we are defining the child element `LineNumber`. Here, to specify the type, we've selected the drop-down list in the *Type* column. As you can see in Figure 6.8, the drop-down list gets converted into an XSD type list if we choose the *XSD Types...* menu option. For the `LineNumber` field, we've chosen the `xsd:integer` type. We'll do the same thing for the `DeliveryDate` field, choosing the `xsd:date` type from the XSD types list.

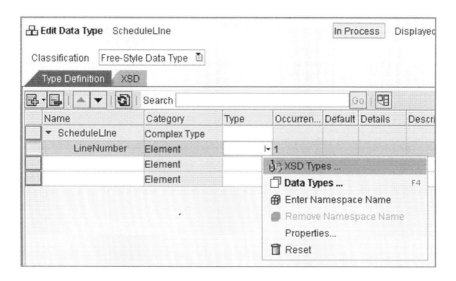

Figure 6.7: Declaring Components in a Data Type Definition (Part 3)

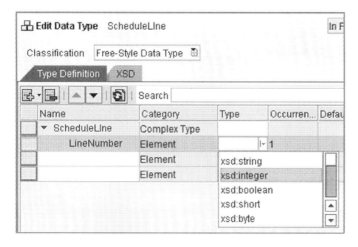

Figure 6.8: Declaring Components in a Data Type Definition (Part 4)

Frequently, it makes sense to define element types in terms of pre-existing types. For example, for the `Quantity` element, we need to define a complex type that provides an attribute called `unitCode` to represent the unit of measure used to quantify the quantity value. In this case, we have defined a new data type called `Quantity` as shown in Figure 6.9.

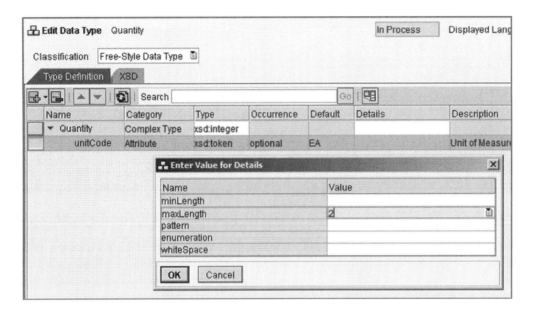

Figure 6.9: Declaring Components in a Data Type Definition (Part 5)

To reference this type in our `ScheduleLine` type definition, we simply click on the drop-down list in the *Type* column and choose the *Data Types...* menu option. Then, in the ensuing *Choose Data Type* dialog box, we can select the target data type and click on the *Apply* button.

Figure 6.10 shows the completed `ScheduleLine` data type. Once we have saved our changes, we can proceed up the document hierarchy to define different aspects of the purchase order document. By repeatedly applying this process, we'll eventually arrive at the definition of a `PurchaseOrder` data type like the one shown in Figure 6.11.

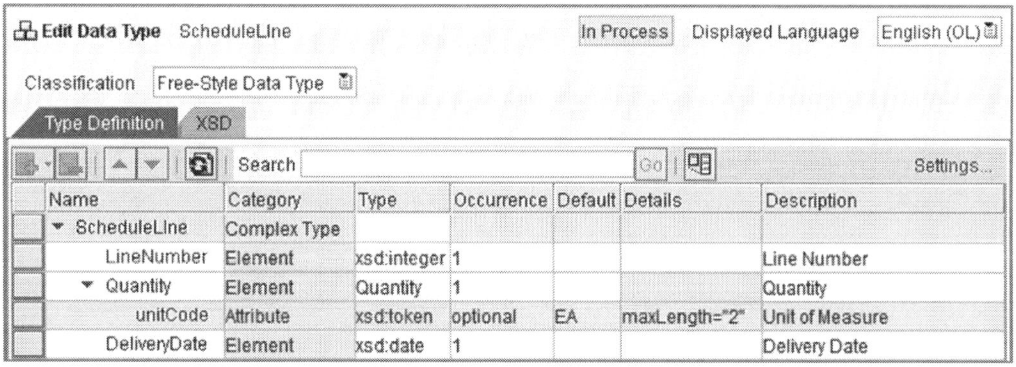

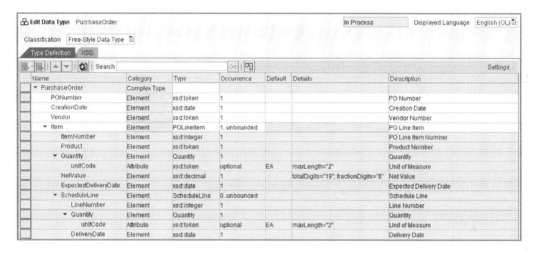

Figure 6.10: Declaring Components in a Data Type Definition (Part 6)
© Copyright 2010. SAP AG. All rights reserved

Figure 6.11: Declaring Components in a Data Type Definition (Part 7)
© Copyright 2010. SAP AG. All rights reserved

6.2.1.2   Core Data Types and Aggregated Data Types

As you saw in Section 6.2.1.1, the XSD editor makes it pretty easy to define data types in the ESR. However, while this free style approach is certainly productive, it is not without its drawbacks. The primary danger here is that, without governance, developers will venture off and formulate their own dialects for describing various business objects. Beyond the obvious incompatibility problems this causes, you also run the risk of redundancy and overlap in data type definitions. Once again, the semantic interoperability problem described in Chapter 5 rears its ugly head.

To combat these problems, the United Nations Centre for Trade Facilitation and Electronic Business (UN/CEFACT) introduced the *Core Component Technical Specification* (CCTS) and *XML Naming and Design Rules* (XML NDR) specifications. These specifications define a methodology for defining a harmonized data model that is easy to understand and use in a wide variety of use cases.

While an in-depth discourse on these topics is beyond the scope of this book, you can find a wealth of information about CCTS and XML NDR on the SAP Developer Network (SDN)[35]. Also, beginning with release 7.1 of SAP NetWeaver PI, you'll also find support for these specifications in the data type editor in the form of *core data types* and *aggregated data types*. For more information on these data type classifications, see the online help documentation under the section entitled *Core Data Types and Aggregated Data Types* (SAP AG).

6.2.1.3 Generating XML Schema

Earlier, we mentioned that data types are defined using the XML Schema language. Within the XSD editor, you can see this on display by clicking on the *XSD* tab as shown in Figure 6.12. Here, you can see the XML Schema generated behind the scenes as you edit a data type.

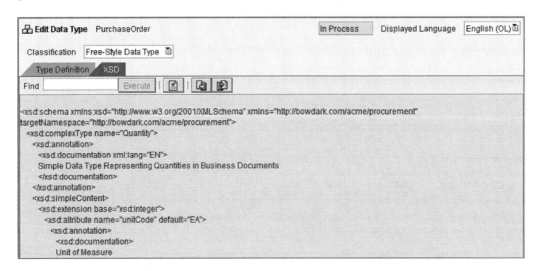

Figure 6.12: Viewing the Generated XML Schema for a Data Type © Copyright 2010. SAP AG. All rights reserved

---

[35] A consolidated list of articles on CCTS is provided at *http://wiki.sdn.sap.com/wiki/display/DataIntegration/Articles+about+CCTS*.

As you can see in Figure 6.12, the XSD view provides you with a search area that you can use to search for specific component declarations, etc. You also have the option to open up the schema definition in an external XML editor (via the 🖺 button) or export the schema as a local file (via the 🖺 button).

6.2.2   Defining Message Types

After you complete the definition of the requisite data types, you must define the *message types* that will be used to specify the service interface operations. From an XML Schema perspective, this is analogous to declaring an element in reference to a data type definition. These elements can then be referenced by the `wsdl:message` definitions contained within a service interface's operation definitions.

To create a new message type, perform the following steps:

1. Choose the SWCV that you want to work with and then right-click on the target namespace. In the popup menu, select the *New* menu option.

2. In the ensuing *Create Object* dialog box, expand the *Interface Objects* submenu in the left-hand navigation area and choose the *Message Type* menu option.

3. Next, enter a name and an optional description for the message type. See the aforementioned SAP NetWeaver How-To guide for naming conventions.

4. Finally, click on the *Create* button to create the new message type.

Figure 6.13 contains an example of a `PurchaseOrder` message type that we have defined within the message type editor. As you can see, there are two basic inputs to a message type definition:

➢ In the *Data Type Used* field, you must select a data type defined within the ESR[36]. This data type describes the structure of the message.

---

[36] This data type must exist within the same SWCV or an underlying SWCV of the SWCV in which the message type is defined.

> ➢ The *XML Namespace* field defines the target namespace for the message type. This value will default to the ESR namespace in which the message type is defined, but you are free to change it as you like.

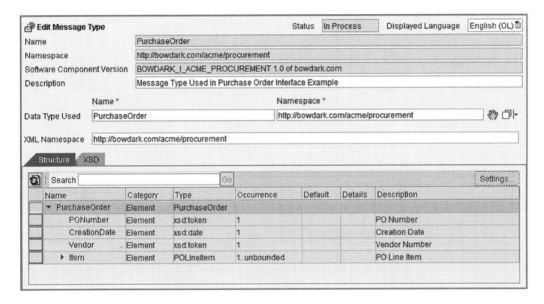

Figure 6.13: Defining a Message Type in the ESR © Copyright 2010. SAP AG. All rights reserved

Much like the XSD editor used to define data types, the message type editor also provides an *XSD* tab that you can use to view the generated XML schema for the message type. The primary difference here is the fact that message types also contain an element declaration like the `PurchaseOrder` element shown in Figure 6.14.

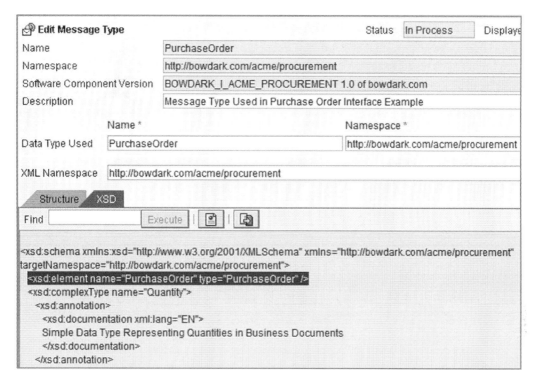

Figure 6.14: Viewing the XML Schema Definition for a Message Type ©
Copyright 2010. SAP AG. All rights reserved

6.2.2.1 Fault Message Types

As you may recall from Chapter 3, service operations can also declare *fault messages* that encapsulate application-specific error messages relayed back to a service consumer. In SOAP-based messaging, these fault messages must adhere to a specific structure. However, that structure can be enhanced with custom data types.

Within the context of the ESR, fault messages are defined using *fault message types*. To create a fault message type, you must perform the following steps:

1. Choose the SWCV that you want to work with and then right-click on the target namespace. In the popup menu, select the *New* menu option.

2. In the ensuing *Create Object* dialog box, expand the *Interface Objects* submenu in the left-hand navigation area and choose the *Fault Message Type* menu option.

3. Next, enter a name and an optional description for the fault message type. See the aforementioned SAP NetWeaver How-To guide for naming conventions.

4. Finally, click on the *Create* button to create the new fault message type.

Figure 6.15 contains a sample fault message type created within the ESR. As you can see, fault message types are defined in much the same way as regular message types. However, unlike normal message types, fault message types are comprised of two different data type definitions:

➢ The core structure of the fault message type is defined by the auto-generated `ExchangeFaultData` type. As you can see in Figure 6.15, you cannot override this definition in the *Standard Data* input field.

➢ Besides the standard data type, you can also specify a custom data type in the *Additional Data* input field. Here, you can choose from any custom data type within the current SWCV or an underlying SWCV. The components of this data type will then be appended to the fault message type underneath the `standard` element in an element called `addition`.

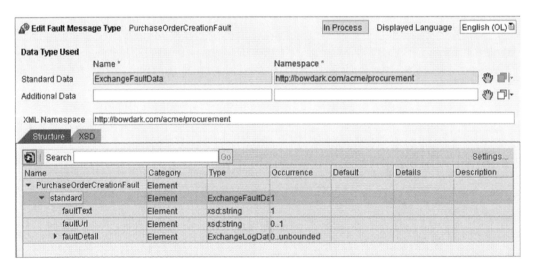

Figure 6.15: Creating a Fault Message Type in the ESR © Copyright 2010. SAP AG. All rights reserved

Whenever you go to save your fault message type, you may be presented with a prompt like the one shown in Figure 6.16. In this case, the editor is advising you that the standard, auto-generated types `ExchangeFaultData` and `ExchangeLogData` have not yet been created within the current namespace. Here, simply click on the *Create* button to allow the system to auto-generate these requisite types.

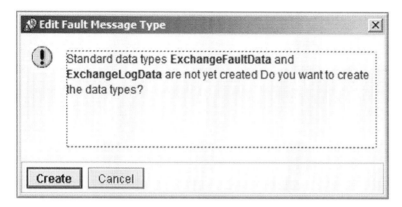

Figure 6.16: Generating Standard Fault Data Types © Copyright 2010. SAP AG. All rights reserved

6.2.3 Defining the Service Interface

The final step in the outside-in approach to interface development is the specification of the service interfaces themselves. We covered most of this already in Section 6.1.3. However, now that you are familiar with the definition of message types, we should take a closer look at how they used to specify service interface operations.

To illustrate how this works, consider the `PurchaseOrderProcessing_In` interface depicted in Figure 6.17. This interface defines operations for creating or updating a purchase order. Looking closely at Figure 6.17, you can see how we have defined the `PurchaseOrderCreate_Async` operation. Of particular note is the specification of the request and error message types contained in the *Messages* table.

In order to be able to plug in message types defined within the ESR, you must select the `Message Type` (or `Fault Message Type`) option in the *Type* column of the *Messages* table. Whenever these options are selected, you can drag-and-drop message types from the left-hand navigation area or search for message types using the provided context-sensitive search helps. Figure 6.17 shows how we declared the messages for the

`PurchaseOrderCreate_Async` operation in terms of the `PurchaseOrder` and `PurchaseOrderCreationFault` message types described in Section 6.2.2.

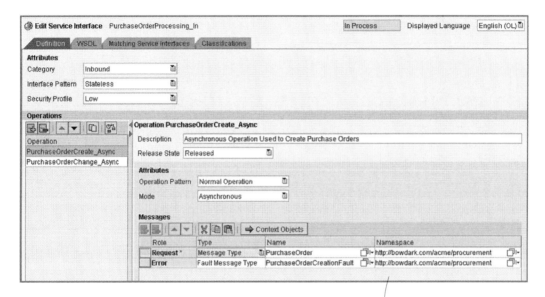

Figure 6.17: Binding Message Types to Service Operations © Copyright 2010. SAP AG. All rights reserved

6.3 Development Using the Inside-Out Approach

For the most part, service interface development using the inside-out approach is relatively straightforward. This is as it should be since most of the analysis/design work has been performed already. Your main task is to import and assemble the external artifacts within the ESR. So, without further adieu, let's see how this is done.

6.3.1 Importing External Definitions

In order to import external artifacts into the ESR, you must create an *external definition* object. External definitions encapsulate these artifacts, allowing you to import pre-existing message definitions from WSDL files, XML Schema files, or even legacy DTD files. The imported message schema can then be utilized in the same way that message types are used to define:

> Request, response, or fault messages in service interface operations.

> The source or target structures for graphical message mappings.

For the most part, you'll find that the process of importing an external artifact is the same regardless of the type of artifact you're working with. The following steps outline this process:

1. Choose the SWCV that you want to work with and then right-click on the target namespace. In the popup menu, select the *New* menu option.

2. In the ensuing *Create Object* dialog box, expand the *Interface Objects* submenu in the left-hand navigation area and choose the *External Definition* menu option.

3. Next, enter a name and an optional description for the external definition. See the aforementioned SAP NetWeaver How-To guide for naming conventions.

4. Finally, click on the *Create* button to create the external definition object.

Figure 6.18 shows the newly created external definition within the ESR. As you can see, there are four basic attributes that you must fill in to define an external definition. Table 6.4 describes each of these attributes in further detail.

Field Name	Description
Category	In this field, you select the type of artifact that you want to import (e.g. WSDL, XSD, and so on).
Messages	This field determines the mode in which message schema are imported. Typically, the default option proposed by the editor will suffice here. However, if you're interested in learning more about the other modes, check out the online help documentation in the section entitled *Working with External Definitions* (SAP AG).
File	In this field, you select the file that you wish to upload. As you can see in Figure 6.18, you can click on the *Import External Definitions* button on the right-hand side of the field to open up a file chooser box to help you locate the target file on your local machine.

Field Name	Description
Source	This field provides a linkage between an external definition within the ESR and the location ID used to reference that artifact within a file. We'll learn more about this feature in Section 6.3.1.1.

Table 6.4: Attributes of External Definitions

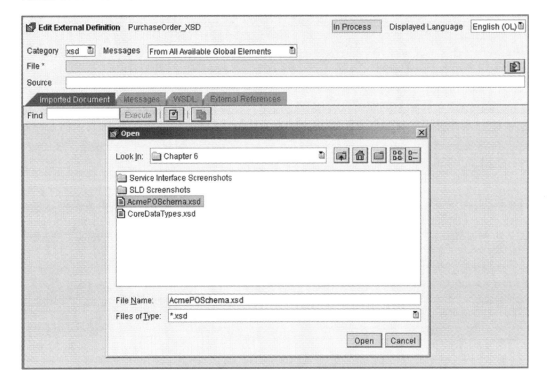

Figure 6.18: Creating an External Definition © Copyright 2010. SAP AG. All rights reserved

Once the document is imported, you can see it displayed on the *Imported Document* tab. Also, as you can see in Figure 6.18, the external definition editor also provides a series of other tab views including:

> The *Messages* tab which displays the schema definition in the same way that message types and data types are represented graphically in the ESR.

> The *WSDL* tab which shows the WSDL wrapper file created by the ES Builder whenever you import non-WSDL files. This wrapper file is

used to simplify the use of message schema elsewhere within the ESR.

➤ The *External References* tab which contains a list of references (e.g. includes/imports) and their relationships to other external definitions within the ESR. More on this in Section 6.3.1.1.

6.3.1.1 Defining External References

Frequently, you may encounter situations where you want to import multiple related files as external definitions. For example, imagine an XSD file called `AcmePOSchema.xsd` that references common types defined in another file named `CoreDataTypes.xsd`. Listing 6.1 demonstrates how this reference might be defined within the `AcmePOSchema.xsd` file. Here, notice how the `schemaLocation` attribute points to a directory path somewhere on a file system. While this location ID makes sense if you're working with the XSD files locally, it has no meaning within a global repository like the ESR.

```
<xsd:schema
    xmlns:xsd="http://www.w3.org/2001/XMLSchema"
    xmlns:core="http://acme.com/schemas/core"
    xmlns:po="http://acme.com/schemas/purchasing"
    targetNamespace="http://acme.com/schemas/purchasing">

  <xsd:import namespace="http://acme.com/schemas/core"
        schemaLocation="CoreDataTypes.xsd" />
  ...
</xsd:schema>
```

Listing 6.1: Defining an Import in an XSD File

To get around this limitation, you must annotate the external definition for the referenced file with the file path that other XSD files use to reference it. For example, Figure 6.19 shows how we have filled in the *Source* field for the aforementioned `CoreDataTypes.xsd` file. Once this field is populated, the system will be able to resolve file references and link everything together. For instance, notice how the system has resolved the reference to the `CoreDataTypes.xsd` file in the `AcmePOSchema` external definition depicted in Figure 6.20.

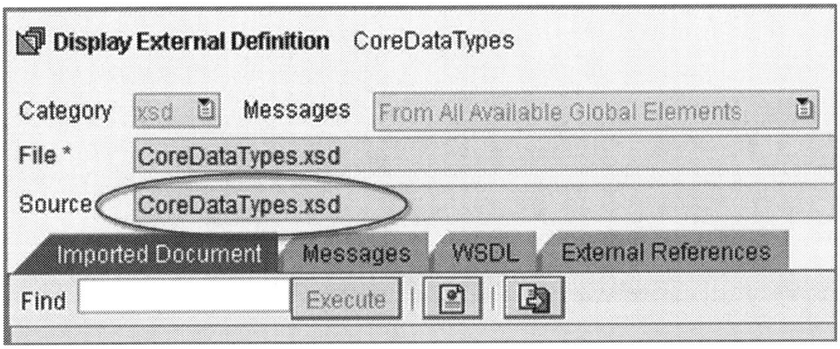

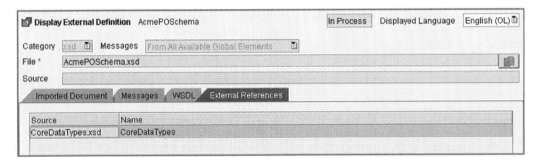

Figure 6.19: Specifying the Source for an External Definition © Copyright 2010. SAP AG. All rights reserved

Figure 6.20: Viewing External References in an External Definition © Copyright 2010. SAP AG. All rights reserved

6.3.1.2 Performing Mass Imports

In the past, if you wanted to import a collection of related definition files into the ESR, you had to perform the imports one at a time. However, with release 7.1 of SAP NetWeaver PI, you can perform mass imports that pull in a series of related artifacts in one fell swoop.

To perform a mass import of external definitions in the ESR, perform the following steps:

1. In the top-level menu bar, select the *Tools → Import External Definitions...* menu option. This will open up the *Import External*

Definitions wizard which will guide you through the import process. After you read over the basic instructions, you can click on the *Continue* button to get started.

2. At the *Choose the Source and Target of Import* step, you'll want to select the SWCV/namespace in which you want to store the imported external definitions. Click the *Continue* button to proceed.

3. Then, at the *Choose File* step, you'll want to navigate to the directory where the target files are stored and select the relevant files/directories[37]. Click the *Continue* button to move to the next step.

4. Finally, on the *Preview/Analysis* step, you can look over the definition proposals made by the tool and perform any last minute tweaks. Assuming you're comfortable with the proposals, you can click on the *Finish* button to generate the external definitions (see Figure 6.21).

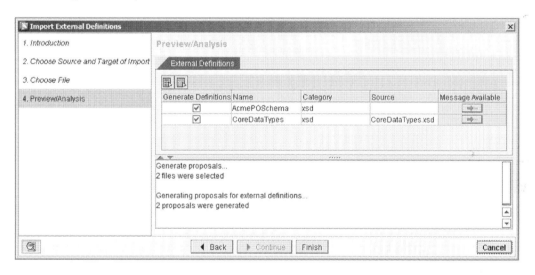

Figure 6.21: Performing a Mass Import of External Definitions © Copyright 2010. SAP AG. All rights reserved

One nice thing about the mass import option is the fact that the system will attempt to resolve references between message definitions automatically.

---

[37] Note: The ES Builder cannot introspect ZIP archives, etc. Therefore, if you want to import definitions from an archive file, you must first unpack it to a local directory.

For example, if you look closely at Figure 6.21, you can see that the system has automatically resolved the reference between the `AcmePOSchema.xsd` and `CoreDataTypes.xsd` schema files.

6.3.1.3 Creating Service Interfaces

Once you have imported message schema as external definitions, you can use them to specify a service interface's operations. Here, for a given operation, you simply select the `External Message` option in the *Type* column of the *Messages* table (see Figure 6.22). Then, you can lookup external messages using the search help provided in the *Name* column. This option is available for request, response, or fault message types.

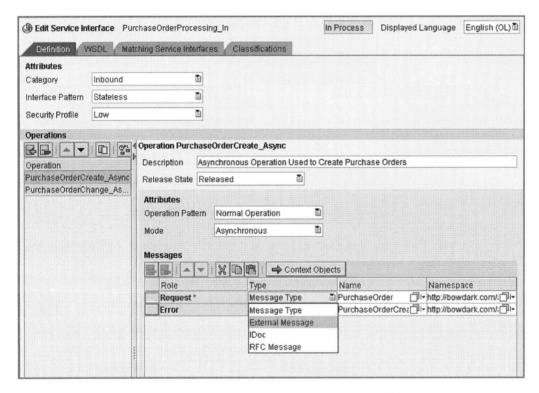

Figure 6.22: Using External Definitions to Define Service Operations
© Copyright 2010. SAP AG. All rights reserved

If the file you're importing is a WSDL definition, then you also have the option of auto-generating an external definition and a service interface at the same time using a wizard provided with the ES Builder. To access this functionality, select the *Tools → Import Service Interface...* menu option from the top-level menu bar. Then, perform the following steps:

1. The first step in the wizard provides you with an overview of what the wizard does. Once you've read through these instructions, click on the *Continue* button to proceed.

2. At the *Choose Source and Target of Import* step, you select the target SWCV/namespace in which you want to store the imported objects. Click the *Continue* button to move to the next step.

3. On the *Choose File* step, you must navigate to the WSDL file that you wish to import. As you can see in Figure 6.23, this step also allows you to choose whether or not you want to define the category of the service interface as *inbound* or *outbound*. Click the *Continue* button to move to the next step.

4. Finally, on the *Preview/Analysis* step, you can view the artifacts that will be generated by the wizard. Assuming you're comfortable with the selections, click on the *Finish* button to let the system create the objects.

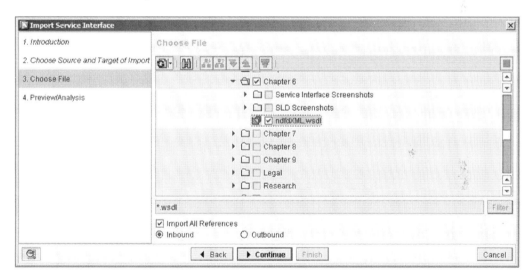

Figure 6.23: Defining a Service Interface Using a WSDL File © Copyright 2010. SAP AG. All rights reserved

Figure 6.24 shows a generated service interface for a publicly available Web service used to lookup forecast information in the U.S. National Oceanic and

Atmospheric Administration (NOAA) database[38]. As you can see, each of the generated service operations are defined using external messages defined in an external definition called `ndfdXML` created by the wizard.

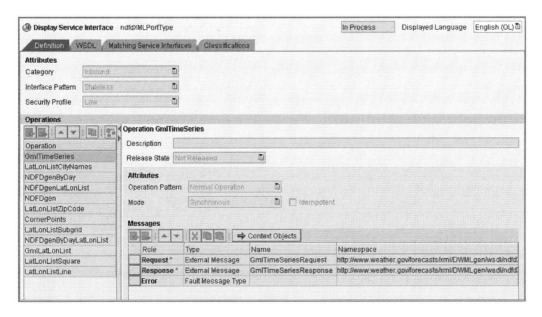

Figure 6.24: Viewing a Generated Service Interface in the ESR © Copyright 2010. SAP AG. All rights reserved

6.3.2 Importing IDocs & RFCs

As you might expect, SAP NetWeaver PI excels at integrating with backend SAP systems. In particular, you'll find that it is very easy to leverage pre-existing ALE IDoc or RFC interfaces within PI. However, in order to do so, you must import the metadata for these definitions into the ESR. In this section, we'll show you how to import and use this metadata in the ESR.

6.3.2.1 Defining Connection Data to the Backend Systems

Before you can import IDoc or RFC metadata into the ESR, you must configure connection data to the backend SAP system that contains the definitions. As you may recall from Chapter 4, this connection data is maintained in the SWCV definition. For example, in Figure 6.25, you can see how we've defined a connection to client 100 of an SAP ECC system called

---

[38] For more information about this service, check out *http://www.weather.gov/forecasts/xml/*.

DEV. As necessary, you can use the *Message Server* and *Group* fields to connect to systems that have load balancing turned on.

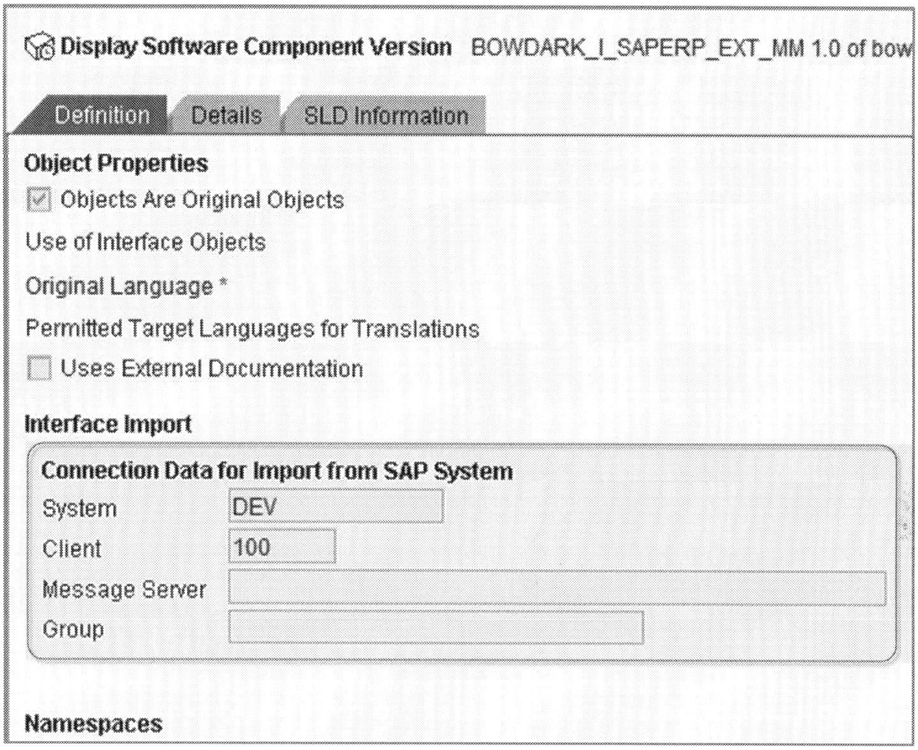

Figure 6.25: Defining Connection Data for Importing IDocs/RFCs from an SAP Backend System © Copyright 2010. SAP AG. All rights reserved

6.3.2.2   Performing an Import

Once the relevant communication settings are in place for your SWCV, you can import an IDoc or RFC definition by performing the following steps:

1. Within the target SWCV, right-click on the *Imported Objects* node and selecting the *Import of SAP Objects* menu option (see Figure 6.26). This will launch the metadata import wizard.

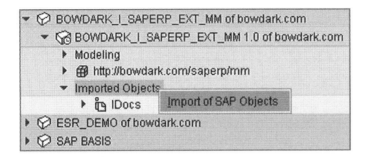

Figure 6.26: Importing IDoc and RFC Metadata (Part 1)

2. On the *Logon* step, you will be prompted to log onto the target backend SAP system (see Figure 6.27). Here, you must plug in the following information:

    a. In the *Application Server* field, you must enter the application server host of the backend SAP system.

    b. In the *System Number* field, you enter the system number of the backend SAP system.

    c. In the *User Name/Password* fields, you must provide the logon credentials for a user account in the backend SAP system. This account must have the proper permissions necessary to introspect IDoc/RFC definitions[39].

---

[39] For a complete list of required authorizations in the backend system, consult the online help documentation underneath the section entitled *Importing IDocs and RFCs* (SAP AG).

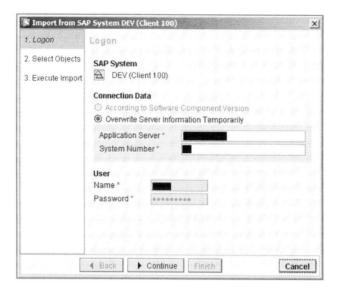

Figure 6.27: Importing IDoc and RFC Metadata (Part 2)

3. On the *Select Objects* step, you can select from the list of IDocs and RFCs that are available within the backend system. This list includes custom-developed modules as well as standard modules delivered by SAP. Once you find the object you're looking for, select its checkbox and click on the *Continue* button.

4. Finally, at the *Execute Import* step, you can click on the *Finish* button to load the selected object into the ESR.

6.3.2.3 Working with Imported IDocs & RFCs

Unlike external definitions, imported IDocs/RFCs play a unique role within the ESR. Indeed, depending upon the usage context, an imported IDoc or RFC could be used as a message type or a service interface. This distinction will become clearer to you as we show you how to leverage these objects in upcoming sections of this book.

6.4　Summary

In this chapter, we explored the ins-and-outs of service interface development within the ESR. Here, you learned how to develop service interfaces using both the outside-in and inside-out approaches. Understanding these concepts is a necessary first step towards developing full-scale integration scenarios.

In the next chapter, we'll move on from service interfaces and begin looking at some of the design objects that you can use to support more complex integration requirements. We'll start this conversation by looking at mapping development techniques in the ESR.

References

SAP AG. (n.d.). *Core Data Types and Aggregated Data Types.* Retrieved December 3, 2010, from SAP Help Library:
http://help.sap.com/saphelp_nwpi711/helpdata/en/45/614fc4c5293bdce100 00000a1553f7/frameset.htm

SAP AG. (n.d.). *How-To Guides for SAP NetWeaver PI 7.1; PI Best Practices: Naming Conventions.* Retrieved December 2, 2010, from SAP Community Network:
http://www.sdn.sap.com/irj/scn/index?rid=/library/uuid/40a66d0e-fe5e-2c10-8a85-e418b59ab36a

SAP AG. (n.d.). *Service Interface.* Retrieved December 2, 2010, from SAP Help Library:
http://help.sap.com/saphelp_nwpi711/helpdata/en/48/5b14cf63424992e100 00000a42189c/frameset.htm

SAP AG. (n.d.). *Supported XML Schema and WSDL (SAP NetWeaver PI 7.1).* Retrieved December 8, 2010, from SAP Developer Network:
http://www.sdn.sap.com/irj/sdn/nw-esr?rid=/library/uuid/40c3a137-1769-2a10-bda9-ad62d508af9c

SAP AG. (n.d.). *Working with External Definitions.* Retrieved December 8, 2010, from SAP Help Library:
http://help.sap.com/saphelp_nwpi711/helpdata/en/26/9e97b0f525d7438829 36c2d6f375c7/frameset.htm

Mapping Development 7

As a PI developer, you will likely spend quite a bit of time developing mapping programs that perform transformations between different XML Schema types. These XML mapping programs bridge the gaps between incompatible sender/receiver interfaces that need to be linked together in order to implement an integration scenario. In this chapter, we will introduce you to some of the basics of mapping development with SAP NetWeaver PI.

After completing this chapter, you will be able to:

❖ Understand what XML mapping programs are and how they are developed in SAP NetWeaver PI.

❖ Develop message mappings using PI's graphical editor tool.

❖ Implement message mappings using industry standard technologies such as Java and XSLT.

7.1   Introduction to Mapping Development

As we have seen throughout this book, integration scenarios in SAP NetWeaver PI consist of two types of interfaces:

> **Sender Interfaces**
> On the sender side of the exchange, a sender system uses a sender interface to send a message to SAP NetWeaver PI.

> **Receiver Interfaces**
> Inbound messages received by PI are then forwarded on to targeted receiver systems via a receiver interface call.

Frequently, the signatures of these sender and receiver interfaces differ from one another. For example, imagine that you're integrating an SAP® ERP system with some 3rd-party system in your landscape. In this scenario, the sender interface might be implemented using IDocs, and the receiver interface via Web services. Besides the obvious differences in protocols, these two interfaces also differ in terms of their *message types*. This is to say that the schema type for the IDoc message varies from the one used in the Web service definition. Therefore, in order to be able to call the Web service, you must first execute a *message mapping* to transform the payload of the IDoc into a format that is compatible with the Web service interface.

In this chapter, and the one that follows, we'll explore the concepts of message mapping with SAP NetWeaver PI. To begin our discussion, we'll take a look at the options you have for developing mapping programs in PI and their relative strengths and weaknesses. From there, we'll delve into specific mapping techniques including graphical message mappings, Java-based mappings, and XSLT. These concepts will provide a foundation upon which more advanced mapping techniques can be explored in Chapter 8.

7.1.1   Options, Options, Options

When it comes to mapping development with SAP NetWeaver PI, one thing that's for sure is that you have a lot of options to choose from. In particular, PI supports the following mapping techniques:

> The development of *message mappings* using a graphical editing tool integrated into the ES Builder.

> The import of custom XML mapping programs written in Java.

> ➤ The import of pre-existing XSLT mapping programs. These programs can be imported directly into the ESR or the ABAP Workbench.

> ➤ The development of custom mapping programs using ABAP Objects.

With all these alternatives to choose from, you might be wondering which technique is the best. The answer is: it depends. It depends on the skills of the developers in your organization, the performance requirements for a particular integration scenario, available system resources on your installation of SAP NetWeaver PI, and so on.

Generally speaking, each of the supported techniques represents a viable alternative for implementing mapping programs. Table 7.1 contains a list of the relative strengths and weaknesses for each of the techniques discussed. You can use this list as a decision matrix to assist you in selecting the right tool for the job.

	Strengths	Weaknesses
Message Mappings	✓ Graphical layout tool integrated into the ES Builder. ✓ Generated Java code is optimized for performance.	✓ Context/queue-based approach can be difficult to learn. ✓ Difficult to implement complex mapping logic involving loops, etc.
Java-Based Mappings	✓ Provides flexibility for implementing maps using a wide variety of XML parsing APIs. ✓ Can be optimized to improve performance when processing larger messages. ✓ Allows you to leverage Java development expertise within your organization.	✓ Typically requires the use of lower-level parsing APIs that are tedious to work with. ✓ Custom developed code must be maintained outside of PI in a separate code repository (e.g. SAP NWDI, Perforce, etc.).

	Strengths	Weaknesses
XSLT (AS Java Stack)	✓ Allows you to develop maps using an XML-based language that is intuitive, productive, and portable. ✓ Tremendous tool support for XSLT within the industry. ✓ Ease of maintenance.	✓ Can be a resource hog; particularly in the case of large messages. ✓ Slower message processing as compared to Java-based approaches.
ABAP Objects/XSLT	✓ Allows you to leverage ABAP development expertise within your organization. ✓ Offers the best performance in certain scenarios since no stack hop is required to execute the message mapping from the Integration Engine. ✓ Source control/logistics provided by the familiar ABAP Workbench toolset.	✓ Parsing XML in ABAP is somewhat cumbersome. ✓ Use of ABAP-based mapping eliminates the possibility for configuring integration scenarios that leverage the performance improvements offered by integrated configurations on the AAE.

Table 7.1: Strengths and Weaknesses of Mapping Techniques in SAP NetWeaver PI

7.2   Developing Message Mappings

Up to this point, all of the XML examples that we've considered have been fairly straightforward and easy to understand. In the real world though, you will frequently find yourself working with XML message types that are much more complicated. In these situations, it is helpful to be able to lay out your mapping logic graphically so that you can see the overall picture. Fortunately, SAP NetWeaver PI provides such a tool in the ES Builder that can be used for this purpose. This tool is called the *mapping editor*, and it is used to interactively create *message mappings* in the ESR.

In this section, we will introduce you to message mappings and show you how you can use the mapping editor to create mapping programs for your integration scenarios. To guide our discussion, we will explore the development of a purchase order mapping program. Here, we'll map the SAP standard `PORDCR102` IDoc type to a custom `PurchaseOrder` schema provided by a fictitious 3rd-party software vendor called AcmeSoft[40].

7.2.1   What are Message Mappings?

Put simply, a message mapping is an ESR object that defines a set of rules for mapping between two types of messages. In XML terms, this means that we're taking a source message with a particular schema type and transforming it into a target message with a different schema type. As mentioned earlier, message mappings are created interactively using the graphical mapping editor tool that is integrated into the ES Builder. Behind the scenes, the mapping editor uses the configured mapping rules to generate Java code that performs the actual XML transformations at runtime.

Conceptually speaking, you can think of a message mapping as an aggregation of *target field mappings*. A target field mapping determines how a field in the target message is populated. As a developer, your task is to define a target field mapping for each of the required fields in the target message. Once these mappings are in place, the message mapping is complete.

To see how this works, let's take a look at a message mapping object in the ES Builder. Figure 7.1 demonstrates a sample message mapping within the mapping editor. As you can see, the editor is partitioned into separate views that help you visually lay out the map:

> ➢ In the *Structure Overview* view, you can select the source/target message types that you want to map between.

---

[40] The functional requirements for this mapping scenario are provided in a spreadsheet called *PORDCR102_to_PurchaseOrder.xlsx* that is included with the source code bundle available online at this book's companion site.

> ➤ In the *Data-Flow Editor* view, you are presented with a palette that can be used to configure individual target field mappings.

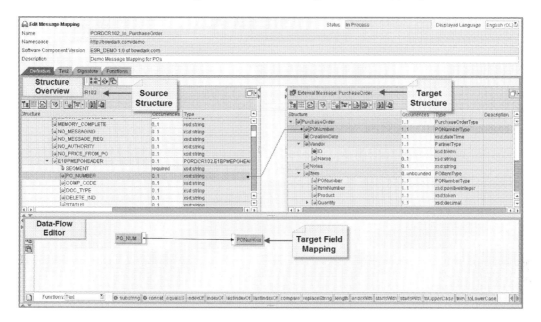

Figure 7.1: Example Message Mapping in the Mapping Editor

In the simplest of cases, you can configure target field mappings by dragging-and-dropping a source field onto a target field. For more advanced requirements, you can use the functions provided in the data-flow editor to implement data conversions, conditional mapping logic, etc. In the upcoming sections, we'll explore these features and show you how they can be used to implement specific message mapping requirements.

7.2.2   Getting Started with the Mapping Editor

Now that you're familiar with the concept of message mappings, let's turn attention towards the process of actually creating one. In this section, we'll introduce you to the mapping editor and show you how to use it to create message mappings.

7.2.2.1 Creating a Message Mapping

To create a new message mapping, log onto the ES Builder and perform the following steps:

1. Select the SWCV that you want to develop in and right-click on the target namespace. In the context menu that appears, select the *New* menu option.

2. In the *Create Object* dialog box that follows, expand the *Mapping Objects* submenu and select the *Message Mapping* menu option. Here, you must provide a name and an optional description for the message mapping.

3. Finally, click on the *Create* button to create the message mapping object. This will open up the mapping editor with an empty message mapping object as shown in Figure 7.2.

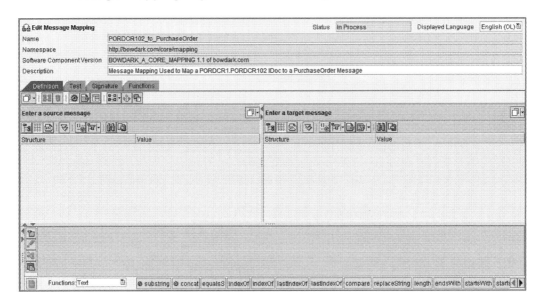

Figure 7.2: Creating a Message Mapping in the ES Builder

As you can see in Figure 7.2, the message mapping editor provides quite a few functions within its toolbars, palettes, etc. In the upcoming sections, we'll discuss many of these features as they relate to mapping development. For a more thorough treatment on each of these functions, consult the online help documentation underneath the section entitled *Message Mappings* (SAP AG).

7.2.2.2 Selecting the Source & Target Message Types

Before you can proceed with the development of your message mapping, you must first select the source and target messages that you wish to map. This can be achieved in one of two ways:

> ➢ By dragging-and-dropping a message from the left-hand navigation bar onto the source/target structure area.

> ➢ By interactively searching for design objects within the ESR.

In the latter case, you can invoke a search help by selecting the button menu adjacent to the source/target structure areas (see Figure 7.3). In the ensuing *Choose Message* dialog, you can choose from design objects such as message types, external definitions, and imported IDocs/RFCs. For example, in Figure 7.4, we have selected an imported PORDCR1.PORDCR102 IDoc type. To apply your changes, click on the *Apply* button. This will load the message into the structure overview area of the mapping editor (see Figure 7.1).

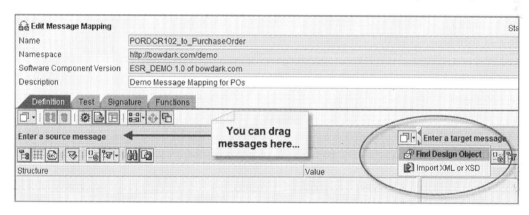

Figure 7.3: Searching for Message Types in the ESR (Part 1) © Copyright 2010. SAP AG. All rights reserved

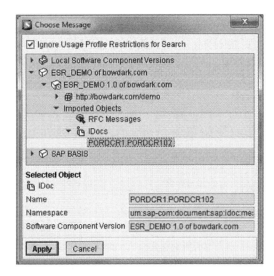

Figure 7.4: Searching for Message Types in the ESR (Part 2) © Copyright 2010. SAP AG. All rights reserved

7.2.2.3 Working with the Data-Flow Editor

Once you have selected the source/target messages that you want to map, you're ready to proceed with the development of the required target field mappings. Here, you can quickly assess the status of the mapping process by looking at the icons displayed next to the fields in the target structure. Table 7.2 describes each of the icon types used in the mapping editor. These icons are further enhanced via a traffic-light coloring scheme which is organized as follows:

> *Red* icons refer to elements or attributes required to complete the mapping that have not yet been mapped.

> *Yellow* icons refer to elements or attributes that have been partially mapped in the data-flow editor.

> *Green* icons mean that the target field mapping is complete.

> *White* icons refer to optional elements or attributes that have not been assigned.

Icon	Description
	This icon refers to an attribute in the target XML structure.
[●]	This icon refers to an element in the target structure.
[●]	This icon refers to an element in the target structure that occurs multiple times.
▽ [●]	If an element contains children, then it will have an expand/contract arrow icon next to it.

Table 7.2: Understanding Icons in the Mapping Editor © *Copyright 2010. SAP AG. All rights reserved*

Generally speaking, there are two ways to implement target field mappings in the mapping editor:

➢ You can create a 1-to-1 mapping between a source and target field by dragging-and-dropping a source field onto a target field.

➢ Alternatively, you can drag source/target fields from the structure overview view into the data-flow editor view and then link them together.

In either case, you'll find yourself spending a lot of time working with data-flow editor at the bottom of the mapping editor screen. Figure 7.5 demonstrates the layout of a target field mapping for the purchase order creation date field. In this case, we're linking the CREAT_DATE field from the IDoc with the CreationDate field in the target message.

Looking closely at the target field mapping in Figure 7.5, you'll notice that there's not a direct line that connects the CREAT_DATE and CreationDate fields. Instead, these fields are indirectly linked via a *function* called DateTrans. This function is used to convert the value of the CREAT_DATE field into a format that is compatible with the target CreationDate field. When linked together, these nodes represent a type of *expression* that defines the mapping of the CreationDate field.

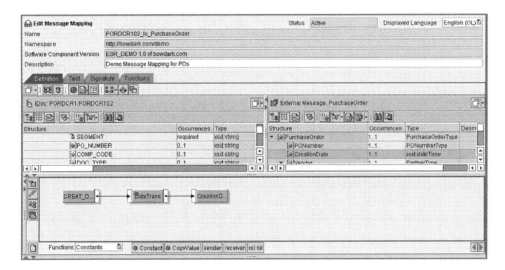

Figure 7.5: Working with the Data-Flow Editor © Copyright 2010. SAP AG. All rights reserved

By default, the mapping editor provides you with many different types of functions to assist you in the mapping process. These functions can be mixed-and-matched to form complex expressions that link together multiple source fields, apply conditional logic, and so on. We'll look at all this and more in the upcoming sections.

7.2.3 Structure Mapping Concepts

Most of the time, whenever people think about target field mappings, they are primarily focused on *value mappings*. A value mapping refers to a mapping of two elementary (or leaf node) elements in the XML structures. For instance, the mapping of the `CreationDate` field described in the previous section is an example of a value mapping.

In addition to the mapping of the leaf nodes, you must also consider the overall structure of the target document being created. Here, the concern is on mapping those complex elements whose content model consists of child elements rather than discrete values. This is important since, without a defined structure, you have no context from which to define your value mappings. For example, getting back to our PO scenario, think about the mapping of a field on the PO line item such as `Product`. Here, we'll define a value mapping between the `MATERIAL` field in the `E1BPMEPOITEM` segment of the `PORDCR102` IDoc type and the `Product` field in the target XML structure. However, since these fields are defined as child elements of the PO line items, and there could be multiple line items, we must first define an overarching *context* for the value mapping. In other words, we need to make sure that we map the `Product` correctly for *each* line item.

In this section, we'll show you how to define structure mappings using the mapping editor. In particular, we will demonstrate how to interact with specialized node functions designed to manipulate complex XML data types. Having an understanding of these concepts is important if you want to get the most out of message mappings.

7.2.3.1 Understanding Queues and Contexts

As we mentioned earlier, message mappings are converted into Java classes that are executed within the SAP NetWeaver PI mapping runtime environment[41]. These classes (and their surrounding framework) utilize the SAX API to parse the source document. As you may recall from Chapter 2, SAX is a very fast and efficient stream-processing API that allows you to extract relevant content from the source XML document as it is being parsed. Of course, in order to do anything useful with this content later on, you need to store it in some kind of intermediate data structure. For this task, message mappings employ the use of a queue-like data structure to store the values for each element/attribute that is mapped from the source structure.

To demonstrate how these queues are organized, let's take a look at an example provided by SAP[42]. Figure 7.6 depicts a sample XML document with a fairly deep hierarchical structure. We'll use this structure to illustrate the concept of *contexts* and *context changes*.

---

[41] You can view the generated source code by selecting the Ctrl-Shift-0 key sequence in the ES Builder. For more information, see *https://forums.sdn.sap.com/thread.jspa?threadID=319199*.

[42] This example was originally described in the online help documentation for SAP NetWeaver PI. From the Message Mappings section described earlier, navigate to *Target Field Mappings → Runtime Procedure → Structure Mapping by Setting the Context*.

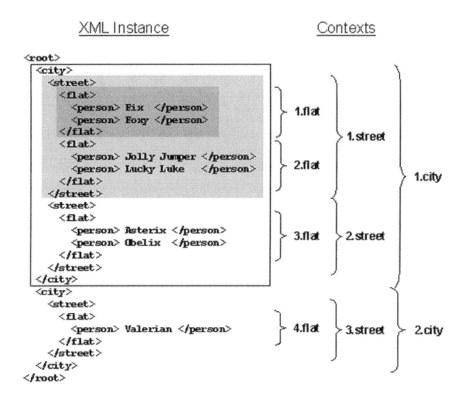

Figure 7.6: Understanding Contexts © Copyright 2010. SAP AG. All rights reserved

If you look closely at Figure 7.6, you'll notice that each element besides the `root` element is defined within the *context* of another element. For instance, the `city` element is a child of the `root` element; the `street` element is a child of `city`; and so on. Therefore, from a data storage perspective, it is not enough to simply create a queue that contains the raw values of each instance of a particular element (e.g. `person`). Rather, there must be a way to identify *context changes* throughout the document so that we know what goes with what. For example, since the `person` element is defined as a child of the `flat` element, there needs to be a context change in the `person` queue at the end of every surrounding `flat` element.

To see how this works, imagine that you're processing the source XML document contained in Figure 7.6. Here, consider the contents of the `person` element queue shown in Figure 7.7. As you can see, the raw values of the `person` element are segregated by context changes (i.e. the shaded rows) that are inserted in conjunction with each surrounding `flat` element (see Figure 7.6). Collectively, this data provides us with the information we need to map the `person` element in context.

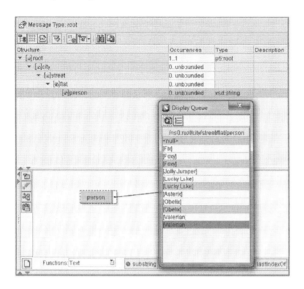

Figure 7.7: Displaying the Queue for an Element in the Mapping Editor

Of course, depending on your requirements, you may want to influence the behavior of these context switches. For example, imagine that you need to come up with a list of people that live on a particular street. In this case, you would want to explicitly define the context of the `person` element in terms of the `street` element as shown in Figure 7.8. Now if you display the contents of the `person` element queue, you'll see that the context switches are inserted in tandem with the `street` element.

If all this still seems confusing, don't worry; a few more examples should help clear you up. Furthermore, in the next section, we'll show you how to work with some specialized node functions specifically designed to operate on these input queues.

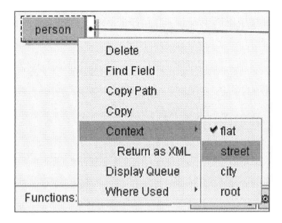

Figure 7.8: Explicitly Setting the Context for a Node in the Data Flow Editor
© Copyright 2010. SAP AG. All rights reserved

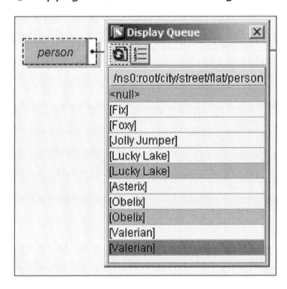

Figure 7.9: Viewing the Contents of a Modified Queue © Copyright 2010.
SAP AG. All rights reserved

7.2.3.2 Working with Node Functions

In many cases, structure mappings can be defined by simply dragging-and-dropping between like structures. For instance, in our PO mapping example, we can map the PO line items by simply linking the E1BPMEPOITEM and Item elements together. This implies that a distinct Item element will be created in the target structure for *each occurrence* of the E1BPMEPOITEM element in the source structure. So long as the cardinalities match, that's pretty much all there is to it. But what if the elements don't match up so nicely?

Frequently, you may need to *flatten* a hierarchical structure into a format that can be received by some legacy system or vice versa. For these kinds of tasks, you'll need to enlist the help of some specialized node functions provided with the mapping editor. Table 7.3 describes some of the node functions that you have at your disposal. These functions can be used to manipulate the queues described in Section 7.2.3.1 in order to generate output at the right level of granularity. In addition, you can also create user-defined functions to satisfy more advanced requirements. We'll learn about user-defined functions in Section 7.2.5.

Function Name	Description
createIf	This function allows you to control the creation of an element based upon some condition. For example, you could use this function to restrict the creation of a Summary element in the PO based upon whether or not there were any line items passed in the source document.
removeContexts	As the name suggests, this function removes all contexts from a queue, yielding a raw array of values.
exists	This function can be used to determine whether or not an element exists in the source document.
splitByValue	This function essentially performs the opposite of removeContexts in that it introduces a context change for each value in a queue. See the online help documentation for parameter options with this function.
collapseContexts	This function copies the first value from each context of the source input queue into a new queue that doesn't contain any context changes.
useOneAsMany	This function enables you to replicate an element that only occurs once as often as some other element in the source document occurs. For instance, in the PO example, this function could be used to copy data from the PO header area down to the line items of the target structure.

sort	This function allows you to sort data from an input queue in ascending or descending order.
sortByKey	This function is similar to sort. The primary difference is that this function allows you to pass in a set of keys to drive the sorting process.

Table 7.3: Node Functions Provided for Structure Mapping

To demonstrate how these node functions work, let's consider an example. In our PO mapping scenario, there's a Notes element in the target structure that will contain header-level notes for the PO. Now, let's imagine that our requirements indicate that this Notes element should only be created if there's an E1BPMEPOTEXTHEADER segment in the IDoc with a TEXT_ID whose value is equal to Z001.

Figure 7.10 illustrates how we would define the structure mapping for the Notes element. Reading from left-to-right, you can evaluate this expression as follows:

1. First, we're comparing the contents of each occurrence of the TEXT_ID field in the E1BPMEPOTEXTHEADER segment with a constant value of Z001. This comparison is implemented using the equalsS function (i.e. "string equals").

2. If an E1BPMEPOTEXTHEADER segment meets the requisite criteria, then the createIf function will append it to an intermediate queue containing matching segments.

3. The results of the createIf function are then passed on to the collapseContexts function, which copies the first element in the results queue into another intermediate queue.

4. Finally, the results of the collapseContexts function as passed on to the Notes element. Thus, if there were E1BPMEPOTEXTHEADER segments that met the criteria, a single instance of the Notes element will be created; otherwise, it will not exist in the target structure.

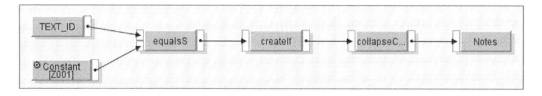

Figure 7.10: Working with Node Functions © Copyright 2010. SAP AG. All rights reserved

At first, you may find it difficult to express certain data relationships using node functions. During these early stages of development, we highly recommend that you consult the online help documentation for message mappings. Here, you will find many examples of common mapping use cases implemented using node functions.

7.2.4 Value Mapping Concepts

Once you align the source and target structures with one another, you can proceed with implementing the various value mappings that are required. As you learned in Section 7.2.2.3, a value mapping is an expression that assigns a value to a field in the target structure. These expressions are built using an assortment of functions that manipulate values from the source structure to define the target field mapping.

In this section, we'll introduce you to some of the functions you have to work with when developing value mappings. We'll also show you how to define variables in the target structure that can be used to simplify certain types of target field mappings.

7.2.4.1 Working with the Standard Functions

By default, the mapping editor provides quite a few standard functions that you can use out of the box to implement value mappings. These functions are analogous to classes and APIs that you have to work with in most programming languages such as ABAP or Java. Indeed, if you're a Java developer, you should find yourself right at home as the standard functions are implemented using core Java classes behind the scenes.

Table 7.4 provides an overview of the available categories of functions that you have to work with. If you have a programming background, then most of these functions will feel fairly intuitive. However, if you have specific questions about a function, you can consult the online help documentation

underneath the section *Message Mappings → Target Field Mappings →
Standard Functions* (SAP AG).

Category	Description
Text	A series of functions used to work with strings. The behavior of these functions is based upon the Java `java.lang.String` API[43].
Arithmetic	This set of functions allows you to perform basic arithmetic operations such as addition or subtraction, etc. In addition, the function `FormatNum` can be used to format numbers for output.
Statistics	These functions allow you to perform various statistical operations such as the calculations of sums and averages.
Date	This set of functions can be used to retrieve the current system date, perform date comparisons, and even format dates for output.
Constants	These functions allow you to populate target fields with constant values.
Boolean	A series of functions for applying Boolean logic operators such as `if`, `and`, `or`, and `not`.
Conversions	These functions can be used to convert between two different domains of values. For instance, you might use the `ValueMapping` function to translate between two different sets of units of measure. We'll learn more about using these conversion functions in Chapter 8.

*Table 7.4: Categories of Standard Functions Provided with the Mapping
Editor*

To demonstrate how to implement value mappings using functions, let's
consider how we would map the `Note` element in our PO mapping example.
As you may recall from Section 7.2.3.2, the target PO structure contains an
element called `Notes` that contains header-level notes for the PO. The `Notes`
element encloses a language-specific child element called `Note` that can
contain up to 100 characters of note text. Figure 7.11 illustrates how we
might implement this mapping. Here, we should point out that the

---

[43] You can find detailed documentation on the `java.lang.String` class at
http://download.oracle.com/javase/1.5.0/docs/api/java/lang/String.html.

overarching context for the value mapping has been set by the mapping of the Notes element as described in Section 7.2.3.2.

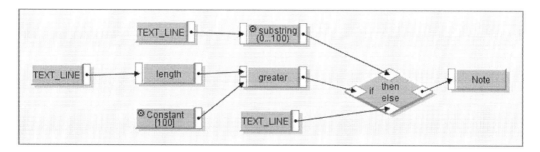

Figure 7.11: Implementing Value Mappings with the Standard Functions ©
Copyright 2010. SAP AG. All rights reserved

As you can see in Figure 7.11, the value mapping for the Note element is controlled by the Boolean function if. In this case, we're mapping the first 100 characters of the TEXT_LINE element (via a call to the Text function substring) *if* the length of the TEXT_LINE element is greater than 100; otherwise, we just map the TEXT_LINE element as-is.

Looking closely at the value mapping illustrated in Figure 7.11, you might be wondering where we got the value 100 in the call to the substring and Constant functions. This value is supplied as a *parameter* to the function. You can tell whether or not a function supports parameters by the presence of that little gear-like icon in the top left-hand corner of the function (see Figure 7.11). To supply parameters to a function, simply double-click on it and fill in the parameters in the popup dialog box (see Figure 7.12).

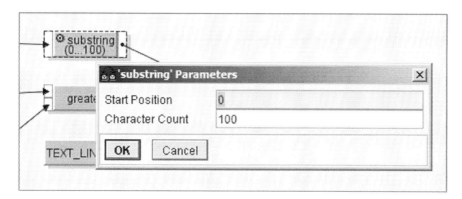

Figure 7.12: Configuring Function Parameters © Copyright 2010. SAP AG. All
rights reserved

One of the things you'll notice about the expression depicted in Figure 7.11 is the fact that multiple source fields/functions were linked together to define the `Note` field mapping. In general, there are no limitations as to how complex an expression can be. However, from a practicality standpoint, you'll want to simplify your expressions as much as possible. This can usually be achieved with careful planning and organization.

7.2.4.2 Working with Variables

Frequently, you may find yourself using a particular value from the source structure over and over again. While certain node functions can be used to facilitate such mappings, it is much easier to capture these values in a *variable*[44]. Once assigned, this variable can then be used to implement each of the target mappings that leverage this value.

Variables are created as children of complex elements within the target structure. For example, in our PO scenario, we might want to define a variable to capture the PO number. Since this is a header-level variable, we would nest it directly underneath the root `PurchaseOrder` element. Similarly, if we defined a PO item variable, we would want to nest it underneath the `Item` element[45].

To create a variable in your message mapping, perform the following steps:

1. First, right-click on the node that you want to nest your variable under and select the *Add Variable* menu option (see Figure 7.13).

---

[44] Variables in message mappings were introduced in release 7.1 of SAP NetWeaver PI.

[45] Keep in mind that variables are not part of the target structure that is output by the message mapping. Rather, they are just used to simplify the creation of other target field mappings within the target structure.

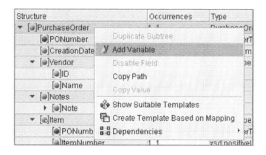

Figure 7.13: Creating Variables in the Target Structure (Part 1)

2. In the *Enter New Variable Name* dialog box that follows, select a name for the variable and click on the *OK* button (see Figure 7.14).

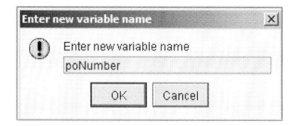

Figure 7.14: Creating Variables in the Target Structure (Part 2)

3. Once this is complete, you'll see the variable listed underneath the selected node with a node-like icon annotated with a V (for *variable* - see Figure 7.15).

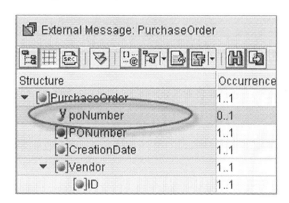

Figure 7.15: Creating Variables in the Target Structure (Part 3)

Once your variables are created, you can use them in target field mappings in much the same way you would map elements from the source structure. This two-step process begins with the mapping of the source element to the variable. Then, once the variable is assigned, you can use drag it into the data-flow editor and use it in expressions in places where a source element is normally expected.

Besides being easy to use, variables can also improve performance for target field mappings based on the `useOneAsMany` function. For instance, in our PO scenario, we need to copy certain header-level fields to the line item and schedule line levels. Without variables, each target field mapping would have to use the `useOneAsMany` function which not only processes the singular header-level element, but also a collection of line items/schedule lines. For even moderately-sized POs with 10s of line items, this process can introduce significant overhead. Therefore, we recommend that you use variables for these kinds of tasks.

7.2.5 Creating User-Defined Functions

In general, most value mapping expressions can be implemented using standard functions. However, sometimes you may find that these expressions are too complex or unwieldy to work with. In these situations, you can define a more specific *user-defined function* (UDF) to simplify matters.

From a technical perspective, UDFs are nothing more than custom-defined methods that are added to the Java class that is created behind the scenes with message mappings. Within the scope of this method, you have access to the Java 2 Standard Edition (J2SE) and Java 2 Enterprise Edition (J2EE) APIs as well as some PI mapping libraries provided by SAP[46]. In addition, you can also import custom-developed classes by creating an *imported archive* in the ESR – something we'll learn about in Section 7.3.3. Collectively, these APIs make it possible to implement just about any kind of mapping requirement imaginable.

UDFs are maintained on the *Functions* tab in the mapping editor. As you can see in Figure 7.16, the editor on this tab page is divided into several sections:

---

[46] For a complete reference on these PI mapping APIs, check out *http://help.sap.com/javadocs*. Under the *Process Integration* section, select the link with the label *PI 7.1 (Adaptcr, Module and Mapping Development)*.

➢ In the *Functions and Java Areas* section, you have access to all of the attributes and methods defined in the local mapping class. Here, in addition to the custom-defined methods, you can define global attributes, helper methods, as well as supporting inner classes. You also have access to two housekeeping methods `init()` and `cleanUp()` that are used to initialize and cleanup attributes used in the mapping class, respectively.

➢ On the *Import Instructions* tab, you can define the imports used within the mapping class.

➢ The *Archives Used* tab contains the imported archives leveraged by the mapping class.

➢ On the right-hand side of the editor, you have a Java source code editor that allows you to maintain your custom Java code.

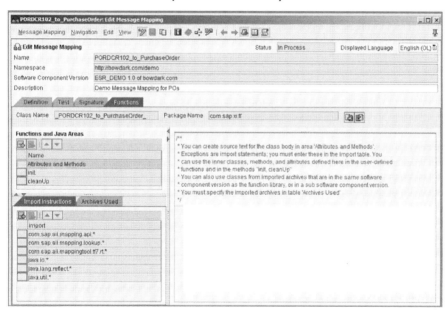

Figure 7.16: Developing User Defined Functions © Copyright 2010. SAP AG. All rights reserved

7.2.5.1 Case Study: Creating a UDF to Sort a Collection

To demonstrate how UDFs work, let's consider an example based on our PO mapping scenario. In the target structure, there's a field at the PO item level called `ExpectedDeliveryDate`. According to the mapping rules, this field should be populated with the latest schedule line date provided within the PO item's schedule lines.

While all this sounds fairly straightforward on paper, there is a little wrinkle to all this. Since the PORDCR102 IDoc type defines PO line items (segment E1BPMEPOITEM) at the same level as PO schedule lines (segment E1BPMEPOSCHEDULE), we cannot simply grab the latest DELIVERY_DATE value from the list of E1BPMEPOSCHEDULE elements. Instead, we must first identify the subset of E1BPMEPOSCHEDULE elements that match the current PO line item in context and then grab the latest DELIVERY_DATE from that subset (see Figure 7.17).

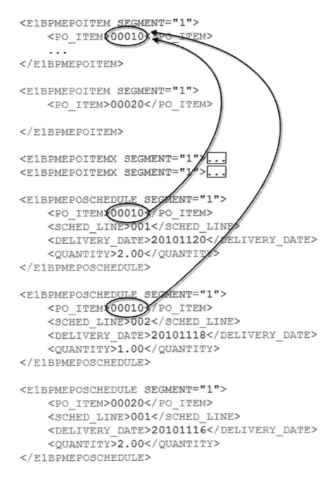

Figure 7.17: Linking PO Schedule Lines with PO Line Items

With all that in mind, let's see how we can encode this logic using a UDF:

1. On the *Functions* tab page of the mapping editor, click on the *Insert Line Below Selection* button in the *Functions and Java Areas* section (see Figure 7.18).

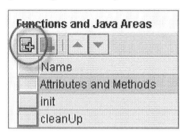

Figure 7.18: Creating a UDF in the Mapping Editor

2. This will add a new line to the *Functions and Java Areas* table. Double-click the generated name and replace it with the desired function name – in this case, getLatestScheduleDate.

3. On the right-hand side of the editor, you must provide the following attributes:

   ❖ The *Title* attribute contains the title for the function that you want to display in the data-flow editor. This attribute should be the same as the function name.
   ❖ The *Description* attribute contains a brief description of the function that will show up as a tooltip in the data-flow editor.
   ❖ For the *Execution Type* attribute, you have three options to choose from:
      a. *Single Values*:
         This option defines a function that processes *single values* of fields in a call. Simple functions like add and subtract are examples of functions that are based on this execution type.

      b. *All Values of Context*:
        This execution type allows you to operate on all of the values of a context within a function call. Here, the elements within the context are copied into an array prior to the invocation of the function.

      c. *All Values of Queue*:
        This option is similar to the *All Values of Context* execution type. However, instead of copying the values of a context into an array, the contents of an entire queue (including context changes) are copied into the array prior to the invocation of the function.

❖ The *Category* attribute can be used to define a function category for the UDF. By default, the category is *User-Defined*. However, it could be reassigned to *Node Functions*, *Text*, etc.

4. Once you configure the basic attributes of the function, you can specify the parameters for the function in the *Signature Variables* table. Here, you can define three different types of variables:

❖ *Argument*:
Variables of this type are used to pass in data from the source structure, constants, etc. In other words, input values normally linked to the left-hand side of the function in the data-flow editor.

❖ *Parameter*:
Variables of this type are used as *parameters* that control the behavior of the function. Figure 7.12 provided an example of parameter assignments for the `substring` function.

❖ *Result*:
For functions with an execution type besides the *Single Values* type, this variable defines a container for returning results to the caller. For more information about this container type, check out the JavaDoc for class `com.sap.aii.mappingtool.tf7.rt.ResultList` in the aforementioned PI mapping API documentation.

Figure 7.19 shows the signature of the `getLatestScheduleDate` function once all of the relevant attributes have been configured. As you can see, this function receives three arguments:

➢ The `poItemKey` argument contains the `PO_ITEM` element for the current `E1BPMEPOITEM` segment being processed.

➢ The `poItems` argument contains a list of PO item keys for the complete set of `E1BPMEPOSCHEDULE` schedule line segments passed with the IDoc.

➢ The `scheduleDates` argument contains a list of delivery dates for the complete set of `E1BPMEPOSCHEDULE` schedule line segments passed with the IDoc.

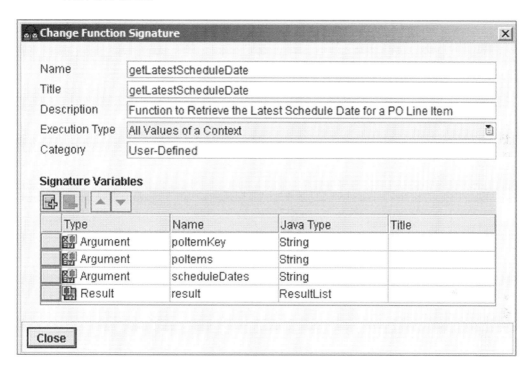

Figure 7.19: Defining the Signature of a UDF © Copyright 2010. SAP AG. All rights reserved

Internally, the `getLatestScheduleDate` function will use the arguments outlined in Figure 7.19 to find the complete set of schedule lines that match the current PO item. Then, it will take that list and sort it by delivery date in descending order. The latest date in that list will then be returned in the `result` variable (see Figure 7.19). This logic is encoded in the sample implementation contained in Listing 7.1.

```java
public void getLatestScheduleDate(String[] poItemKey,
                                  String[] poItems,
                                  String[] scheduleDates,
                                  ResultList result,
                                  Container container)
  throws StreamTransformationException
{
  // Retrieve the cached PO item/schedule date map from the
  // mapping program container:
  HashMap<String, List<String>> dateMap =
    (HashMap<String, List<String>>)
      container.getParameter("ItemScheduleDates");

  // If the map doesn't exist yet in memory,
  // then we need to create it:
  if (dateMap == null)
  {
    dateMap = new HashMap<String, List<String>>();

    // Then, we'll build a matrix that indexes the schedule line
    // delivery dates by PO line item:
    for (int itemIdx = 0; itemIdx < poItems.length; itemIdx++)
    {
      // Since each line item could have multiple schedule lines,
      // we need to make sure that we append the schedule dates
      // to the proper index record:
      List<String> itemDates = dateMap.get(poItems[itemIdx]);
      if (itemDates == null)
      {
        itemDates = new ArrayList<String>();
        dateMap.put(poItems[itemIdx], itemDates);
      }
      itemDates.add(scheduleLines[itemIdx]);
    } // -- End for (PO Items) -- //

    // Cache the map in memory to speed up lookups in
    // future calls:
    container.setParameter("ItemScheduleDates", dateMap);
  } // -- End if (Cached map exists?) -- //

  // Take the latest date from the list:
  String poItem = poItemKey[0];
```

```
List<String> itemDates = dateMap.get(poItem);
Collections.sort(itemDates);
String scheduleDate = itemDates.get(itemDates.size() - 1);

// Store the value in the result set passed back to the
// mapping program:
result.addValue(scheduleDate);
} // -- function getLatestScheduleDate() -- //
```

Listing 7.1: Implementing the getLatestScheduleDate() UDF

Once your UDF is defined, you can leverage it to build target field mappings in the same way that you use standard functions. Unless you changed the default function category, you can locate your UDF in the *User-Defined* category of functions in the data-flow editor (see Figure 7.20). From there, you can drag it into the data-flow editor and configure your target field mappings as per usual (see Figure 7.21).

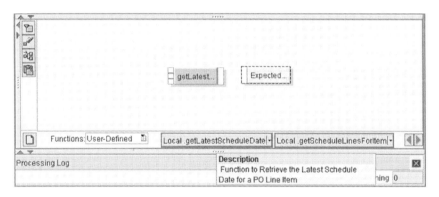

Figure 7.20: Inserting UDFs into the Data-Flow Editor © Copyright 2010. SAP AG. All rights reserved

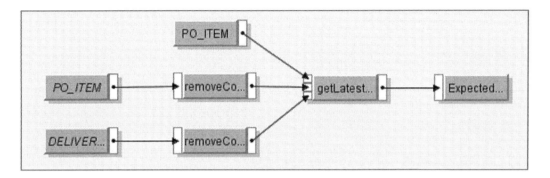

*Figure 7.21: Building Target Field Mappings Using UDFs © Copyright 2010.
SAP AG. All rights reserved*

7.2.6   Testing Message Mappings

In the next chapter, we'll show you how to create *operation mappings* that
allow you to integrate your mapping programs into integration scenarios at
runtime. In the meantime, short of having an interface configured end-to-
end, you'll need a way to test your message mapping programs to make
sure that they're working correctly. Fortunately, the mapping editor provides
just such a tool.

You can test your message mapping programs by selecting the aptly named
Test tab page. As you can see in Figure 7.22, the test environment looks
similar to the normal mapping editor. However, in this perspective, the
source/target structures refer to actual XML instance documents rather than
generic schema types.

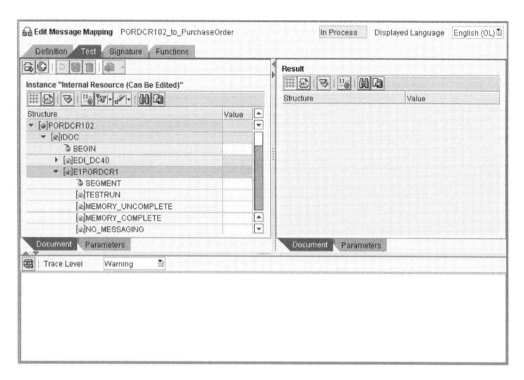

Figure 7.22: Testing Message Mappings © Copyright 2010. SAP AG. All rights reserved

To conduct a test, you'll need to load some sample XML into the source structure. This can be achieved several ways:

> ➢ You can use the graphical editor to populate a sample XML document with values. Here, you can simply key in or paste values into the *Value* column (see Figure 7.22).
> ➢ If you have an existing XML document somewhere on your local machine, you can import it into the testing tool by clicking on the *Load Test Instance* 🔲 toolbar button.
> ➢ You can click on the *Source Text View* 🔲 toolbar button to switch the source structure editor from graphical mode to text editor mode. Here, you can copy-and-paste snippets of raw XML from a sample file, etc.

Once the source structure is loaded with some sample XML, you can execute the test by clicking on the *Start the Transformation* 🔲 button. This will trigger the execution of the mapping code and, assuming all goes well, generate the resultant target structure. From there, you can view the generated XML graphically or via the source text view in the target structure.

7.2.7 Debugging Techniques

While it is useful to be able to test message mappings as a whole, there are often situations where you need to debug certain troublesome areas of the mapping logic. In particular, it is useful to see the inputs and outputs of the various functions that are chained together to build target field mappings.

While there is no debugger provided in the mapping editor that allows you to step through the mapping code line-by-line, there is a way to view the contents of the queues for each node in an expression. Figure 7.23 demonstrates this queue browser for a UDF called getScheduleLinesForPOItem. As you can see, the browser not only displays the contents of the queues, but also the context changes.

To browse the contents of queues in your message mapping, perform the following steps:

1. Open up the message mapping and load a test XML document into the source structure on the *Test* tab.

2. Then, navigate back to the *Definition* tab page and select the target field mapping that you want to debug by double-clicking on the target field.

3. In the data-flow editor, you can browse a queue by right-clicking on a node and selecting the *Display Queue* menu option (see Figure 7.23).

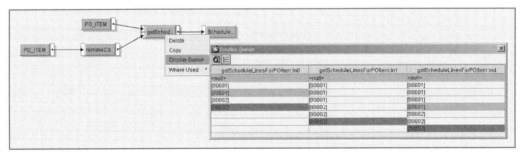

Figure 7.23: Viewing the Contents of a Queue © Copyright 2010. SAP AG. All rights reserved

Another debugging option you have at your disposal for UDFs is the MappingTrace API that provides you with methods for outputting messages to the console. You can access this API from a UDF via the container parameter's getTrace() method. Listing 7.2 demonstrates how this works.

```
public void someFunction(Container container)
  throws StreamTransformationException
{
  container.getTrace().addInfo("In someFunction()...");
} // -- public void someFunction() -- //
```

Listing 7.2: Outputting Trace Messages to the Console

The trace messages are output in the console whenever you execute a test in the test environment. You can use these messages to literally trace through the UDF logic step-by-step.

7.3 Developing Mapping Programs Using Java

Technically speaking, you can implement just about any kind of mapping requirement using message mappings. However, in certain scenarios, it may be easier or more efficient to implement your mapping program using a full-fledged programming language such as Java. Or, perhaps you're just not a draggy-droppy, pointy-clicky kind of person. In any case, SAP NetWeaver PI allows you to develop mapping programs externally in Java and then import them into the ESR.

In this section, we'll show you how to implement mapping programs in Java. Of course, realistically, a detailed explanation of XML processing in Java is beyond the scope of this book. Therefore, we'll limit our discussion to basic framework issues. Once you understand the framework, you should have no problems developing mapping programs using your favorite parsing API.

7.3.1 Java Mapping Overview

For the most part, SAP makes it very easy to develop mapping programs in Java. Indeed, the only requirement for implementing a Java-based mapping program is that you inherit from an abstract class called AbstractTransformation. Figure 7.24 contains a UML class diagram that depicts the relationship between this class and some other core framework

classes. As you can see, these classes are provided in the
`com.sap.aii.mapping.api` package[47].

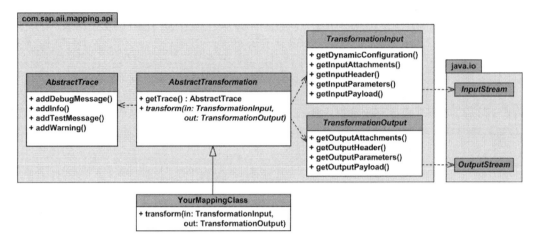

Figure 7.24: UML Class Diagram for Java Mapping API

Within your custom mapping class, you must provide an implementation of
the `transform()` method. As you can see in Figure 7.24, this method
receives two parameters:

> ➤ A parameter of type `TransformationInput` that contains relevant
> information about the source message.

> ➤ A parameter of type `TransformationOutput` that will contain the
> generated target message.

Generally speaking, you are free to implement the `transform()` method
however you like. If you look closely at the UML class diagram shown in
Figure 7.24, you'll notice that both the `TransformationInput` and
`TransformationOutput` types have a dependency on the `java.io` classes
`InputStream` and `OutputStream`, respectively. This implies that you can
manipulate the raw payloads of the source/target documents directly as
demonstrated in Listing 7.3.

---

[47] You can find comprehensive JavaDoc documentation for this package
online at *http://help.sap.com/javadocs*. Here, click the link entitled *PI 7.1
(Adapter, Module and Mapping Development)*.

```
public class SomeMappingClass
  extends AbstractTransformation
{
  @Override
  public void transform(TransformationInput in,
                        TransformationOutput out)
    throws StreamTransformationException
  {
    // Extract the source XML payload as a
    // java.io.InputStream:
    InputStream is =
      in.getInputPayload().getInputStream();
    ...

    // Transformation logic goes here...
    ...

    // Obtain a reference to a java.io.OutputStream
    // to serialize the generated XML document:
    OutputStream os =
      out.getOutputPayload().getOutputStream();

    // Serialization logic goes here...
    ...
  } // -- public void transform() -- //
} // -- End of class SomeMappingClass -- //
```

Listing 7.3: Accessing XML Payloads in a Java Mapping Class

Having access to the raw input and output streams of the source/target documents gives you tremendous flexibility as these native types are supported by all Java-based XML processing APIs in one way or another. By default, you have instant access to the Java API for XML Processing (JAXP) to implement mapping programs using the SAX or DOM APIs. In addition, you also have the option of leveraging 3rd-party XML processing libraries such as JDOM, the XML Pull Parser (XPP), and so on.

Programming Restrictions

While the SAP mapping API for Java doesn't impose many limitations on you in terms of how you go about implementing your XML transformations, there are certain programming restrictions that you need to be aware of from a runtime perspective.

The basic notion to keep in mind here is that, unlike standalone Java programs, your mapping programs execute within a *container* in the Java runtime environment of the SAP NetWeaver PI AS Java server. Consequently, there are steps that you have to take as a developer to ensure that your mapping programs behave consistently across different runtime environments. For example, if the AS Java server happens to be clustered, then your mapping programs will be distributed across multiple AS Java server nodes. In this scenario, use of static variables could prove disastrous as the value of these variables would most likely be different on each server node. Similarly, use of I/O resources such as files and network sockets can also lead to unpredictable results.

In general, you should think of your mapping classes as being *stateless*. This is to say that you should avoid using attributes and other resources to maintain the state of your mapping program. If you've ever programmed using the Enterprise JavaBeans (EJB) component model, then you're probably already familiar with many of these concepts. If not, you can find a comprehensive list of no-no's by reading through *Section 21.1.2: Programming Restrictions* in the EJB 3.0 specification[48].

Regardless of the XML processing APIs you choose to work with, the mapping procedure in Java is essentially the same each time:

1. Obtain a reference to the source document's `InputStream`.

2. Use the `InputStream` to parse the source document using your preferred XML processing API (e.g. SAX).

3. Use the parsed input to generate the target document using your preferred XML processing API (e.g. DOM).

4. Serialize the target document onto the target document's `OutputStream` using serialization methods supported by your preferred XML processing API.

One final note we should make here is that you should avoid any temptations to use Java mapping programs as a type of *user exit* for hanging other non-mapping related logic. In general, mapping programs should not produce any

---

[48] You can download the EJB 3.0 specification online at *http://jcp.org/aboutJava/communityprocess/final/jsr220/index.html*. From there, locate the document entitled *JSR-000220 Enterprise JavaBeans 3.0 Final Release (ejbcore)*.

side-effects. Examples of such side-effects include updates to a database, calls to RFC functions that change the state of a business object, etc. While these requirements may well be legitimate, there are other more appropriate places to implement these types of requests. We'll learn more about these options as we proceed further along in the book.

7.3.2 Creating a Java Mapping Program

For the most part, there are no special requirements for developing Java mapping programs. Indeed, if you were so inclined, you could implement your mapping programs using text editor and the JDK. However, since this is a book about SAP software, it only makes sense that we demonstrate the creation of Java mapping programs using the SAP NetWeaver® Developer Studio (NWDS).

To develop your Java mapping program, open up the NWDS and create a new Java project[49]. Before you proceed any further, you need to make sure that the PI mapping library is included in your project's build path. With the NWDS 7.11, you can add this library to your build path as follows:

1. Right-click on your project and select the *Properties* menu option.

2. In the ensuing dialog box, select the *Java Build Path* link on the left-hand side and then click on the *Libraries* tab page (see Figure 7.25).

---

[49] If you use the SAP NetWeaver Development Infrastructure (NWDI) to manage your Java software logistics, then most of the same concepts apply to Java DCs. The primary difference is in the way you assign the PI mapping libraries to your build path (e.g. via an *External Library* DC).

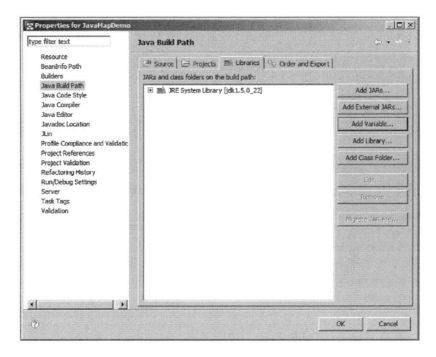

Figure 7.25: Adding the PI Mapping Library to the Build Path (Part 1)

3. Next, click on the *Add Variable...* button to add a new variable to the build path. Here, you will want to extend the SAP_SYSTEM_ADD_LIBS variable (see Figure 7.26).

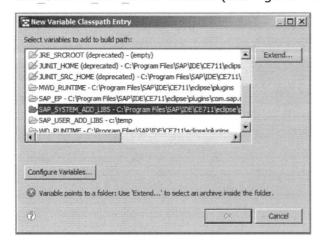

Figure 7.26: Adding the PI Mapping Library to the Build Path (Part 2)

4. If the `SAP_SYSTEM_ADD_LIBS` variable doesn't yet exist in your environment, click on the *Configure Variables...* button (see Figure 7.26). Then, in the *Classpath Variables* dialog box, click on the *New...* button and add the variable as shown in Figure 7.27. Here, the path should point to:

   `{NWDS Home}/eclipse/plugins/com.sap.tc.ap_XXX.`

   Hit the *Enter* key to create the variable entry and then click the *OK* button to return to the variable editor dialog box.

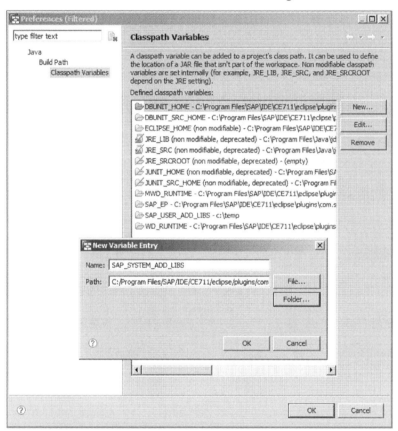

Figure 7.27: Adding the PI Mapping Library to the Build Path (Part 3)

5. After you locate the `SAP_SYSTEM_ADD_LIBS` variable, you must extend it by clicking on the *Extend...* button (see Figure 7.26). Here, you can add the PI mapping archive by navigating to

   `comp/SAP_XIAF/DCs/sap.com/com.sap.aii.mapping.lib.facade/`

`comp/gen/default/public/api/lib/java/com.sap.aii.mapping.`
`api.filter.jar`. Select the JAR file and click the *OK* button to
extend the variable (see Figure 7.28).

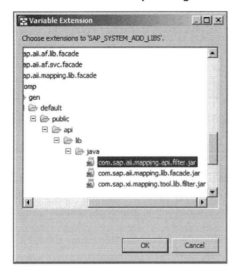

Figure 7.28: Adding the PI Mapping Library to the Build Path (Part 4)

6. Finally, click the *OK* button one last time to confirm your changes.

Once the PI mapping library is on the build path, you are ready to proceed
with the development of your Java mapping program. Here, you simply
create a class in your Java project as per usual. Of course, you'll want to
make sure that the new class inherits from the
`com.sap.aii.mapping.api.AbstractTransformation` super class (see
Figure 7.29).

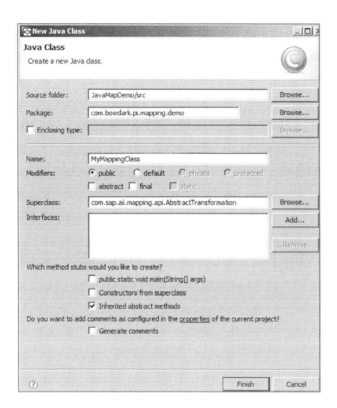

Figure 7.29: Creating a Java Mapping Program in the NWDS (Part 1)

Figure 7.30 shows the skeleton of the class that gets generated in the NWDS. At this point, you should have all the framework pieces in place to begin development. However, if you're the kind of person that prefers to work off of a reference model, then you can find a sample implementation based upon the JDOM API in the source code bundle for this chapter online. Another useful resource to help get you started is Arthur Griffith's *Java, XML, and JAXP* (Griffith, 2002).

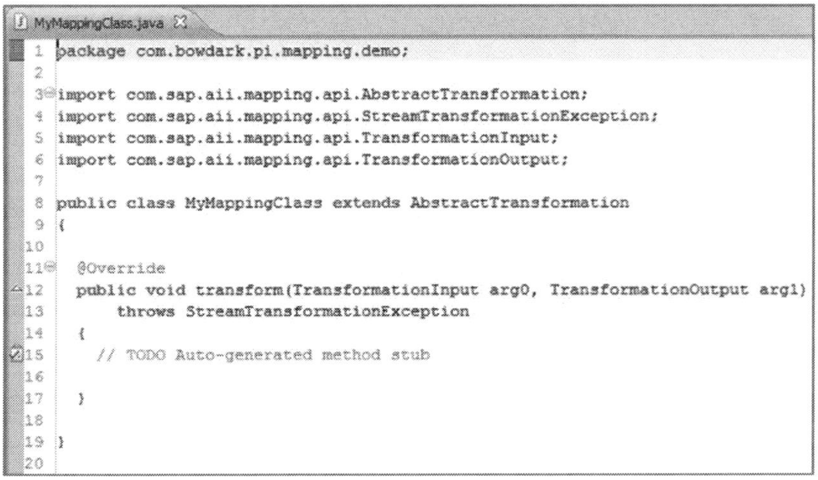

```
MyMappingClass.java 23
 1  package com.bowdark.pi.mapping.demo;
 2
 3  import com.sap.aii.mapping.api.AbstractTransformation;
 4  import com.sap.aii.mapping.api.StreamTransformationException;
 5  import com.sap.aii.mapping.api.TransformationInput;
 6  import com.sap.aii.mapping.api.TransformationOutput;
 7
 8  public class MyMappingClass extends AbstractTransformation
 9  {
10
11      @Override
12      public void transform(TransformationInput arg0, TransformationOutput arg1)
13              throws StreamTransformationException
14      {
15          // TODO Auto-generated method stub
16
17      }
18
19  }
20
```

Figure 7.30: Creating a Java Mapping Program in the NWDS (Part 2)

7.3.3 Importing Java Mapping Programs into the ESR

After you finish writing your Java mapping program, the next step is to import it into the ESR. However, you cannot simply upload the generated class file(s) directly; rather, you must package them in a JAR (or *Java ARchive*) file. Then, you can upload the JAR file into the ESR as an *imported archive*. In this section, we'll show you how to perform both of these tasks.

7.3.3.1 Generating JAR Files

If you haven't worked with JAR files before, you can think of them as a special type of ZIP file that requires you to place certain artifacts in specific folders. In the case of imported archives, it's simply a matter of zipping up the relevant class files that make up your Java mapping program.

To export a JAR file for your Java project in the NWDS, perform the following steps[50]:

1. Select your project in the Package Explorer on the left-hand side of the screen and select the *File → Export...* menu option.

2. In the ensuing *Export* dialog box, select the export destination *Java → JAR File* (see Figure 7.31). Then, click the *Next >* button.

---

[50] If you have more sophisticated archive requirements, you might want to consider using a build tool like Apache Ant. For more information about Ant, check out *http://ant.apache.org*.

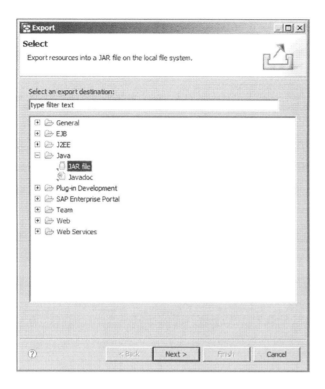

Figure 7.31: Creating a JAR File in the NWDS (1)

3. On the following screen, you'll want to select the project resources that you want to include in the generated JAR file. For example, in Figure 7.32, we have selected the *Export generated class files and resources* and *Export Java source files and resources* checkboxes to include the generated Java class files and source files, respectively.

4. In the *Select the export destination* input field, you'll want to provide the path to the JAR file that you want to generate. You also have some options below this field that determine how the JAR file gets created (see Figure 7.32).

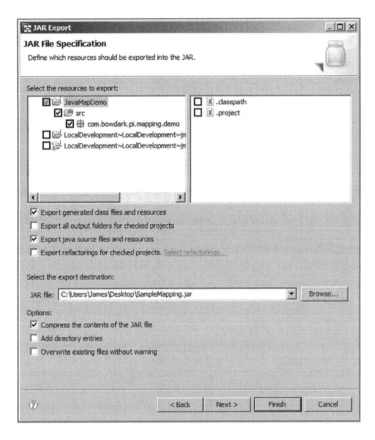

Figure 7.32: Creating a JAR File in the NWDS (2)

5. Finally, you can click on the *Finish* button to generate the target JAR file.

7.3.3.2 Creating an Imported Archive

After you generate your JAR file, you can then import it into the ESR by creating an *imported archive* in the ES Builder. To create an imported archive, perform the following steps:

1. In the ES Builder tool, select the SWCV that you want to develop in and right-click on the target namespace. In the context menu that appears, select the *New* menu option.

2. In the *Create Object* dialog box, expand the *Mapping Objects* submenu and choose the *Imported Archive* menu option.

3. Next, you must enter a name and description for the imported archive. To continue, click the *Create* button.

4. In the following *Edit Imported Archive* view, click on the *Import Archive* button to open up a file selection dialog box that you can use to search for JAR files. Once you find the JAR file you're looking for, click the *Open* button to load the JAR file into the imported archive (see Figure 7.33).

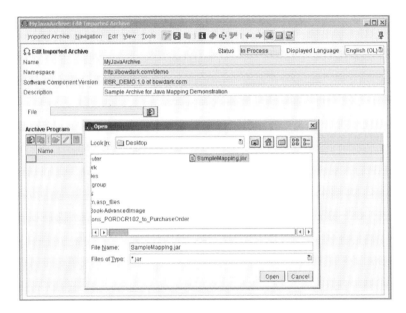

Figure 7.33: Creating an Imported Archive (Part 2)

5. Finally, click on the *Save* button to save your changes.

7.3.4 Classloading Concepts

Up until now, our view of Java mapping programs has been limited to simple cases involving the development of a single mapping class. Of course, in real-world scenarios, you may want to develop a number of supporting classes to assist you in the mapping development process. Or, you might want to enlist the help of some 3rd-party library that are already packaged up in a JAR file. In either case, you can use imported archives to upload these classes. However, there are certain classloading issues to be aware of.

According to the SAP online help documentation (SAP AG), the search paths for classes in Java mapping programs are organized as follows:

1. The paths of the JRE of the underlying AS Java instance. This includes the core Java libraries as well as extension libraries loaded into the `lib\ext` folder of the JRE home directory.

2. The path in which the SAP mapping API library is saved as well as the paths to certain standard libraries such as the SAP XML Toolkit, the SAP Java Connector (JCo), the SAP Logging Service, and so on.

3. Classes in imported archives contained within the same software component version/namespace as the Java mapping program. This also includes other classes within the same imported archive as the Java mapping program.

4. Classes that are in imported archives in the same namespace and a subordinate (basis) software component version.

5. Classes that are in imported archives in other namespaces of the software component version.

6. Classes that are in imported archives in other namespaces of subordinate (basis) software component versions.

At runtime, the runtime environment will scan these paths in order as it loads mapping programs into context. Whenever a match is found for a particular class or resource, the classloader will end the search. Therefore, it some cases, you'll want to be careful about where you upload imported archives.

What about Message Mappings and UDFs?

The classloading concepts described in this section also apply to UDF development with message mappings. This implies that you can leverage custom classes and/or external libraries in your UDFs by importing them in the ESR as an imported archive. Looking back at Section 7.2.5, you'll recall that the *Functions* tab editor page included a sub-tab called *Archives Used*. Here, you can define references to imported archives and then import their constituent classes on the *Import Instructions* tab (see Figure 7.16).

As a best programming practice, we recommend that you define a base software component version that contains core mapping libraries for your organization. You can then use this base software component as a prerequisite software component version for all of your custom mapping developments. That way, each newly-developed mapping component inherits this core functionality by default and you don't have to worry about collisions, etc.

7.4   Developing Mapping Programs Using XSLT

XML processing models such as DOM make it very easy to scan through and manipulate an XML document. However, if you need to copy the content of one XML document into another, the process can be somewhat tedious. The primary challenge here is that you have to account for the creation of all XML content when, in reality, only a fraction of the content is dynamic in nature. Ideally, it would be much more productive if we could use a *template* to define the bulk of the static content and then weave in the dynamic content at runtime. Recognizing the need for a more economical development model, the W3C defined the *Extensible Stylesheet Language Transformations* (XSLT) language for this purpose.

In this section, we'll provide a brief introduction to XSLT and show you how you can use it to create mapping programs that can be deployed to the ESR[51]. Given the breadth of the XSLT language specification, it's not realistic for us to present a thorough treatment of XSLT here. Instead, we provide a basic introduction that you can use as a foundation for more advanced study. An excellent resource to begin with is Bob DuCharme's *XSLT Quickly* (DuCharme, 2001). Also, if you're interested in learning more about developing XSLT programs on the AS ABAP stack, you should check out *XML Data Exchange Using ABAP* (Trapp, 2006).

7.4.1   What is XSLT?

Initially, XSLT was positioned as a language that could be used to simplify the creation of HTML markup. Over time, it has evolved into a more general-purpose language that can be used to perform all kinds of transformations. Regardless of the source and target content types, the process is essentially the same: an XSLT processor uses an XML document called a *stylesheet* as a template for transforming a source data object into a target data object. Here, even though the process is described as a *transformation*, the source data object isn't changed. Rather, its contents are used as a data source for building the target data object. Figure 7.34 illustrates this process as it relates to the transformation of XML documents.

---

[51] Note: The mapping runtime environment only provides support for XSLT version 1.0.

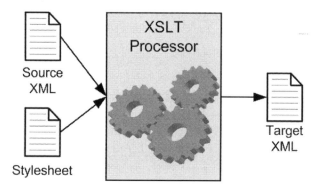

Figure 7.34: XSLT Processing Model

Unlike conventional programming languages, XSLT uses a *declarative approach* that tells the XSLT processor what to do when it encounters specific nodes within the source XML document. In XSLT parlance, these processing instructions are called *template rules*. A template rule blends static content with various types of functional expressions to create portions of the target data object. Collectively, an XSLT stylesheet combines these template rules together to define the transformation logic that the XSLT processor should recursively apply towards the creation of the target data object. Next, we explain how all of this fits together as we investigate the creation of XSLT stylesheets.

7.4.2   Creating XSLT Stylesheets

An XSLT stylesheet is an XML document whose vocabulary is defined by the W3C (W3C, 1999). The root element of a stylesheet can be either `transform` or `stylesheet`; though in the context of mapping development, it should be `transform`. In either case, the root element (and all XSLT-specific elements) must be qualified using the `http://www.w3.org/1999/XSL/Transform` namespace (commonly prefixed with the `xsl` namespace prefix). This requirement is necessary so that XSLT processors can recognize specific language elements within a stylesheet at runtime. Listing 7.4 shows how this root element is defined.

```
<xsl:transform version="1.0"
  xmlns:xsl="http://www.w3.org/1999/XSL/Transform">
  ...
</xsl:transform>
```

Listing 7.4: Creating an XSLT Stylesheet

7.4.2.1 Template Rules and Match Patterns

As mentioned earlier, XSLT stylesheets are comprised of a series of *template rules*. Template rules provide a set of instructions that tell the XSLT processor what to do whenever it encounters a particular pattern in the source XML document. Such instructions can include the output of static content, content from the source document, and even the call to other templates that behave like subroutines.

Listing 7.5 demonstrates the basic syntax used to define template rules. As you can see, template rules are defined using the `xsl:template` element. The `match` attribute contains a *match pattern* that helps the XSLT processor know when to apply the template rule. For example, the template rule shown in Listing 7.5 would be executed whenever the XSLT processor encounters the `IDOC` element within the `PORDCR102` source XML structure.

```
<xsl:transform version="1.0"
  xmlns:xsl="http://www.w3.org/1999/XSL/Transform">
  <!-- Template rule matching the root IDoc element -->
  <xsl:template match="PORDCR102/IDOC">
    <!-- Static content -->
    <PurchaseOrder>
      <PONumber>
        <!-- XSLT Expression -->
        <xsl:value-of
          select="\E1PORDCR1\E1BPMEPOHEADER\PO_NUMBER" />
      </PONumber>
      ...
    </PurchaseOrder>
  </xsl:template>
</xsl:transform>
```

Listing 7.5: Creating Template Rules in XSLT

Match patterns are specified using a specialized XML query language prescribed by the W3C called the *XML Path Language* (or XPath). XPath expressions define a *location path* that is separated by slashes (`/`) into a series of *location steps*. According to the XPath specification (W3C, 1999), each location step can be broken up into three parts:

➢ **Axes**
Axes are used to orient the search towards a particular node direction within the XML tree structure. XPath defines many axes such as *child*,

parent, *ancestor*, *descendent*, and so on. Figure 7.35 illustrates the orientation of some of these axes using our PO example. In XSLT, if no axis is selected explicitly, an XSLT processor assumes that the default child axis should be used[52].

> **Node Tests**
  Node tests identify the node (or nodes) to search for within the selected axis.

> **Predicates**
  Predicates are optional components that can be used to filter search results based upon the results of a logical expression. Predicates can be used in much the same way that WHERE clauses are used in SQL.

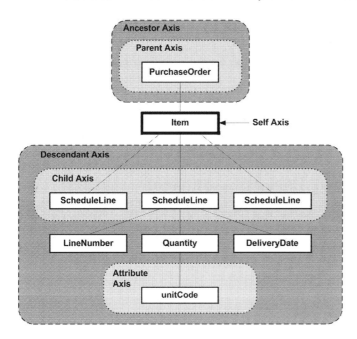

Figure 7.35: Understanding XPath Axes

Listing 7.6 demonstrates the complete syntax diagram of an XPath location step. Of course, in terms of everyday use, you'll find that most XPath location steps simply consist of a node test component. This usage style lends itself well to developing location paths that mirror familiar file system lookup patterns. For example, to look up the name of the supplying vendor

---

[52] For a complete list of supported axes, check out *http://www.w3.org/TR/xpath/#axes*.

in our PO example, you could build the XPath location path
`/PORDCR102/IDOC/E1PORDCR1/E1BPMEPOHEADER/VENDOR`.

`axis::node_test[predicate]`

Listing 7.6: Syntax Diagram of XPath Location Steps

In some cases, you can simplify the direction XPath location steps through the use of some abbreviated syntax. Table 7.5 illustrates this abbreviated syntax.

Symbol	Meaning	Usage
@	Shorthand for the `attribute` **axis**.	Instead of having to write `/Note/attribute::lang` to access the `Note` element's `lang` attribute, you could define your location path as `/Note/@lang`.
.	Shorthand for the `self` **axis**.	Frequently used to pass the current node in context to XPath functions, etc.
..	Shorthand for `parent` **axis**.	Used to go up one level in the XML document's hierarchy. For example, if you're operating at the item level in our PO example, you could use this shorthand to navigate up to header-level data like this: `../CreationDate`.
/	Shorthand for the `child` **axis**.	Typically used to define location paths that traverse up the XML tree. For instance, notice how it is used to access the `CreationDate` child element off of the PO root element in the example above.
//	Shorthand for `descendant-or-self` **axis**.	Used to refer to a context node's children, its children's children, and so on.

Table 7.5: XPath Abbreviated Syntax for Axes

7.4.2.2 Generating Output

Once you outline your template rules and identify your match patterns, the next step in the XSLT development process is to fill in these template rules with static content and expressions for generating output. Table 7.6 contains a list of most of the common XSLT elements you have at your disposal. A more thorough treatment of these elements can be found in *XSLT Quickly*

(DuCharme, 2001). There, you'll also find a reference on certain XPath functions that allow you to perform string manipulations, mathematical operations, and so on.

XSLT Element	Description
`<xsl:variable>`	Used to define a variable in XSLT. The value of this variable can be assigned using the `select` attribute which contains an XPath expression like this: ``` <xsl:variable name="poDate" select="/PurchaseOrder/CreationDate" /> ``` You can also assign variable values by embedding more complex expressions inside the `<variable>` element. In either case, once the assignment is made, you cannot change the value of the variable. You can refer to variables elsewhere in the document by prefixing the variable name with the `$` prefix (e.g. `$poDate`).
`<xsl:value-of>`	Used to output data to the target structure. This data could be from the source structure, a variable, etc. ``` <xsl:value-of select="/PurchaseOrder/Vendor/Name" /> ```
`<xsl:if>`	Used to conditionally output content in the target structure. The conditional logic is expressed using the `test` attribute as shown below. ``` <xsl:if test="$quantity > 5"> <!-- Content goes here --> </xsl:if> ```

XSLT Element	Description

`<xsl:choose>`	The `<choose>` element is similar to a switch or case statement in other languages. For example, below, we've implement a kind of `if...else` statement.
	
	``xml
	<xsl:choose>
	  <xsl:when test="$quantity > 0">
	    <!-- Content goes here -->
	  </xsl:when>
	  <xsl:otherwise>
	    <!-- Content goes here -->
	  </xsl:otherwise>
	</xsl:choose>
	``

`<xsl:sort>`	Used to sort a node set in ascending or descending order according to some criteria.

`<xsl:for-each>`	Used to iterate (or loop) over a node set. For example, the following XSLT snippet will output the product number for each of the line items in our PO example.
	
	``xml
	<xsl:for-each
	   select="/PurchaseOrder/Item">
	  <!-- Note: Each iteration loads the
	            current line item into
	            context -->
	  <xsl:value-of select="Product" />
	</xsl:for-each>
	``

`<xsl:element>`	Used to dynamically generate an element in the target document. For example:
	
	``xml
	<xsl:element name="{$elementName}">
	  <!-- Element content goes here -->
	</xsl:element>
	``

`<xsl:attribute>`	Used to dynamically generate an attribute for an element in the target document:
	
	``xml
	<xsl:attribute name="unitCode">
	  <!-- Attribute value goes here -->
	</xsl:attribute>
	``

Table 7.6: Some Common XSLT Logic Elements

7.4.2.3 Modularization Techniques

As mentioned in Section 7.4.2.1, XSLT stylesheets are composed of a series of template rules. Technically speaking, you can implement most maps using only a single template rule. This is analogous to writing a program in a normal programming language and embedding all of the code in a module called `main`, etc.

Since this is a book for programmers, we won't belabor the importance of modularization. Instead, we'll focus on the XSLT language elements that make it possible:

> ➤ The `<xsl:apply-templates>` element allows you to implicitly invoke other templates that match the current node(s) in context. This approach can allow you to recursively process the source document in a top-down fashion.

> ➤ The `<xsl:call-template>` element is used to explicitly call a named template. You can use the child element `<xsl:with-param>` to pass parameters to the template just like you would in a call to a subroutine in other languages.

> ➤ The `<xsl:include>` element allows you to include the content of other stylesheets in your stylesheet. Thus, for example, you could create a standalone stylesheet containing some utility template rules and then include that library in your mapping programs. The only requirement here is that the included stylesheets be accessible from the including stylesheet.

As you get more comfortable with XSLT, you will want to think about ways that you can use these elements to modularize your mapping programs and increase reuse.

7.4.2.4 Working with Java Enhancements

Sometimes, you may stumble across requirements that are almost impossible to implement using standard XSLT functionality. Here, for example, you might need to implement a complicated algorithm, perform advanced string parsing, etc. In these situations, you can employ the use of *Java enhancements* in your XSLT mappings.

Note

Though the XSLT 1.0 specification proposes an enhancement mechanism to enable external calls from XSLT programs, the means by which the calls are carried out is non-standardized. Therefore, while SAP's implementation of this feature is not unlike other implementations, it is nevertheless proprietary. So, if your goal is to develop vendor-agnostic XSLT files, you may want to be careful about how you use this feature.

For the most part, the implementation of a Java enhancement in an XSLT mapping program is fairly straightforward. In general, the steps required for implementation are as follows:

1. Implement a Java class that provides static methods that encapsulate the functionality you wish to leverage.

2. Add a customized XML namespace declaration in your XSLT program to declare the use of the class.

3. Plug in the function call in your XSLT program wherever you would normally access an XPath function, etc.

The following subsections describe each of these steps in more detail.

Implementing the Java Class

Generally speaking, you develop Java enhancement classes in much the same way that you would develop helper classes for Java mappings or graphical message mappings. Here, aside from the programming restrictions outlined in Section 7.3.1, the only other stipulation is that the enhancement functionality be exposed via *static methods*. For example, in Listing 7.7, you can see how we've implemented a string utilities class called `StringUtils`. This class provides a static method called `removeLeadingChars()` that can be used to remove a series of leading characters off of a string value.

```
package com.bowdark.util;

public class StringUtils
{
  public static String removeLeadingChars(String source,
                                                  char c)
  {
    char[] sourceChars = source.toCharArray();
    int index = 0;

    for (index = 0; index < sourceChars.length; index++)
    {
      if (sourceChars[index] != c)
        break;
    } // -- End for (Characters) -- //

    return source.substring(index);
  } // -- public static String removeLeadingChars() -- //
} // -- End of class StringUtils -- //
```

Listing 7.7: Implementing an Enhancement Class in Java

As is the case with Java mapping programs, enhancement classes are loaded into the ESR as part of an imported archive. This could be a standalone archive, or part of the archive used to upload the leveraging XSLT program. We'll show you how to achieve the latter option in Section 7.4.3.

Importing a Java Class into an XSLT Program

To load a Java class into context, you must define a specialized XML namespace at the beginning of your XSLT program. Listing 7.8 demonstrates the syntax of this namespace declaration. As you can see, instead of a typical URI reference, this namespace declaration uses a specialized syntax of the form `java:` plus the fully qualified class name of your Java class. You are free to assign whatever namespace prefix you prefer.

```
<xsl:stylesheet version="1.0"
    xmlns:xsl="http://www.w3.org/1999/XSL/Transform"
    xmlns:bowdark="java:com.bowdark.util.StringUtils">
  ...
</xsl:stylesheet>
```

Listing 7.8: Importing a Java Class into an XSLT Program

Calling Java Methods from an XSLT Program

Once a Java enhancement class has been loaded into context, you can call its methods using the same syntax you use to call XPath functions. For example, Listing 7.9 shows how we're calling the `removeLeadingChars()` method defined in class `StringUtils` (see Listing 7.7). As you can see, we're defining the parameters to this method using the `xsl:param` element.

```
<xsl:stylesheet version="1.0"
    xmlns:xsl="http://www.w3.org/1999/XSL/Transform"
    xmlns:javamap="java:com.bowdark.util.StringUtils">

  <!-- Declare parameters to pass to the Java method -->
  <xsl:param name="docNo">
    <xsl:value-of select="//DocumentNumber" />
  </xsl:param>

  <!-- This parameter is assigned by the mapping runtime and
       provides you with access to the mapping trace, etc.
       To pass it to your method, simply define a parameter
       called inputparam and assign it the type
       java.util.Map. -->
  <xsl:param name="inputparam" />

  <xsl:template match="/">
    <SomeBusinessTransaction>
      <DocumentNumber>
        <xsl:if
          test="function-available('bowdark:removeLeadingChars')">
          <xsl:value-of
            select="bowdark:removeLeadingChars($docNo)" />
        </xsl:if>
      </DocumentNumber>
    </SomeBusinessTransaction>
  </xsl:template>
</xsl:stylesheet>
```

Listing 7.9: Calling a Java Method from an XSLT Program

Looking closely at the source code depicted in Listing 7.9, you can see that we wrapped an `xsl:if` element around the method call to check to see that the function (method) is available. It is a good idea to get into the practice of this since it is possible that the class/method might not be available at runtime due to some kind of classloading error. In this situation, the XSLT program will generate a runtime error if the method you try to call is unavailable. Therefore, it might make sense to use the `xsl:choose` element to define an alternative path in the mapping logic.

7.4.3   Importing XSLT Stylesheets into the ESR

The process for importing XSLT stylesheets into the ESR is quite similar to the one used to import Java mapping programs. Here, just as before, you create an imported archive to upload the XSLT program. The primary difference in this case is that the XSLT program (and its included templates) is packaged up in a ZIP file rather than a JAR file.

Generally speaking, the steps for creating XSLT imported archives are the same as the ones described in Section 7.3.3. Of course, whenever you click on the *Import Archive* button, you'll want to browse to the ZIP archive containing your XSLT program (see Figure 7.36).

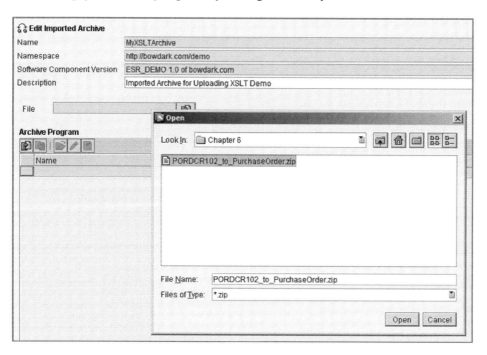

Figure 7.36: Uploading an XSLT Archive into the ESR © Copyright 2010. SAP AG. All rights reserved

7.5   Summary

In this chapter, you learned some of the basics of mapping development using SAP NetWeaver PI. In particular, we explored the creation of graphical message mappings, Java-based mappings, and XSLT-based mappings. Now that you are familiar with these concepts, you are ready to move on and tackle some more advanced topics – the subject of our next chapter.

References

DuCharme, B. (2001). *XSLT Quickly.* Manning Publications.

Griffith, A. (2002). *Java™, XML, and JAXP.* Wiley Computer Publishing.

SAP AG. (n.d.). *Message Mappings.* Retrieved December 7, 2010, from SAP Help Library:
http://help.sap.com/saphelp_nwpi711/helpdata/en/49/1ebc6111ea2f45a994
6c702b685299/frameset.htm

SAP AG. (n.d.). *Runtime Environment (Java Mappings).* Retrieved November 5, 2010, from SAP Help Library:
http://help.sap.com/saphelp_nwpi711/helpdata/en/bd/c91241c738f423e100
00000a155106/frameset.htm

Trapp, T. (2006). *XML Data Exchange Using ABAP.* SAP PRESS.

W3C. (1999, November 16). *XML Path Language (XPath) Version 1.0.*
Retrieved November 9, 2010, from W3C Standards and Drafts:
http://www.w3.org/TR/xpath/

W3C. (1999, November 16). *XSL Transformations (XSLT) Version 1.0.*
Retrieved November 9, 2010, from W3C Standards and Drafts:
http://www.w3.org/TR/xslt

Advanced Mapping Development 8

In the previous chapter, you learned some of the basics of mapping development in SAP NetWeaver PI. In this chapter, we'll expand on these concepts and show you how to implement more sophisticated requirements in your mapping programs.

After completing this chapter, you will be able to:

- ❖ Understand how operation mappings are used to determine which mapping programs should be used to map between pairs of service operations.

- ❖ Build reusable function libraries that are shared between message mappings.

- ❖ Perform mapping lookups to translate between different domains of values.

- ❖ Develop mapping programs using the ABAP Workbench.

8.1   Operation Mappings

Up until now, our discussion on mapping development has been focused strictly on XML transformation concepts. This is all fine and good, but you might be wondering how these mapping programs fit into the larger picture. In other words, if you have a sender interface A and a receiver interface B, how do you plug in a mapping program to convert the data from the sender interface into a format that is compatible with the receiver interface? In SAP NetWeaver PI, this relationship is defined using an *operation mapping*.

8.1.1   Creating Operation Mappings

Operation mappings, as the name suggests, register mapping programs with a pair of service operations. To demonstrate how all these pieces fit together, let's look at how operation mappings are maintained within the ES Builder. Here, you can create an operation mapping by performing the following steps:

1. To begin, right-click on the target SWCV/namespace that you want to develop in and select the *New* menu option.

2. In the ensuing *Create Object* dialog box, expand the *Mapping Objects* submenu and select the *Operation Mapping* menu option.

3. Next, you must enter a name[53] and an optional description for your operation mapping. Click on the *Create* button to continue.

4. Once the operation mapping is created, you will be routed to the operation mapping editor screen shown in Figure 8.1. Here, there are three basic elements that you must define to create the operation mapping:

   a. On the *Source Operation* view on the left-hand side of the editor, you must select an operation from the source service interface. Here, you can either drag-and-drop in a service interface (operation) from the left-hand navigation area or use the value help in the *Name* field to select the desired service operation.

   b. In the *Target Operation* view on the right-hand side of the editor, you must select an operation from the target service

---

[53] Consult the SAP NetWeaver How-To Guide entitled *PI Best Practices: Naming Conventions* (SAP AG) for naming conventions.

interface. Here, once again, you can either drag-and-drop in a service interface (operation) from the left-hand navigation area or use the value help in the *Name* field to select the desired service operation.

c. After the source/target operations are loaded into the editor (which is achieved by clicking on the *Read Operations* button shown in Figure 8.1), you can assign your mapping program to the operation mapping using the *Mapping Program* table at the bottom of the screen. As you can see in Figure 8.1, you can choose between several different mapping program types here using the dropdown list in the *Type* column. Then, once the mapping program type is selected, you can use the search help in the *Name* column to assign your mapping program to the operation mapping.

5. Finally, click the *Save* button to save your changes.

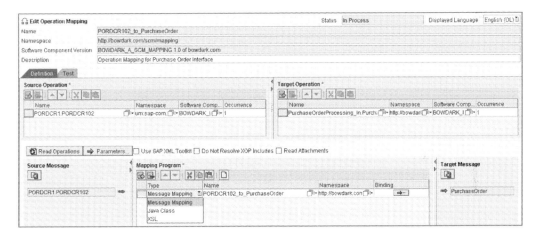

Figure 8.1: Editing an Operation Mapping in the ESR © Copyright 2010. SAP AG. All rights reserved

Chaining Mapping Programs Together

If you look closely at Figure 8.1, you'll notice that the *Mapping Program* table in the bottom portion of the operation mapping editor lets you assign *multiple* mapping programs to an operation mapping. This option allows you to effectively daisy chain multiple mapping programs together to define your operation mapping. In this case, the output of the proceeding mapping program is passed on to the next program as the system recursively works its way down the list.

8.1.2 Configuration Options

Looking closely at the operation mapping editor screen shown in Figure 8.1, you can see that there are several other settings that influence the behavior of an operation mapping. These options are described in detail in Table 8.1.

Configuration Option	Description
Use SAP XML Toolkit	This setting is a carry-over from previous versions of SAP NetWeaver PI. In version 7.1, the SAP XML Toolkit is replaced by enhanced XML processing capabilities bundled with JDK 5. In general, this default functionality is preferable to use of the SAP XML Toolkit for performance reasons. However, one place where you will need to specify this option is with XSLT programs that utilize Java enhancements. Here, the SAP XML Toolkit is needed to support the proprietary extension mechanism defined by SAP.
Do Not Resolve XOP Includes	The term "XOP" here refers to an *XML-Binary Optimized Packaging*; a feature common to the *SOAP Message Transmission Optimization Mechanism* (MTOM)[54]. You can think of an XOP include as a kind of hyperlink that points to a message attachment. By default, the mapping runtime will resolve these XOP includes, reassembling the message by embedding the binary attachments as an `xsd:Base64Binary` payload. Selecting this checkbox turns off this behavior within the mapping runtime.
Read Attachments	This setting determines whether or not attachments are passed to the mapping at runtime. Without this option, only the main payload of the message is transferred at runtime.

---

[54] Refer to *http://www.w3.org/TR/soap12-mtom/* for more details.

Table 8.1: Configuration Options for Operation Mappings

8.1.3 Parameterization Techniques

Oftentimes, you may encounter situations in which the same mapping logic is required for multiple interfaces. For instance, imagine that we extended the scope of our purchase order interface example from Chapter 7 to also support modifications and cancelations. Here, it is likely that much of the same mapping logic applies to each of the interface scenarios; the only difference might be the mapping of some kind of *transaction type* field that is used to distinguish between the various transaction types.

One way to deal with these slight variations in mapping logic is to define a series of *parameters* that influence the behavior of a mapping program at runtime. For example, with our PO mapping program, we need to pass in a transaction type parameter that will allow the program to distinguish between different kinds of requests. As you may have guessed, operation mappings represent a fairly logical place for performing such parameter assignments.

In this section, we'll show you how to parameterize mapping programs using operation mappings. These techniques will help you get more reuse out of your mapping programs.

8.1.3.1 Defining Parameters in Operation Mappings

In Section 8.1.1, you learned how operation mappings select the mapping programs that should be called whenever the system needs to perform a transformation between a pair of service operations. It is here within these assignments that you define the parameters that are passed to mapping programs at runtime. Figure 8.2 illustrates these assignments, showing you how parameters are linked between an operation mapping and a mapping program.

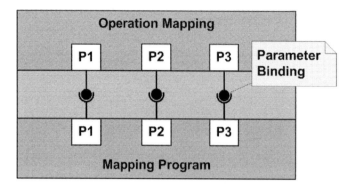

Figure 8.2: Defining Parameter Bindings between Operation Mappings and Mapping Programs

In order to implement the parameter bindings shown in Figure 8.2, you must first define the parameters that are passed to the operation mapping. These parameters can be defined within the operation mapping editor by clicking on the *Parameters...* button (see Figure 8.3). This will open up the *Parameters* view in the bottom portion of the editor screen (see Figure 8.4).

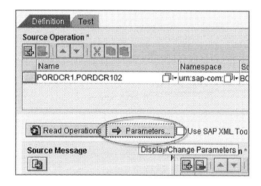

Figure 8.3: Defining Parameters in an Operation Mapping (Part 1)

Parameters

Define the parameters used in the binding of the mapping programs. You assign values to the parameters in the interface determination editor in the Integration Directory.

Name	Category	Type	Parameter	Description
TRANS_TYPE	Simple Type	xsd:string	Import	Transaction Type

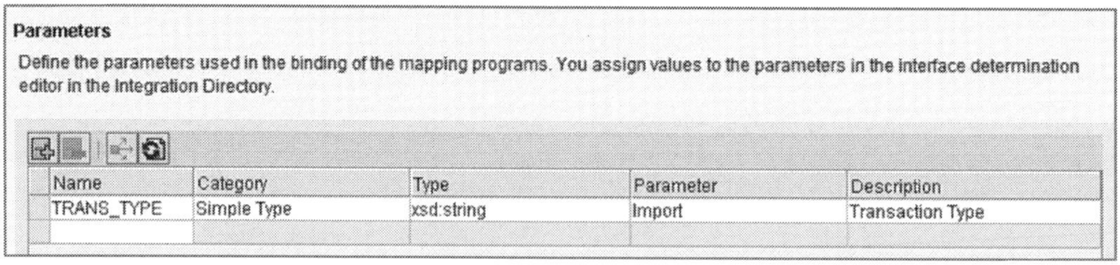

Figure 8.4: Defining Parameters in an Operation Mapping (Part 2)

As you can see in Figure 8.4, each parameter definition supports the specification of several attributes. Table 8.2 describes each of these attributes in detail.

Attribute	Possible Values	Description
Name	N/A	In this field, you specify a name for the parameter. The name must not contain any spaces.
Category	Simple Type Adapter	This field allows you to choose the *category* of the parameter. Here, you can choose between simple XSD types and adapter types which are used to facilitate mapping lookups. We'll learn more about mapping lookups in Section 8.5.
Type	Simple Types: xsd:string xsd:integer Adapter: JDBC RFC SOAP	In this field, you select a data type for the parameter. These value sets are static, and depend on the value selected in the category column.
Parameter	Import Export	In this field, you determine whether or not the parameter is an *importing* parameter or an *exporting* parameter. Exporting parameters can be returned to integration processes for subsequent evaluation.
Description	N/A	In this field, you can enter an optional description for the parameter.

Table 8.2: Attributes of Parameters in Operation Mappings

Once you define the requisite parameters for your operation mapping, you have effectively updated the *signature* of the operation mapping. In other words, whereas before the operation mapping was called without specifying any parameters; now it must be called with actual parameters. These parameter values are defined at configuration time within the Integration Directory. We'll learn how these values are assigned in Chapter 12. For now, suffice it to say that these parameter values will be passed to your operation mappings at runtime (by magic).

8.1.3.2 Parameterized Message Mappings

In order to pass parameters to graphical message mappings, you must add these parameters to the message mapping's *signature*. Here, the signature is defined on the aptly named *Signature* tab within the mapping editor. As you can see in Figure 8.5, you can maintain parameters for message mappings in much the same way that you define parameters for operation mappings.

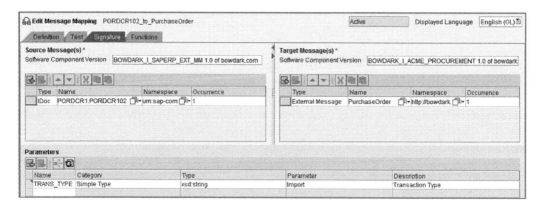

Figure 8.5: Defining Parameters for Message Mappings © Copyright 2010. SAP AG. All rights reserved

Once you have defined the signature of your message mapping, the next step is to link the parameters in your message mapping to the ones defined within the operation mapping that executes your message mapping at runtime. To implement these bindings, perform the following steps:

1. Open up the operation mapping and find the row in the *Mapping Program* table where the target message mapping is assigned (see Figure 8.6).

2. Then, click on the arrow button in the *Binding* column to open up the binding editor (see Figure 8.6).

3. Finally, in the binding editor, you can use the value helps to bind parameters defined in the operation mapping to parameters defined in the message mapping. Click the *OK* button to confirm your assignments.

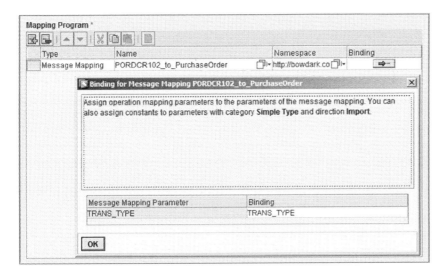

Figure 8.6: Binding Parameters between Operation Mappings and Message Mappings © Copyright 2010. SAP AG. All rights reserved

You can access parameter values in your message mappings using the `Constant` function. To demonstrate how this works, consider the value mapping shown in Figure 8.7. Here, we're using the `Constant` function to assign a value to the `TransactionType` field. In this case, the parameter value is selected in the `Constant` function's parameters using the value help provided with the *Value* field. As you can see in Figure 8.7, the parameter name is escaped on either side by the `$` character.

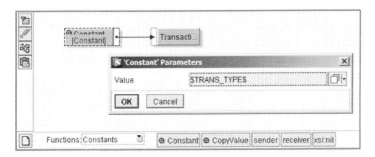

Figure 8.7: Accessing Parameters in Message Mappings © Copyright 2010. SAP AG. All rights reserved

8.1.3.3 Parameterized Java Mapping Programs

To access parameters in a Java mapping program, you must use the API methods provided in package com.sap.aii.mapping.api[55]. Listing 8.1 demonstrates how this works in a sample Java mapping program.

```java
public class ParameterizedMap
  extends AbstractTransformation
{
  public void transform(TransformationInput in,
                        TransformationOutput out)
    throws StreamTransformationException
  {
    // Accessing import parameters...
    String sParam =
      in.getInputParameters().getString("I_STR_PARAM");
    int iParam =
      in.getInputParameters().getInt("I_INT_PARAM");
    Channel cParam =
      in.getInputParameters().getChannel("I_CHL_PARAM");

    // Mapping logic goes here...

    // Populating export parameters:
    out.getOutputParameters().setString("E_STR_PARAM","Paige");
    out.getOutputParameters().setInt("E_INT_PARAM", 7);
    out.getOutputParameters().setValue("E_OBJ_PARAM", someObj);
  } // -- public void transform() -- //
} // -- End of class ParameterizedMap -- //
```

Listing 8.1: Accessing Parameters from a Java Mapping Program

As you can see in Listing 8.1, parameters are accessed via the getInputParameters() and getOutputParameters() methods provided by classes TransformationInput and TransformationOutput, respectively. These methods provide you with access to bean-like objects that allow you to retrieve or set the values of various parameters. From a code perspective, that's all there is to it.

---

[55] You can access the JavaDocs for this package by logging onto *http://help.sap.com/javadocs/* and clicking on the *PI 7.1 (Adapter, Module and Mapping Development)* link.

However, before you can access these parameters in your Java mapping program, you must define parameter bindings in the operation mapping that calls it. This procedure is almost identical to the one described for message mappings in Section 8.1.3.2. However, with Java mappings, you define the names of the parameters within the binding assignment (see Figure 8.8). The configured names are the same names you will use to access the parameter via the API calls demonstrated in Listing 8.1.

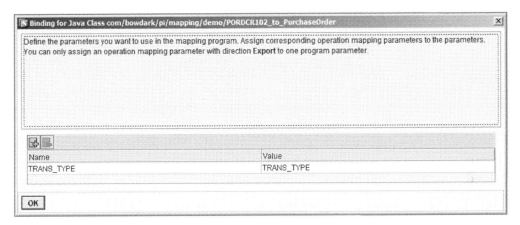

Figure 8.8: Binding Parameters to Java Mapping Programs © Copyright 2010. SAP AG. All rights reserved

8.1.3.4 Parameterized XSLT Mapping Programs

Unlike graphical message mappings or Java mappings, there is no direct or standard way to pass parameters to XSLT mapping programs. However, that's not to say that it is impossible to implement – just tedious. If you're interested in seeing how all this works, check out the SAP SDN blog entitled *PI Parameterized XSLT - A Flexible Alternative* (Glas).

8.2   Function Libraries

In Chapter 7, you learned how to create user-defined functions (UDFs) to simplify complex mapping requirements. By default, these UDFs are saved as part of a local function library within the message mapping. This implies that the UDFs are only visible within the message mapping that defines them.

Sometimes, you may want to reuse a UDF in multiple mapping scenarios. In this case, instead of copying-and-pasting the UDF from one message mapping to next, it makes sense to define the UDF as part of a global *function library*. That way, other message mappings can leverage the same

UDF as needed. Furthermore, if you ever need to update the UDF logic down the road, you only have to modify it in one place.

8.2.1 Creating a Function Library

For the most part, you'll find that function libraries are maintained in much the same way that local UDFs are maintained within the mapping editor. To create a new function library, perform the following steps:

1. To begin, right-click on the target SWCV/namespace that you want to develop in and select the *New* menu option.

2. In the ensuing *Create Object* dialog box, expand the *Mapping Objects* submenu and select the *Function Library* menu option.

3. Next, you must enter a name[56] and an optional description for your function library. Click on the *Create* button to continue.

4. Finally, your new function library will be opened up in the function library editor shown in Figure 8.9. As you can see, the function library editor is identical to the one used to edit local UDFs within message mappings.

---

[56] Consult the SAP NetWeaver How-To Guide entitled *PI Best Practices: Naming Conventions* (SAP AG) for naming conventions.

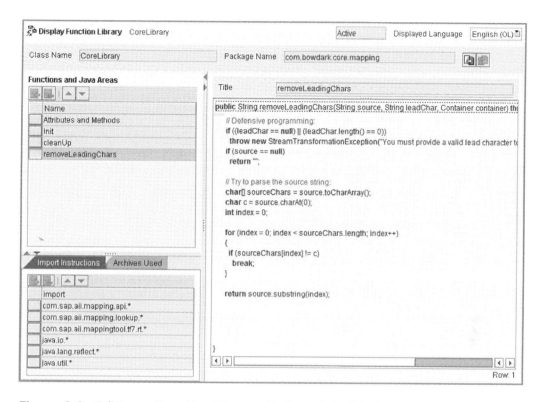

Figure 8.9: Editing a Function Library © Copyright 2010. SAP AG. All rights reserved

Behind the scenes, a function library is implemented as a Java class whose fully qualified class name is defined in terms of the values in the *Package Name* and *Class Name* input fields shown in Figure 8.9. By default, these classes include two lifecycle methods called `init()` and `cleanUp()` that are used to initialize and clean up resources used by the function library. The `init()` method is called just before the message mapping executes; while the `cleanUp()` method is called after the message mapping is complete.

Since the process of maintaining UDFs within a function library is the same as the one described for local UDFs in Chapter 7, we won't re-hash it here. Furthermore, as you would expect, you can supplement your UDFs in function libraries with the same functionality afforded to local UDFs. The list of supported options here includes:

> ➤ Global attributes
> ➤ Private helper methods

> ➤ Inner classes

> ➤ Classes provided with the core J2SE/J2EE libraries

> ➤ Classes provided in the PI mapping API

> ➤ Classes imported via imported archives

For more information about each of these features, we recommend that you check out the online help documentation underneath the section entitled *Function Libraries* (SAP AG).

8.2.2 Importing Function Libraries

In order to utilize a function library within your message mapping, you must define a dependency to it. This can be accomplished via the following steps:

1. Open up a message mapping and click on the *Show Used Function Libraries* button on the left-hand toolbar of the data-flow editor (see Figure 8.10).

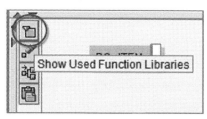

Figure 8.10: Importing a Function Library (Part 1)

2. Next, in the expanded *Used Libraries* view, click the insert line button to add a new function library reference (see Figure 8.11).

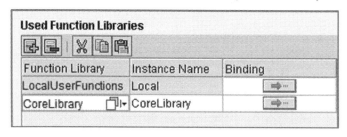

Figure 8.11: Importing a Function Library (Part 2)

3. To create the library reference, use the provided search help in the *Function Library* column shown in Figure 8.11[57].

Once you have imported the library into your message mapping, you'll notice a new category of functions available in the data-flow editor. In this case, the category name will match the value in the *Instance Name* column shown in Figure 8.11. Naturally, you can use the functions defined within this category just as you would any normal function within the data-flow editor (see Figure 8.12).

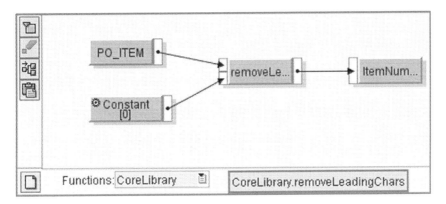

Figure 8.12: Accessing UDFs Defined in a Function Library © Copyright 2010. SAP AG. All rights reserved

8.3 Multi-Mappings

So far, each of the mapping scenarios that we have considered has transformed a single source message into a single target message. However, there may be times in which you'll need to split a source message into multiple target messages or vice versa. For instance, thinking about the PO interface example considered over the course of the past few chapters, imagine that the downstream 3rd-party system maintains PO data at the line item level. In this scenario, you would need to generate multiple target messages: one for each line item provided in the source PO message. Within SAP NetWeaver PI, such functionality can be realized using *multi-mappings*.

According to SAP, a multi-mapping is "...a mapping program that is not restricted to the transformation of one source message to one target message" (SAP AG). As such, multi-mappings can be used as follows:

---

[57] Keep in mind that message mappings can only utilize function libraries defined within the same SWCV or an underlying SWCV.

> ➤ In normal mapping scenarios where you need to split a source message into multiple (smaller) target messages.

> ➤ Within an integration process, multi-mappings can be used to perform one-to-many, many-to-one, and many-to-many transformations. We'll learn more about this usage type in Chapter 9.

Generally speaking, you can implement multi-mappings using any of the mapping techniques supported by SAP NetWeaver PI. In the upcoming sections, we'll show you how to develop multi-mappings within the ESR. Then, in Chapter 12, we'll follow up and show you how multi-mappings can be interjected into the logical routing process at runtime.

8.3.1   Organizational Concepts

From a functional standpoint, multi-mappings behave just like any other message mapping in that they receive a single input message and generate a single output message. To understand how this works, consider the sample message structure contained in Listing 8.2.

```
<sm:Messages xmlns:sm="http://sap.com/xi/XI/SplitAndMerge">
   <!-- A MessageN element occurs for each distinct
        message type utilized in the source/target
        message; e.g. Message1, Message2, etc. -->
   <sm:Message1>
     <OrderHeader>
       ...
     </OrderHeader>
   </sm:Message1>

   <!-- Messages of a particular type can recur multiple
        times within a MessageN element. For example,
        notice how we have embedded multiple OrderItem
        messages within the Message2 element below. -->
   <sm:Message2>
     <OrderItem>
       ...
     </OrderItem>

     <OrderItem>
       ...
```

```
      </OrderItem>
    </sm:Message2>
  </sm:Messages>
```

Listing 8.2: Anatomy of a Split-and-Merge Message Structure

As you can see in Listing 8.2, multi-mappings operate on a composite message structure whose root element is `Messages`[58]. Underneath the `Messages` element, you have a series of numbered `Message` elements: one for each distinct message type provided to/generated by the multi-mapping (e.g. `Message1`, `Message2`, and so on). Within the `MessageN` elements, you have the embedded source/target messages that are passed to/from the multi-mapping.

8.3.2   Developing Multi-Mappings

Once you understand how to work with the multi-mapping message structure, the process of developing a multi-mapping is not much different than the one used to develop normal message mappings. Here, you simply break the message(s) apart, apply your mapping logic, and generate output that conforms to the layout outlined in Listing 8.2. Of course, there are a few subtleties that you'll need to account for. In the following sections, we'll touch on these details.

8.3.2.1 Developing Multi-Mappings in the Mapping Editor

To develop multi-mappings in the graphical mapping editor, you must adjust the *signature* of the mapping. This can be accomplished by opening up the mapping editor and navigating to the *Signature* tab page. Here, you can alter the occurrence value for a source/target message by choosing a value from the drop-down list provided in the *Occurrence* column (see Figure 8.13). Furthermore, you can also specify additional source/target messages by clicking on the *Insert Line Below Selection* ( ) button in the *Source Messages* and *Target Messages* areas, respectively.

As soon as you modify the signature of your message mapping, the mapping editor will adjust the source/target message structures in accordance with the split-and-merge structure outlined in Listing 8.2. For example, Figure 8.14 depicts the structure overview area for a multi-mapping based on our

---

[58] According to the SAP documentation, the `Messages` element must be assigned to the `http://sap.com/xi/XI/SplitAndMerge` namespace (SAP AG).

PO scenario. From here, you simply create your target field mappings as per usual.

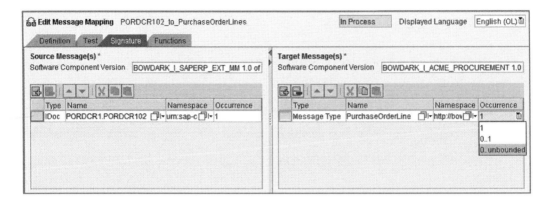

Figure 8.13: Defining the Cardinalities for Message Mappings © Copyright 2010. SAP AG. All rights reserved

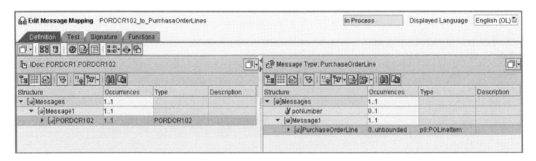

Figure 8.14: Editing a Multi-Mapping in the Mapping Editor © Copyright 2010. SAP AG. All rights reserved

8.3.2.2 Developing Multi-Mappings Externally

Generally speaking, there are no special requirements for multi-mappings developed in Java or XSLT. Here, you simply define a mapping program based upon the schema structure outlined in Listing 8.2 and import it as an imported archive as per usual. That's all there is to it.

8.3.3 Configuring Operation Mappings

To utilize your multi-mapping program at runtime, you must integrate it with an operation mapping. For the most part, this process mirrors the one described in Section 8.1. However, in this case, you'll need to adjust the cardinalities of the source/target messages to reflect the cardinalities defined within the multi-mapping. Furthermore, you can also specify additional source/target operations as necessary. Figure 8.15 demonstrates the options you have for specifying these attributes.

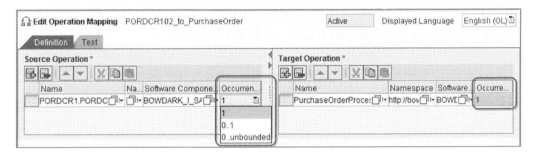

Figure 8.15: Defining the Cardinalities for Operation Mappings © Copyright 2010. SAP AG. All rights reserved

8.3.4 Usage Scenarios

Unlike regular mapping programs, multi-mappings have a more limited set of use cases. In particular, multi-mappings can be used in the following scenarios:

> Multi-mapping programs that split a message into multiple sub-messages (e.g. a 1:n transformation) can be used to implement *mapping-based message splits*. In this case, each of the generated sub-messages will be routed to their target receiver system in sequence.

> Multi-mapping programs can also be used in integration processes. In this case, any type of transformation is fair game. We'll learn more about this feature in Chapter 9.

8.4 Value Mappings

Whenever you develop interfaces between two different systems, you'll often encounter discrepancies in the way that certain objects are represented. For example, in one system the country code value used for the United States of America might be US, while another system uses the value USA. From a mapping perspective, this implies that you will need to perform a translation between these different value domains.

Within SAP NetWeaver PI, you can define value mapping tables that map between these different representations. These value mapping tables are maintained within the Integration Directory using a configuration object called *value mapping group*. In the upcoming sections, we'll show you how to define value mapping groups and use them to perform value mappings within your mapping programs.

8.4.1   Defining Value Mapping Groups

Value mapping groups collect different representations of an object. Within a value mapping group definition, each representation of an object must be uniquely qualified by a pair of *identifiers* as described in Table 8.3.

Identifier Type	Description
Issuing Agency	According to SAP, an issuing agency is an entity that "…produces one or more identification schemes to identify objects uniquely" (SAP AG). In some cases, the issuing agency may represent an actual company that publishes identification schemes. For example, Dun & Bradstreet indexes the list of companies it maintains using a *D-U-N-S number*. Therefore, if you need to represent a company within a value mapping group, you might want to leverage this common identification scheme. On the other hand, some value domains are proprietary to a particular software vendor, business system, etc. In this case, you can define an arbitrary issuing agency to describe the identification scheme.
Identification Scheme	An identification scheme provides "…a frame of reference within which it is possible to identify an object uniquely" (SAP AG). In cases where the issuing agency does not specify a formal identification scheme (e.g. like a D-U-N-S number), you can define arbitrary identification schemes.

Table 8.3: Identifiers for Objects in a Value Mapping Group

To define a value mapping group, you must log onto the Integration Directory and perform the following steps:

1. From the top-level menu, select the menu option *Object → New*.

2. In the ensuing *Create Object* dialog box, expand the *Configuration Objects* submenu and select the *Value Mapping Group* menu option.

3. Next, you will need to enter a name and optional description for the value mapping group[59].

4. Finally, click on the *Create* button to create the value mapping group.

Once the value mapping group is created, you can begin filling in different representations using the table shown in Figure 8.16. Here, you can select from pre-existing agencies/identification schemes or key in new ones. As you can see, the red asterisks next to the field names indicate that all three fields are required to define a unique representation for the object.

To illustrate how all this works, consider the value mapping group called CountryUS shown in Figure 8.16. As you might expect, this value mapping group contains different representations of the U.S. country code. In this example, we have specified two different representations for the country code: one for an SAP ECC system; the other for a fictitious 3rd-party system. If we were to later encounter some other system that represented the U.S. country code using a different value, we would simply add another row to the value mapping group and specify it accordingly.

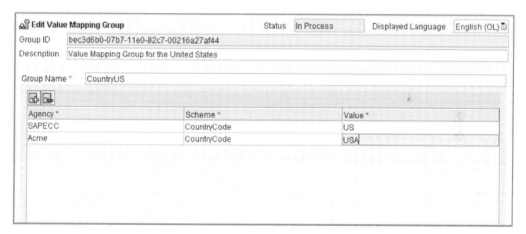

Edit Value Mapping Group		Status In Process		Displayed Language	English (OL)

Group ID   bec3d6b0-07b7-11e0-82c7-00216a27af44
Description Value Mapping Group for the United States

Group Name * CountryUS

Agency *	Scheme *	Value *
SAPECC	CountryCode	US
Acme	CountryCode	USA

Figure 8.16: Editing Value Mapping Groups in the Integration Directory © Copyright 2010. SAP AG. All rights reserved

Automating the Population of Value Mapping Groups

[59] You can find naming conventions for value mapping groups in the SAP NetWeaver How-To Guide entitled *PI Best Practices: Naming Conventions* (SAP AG).

As you can imagine, the process of maintaining value mapping groups can become tedious in a hurry. Fortunately, SAP provides a series of interfaces that you can use to automate this process. For more information on these interfaces, check out the online help documentation underneath the section entitled *Value Mapping Replication for Mass Data* (SAP AG). You can also find an interesting application of these interfaces on the SAP SDN in the weblog entitled *Value Mapping Replication Scenario* (Martens).

8.4.2   Performing Value Mappings in Message Mappings

Once you have created the necessary value mapping groups in the Integration Directory, you can use them to define lookups in your message mappings. For this task, you'll utilize the standard Value mapping function provided in the Conversions category of functions within the data-flow editor. Figure 8.17 demonstrates the properties provided by this function.

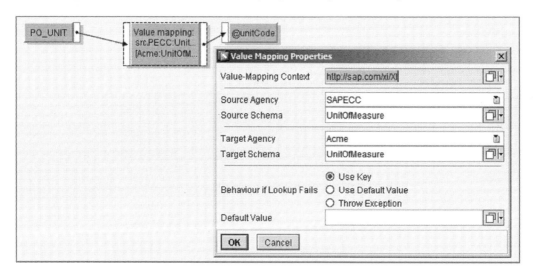

Figure 8.17: Using the Value Mapping Function in the Data-Flow Editor

In general, there are four basic properties that you must configure when using the Value mapping function:

> ➢ In the *Value-Mapping Context* field, you must select the context for the value mapping. In almost all cases, the default http://sap.com/xi/XI value will suffice here.

➢ In the *Source Agency* and *Source Schema* fields, you specify an identifier that is used as a key for locating the value mapping group in which the source value is defined.

➢ In the *Target Agency* and *Target Schema* fields, you specify an identifier that is used as a key for locating the target value within the selected value mapping group.

➢ In the bottom section of the *Value Mapping Properties* dialog box, you can determine how the function will behave if the lookup fails. Here, you can choose to keep the source value, plug in a default value, or raise an exception.

8.4.3   Performing Value Mappings in Java Programs

To perform value mapping lookups in Java programs, you must use the API classes provided in the `com.sap.aii.mapping.value.api` package[60] of the PI mapping library. Listing 8.3 demonstrates how to work with this API.

```
import com.sap.aii.mapping.value.api.IFIdentifier;
import com.sap.aii.mapping.value.api.XIVMFactory;
import com.sap.aii.mapping.value.api.XIVMService;
import com.sap.aii.mapping.value.api.ValueMappingException;

public class AcmeValueMappingProxy
{
  private static final String SAP_AGENCY = "SAPECC";
  private static final String ACME_AGENCY = "Acme";
  private static final String UOM_SCHEME = "UnitOfMeasure";

  public static String getAcmeUOMForSAPUOM(String sapUom)
  {
    try
    {
      IFIdentifier sourceId =
        XIVMFactory.newIdentifier(SAP_AGENCY, UOM_SCHEME);
      IFIdentifier targetId =
        XIVMFactory.newIdentifier(ACME_AGENCY, UOM_SCHEME);
      String acmeUom =
        XIVMService.executeMapping(sourceId, targetId, sapUom);
```

---

[60] You can access the JavaDocs for these API classes online at *http://help.sap.com/javadocs*. From the main page, click on the *PI 7.1. (Adapter, Module, and Mapping Development)* link.

```
      return acmeUom;
   }
   catch (ValueMappingException vme)
   {
      return sapUom;
   }
   } // -- public static String getAcmeUOMForSAPUOM() -- //
} // -- End of class ValueMappingProxy -- //
```

Listing 8.3: Working with the Value Mapping API

For the most part, the logic encoded in Listing 8.3 should have a similar feel to its graphical counterpart. Here, you simply specify the source/target identifiers and then perform a lookup using the static `executeMapping()` method provided by the `XIVMService` class. If an exception occurs during the lookup process, you can decide whether or not you wish to propagate the exception or return some kind of default value. The latter approach is demonstrated in Listing 8.3.

8.4.4   Performing Value Mappings in XSLT Programs

By default, XSLT programs do not have the capability to perform value mapping lookups. However, if you encapsulate the mapping lookup within a static Java method like the one shown in Listing 8.3, you can incorporate these lookups into your XSLT programs using the Java enhancement technique described in Chapter 7.

8.4.5   Performance Considerations

At runtime, value mapping lookups are performed against a cache of values stored within the mapping runtime environment. From a performance perspective, this implies that value mapping lookups run much faster than JDBC lookups, etc.

8.5   Mapping Lookups

Value mappings are useful if you need to map between two domains of values that are relatively static. However, sometimes you may encounter requirements that call for more complex mapping logic. For example, you might need to execute a query in an external database or call a function in a backend SAP system. In this section, we'll show you how to use the lookup API provided by the mapping runtime to perform these types of advanced mapping functions.

8.5.1   Conceptual Overview

From a development perspective, it is technically possible to implement mapping lookups directly by simply using core Java and SAP libraries. However, there are several downsides to this approach:

- ➢ The connection parameters used to initiate the call are typically concealed inside the mapping logic. This can cause logistical headaches as mapping programs are transported from system to system.

- ➢ You must pay careful attention to ensure that resources are managed properly (i.e. to avoid resource leaks, etc.).

- ➢ In some cases, the process of allocating connections on the fly within a mapping program can introduce significant overhead at runtime.

The aforementioned lookup API addresses these kinds of problems. As you can see in Figure 8.18, the lookup API provides an abstraction between a mapping program and connectivity brokered by the AAE. Not only does this abstraction simplify the way that connections are established, it also makes it easier to streamline the lookup process since developers only have to work with a single API.

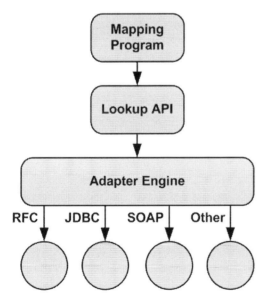

Figure 8.18: Understanding the Positioning of the Lookup API

The lookup API is available for use with any of the mapping techniques we have demonstrated thus far. In the upcoming sections, we'll show you how it can be used in different contexts.

8.5.2 Providing Connectivity

Before you can proceed with the development of a mapping lookup, you must adjust the signature of your operation mappings/mapping programs to receive a parameter of type *Adapter*. At configuration time, these parameters are bound to communication channels within the Integration Directory. Since we have not had much of an opportunity to explore communication channels thus far, suffice it to say that this assignment provides a mapping program with a physical connection to an external resource. At runtime, this connection is used by the lookup API to perform queries or execute functions.

Figure 8.19 demonstrates how you can define adapter parameters within an operation mapping. Here, we have defined a parameter called `LOOKUP_CONN` that is of type *JDBC*. At configuration time, this parameter will be bound with a receiver communication channel whose adapter type is the JDBC adapter.

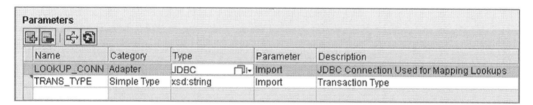

Figure 8.19: Defining Adapter Type Parameters in Operation Mappings

Besides the different category and type assignments, you'll find that adapter parameters work just like the simple parameter types described in Section 8.1.3. As such, you'll still need to define a binding between parameters of operation mappings and mapping programs.

8.5.3 Implementing Mapping Lookups

Regardless of the type of mapping lookup you're performing, you'll find that the steps required to perform a lookup using the lookup API are pretty much the same. In this section, we'll explore this process, highlighting some of the key functionality that you have at your disposal.

8.5.3.1   Working with the Java-Based Lookup API

Unlike a lot of complex APIs that are made up of hundreds of classes, the lookup API is relatively compact and easy to work with. Figure 8.20 contains a UML class diagram that depicts the relationships between the core classes in the `com.sap.aii.mapping.lookup` package[61]. As an extension of the mapping API, these classes can be used to perform lookups in UDFs, Java mapping programs, and XSLT programs that utilize Java enhancements.

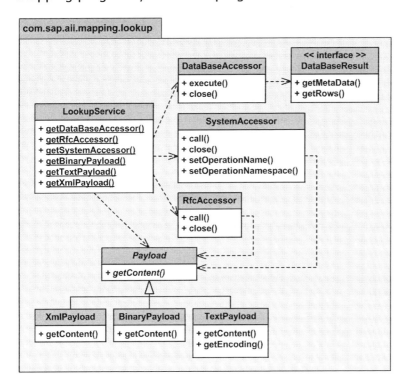

Figure 8.20: UML Class Diagram of Lookup API

To demonstrate how to work with the lookup API, let's consider an example. Here, let's imagine that you need to perform a lookup to determine a user's full name based upon their user account. Since this information is available in a backend SAP system, you want to call the RFC-enabled `BAPI_USER_GET_DETAIL` function to perform the lookup.

---

[61] You can find the JavaDocs for this package online at *http://help.sap.com/javadocs/*. From the main page, select the *PI 7.1 (Adapter, Module and Mapping Development)* link.

Listing 8.4 demonstrates how you could use the lookup API to execute this RFC call for a Java mapping class called RFCLookupDemo. As you can see, the majority of the heavy lifting has been delegated to a method called getUserFullName(). This method receives the configured adapter channel (in this case, of type RFC) and performs the following steps:

1. First, it uses the getRfcAccessor() factory method of class LookupService to obtain a reference to an RfcAccessor instance. This class is used to broker the RFC call.

2. Next, it builds the RFC request payload (as XML) and then serializes it to a java.io.InputStream.

3. Once the raw payload is built, it must be converted into a Payload instance that is compatible with the lookup API.

4. The RFC call is then executed via a call to the RfcAccessor class' call() method.

5. Finally, the response Payload instance is parsed and the results are passed back to the caller.

```java
import com.sap.aii.mapping.api.AbstractTransformation;
import com.sap.aii.mapping.api.StreamTransformationException;
import com.sap.aii.mapping.api.TransformationInput;
import com.sap.aii.mapping.api.TransformationOutput;
import com.sap.aii.mapping.lookup.*;

public class RFCLookupDemo
  extends AbstractTransformation
{
  public void transform(TransformationInput in,
                        TransformationOutput out)
    throws StreamTransformationException
  {
    try
    {
      // Retrieve the provided channel parameter:
      Channel channel =
        in.getInputParameters().getChannel("RFC_CHANNEL");

      // Perform message transformation as per usual...
      String userName = null;
```

```
    ...

    // Execute a mapping lookup:
    String fullName = getUserFullName(channel, userName);

    // Add the result to the generated target message:
    ...
  }
  catch (Exception ex)
  {
    // Exception Handling goes here...
  }
} // -- public void transform() -- //

private String getUserFullName(Channel channel,
                               String userName)
{
  // Method-Local Data Declarations:
  RfcAccessor accessor = null;

  // Process the lookup request:
  try
  {
    // Obtain a reference to a RfcAccessor instance:
    accessor = LookupService.getRfcAccessor(channel);

    // Build the RFC request payload (as XML) and convert it
    // to a java.io.InputStream:
    java.io.InputStream inputStream = null;
    ...

    // Use the LookupService class to build the request
    // payload:
    Payload payload = LookupService.getXmlPayload(inputStream);

    // Execute the lookup function:
    Payload result = accessor.call(payload);

    // Parse the result payload and return the results:
    ...
  }
  catch (Exception ex)
```

```
  {
    // Exception Handling goes here...
  }
  finally
  {
    // Close the accessor to release its resources:
    if (accessor != null)
      accessor.close();
  }
} // -- private String getUserFullName() -- //
} // -- End of class RFCLookupDemo -- //
```

Listing 8.4: Executing an RFC Call Using the Lookup API

For the most part, you'll find that the same steps outlined above also apply to other types of lookups. The primary difference is in the type of accessor class used to perform the lookup. Table 8.4 describes the different accessor classes provided with the lookup API.

Accessor Class	Usage
DataBaseAccessor	This accessor class is used to perform JDBC lookups using a provided JDBC receiver channel. In this case, instead of passing an XML payload, you pass in the SQL statement used to perform the query. The results are then passed back as a DataBaseResult class which is somewhat analogous to the java.sql.ResultSet class used in JDBC. See the API documentation for more details.
RFCAccessor	As demonstrated in Listing 8.4, the RfcAccessor class can be used to facilitate calls to RFC-enabled functions on a backend SAP system.
SystemAccessor	This accessor class is used for all other types of lookups (e.g. SOAP calls or synchronous calls made by some other compliant adapter type).

Table 8.4: Accessor Classes Provided by the Lookup API

8.5.3.2 Defining Lookups in Message Mappings

As you learned in Section 8.5.3.1, you can use the lookup API in graphical message mappings by defining UDFs. However, if you prefer not to work with UDFs, there is another alternative. Among the standard functions underneath the *Conversions* category, you'll find two functions that can be used to perform mapping lookups: JDBC lookup and RFC lookup. These functions can be used to model lookup functions using the JDBC and RFC adapters, respectively.

To demonstrate how these functions work, let's consider yet another extension of our example PO interface scenario. Here, imagine that the unit of measure values maintained in SAP ERP and the 3rd-party supply chain system differ from one another. Furthermore, let's suppose that the cross-reference table used to map between these two value domains is maintained in the 3rd-party system's database. Therefore, at runtime, we need to perform a query against that cross-reference table to look up the target unit of measure value. For this task, we'll utilize the JDBC lookup function.

For the most part, the process of modeling queries using the JDBC lookup function is relatively straightforward:

1. First off, you need to import metadata for the table that you wish to query against. This metadata is imported as a special type of external definition within the ESR.

2. Once the table metadata is imported, you can drag the JDBC lookup function into the data-flow editor.

3. By default, the JDBC lookup function does not define any inputs or outputs. Therefore, you must use fields from the imported table definition to define these parameters for the function.

4. Finally, after the parameters are defined, you can implement your value mappings as per usual by linking source/target fields with the function in the data-flow editor.

In the upcoming sections, we'll show you how to perform each of these tasks in turn. For the most part, you'll find that similar concepts apply when using the RFC lookup function.

Importing Table Metadata

In order to import table metadata into the ESR, you must create a special kind of external definition. The process for creating these external definitions is as follows:

1. To begin, right-click on the target SWCV/namespace that you want to develop in and select the *New* menu option.

2. In the ensuing *Create Object* dialog box, expand the *Interface Objects* submenu and select the *External Definition* menu option. Then, click on the *Create* button to create the new external definition.

3. In the external definition editor, select the category value `dbtab` and click on the search help button adjacent to the *Communication Channel* field.

4. This will open up the *Table Import* wizard shown in Figure 8.21. On the *Select Database* step, you'll browse to a JDBC receiver channel that is set up to connect to the target database. For now, we'll assume that someone has graciously created this receiver channel on your behalf. Click the *Continue* button to proceed.

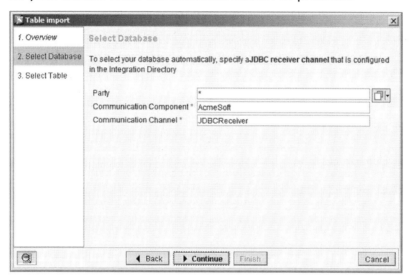

Figure 8.21: Importing Table Metadata into the ESR (Part 1)
© Copyright 2010. SAP AG. All rights reserved

5. Finally, on the *Select Table* step, you can use the search help provided for the *Table Name* input field to locate the target table. Once you find the table you're looking for, select it by double-clicking on it and then click on the *Finish* button to import the table's metadata (see Figure 8.22).

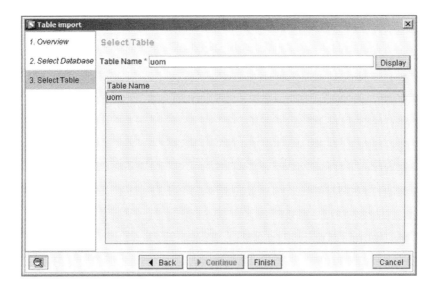

Figure 8.22: Importing Table Metadata into the ESR (Part 2)

Figure 8.23 shows what the external definition looks like after the table metadata is imported. Be sure to save your changes.

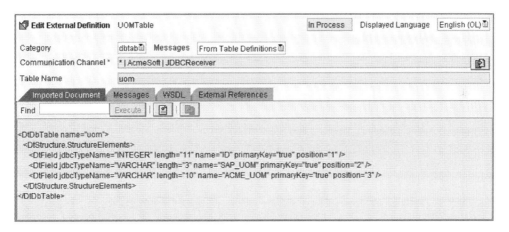

Figure 8.23: An External Definition Containing Table Metadata

Modeling the Query

Once you have imported the metadata for the table you wish to query from, you can begin modeling the query in the mapping editor by dragging the `JDBC lookup` function onto the data-flow editor canvas. Then, double-click on the function in the data-flow editor to bring up the *JDBC Lookup* dialog box shown in Figure 8.24. Here, there are three basic properties you must configure:

> ➢ In the drop-down list at the top of the window, you must select the adapter parameter that will be used to perform the lookup at runtime. Here, the parameter type must be JDBC.

> ➢ In the next field, you must select the external definition that contains the metadata for the table you wish to query against. You can use the provided value help to locate the external definition within the ESR.

> ➢ In the bottom portion of the editor, you must define the parameters used to execute the query as well as the result parameters. This can be achieved by selecting table fields from the center of the screen and clicking on the left and right arrows shown in Figure 8.24.

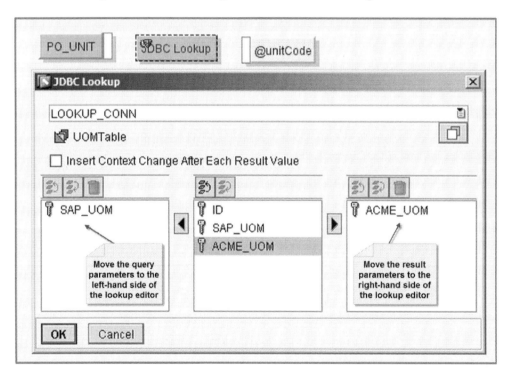

Figure 8.24: Modeling a JDBC Lookup in the Mapping Editor © Copyright 2010. SAP AG. All rights reserved

After the query is defined, you can click on the *OK* button to confirm your changes. At this point, the icon for the JDBC lookup function will be updated to reflect these parameter definitions. From here, you can define your target field mapping as per usual (see Figure 8.25).

Figure 8.25: Using the JDBC Lookup Function to Define a Value Mapping

8.5.4 Performance Considerations

Though mapping lookups are similar conceptually to value mappings, it would be a mistake to think that these features are interchangeable in terms of performance. With value mappings, the lookups are performed against a cache of values stored within the mapping runtime. Conversely, mapping lookups incur the overhead of connection allocation, message transmission, and so on.

The basic takeaway here is that, while mapping lookups are powerful, they should be used sparingly in order to conserve resources within the Integration Server. Obviously, if you can implement a mapping lookup using value mappings, you should strive to do so. Furthermore, in some cases, you might be able to redesign the sender/receiver interfaces to avoid such overhead. If the lookup can't be avoided, then so be it, but at least you tried your best to be a good steward of system resources.

8.6 Mapping Development in ABAP

One of the tricky things about staffing PI projects is the fact that most SAP developers are more at home with ABAP than they are with Java. Of course, while it certainly helps to have a Java developer or two on hand, this ABAP expertise doesn't have to go to waste. Besides the mapping techniques considered thus far, PI also supports the development of mapping programs in the ABAP Workbench. In this section, we'll show you how to create mapping programs using ABAP.

8.6.1 Configuring Support for ABAP Mappings

By default, support for ABAP mappings is not configured as part of a normal SAP NetWeaver PI installation. Therefore, if you want to develop mapping programs in ABAP, you'll need to work with your Basis staff to adjust the SAP NetWeaver PI *Exchange Profile*.

To configure support for ABAP mappings in PI, perform the following steps:

1. Log onto the Exchange Profile editor via the URL *http(s)://{AS Java Host}:{AS Java HTTP(s) port}/exchangeProfile/index.html*.

2. From the main page, expand the *IntegrationBuilder.Repository* node on the left-hand side of the page. Then, click on the node entitled *com.sap.aii.repository.mapping.additionaltypes*.

3. In the edit mask on the right-hand side of the screen, you'll need to enter the following value into the *com.sap.aii.repository.mapping.additionaltypes* input field:
   `R3_ABAP|ABAP Class;R3_XSLT|XSL (ABAP Engine).`

4. Finally, click on the *Save* button to save your changes. The changes will take effect after the next restart of the Integration Server.

Once the configuration changes are in place, you'll notice that the selected ABAP mapping program types will show up in the *Type* column contained within the *Mapping Program* table on the bottom portion of the operation mapping editor (see Figure 8.26). This will allow you to assign your ABAP-based mapping programs to an operation mapping as per usual.

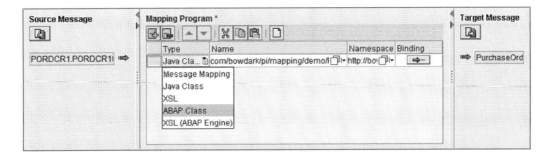

Figure 8.26: Selecting ABAP Mapping Programs in an Operation Mapping

8.6.2 Developing Mapping Classes in ABAP

ABAP mapping programs are developed using the familiar ABAP Workbench tool on the PI AS ABAP stack. As such, you'll find that they are managed just like any other ABAP-based development object in terms of activation, versioning, and so on. Furthermore, they are transported from one PI system to the next using the customary *Change and Transport System* (CTS).

Unlike some of the other ABAP-based development objects you might be accustomed to working with, ABAP mapping programs are developed as ABAP Objects classes. Therefore, in the upcoming sections, we'll show you how to develop mapping classes in ABAP. If you're not familiar with object-oriented programming in ABAP, don't worry – we'll show you what you need to know. However, if you're interested in learning more about these concepts, check out *Object-Oriented Programming with ABAP Objects* (Wood, 2009).

8.6.2.1 Creating a Mapping Class

For the most part, you'll find that PI mapping classes are created just like any normal ABAP Objects class. Indeed, the only PI-centric requirement is the implementation of an interface called `IF_MAPPING`. To create an ABAP mapping class in the ABAP Workbench, perform the following steps:

1. Log onto the AS ABAP stack and open up the Object Navigator (transaction SE80).

2. In the left-hand navigation area, select the `Package` option in the *Object List* and then fill in the package in which you wish to develop

your mapping class. Hit the *Enter* key to load the package into context (see Figure 8.27).

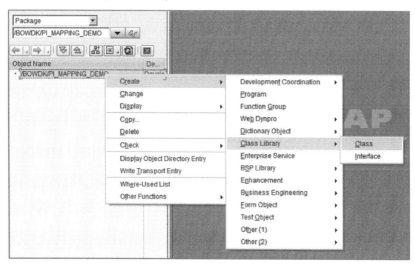

Figure 8.27: Creating a PI Mapping Class (Part 1)

3. Once the package is loaded, select it by right-clicking on it and then choose the menu option *Create → Class Library → Class* (see Figure 8.27).

4. In the ensuing *Create Class* dialog box shown in Figure 8.28, you must enter the following properties:

    a. In the *Class* and *Description* fields, you assign a name and an optional description for the class.

    b. In the *Instantiation* drop-down list, you'll want to keep the default `Public` instantiation context.

    c. In the *Class Type* area, you'll keep the default *Usual ABAP Class* selection.

    d. In the *Final* checkbox, you can determine whether or not the mapping class can be extended (or inherited from) in the future.

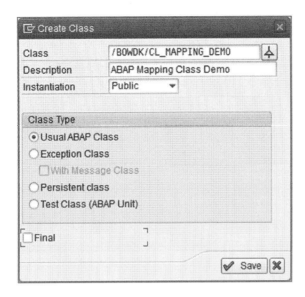

Figure 8.28: Creating a PI Mapping Class (Part 2)

5. Finally, you'll click on the *Save* button to create your new mapping class. Here, you will be prompted to confirm your package assignment and also assign the class to a transport request.

Once your mapping class is created, it will be loaded into Class Builder tool shown in Figure 8.29. Here, the first thing you will want to do is click on the *Interfaces* tab and implement the IF_MAPPING interface. This can be achieved by filling in the IF_MAPPING interface in the *Interface* column shown in Figure 8.29 and hitting the *Enter* key.

As soon as the interface implementation assignment as been made, you'll notice that the signature of the mapping class has been adjusted to include an implementation of the method EXECUTE() (see Figure 8.30). This method is analogous to the transform() method called in Java mappings in that it is the main method called when the mapping program is executed. As such, it will perform all of the heavy lifting at runtime.

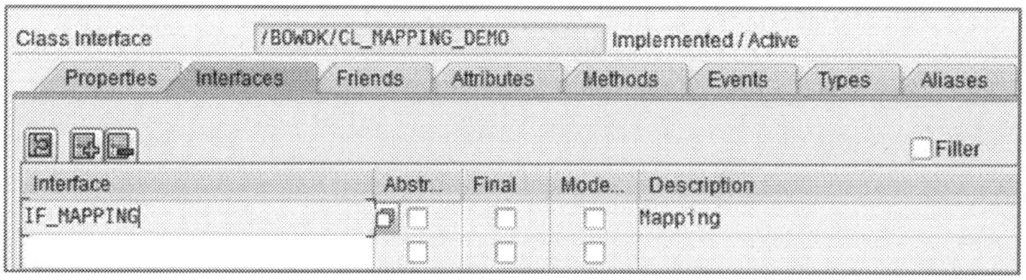

Figure 8.29: Editing a Mapping Class in the Class Builder (Part 1)

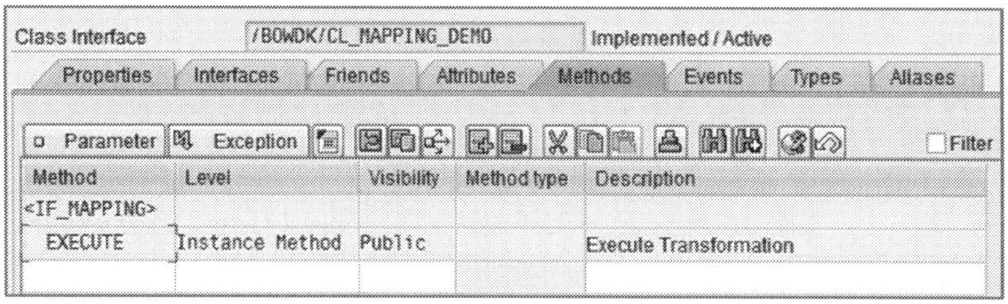

Figure 8.30: Editing a Mapping Class in the Class Builder (Part 2)

As you look at the signature of the EXECUTE() method, you'll discover that there are a number of parameters that you have to work with. Besides the obvious SOURCE and RESULT message parameters, you'll also find parameters for accessing mapping parameters, outputting trace messages, and so on. Table 8.5 describes each of these parameters in detail.

Parameter Name	Description
SOURCE	This parameter contains the raw payload of the source XML message passed to the mapping. It is of type XSTRING, which is the ABAP equivalent of a byte array in Java.
PARAM	This parameter allows you to retrieve runtime information about the mapping (e.g. the sender/receiver services, etc.). You can obtain these values by calling the GET() method defined in interface IF_MAPPING_PARAM.
TRACE	This parameter provides you with a reference to an object that can be used to output messages to the mapping trace. See interface IF_MAPPING_TRACE for more details.
PARAMETERS	This parameter can be used to access parameters that are passed from the encapsulating operation mapping. See interface IF_MAPPING_PARAMETERS for more details.
DYNAMIC_CONFIGURATION	This parameter can be used to manipulate adapter-specific message attributes. This API is described in the documentation for interface IF_MAPPING_DYNAMIC_CONF.
ATTACHMENTS	This parameter can be used to access attachments in the event that a message is passed with attachments. See interface IF_MAPPING_ATTACHMENTS for more details.
RESULT	You will use this parameter to serialize the target XML message that you generate during the mapping process. Like the SOURCE parameter, the RESULT parameter is also of type XSTRING.

Table 8.5: Parameters for Method IF_MAPPING~EXECUTE()

At this point, you should have everything in place to begin the development of your mapping class. However, even if you're familiar with ABAP, you might not know how to process XML with it. Therefore, in the next section, we'll show you how to process XML in ABAP.

8.6.2.2 Working with the iXML Library

Beginning with release 4.6C of the Basis kernel (which was the predecessor to the AS ABAP), SAP decided to integrate an XML 1.0-compliant parser into the ABAP runtime environment. This parser, along with the ABAP Objects-based API used to interface with it, makes up the *iXML Library*. Like most XML processing libraries, the iXML library allows you to process XML documents using DOM-based and event-based processing models. In addition, the iXML library also provides tools that make it easy to serialize documents to various output types, and so on.

Figure 8.31 contains a UML class diagram that highlights the core classes and interfaces that you'll be working with when using the iXML library. As you can see, the entry point into this API is the CL_IXML factory class. This class contains a public factory class method called CREATE() that can be used to return an instance of a class that implements the IF_IXML interface. The IF_IXML interface defines a series of instance methods that return references to objects that you can use to parse XML documents, create new XML documents from scratch, and so on.

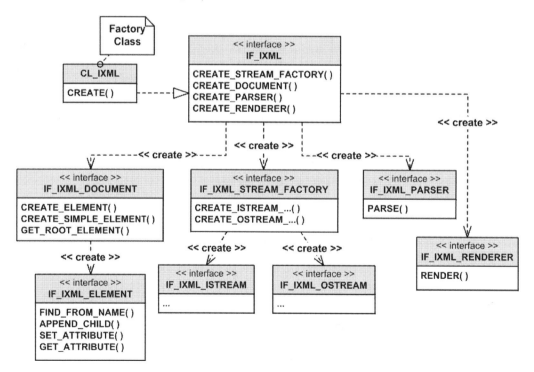

Figure 8.31: UML Class Diagram of iXML Library Classes

Note

The core of the iXML library is implemented using the C++ programming language, which has better support for raw stream-based I/O than ABAP. This implies that the ABAP portion of the iXML library is implemented via *kernel methods*. The interfaces defined in the iXML library shield developers from these low-level details, freeing SAP to swap out XML parser implementations as needed.

Now that you understand the positioning of the iXML library, let's see how it can be used to create mapping programs. In the following subsections, we'll show you how different classes/interfaces in the API can be used to implement various mapping requirements.

Parsing the Source Message

Before you can begin implementing your mapping logic, you must first parse the source message in a format that you can work with. For this task, you can choose between DOM-based parsing and event-based parsing. Which method you choose is mostly a matter of preference. However, as you learned in Chapter 2, the event-based model can prove to be more efficient in situations where you only need to process a fraction of the incoming data.

Listing 8.5 contains a code excerpt that demonstrates how to parse a source message using the iXML DOM API. As you can see, there are three basic steps required here:

1. First, we obtain a reference to the iXML library by calling the `CREATE()` method of factory class `CL_IXML`.

2. Then, we create a stream factory that is used to convert the raw source message into an input stream that is compatible with the iXML parser. For this, we're using the `CREATE_ISTREAM_XSTRING()` method that is designed to operate on raw `XSTRING` payloads.

3. Finally, we use the built-in parser implementation to generate a DOM-based document object that implements the `IF_IXML_DOCUMENT` interface.

If there are any errors discovered during the parsing process, you can iterate through them using methods provided via the `IF_IXML_PARSER` interface. For PI mapping programs, you'll want to propagate such errors back to the

Integration Engine so that they are captured in the message logs. This can be achieved by raising an exception of type CX_MAPPING_FAULT.

```
DATA:
  lo_ixml_factory    TYPE REF TO if_ixml,
  lo_stream_factory  TYPE REF TO if_ixml_stream_factory,
  lo_istream         TYPE REF TO if_ixml_istream,
  lo_document        TYPE REF TO if_ixml_document,
  lo_parser          TYPE REF TO if_ixml_parser,
  lo_exception       TYPE REF TO cx_root.

TRY.
  "Obtain a reference to the iXML factory class:
  lo_ixml_factory = cl_ixml=>create( ).

  "Convert the raw source message into an input stream:
  lo_stream_factory =
    lo_ixml_factory->create_stream_factory( ).

  lo_istream =
    lo_stream_factory->create_istream_xstring( im_source ).

  "Parse the source document:
  lo_document = lo_ixml_factory->create_document( ).

  lo_parser =
    lo_ixml_factory->create_parser(
      stream_factory = lo_stream_factory
      istream        = lo_istream
      document       = lo_document ).

  IF lo_parser->parse( ) NE 0.
    "Error handling goes here...
  ENDIF.
CATCH cx_root INTO lo_exception.
  RAISE EXCEPTION TYPE cx_mapping_fault
    EXPORTING
      previous = lo_exception.
ENDTRY.
```

Listing 8.5: Parsing a Document Using DOM

Assuming all goes well with the parsing process illustrated in Listing 8.5, the next step is to extract the relevant values from the source message that will be copied into the target message. This can be accomplished through methods defined in interfaces IF_IXML_DOCUMENT and IF_IXML_ELEMENT, respectively.

Listing 8.6 contains a code excerpt that demonstrates how these API methods work. As you can see, the first step is to obtain a reference to the root element of the source document. From there, you can iteratively scan through the document using methods defined in interface IF_IXML_ELEMENT. You can find detailed documentation for these methods in the online help documentation underneath the section entitled *XML Library* (SAP AG). Another useful reference is *XML Data Exchange Using ABAP* (Trapp, 2006).

```
DATA: lo_root_elem        TYPE REF TO if_ixml_element,
      lo_idoc_elem        TYPE REF TO if_ixml_element,
      lo_e1pordcr1_item   TYPE REF TO if_ixml_element,
      lo_header_elem      TYPE REF TO if_ixml_element,
      lo_po_number_elem   TYPE REF TO if_ixml_element,
      lv_po_number        TYPE string.

lo_root_elem = lo_source_doc->get_root_element( ).
lo_idoc_elem =
  lo_root_elem->find_from_name_ns( name = 'IDOC' ).
lo_e1pordcr1_elem =
  lo_idoc_elem->find_from_name_ns( name = 'E1PORDCR1' ).
lo_header_elem =
  lo_e1pordcr1_elem->find_from_name_ns( name = 'E1BPMEPOHEADER' ).

lo_po_number_elem =
  lo_e1bpmepoheader_elem->find_from_name_ns( 'PO_NUMBER' ).
lv_po_number =
  lo_po_number_elem->get_value( ).
```

Listing 8.6: Extracting Data from the Source Document

Note

Looking at the code excerpt in Listing 8.6, you can see that the code can get tedious in a hurry. Therefore, for simplicity's sake (and to improve program readability), we recommend that you copy the values from the source structure into an intermediate data structure (e.g. a structure or ABAP Objects class) that is easier to work with.

Building the Target Document

Once you have parsed the source document, you can use its contents to build the target document. Here, once again, you will use the DOM API to create the target document and fill in its structure. Listing 8.7 contains a code excerpt that demonstrates how this works.

```abap
DATA:
  lo_ixml_factory TYPE REF TO if_ixml,
  lo_target_doc   TYPE REF TO if_ixml_document,
  lo_po           TYPE REF TO if_ixml_element,
  lo_trans_type   TYPE REF TO if_ixml_element,
  lo_exception    TYPE REF TO cx_root.

TRY.
  "Obtain a reference to the iXML library:
  lo_ixml_factory = cl_ixml=>create( ).

  "Create the target document:
  lo_target_doc =
    lo_ixml_factory->create_document( ).

  lo_po =
    lo_target_doc->create_simple_element_ns(
      name   = 'PurchaseOrder'
      parent = lo_target_doc
      prefix = 'acme'
      uri    = `http://acme.com/schemas/purchasing` ).

  "Map the TransactionType element:
  lo_trans_type =
    lo_target_doc->create_simple_element_ns(
      name   = 'TransactionType'
      parent = lo_po ).
  lo_trans_type->set_value( 'Create' ).
  ...
CATCH cx_root INTO lo_exception.
  RAISE EXCEPTION TYPE cx_mapping_fault
    EXPORTING
      previous = lo_exception.
```

```
ENDTRY.
```

Listing 8.7: Building the Target Document Using DOM

As you can see in Listing 8.7, you create the target document using the `CREATE_DOCUMENT( )` method provided via the core `IF_IXML` interface. From there, you can map each of the underlying elements using the `CREATE_SIMPLE_ELEMENT_NS( )` method provided in interface `IF_IXML_DOCUMENT`.

Serializing the Results

The last step in the mapping development process is the serialization of the target document onto the result stream that gets passed back to the calling Integration Engine. Listing 8.8 contains a code excerpt that demonstrates how this can be accomplished. As you can see, there are essentially three steps required to serialize the target document:

1. First, you must generate an output stream that encapsulates the `RESULT` parameter. This is accomplished using the `CREATE_OSTREAM_XSTRING( )` method provided with interface `IF_IXML_STREAM_FACTORY`.

2. Next, you can optionally set the encoding of the output as the message is serialized using interface `IF_IXML_ENCODING`.

3. Finally, you create a *renderer* object (i.e. of type `IF_IXML_RENDERER`) to serialize the document. This is realized via a call to the `RENDER()` method.

```
DATA: lo_ixml_factory     TYPE REF TO if_ixml,
      lo_target_doc       TYPE REF TO if_ixml_document,
      lo_stream_factory   TYPE REF TO if_ixml_stream_factory,
      lo_ostream          TYPE REF TO if_ixml_ostream,
      lo_encoding         TYPE REF TO if_ixml_encoding,
      lo_renderer         TYPE REF TO if_ixml_renderer,
      lo_exception        TYPE REF TO cx_root.

TRY.
  "Obtain a reference to the iXML library:
  lo_ixml_factory = cl_ixml=>create( ).

  "Populate the target document:
  lo_target_doc =
```

```
    lo_ixml_factory->create_document( ).
  ...


  "Create an output stream for the results:
  lo_stream_factory =
    lo_ixml_factory->create_stream_factory( ).
  lo_ostream =
    lo_stream_factory->create_ostream_xstring( result ).

  "Set the encoding of the output stream to UTF-8:
  lo_encoding =
    lo_ixml_factory->create_encoding( character_set = 'UTF-8'
                                      byte_order = 0 ).
  lo_ostream->set_encoding( lo_encoding ).

  "Serialize the results:
  lo_renderer =
    lo_ixml_factory->create_renderer(
      ostream  = lo_ostream
      document = lo_target_doc ).

  IF lo_renderer->render( ) NE 0.
    RAISE EXCEPTION TYPE cx_mapping_fault.
  ENDIF.
CATCH cx_root INTO lo_exception.
  RAISE EXCEPTION TYPE cx_mapping_fault
    EXPORTING
      previous = lo_exception.
ENDTRY.
```

Listing 8.8: Serializing the Results of a Target Document

Putting it all Together

For brevity's sake, we could not include a complete ABAP mapping program example in this text. However, we have provided a transport package that contains a sample ABAP mapping program in the source code bundle available for this chapter online.

8.6.2.3 Parameterized ABAP Mapping Programs

In addition to parameterized mapping programs on the Java stack, you can also pass parameters to ABAP mapping programs via the PARAMETERS parameter passed to the IF_MAPPING~EXECUTE() method. Here, you can access the parameters within your mapping program by calling the relevant getter methods provided with the `IF_MAPPING_PARAMETERS` interface. The parameter bindings are configured in the same way that you define bindings for Java mapping programs.

8.6.3   Creating XSLT Mappings on the ABAP Stack

Another option you have for developing mapping programs in the ABAP Workbench is to create XSLT mapping programs using the *Transformation Editor*. Here, the development model is essentially the same as the one described for Java-based XSLT mapping programs in Chapter 7.

To create an XSLT mapping program in the ABAP Workbench, perform the following steps:

1. Log onto the AS ABAP stack and open up the Object Navigator (transaction SE80).

2. In the left-hand navigation area, select the `Package` option in the *Object List* and then fill in the package in which you wish to develop your mapping class. Hit the *Enter* key to load it into context.

3. Once the package is loaded, select it by right-clicking on it and then choose the menu option *Create* → *Other (1)* → *Transformation* (see Figure 8.32).

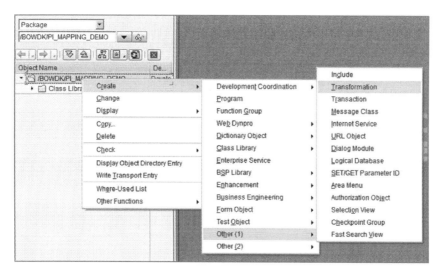

Figure 8.32: Creating an XSLT Transformation (Part 1)

4. In the ensuing *Create Transformation* dialog box, you must fill in the following properties:

    a. In the *Transformation* input field, you must select a name for the transformation program.

    b. In the *Short Description* field, you can provide an optional description for the transformation program.

    c. In the *Transformation Type* field, you'll want to select the value XSLT Program.

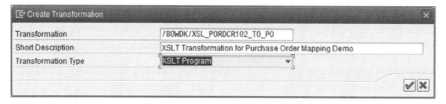

Figure 8.33: Creating an XSLT Transformation (Part 2)

5. Finally, hit the *Enter* key to create the transformation program. Here, you will be prompted to confirm your package assignment and assign the transformation program to a transport request.

Once your transformation program is created, you can edit it in the Transformation Editor screen shown in Figure 8.34. Here, you'll find syntax highlighting, syntax check tools, as well as some testing tools that you can use to determine whether or not your mapping logic is correct. The aforementioned *XSLT Data Exchange Using ABAP* (Trapp, 2006) describes each of these features in great detail.

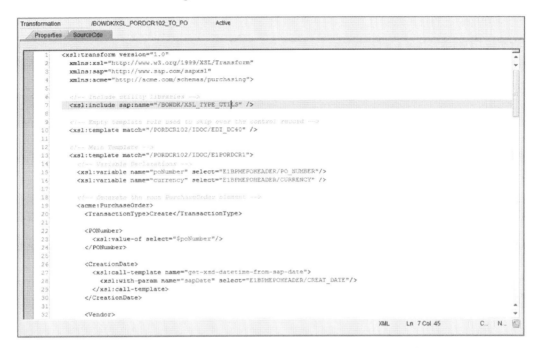

Figure 8.34: Editing an XSLT Program in the Transformation Editor

8.7   Summary

In this chapter, we explored some advanced message mapping topics within SAP NetWeaver PI. While you may not use all of these tools in your normal day-to-day development, it's nice to know that they're there when you need them. In the next chapter, we'll move on from mapping and take a look at another type of design object that can be used for mediated collaboration: *integration processes*.

References

Glas, P. (n.d.). *PI Parameterized XSLT - A Flexible Alternative.* Retrieved March 23, 2011, from SAP Developer Network (SDN): http://www.sdn.sap.com/irj/scn/weblogs?blog=/pub/wlg/20742

Martens, U. (n.d.). *Value Mapping Replication Scenario.* Retrieved December 4, 2010, from SAP SDN: http://www.sdn.sap.com/irj/scn/weblogs?blog=/pub/wlg/13812

SAP AG. (n.d.). *Function Libraries.* Retrieved December 12, 2010, from SAP Help Library: http://help.sap.com/saphelp_nwpi711/helpdata/en/43/78bd467afa345ae100 00000a422035/frameset.htm

SAP AG. (n.d.). *Multi-Mappings.* Retrieved December 13, 2010, from SAP Help Library: http://help.sap.com/saphelp_nwpi711/helpdata/en/21/6faf35c2d74295a3cb9 7f6f3ccf43c/frameset.htm

SAP AG. (n.d.). *PI Best Practices Naming Conventions.* Retrieved December 9, 2010, from SAP Developer Network: http://www.sdn.sap.com/irj/scn/index?rid=/library/uuid/40a66d0e-fe5e-2c10-8a85-e418b59ab36a

SAP AG. (n.d.). *Value Mapping.* Retrieved December 14, 2010, from SAP Help Library: http://help.sap.com/saphelp_nwpi711/helpdata/en/4a/3642f503df044fe1000 0000a421937/frameset.htm

SAP AG. (n.d.). *Value Mapping Replication for Mass Data.* Retrieved December 14, 2010, from SAP Help Library: http://help.sap.com/saphelp_nwpi711/helpdata/en/4a/3626a9d5e92ab1e10 000000a42189c/frameset.htm

SAP AG. (n.d.). *XML Library.* Retrieved December 16, 2010, from SAP Help Library: http://help.sap.com/saphelp_nwpi711/helpdata/en/47/b5413acdb62f70e100 00000a114084/frameset.htm

Trapp, T. (2006). *XML Data Exchange Using ABAP.* Boston: Galileo Press, Inc.

Wood, J. (2009). *Object-Oriented Programming with ABAP Objects.* Boston: Galileo Press, Inc.

Integration Processes

9

Interfaces rarely exist in isolation. Most of the time, you'll find that systems exchange a series of related messages back and forth with one another in coordinated fashion. Sometimes, these interactions may require an intermediary to direct traffic or deal with exceptions. In SAP NetWeaver PI, such mediated collaboration can be implemented using *integration processes*.

After completing this chapter, you will be able to:

❖ Understand what integration processes are and realize how they are used to orchestrate complex integration scenarios.

❖ Use the process editor to define and edit integration processes.

❖ Recognize situations in which integration processes should and shouldn't be used.

9.1 Basic Concepts

As a developer down in the trenches, it is often difficult to see the big picture when it comes to interface development. For instance, you may be tasked to work on a couple of interfaces going one direction while your teammates develop interfaces going the other direction. Nevertheless, you can rest assured that interface requirements do not simply appear out of thin air. Rather, they are identified by business analysts as being part of a larger business process that may span system and/or corporate boundaries.

In Part 3 of this book, we'll see how these business processes come together in the Integration Directory. Here, for the most part, you'll find that the vast majority of distributed business processes can be realized by simply exchanging messages between systems in asynchronous fashion. However, there are times when more sophisticated message choreography is required. In these situations, you can enlist the aid of *integration processes*.

In this chapter, we'll introduce you to integration processes and show you where and when they can be used to enhance message processing within SAP NetWeaver PI.

9.1.1 What are Integration Processes?

According to SAP, an integration process is "...an executable cross-system process for processing messages. Integration processes are applied whenever you want to define, control, and monitor complex business processes that extend beyond the enterprise and application boundaries" (SAP AG). In this light, you can think of integration processes as a programmable layer within the Integration Server, allowing you to plug in the logic needed to handle more complex business requirements.

From a development perspective, the term *integration process* takes on different meanings depending upon where you are in the interface development process:

> **Design Time**
> At design time, an integration process is defined as a repository object within the ESR. Here, you can use a graphical editor tool to design and maintain integration processes (see Figure 9.1).

> **Configuration Time**
>
> At configuration time, an integration process is positioned as a type of logical communication component that can exchange messages with other communication components (i.e. business systems, business components, and even other integration processes).

> **Runtime**
>
> At runtime, integration processes run within the *Business Process Engine* (BPE). As an extension of the WebFlow Engine used to process SAP Business Workflow processes, the BPE provides a container that supports stateful processing, event handling, and so on.

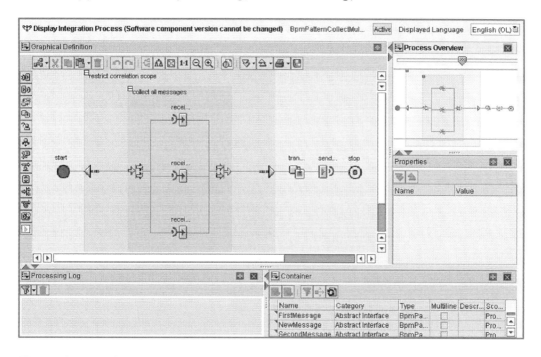

Figure 9.1: Maintaining Integration Processes in the ESR © Copyright 2010. SAP AG. All rights reserved

Behind the scenes, the process editor encodes the business process logic defined within an integration process using the industry standard *Web Services Business Process Execution Language* (WS-BPEL) language[62]. Whenever an integration process is activated, the system uses this meta model as the basis for generating a workflow definition on the backend AS

---

[62] For more information about WS-BPEL, check out *http://docs.oasis-open.org/wsbpel/2.0/wsbpel-v2.0.html*.

ABAP system. It is this workflow definition that executes at runtime within the BPE.

9.1.2   When Should Integration Processes be Used?

Among all of the various features offered by SAP NetWeaver PI, integration processes are perhaps the most misunderstood. Some developers avoid them like the plague, while others tend to overuse them in situations where they don't really make sense. In order to strike a balance between these two extremes, you must find a way to identify the places where integration processes should and shouldn't be used.

The first and most basic rule of thumb here is to only use integration processes in places where you actually need them. For example, if you're implementing a simple point-to-point interface with no complex message orchestration requirements, plugging in an integration process is overkill. Beyond this basic principle, some other design prerequisites that you should take into account are as follows:

> ➢ The messages exchanged within the integration process should be closely related in terms of their semantic meaning.

> ➢ When dealing with related messages, the criteria used to establish linkages between messages must be unambiguous.

> ➢ Though integration processes execute within a workflow engine, they are not a replacement for workflow. In particular, they should not be used to implement processes that require user interactions, etc.

> ➢ Integration processes should not incorporate business logic that belongs on the endpoint systems.

> ➢ The business process(es) that you model with integration processes must have a defined end state.

If you're unsure as to whether or not your particular integration scenario meets the basic criteria, we recommend that you review the checklist that SAP has published with their online help documentation. Underneath the section entitled *Defining and Managing Integration Processes* select the link *Checklist: Making Correct Use of Integration Processes* (SAP AG).

9.1.3   Performance Considerations

Though integration processes are powerful, that power comes at a price. In order to implement stateful and event-driven processing, the BPE must keep track of every aspect of the business process. This includes copies of messages that are being exchanged, overall status information for the process, and so on. If you're only dealing with a handful of messages at a time, then the additional overhead is probably not of much concern. However, in situations where the system is processing thousands of messages an hour, the increase in the demand for system resources can increase exponentially.

The basic takeaway from all this is to be careful not to disregard performance issues when designing integration processes. Otherwise, you may find yourself in the unenviable situation of trying to troubleshoot bottlenecks in message processing, etc. For specific questions about performance issues with integration processes, see SAP Note 857530.

9.2   Working with the Process Editor

Before we embark on a detailed discussion on the ins-and-outs of integration processes, it is first a good idea to get acquainted with the tool that you'll use to define them: the *process editor*. This complex editor tool streamlines the development process, compartmentalizing various aspects of integration process development into a series of interchangeable views.

9.2.1   Creating an Integration Process

Before we can demonstrate the functions and features of the process editor, we first need to show you how to create an integration process. Here, you must perform the following steps:

1. To begin, right-click on the target SWCV/namespace that you want to develop in and select the *New* menu option.

2. In the ensuing *Create Object* dialog box, expand the *Process Integration Scenario Objects* submenu and select the *Integration Process* menu option.

3. Next, you must enter a name[63] and an optional description for your integration process. Click on the *Create* button to continue.

4. Once your integration process is created, it will be loaded into the process editor screen shown in Figure 9.2. Click the *Save* button to save your changes.

9.2.2   Navigating within the Process Editor

As you'll soon see, you can do a lot with integration processes. Therefore, in order to support you in the configuration of all these features, SAP had to cram a lot of functionality into the process editor. To maximize space, the process editor screen was split into a series of *editor areas* that contain related views. Figure 9.2 illustrates how the editor areas are laid out within the process editor screen.

Table 9.1 describes the function of each of the editor areas outlined in Figure 9.2. Within these editor areas, you can toggle between different views by clicking on the ▣ button on the top left-hand corner of the area. You can also maximize or close a particular editor area by clicking on the ▣ and ▣ buttons on the top right-hand corner of an area, respectively.

---

[63] Consult the SAP NetWeaver How-To Guide entitled *PI Best Practices: Naming Conventions* (SAP AG) for naming conventions.

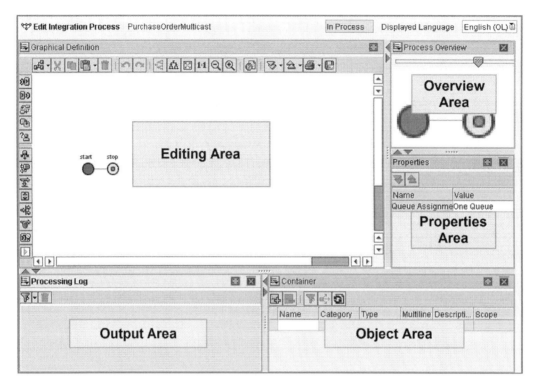

*Figure 9.2: Navigating within the Process Editor © Copyright 2010. SAP AG.
All rights reserved*

Editor Area	Provided Views	Description
Editing Area	Graphical Definition	In this view, you implement the core logic of your integration process by linking together a series of step definitions.
	BPEL Display	You can switch to this view to see the WS-BPEL code being generated behind the scenes by the process editor.
	Correlation Editor	This editor view enables you to define and configure *correlations*. We'll learn more about correlations in Section 9.3.9.

Editor Area	Provided Views	Description
Overview Area	Process Overview	This view allows you to observe an integration process at different levels of magnification. You can view the whole process, or zoom in on specific parts.
	Dependent Objects	In this view, you can generate a "where-used" list of repository objects utilized by the integration process.
	Process Outline	You can use this view to visualize the integration process in a hierarchical manner. Here, the individual steps are displayed in an editable list that allows you to rearrange the process flow.
Properties Area	N/A	This view is used to maintain the various properties of a selected step in the graphical definition view.
Output Area	Processing Log	This view displays the various messages issued by the editor as you proceed through the development process.
	Tasks	This view contains messages issued by the syntax check function integrated into the process editor.
	Search Result	This view contains search results for step searches launched via the *Search for Steps* 🔍 button in the top-level toolbar of the graphical definition view.
Object Area	Container	In this view, you define the *container elements* (or variables) used to maintain state within the integration process.

Editor Area	Provided Views	Description
	Correlation List	This view is used to define correlations.
	Process Signature	This view displays the *signature* of the integration process in terms of the abstract messages it sends and receives.
	Configurable Parameters	In this view, you can define the parameters that an integration process will receive at runtime. See the online help documentation for more details.

Table 9.1: Editor Areas within the Process Editor

9.3　Functional Overview

Integration processes are initiated by the receipt of a message passed in from the Integration Engine. From here, the process flow is directed by a series of *processing steps* defined within the integration process. These processing steps correspond with typical programming language elements such as loops, conditional logic statements, and so on. Collectively, you can assemble processing steps to implement the requisite business process logic.

In this section, we'll explore the functions that you can use to define integration processes. However, as a detailed treatment on each of these functions could fill an entire book, we'll focus our discussion on some of the more common functions used to create process definitions[64].

9.3.1　Step Types

As you develop integration processes within the process editor, you'll find yourself spending a lot of time in the graphical definition view of the main editing area. As you can see in Figure 9.3, this view contains a number of toolbar buttons on the left-hand side of the screen that enable you to select the processing steps required for your integration process.

---

[64] You can find reference material for all of the supported functions in the online help documentation underneath the section entitled *Defining an Integration Process* (SAP AG).

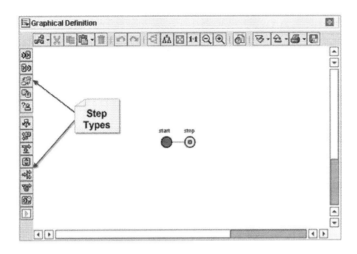

Figure 9.3: Configurable Step Types within the Process Editor © Copyright 2010. SAP AG. All rights reserved

To add a processing step to your integration process, you simply click on a step type in the toolbar and then drag it over to the desired location within the process flow. Here, the orange brackets will guide you in positioning the step in the proper location within the process definition (see Figure 9.4).

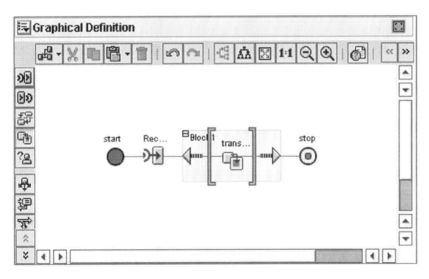

Figure 9.4: Inserting a Processing Step into an Integration Process © Copyright 2010. SAP AG. All rights reserved

For the most part, you'll find that the available step types within the process editor are fairly intuitive. All the same, Table 9.2 describes each of these step types in detail.

Step Type	Icon	Description
Receive Step		The receive step is used to receive messages into an integration process. As such, it is always the first step defined within an integration process. Of course, it can also be used to receive messages later on in an event-based fashion.
Send Step		This step is used to send messages from an integration process. The receiver components can be business systems, logical business components, or even other integration processes. Messages can be sent synchronously or asynchronously.
Receiver Determination Step		With this step type, you can dynamically determine the receiver(s) of a message using a receiver determination configured in the Integration Directory. The receiver list can then be used in conjunction with the send step to forward messages on to receivers.
Transformation Step		This step type can be used to call operation mappings defined within the ESR. Here, you can perform simple 1-to-1 transformations or use multi-mappings to split messages apart or merge messages together.

Integration Processes | 331

Step Type	Icon	Description
User Decision Step		You can use this step type to allow users to make decisions about how to proceed with a process in situations where certain conditions are not met. Users receive the decision requests as work items in their workflow inbox on the PI AS ABAP stack (Transaction SBWP). To understand how user decision steps work, imagine that you are using an integration process to collect a series of messages and forward them on to some target system. If all of the source messages have not been received within a given amount of time, you might use a user decision step to allow a user to determine how the process should proceed. Here, you could configure different user options to allow a user to extend the deadline, terminate the process, and so on.
Switch Step		This step type behaves similarly to the `switch` statement in Java or the `CASE` statement in ABAP in that it allows you to define multiple branches within the process logic based upon certain logical conditions.
Container Operation		This step type is used to build simple expressions that initialize container elements, increment counters, and so on.
Control Step		The control step can be used to: ➤ Terminate the integration process. ➤ Raise an exception. ➤ Trigger an alert that is forwarded on to key stakeholders involved in the process.
Block		The block step type is used to define a *block* in which related steps are combined. As such, it behaves similarly to a try block in modern programming languages such as ABAP Object or Java. Here, you can group together steps that make up a logical unit of work (LUW) and define common exception handling routines, transactional behavior, and so on. We'll explore these concepts further in Section 9.3.8.

Step Type	Icon	Description
Fork Step		The fork step type allows you to split the integration process flow into independent branches (or threads) that run in parallel. These branches come back together whenever a specified condition is met.
Loop Step		The loop step type is the functional equivalent of `while` loops found in programming languages such as ABAP or Java.
Wait Step		The wait step type is used to interject a delay in the process. The duration of the wait time can be in minutes, hours, days, or even months and years. Wait steps can be useful in situations where you are waiting for some condition to be met before proceeding. Here, you might have your process sit in a tight loop, periodically checking on the availability of some resource. If the resource is not found, you can wait a given amount of time before checking again to avoid unnecessary resource consumption.
Undefined Step		You can use this step type as a placeholder for some step that has not yet been defined. Such steps are not taken into account at runtime.

Table 9.2: Step Types for Integration Processes

9.3.2 Defining Abstract Interfaces

As we mentioned earlier, integration processes take on the role of communication component at runtime. In order to communicate with these intermediary components, you must define the component's *interface* (or *signature*). This interface makes it possible for the Integration Server to exchange messages with an integration process instance at runtime.

To model the signature of an integration process, you must define *abstract service interfaces*. For the most part, you'll find that the process of defining abstract interfaces is the same as the one used to define concrete service interfaces. The primary difference here is in the selection of the `Abstract` category value (see Figure 9.5).

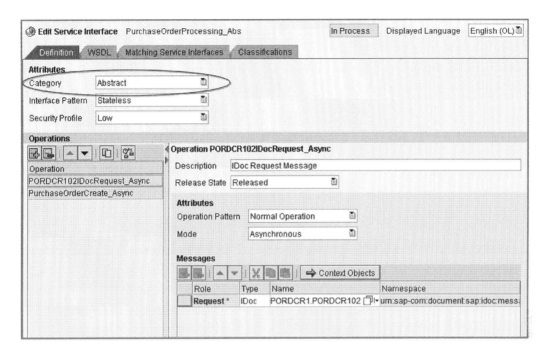

Figure 9.5: Defining Abstract Interfaces in the ESR © Copyright 2010. SAP AG. All rights reserved

Within an integration process, abstract service interfaces are also used to define the messages created in a transformation step, sent or received from a synchronous send step, and so on. Therefore, your approach to abstract service interface development will be slightly different than the one described in Chapter 6. For example, to model a synchronous interface in an integration process, you would generally require three abstract service interfaces:

> ➢ An abstract interface that defines a synchronous operation to represent the synchronous interface call.

> ➢ An abstract interface that defines an asynchronous operation to represent the request message in the synchronous call.

> ➢ And an abstract interface that defines an asynchronous operation to represent the response message from the synchronous call.

In the upcoming sections, all of this will become much clearer as you see how messages are sent and received by integration processes.

Design Tip

Integration processes require referenced objects such as abstract interfaces to be defined within the same SWCV or an underlying SWCV. Since these artifacts in turn usually depend on repository objects defined in other SWCVs (e.g. message type definitions, etc.), we recommend that you define a usage dependency in the SLD between the SWCV that defines your integration process and those SWCVs that contain the repository objects needed to create the abstract interfaces.

9.3.3 Working with Container Elements

In order to implement stateful processing, integration processes need to keep track of various pieces of information. Examples of these data elements include:

> Copies of the messages that are being exchanged.

> Simple variables such as counters or flags.

> A list of receivers that should receive a particular message.

Within an integration process, these variables are defined as *container elements*.

Container elements are maintained within the *Container* view in the lower-right hand object area of the process editor. As you can see in Figure 9.6, this view contains a table in which you can define individual container elements. Table 9.3 describes each of the attributes you can configure within this table.

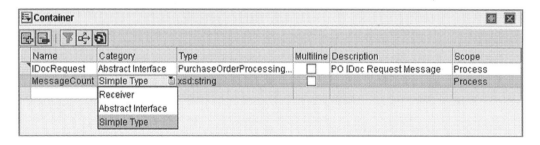

Figure 9.6: Defining Container Elements in the Process Editor © Copyright 2010. SAP AG. All rights reserved

Attribute	Possible Values	Description
Name	N/A	This attribute specifies the name of the container element that will be used in step definitions, etc.
Category	Receiver Abstract Interface Simple Type	The Category attribute determines the *role* of the container element: ➢ For simple variables such as counters or flags, you'll select the value Simple Type. ➢ The Abstract Interface category is used to define container elements that represent the messages that are processed by the integration process. ➢ The Receiver category is used to define container elements that represent a list of receivers dynamically derived via the receiver determination step.
Type	If the category value is Abstract Interface, then the Type attribute will point to an abstract service interface definition in the ESR. If the Category value is Simple Type, then you can choose between the following XSD built-in types: ➢ xsd:string ➢ xsd:integer ➢ xsd:date ➢ xsd:time	This attribute is used to further specify the type of the container element. Here, the possible values to choose from will depend upon the selection of the Category attribute.

Attribute	Possible Values	Description
Multiline	True or False	If this attribute is checked, the container element will expand to hold a collection of values. Multiline container elements are similar to arrays in Java or internal tables in ABAP.
Description	N/A	This attribute can be used to provide a brief description about a container element.
Scope	`Process {Block}`	This attribute is used define the *scope* of the container element. Here, you can assign a process-wide scope, or narrow the scope down to a particular block definition within the integration process.

Table 9.3: Container Element Attributes

9.3.3.1 Performing Container Operations

In the upcoming sections, we'll see how container elements are used to define the inputs and outputs of various step types. In addition to these implicit assignments, you can also use the container operation step to explicitly assign values to container elements. Here, container operations are used to increment counters, toggle flags, and perform various other housekeeping tasks for container elements.

You can insert a container operation step into your process definition by clicking on the *Container Operation* button and dragging it onto the canvas at the desired location. Then, you can configure the operation in the properties area on the right-hand side of the editor screen. For example, Figure 9.7 illustrates how we have defined a container operation that is used to increment a counter variable. Here, the properties are configured as follows:

> ➢ In the *Step Name* and *Description* properties, we have assigned a name and optional description for the container operation.

> ➢ In the *Target* property, we have selected the container element `MessageCount`, which is of type `xsd:integer`. This container element represents the l-value in the expression.

> ➢ With the *Operation* property, you can determine whether or not the operation will assign a value to a simple container element, or append a record to a multiline container element.

> ➢ For assignment operations, you can use the *Expression* and *Operator* properties to build an assignment expression. For example, in Figure 9.7, we are incrementing the `MessageCount` variable by a constant value of 1.

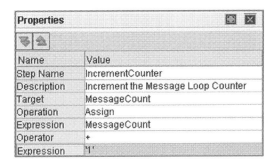

Figure 9.7: Configuring a Container Operation © Copyright 2010. SAP AG. All rights reserved

9.3.4   Switches, Loops, and Forks

One of the most powerful features of integration processes is their ability to control the flow of messages as they travel in and out of the system. This capability is driven by step types that behave similarly to familiar control statements found in programming languages such as Java or ABAP. In this section, we'll explore the control steps that you have at your disposal with integration processes.

9.3.4.1 Conditional Logic with Switches

You can define conditional logic within your process definition using the *switch step*. With this step, you can configure different branches in the process logic that are controlled by Boolean expressions referred to as *conditions*. An example of a condition might be a check to see if a particular element within the source document's payload is equal to some constant value, etc.

At runtime, the conditions for each branch in a switch step are checked sequentially until a match is found. If no match is found for any of the specified conditions, control will continue with the default *Otherwise* branch that is automatically created by the system.

Figure 9.8 illustrates the graphical representation of a switch step. As you can see, each branch within the switch defines a boxed area in which you can insert a series of steps that should be performed whenever a condition is met. You can insert additional branches into the switch step by right-clicking on it and selecting the menu option *Insert → Branch*.

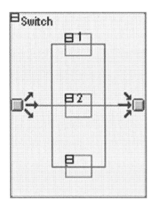

Figure 9.8: Working with Switches © Copyright 2010. SAP AG. All rights reserved

To configure the condition for a particular branch, select the branch in the graphical definition view and then click on the value help provided with the *Condition* property in the properties area on the right-hand side of the screen. This will open up the *Condition Editor* dialog box shown in Figure 9.9. Here, you can combine Boolean operators with values found in container elements or source messages to build logical expressions. For more information about how to define conditions using this tool, consult the online help documentation underneath the section entitled *Define a Condition* (SAP AG).

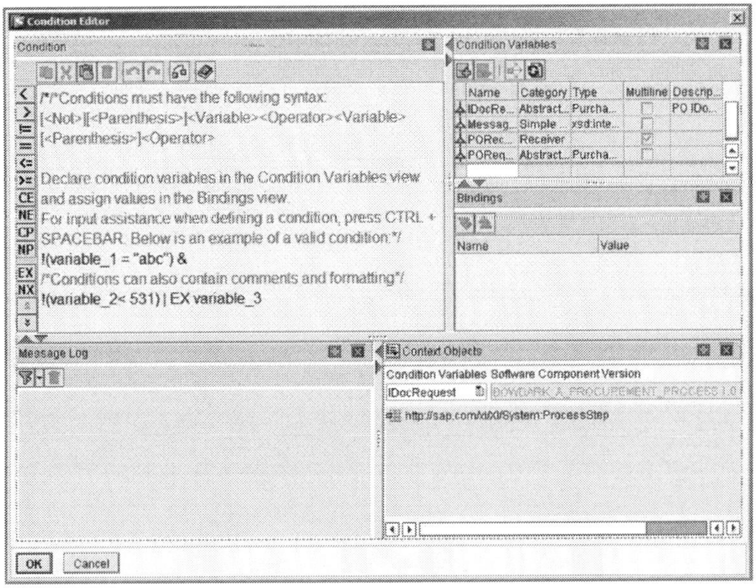

Figure 9.9: Defining Conditions in the Condition Editor © Copyright 2010. SAP AG. All rights reserved

9.3.4.2 Defining Loops

From a behavioral standpoint, the loop step is functionally equivalent to the while loop found in most programming languages. Here, the loop is controlled by a condition which is configured using the condition editor tool described in Section 9.3.4.1. If the specified condition is met, then the loop will continue to run until that condition no longer applies. Of course, if the specified condition is never true, then the loop won't execute at all.

Figure 9.10 illustrates how the loop step is depicted within a process definition. Within this step, you can insert the steps that should be executed within a given loop iteration.

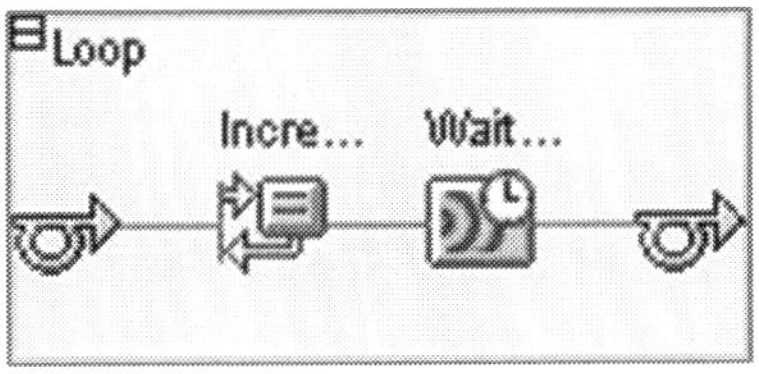

Figure 9.10: Working with Loops © Copyright 2010. SAP AG. All rights reserved

9.3.4.3 Parallelization with Forks

As you learned in Section 9.3.1, forks are used to split the process flow into separate branches that run in parallel. Like the switch step, each branch in a fork step is controlled by a condition. As particular conditions are met, the process flow splits off and executes the steps defined within the related branches. Ultimately, everything comes back together whenever one of the following conditions is met:

> ➤ Each of the defined branches has executed to completion.

> ➤ The specified end condition for the fork step is met.

In the latter case, the end condition is specified using the condition editor described previously. Here, for example, you might define a condition that states that the fork should end whenever x number of messages have been received, and so on.

Figure 9.11 illustrates how SAP is using the fork step to collect messages in the sample `BpmPatternCollectMultiIf` process provided with the `SAP BASIS` software component. Here, the fork step is defined with three branches that wait to receive a particular type of message. Once all three messages have been received, the process continues with the next step.

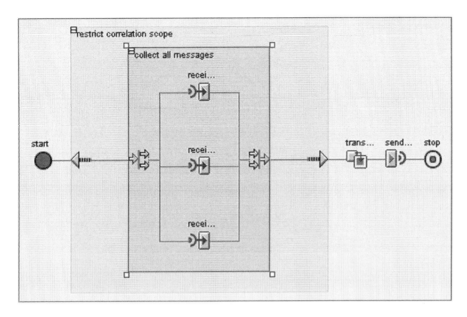

Figure 9.11: Working with Forks © Copyright 2010. SAP AG. All rights reserved

9.3.5   Sending and Receiving Messages

As we mentioned earlier, an integration process is triggered by the receipt of a message. Therefore, the first step in every integration process definition is always the receive step. From there, an integration process can use the send and receive steps to interactively communicate with other communication components. In this section, we'll see how all this works.

9.3.5.1   Receiving Messages with the Receive Step

For the most part, you'll find that the receive step is very easy to work with. In general, you can configure this step as follows:

1. First, you simply click on the *Receive* button in the left-hand toolbar of the graphical definition view and drag it over into the proper position within your process definition.

2. Then, in the properties area on the right-hand side of the screen, you must select a name and optional description for the step.

3. Finally, in the *Message* input field, you assign the incoming message to a container element whose category value is `Abstract Interface`.

To some extent, you'll find that the configuration process varies slightly depending upon whether or not the receive step initiates the integration process. If it does, then there are two additional properties that you will need to configure (see Figure 9.12):

➢ The *Start Process* checkbox is used to indicate that the receive step kicks off the integration process. This checkbox can only be checked for the first receiver step in the process definition. However, you can use a fork step to split the process such that there are multiple initial receiver steps that run in parallel.

➢ In the *Mode* input field, you can choose between asynchronous and synchronous processing. In the latter case, the receive step opens up a "Sync-to-Async" bridge that allows the integration process to interactively fulfill a synchronous interface request.

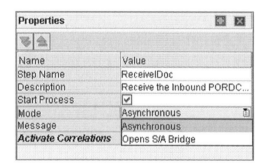

Figure 9.12: Maintaining the Properties of the Receive Step © Copyright 2010. SAP AG. All rights reserved

As you look over the properties of the receive step, you'll notice that you have the choice to use or activate *correlations*. We'll defer a discussion on correlations to Section 9.3.9.

9.3.5.2 Sending Messages with the Send Step

To send a message from your integration process, you must add a send step to your process definition. This can be accomplished by dragging-and-dropping the receive step into the proper location within your process definition. From here, it's simply a matter of configuring the parameters for message exchange.

Unlike the receive step in which you only need to configure a handful of parameters, you'll find that the configuration of the send step is slightly more involved. Much of this complexity stems from the multitude of configuration options tied to each of the supported modes of execution. For instance, the properties used to define an asynchronous call vary from the ones used to implement a synchronous call, etc. Figure 9.13 illustrates the properties editor for the send step. Table 9.4 describes these properties in further detail.

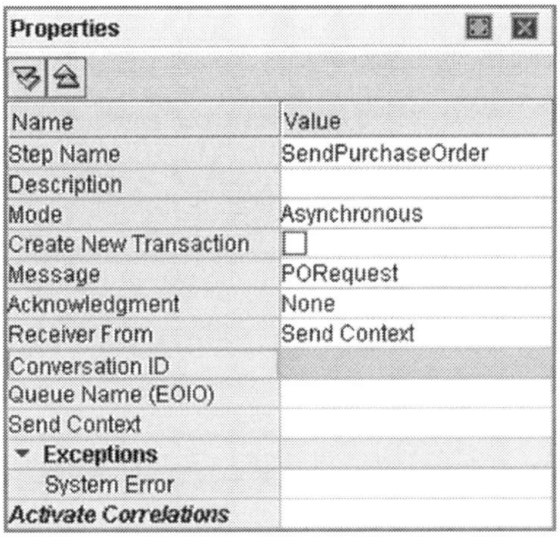

Figure 9.13: Maintaining the Properties of the Send Step © Copyright 2010. SAP AG. All rights reserved

Property	Possible Values	Description
Step Name	N/A	The name assigned to the send step.
Description	N/A	An optional description for the send step.
Mode	Asynchronous Synchronous Acknowledgment Closes S/A Bridge	You use this property to determine the mode of the transmission. Besides the obvious Asynchronous and Synchronous modes, you can also configure the send step to send acknowledgments or close a sync-to-async bridge.

Property	Possible Values	Description
Create New Transaction	True or False	When this option is checked, the send step will be executed within a new transaction. We'll learn more about transactions in Section 9.3.8.
Message(s)	Any container element with the category value Abstract Interface.	This property will vary based upon the selected mode value. For example, in asynchronous mode, this property will point to a container element containing the request message. Conversely, in synchronous mode, you must specify the request and response messages as well as the abstract service interface that defines the synchronous operation to be called.
Acknowledgment	None Transport Application	In asynchronous mode, you can specify whether or not the send step will await an acknowledgment from the receiver system. Here, keep in mind that this is only possible if the adapter used to communicate with the receiver system supports acknowledgments.
Receiver From	Send Context Receivers List Response to Message	This property determines how the receiver of the message will be derived. In the normal case, you will select the default Send Context value to apply a receiver determination defined in the Integration Directory. Alternatively, you can plug in a list of receivers derived via a receiver determination step or allow the system to respond to a message that was received previously.

Property	Possible Values	Description
Conversation ID	A container element with the type `xsd:string`.	This property allows you to specify a *conversation ID* that can be used to identify messages that should be grouped together semantically. See the online help documentation for more details about this feature.
Queue Name (EOIO)	A 16-character string value that may consist of alphanumeric characters, slashes (/), underscores ( ), or hyphens (-).	If you want the messages to be sent to the target receiver system in order, you can configure EOIO processing and use this property to specify the name of the queue used to serialize the messages.

Table 9.4: Properties of the Send Step

9.3.6 Applying Transformations

Within an integration process, there are often times when you need to apply a transformation between a pair of messages. For example, when developing a sync-to-async bridge, you generally need to apply a transformation between the request and response messages. For this task, you can use the transformation step.

For the most part, you can think of transformation steps as nothing more than a wrapper around an operation mapping. The only difference in this case is that the operation mapping defines a mapping between abstract service operations. Figure 9.14 shows the properties that you must configure when defining a transformation step. As you can see, there are three basic elements of a transformation step definition:

> **Operation Mapping**
> Here, you assign the operation mapping that will be used to perform the transformation.

> **Source Messages**
> With this property, you enter the source message(s) that are passed to the operation mapping. The messages are represented as container elements.

> ➤ **Target Messages**
> You use this property to bind the results of the operation mapping with one or more container elements.

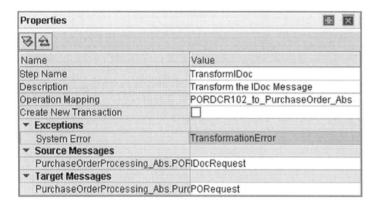

Figure 9.14: Configuring a Transformation Step © Copyright 2010. SAP AG. All rights reserved

9.3.7 Determining Receivers

A common use case for integration processes is to take a single input message and dispatch (or multicast) it to multiple receivers. In this scenario, you need to determine the receivers of a message up front so that you know where to send the messages. For this task, you can utilize the receiver determination step.

Figure 9.15 depicts the properties that you must configure whenever you define a receiver determination step. Here, there are three basic properties that you must take into account:

> ➤ In the *Message* property, you plug in the message that you want to send to the receiver(s). This message is defined as a container element.

> ➤ In the *Send Context* property, can specify a *send context* that allows you to send the same interface to different receivers using different send steps. Here, the send context is simply an arbitrary string value that can be queried within the receiver determination definition in the Integration Directory.

> ➤ In the *Receivers* property, you select a container element with the category type `Receiver`. Most of the time, this container element will be defined as a multiline container element.

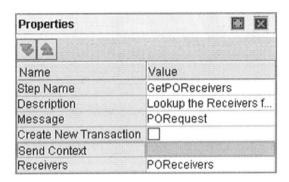

Figure 9.15: Configuring a Receiver Determination Step © Copyright 2010. SAP AG. All rights reserved

9.3.8   Working with Blocks

As you learned in Section 9.3.1, blocks can be used to group together a series of related steps. This grouping offers many benefits when it comes to transaction management, exception handling, and so on. In this section, we'll look at some of the features that blocks have to offer.

9.3.8.1 Transaction Management

Normally, the system will create a new transaction for each step within an integration process. However, these days, you can override this default behavior for particular step types. For example, in a transformation step, you can choose whether or not to start a new transaction using the *Create New Transaction* property shown in Figure 9.16. If you don't select this checkbox, then the transformation step will operate within the currently open transaction (which, in turn, eliminates a database access, etc.). The same also applies for send steps and receiver determination steps.

Properties	⊡ ☒

Name	Value
Step Name	TransformIDoc
Description	Transform the IDoc Me...
Operation Mapping	PORDCR102_to_Purc...
Create New Transaction: ☐	
▼ **Exceptions**	
System Error	TransformationError
▼ **Source Messages**	
PurchaseOrderProce:IDocRequest	
▼ **Target Messages**	
PurchaseOrderProce:PORequest	

Figure 9.16: Configuring the Transactional Behavior for Particular Step Types

Oftentimes, it makes sense to combine these steps into a separate *logical unit of work* (LUW) that executes within its own transactional context. For example, you might want to combine a transformation and send step together in a single LUW that either executes to completion, or not at all. Such behavior can be realized by grouping the steps together in a block (see Figure 9.17).

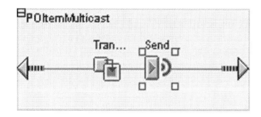

Figure 9.17: Grouping Steps Together in a Block

Once you have grouped together a series of related steps within a block, you can define the transactional behavior of that block by configuring the *Block Start* and *Block End* properties shown in Figure 9.18. Here you can determine whether or not a new transaction should be started before/after the block executes. If a new transaction is started within a block, then that transaction is the one that will be adopted by those steps in which you choose not to create a new transaction.

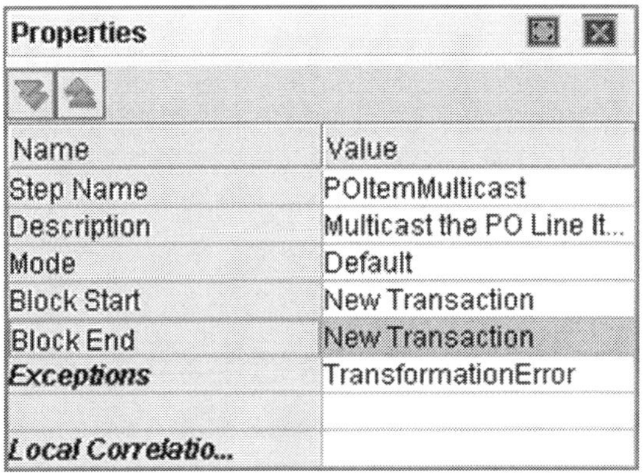

Figure 9.18: Defining the Transactional Behavior of a Block © Copyright 2010. SAP AG. All rights reserved

9.3.8.2 Exception Handling

Sometimes, certain steps within an integration process may not be able to execute correctly at runtime. Here, for example, you might encounter a situation where a synchronous send step tries to communicate with a receiver system that is unavailable. These exceptions, if left unchecked, will cause the integration process to fail in unexpected ways. Fortunately, within a block definition, you can define more graceful ways of dealing with exceptions.

Whenever you create a block, you have the option of specifying a series of *exceptions* within the properties editor (see Figure 9.19). These exceptions are simply arbitrary strings that you use to describe the types of exceptions that may be triggered by steps within the block definition. Once these exceptions are defined, you can reference them in steps defined within the block. For example, Figure 9.20 shows how we have assigned an exception called `TransformationError` to a transformation step. At runtime, if an error occurs within the defined operation mapping, an exception of this type will be raised by the transformation step.

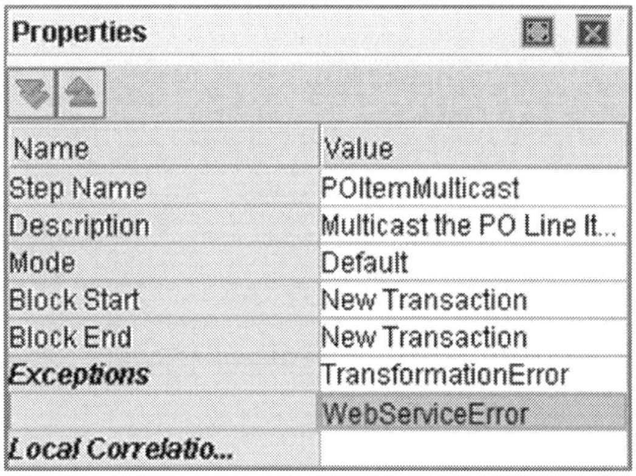

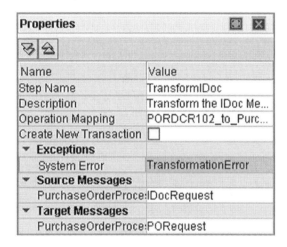

Figure 9.19: Defining Exceptions in a Block Definition © Copyright 2010. SAP AG. All rights reserved

Figure 9.20: Defining the Exception Type Thrown by a Transformation Step © Copyright 2010. SAP AG. All rights reserved

In order to handle the exceptions raised within the individual steps within a block definition, you must define *exception branches*. These branches contain steps that are used to gracefully react to an error situation. For example, if we are unable to communicate with a target system, we might send out an acknowledgment or alert so that interested parties are made aware of the problem.

To define an exception branch within your block definition, simply right-click on it and select the menu option *Insert → Exception Branch*. For each exception branch defined, you must determine which exception you want it to handle (see Figure 9.21). Once you have defined these branches, you can insert the necessary steps for dealing with the error situation. For example, Figure 9.22 shows how we have defined two exception branches for a block used to multicast messages: one for transformation errors and one for handling errors in the send step. In either case, we are using the control step to terminate the workflow process.

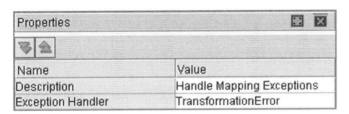

Figure 9.21: Defining Exception Branches in a Block Definition (Part 1)

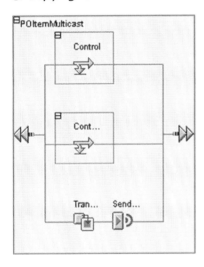

Figure 9.22: Defining Exception Branches in a Block Definition (Part 2)

9.3.8.3 Deadline Monitoring

In addition to the exception handling capabilities described in the previous section, you can also specify deadlines for completing processing within a block. This capability is useful in cases where you need to react to situations where the process stalls out. For example, if you have not received a response message from a particular system within 24 hours, you might want to send an alert or terminate the process.

To configure deadline monitoring for your block definition, simply right-click on it and select the menu option *Insert → Deadline Branch*. This will add branch to the block definition that is similar to the exception branches described in the previous section. Within this branch, you can insert various steps to react to the expired deadline.

Figure 9.23 shows how you can configure a deadline branch in the properties editor. Here, there are three basic properties that you must configure:

➢ In the *Reference Date/Time* property, you provide a reference for the system to derive the deadline. Here, you have several options to choose from:

    ○ **Creating the Step**
    In this case, the clock starts as soon as the step is created within the BPE.

    ○ **Creating the Process**
    In this case, the time interval begins whenever the process itself is started.

    ○ **Expression**
    This option allows you to define an arbitrary deadline in terms of a date/time value within the message, a constant value, and so on.

➢ With the *Unit* property you determine the time unit used to measure the deadline interval. Here, you can choose between minutes, hours, days, and even months or years.

➢ In the *Duration* property, you specify the duration of the deadline interval in terms of the defined unit value.

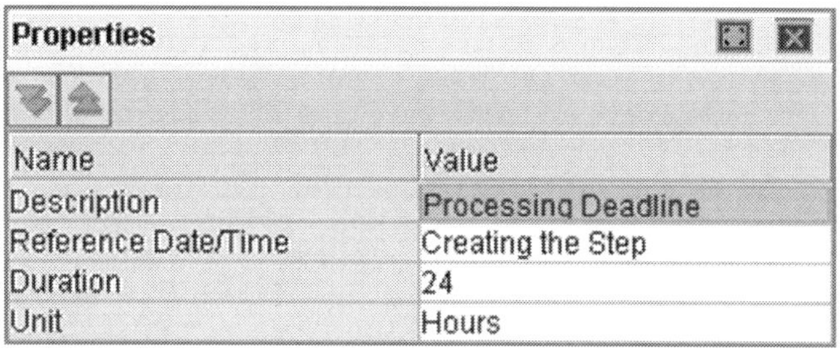

Properties	
Name	Value
Description	Processing Deadline
Reference Date/Time	Creating the Step
Duration	24
Unit	Hours

Figure 9.23: Configuring Deadline Monitoring © Copyright 2010. SAP AG. All rights reserved

9.3.8.4 Implementing For-Each Loops

By default, the steps defined within a block are executed one time. Besides this default behavior, blocks can also be configured as a type of "For-Each" loop in which the steps defined within the block are executed for each line within a multiline container element. Here, for example, you might use a block to process each of the messages generated by a multi-mapping.

Figure 9.24 demonstrates how you can configure the mode for a block definition. In this case, we've selected the ForEach mode to process each of the messages in the POLineItems container element in sequential fashion. Alternatively, we could have chosen the ParForEach mode to process each of the messages in parallel.

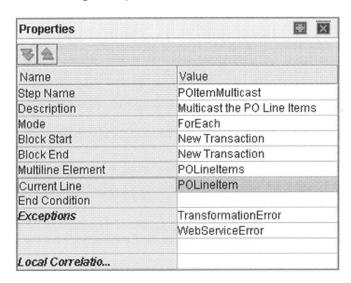

Name	Value
Step Name	POItemMulticast
Description	Multicast the PO Line Items
Mode	ForEach
Block Start	New Transaction
Block End	New Transaction
Multiline Element	POLineItems
Current Line	POLineItem
End Condition	
Exceptions	TransformationError
	WebServiceError
Local Correlatio...	

Figure 9.24: Specifying the Dynamic Mode for a Block Definition © Copyright 2010. SAP AG. All rights reserved

At the beginning of each loop iteration, the current line from the source multiline container element is copied to the message defined in the *Current Line* property shown in Figure 9.24. Here, the current line element must be defined within the scope of the block definition rather than the process as a whole (see Figure 9.25).

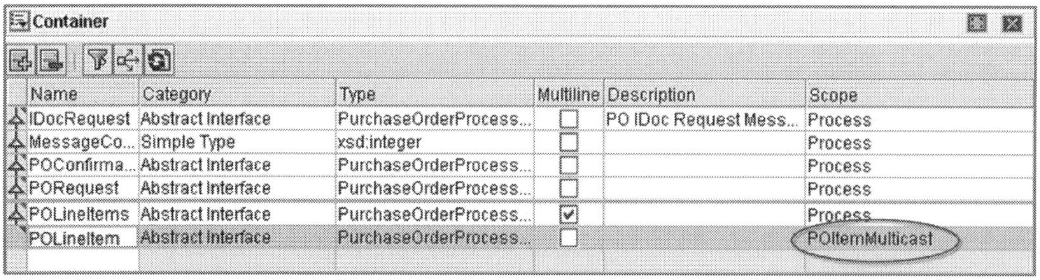

Name	Category	Type	Multiline	Description	Scope
IDocRequest	Abstract Interface	PurchaseOrderProcess...	☐	PO IDoc Request Mess...	Process
MessageCo...	Simple Type	xsd:integer	☐		Process
POConfirma...	Abstract Interface	PurchaseOrderProcess...	☐		Process
PORequest	Abstract Interface	PurchaseOrderProcess...	☐		Process
POLineItems	Abstract Interface	PurchaseOrderProcess...	☑		Process
POLineItem	Abstract Interface	PurchaseOrderProcess...	☐		POItemMulticast

Figure 9.25: Adjusting the Scope of a Container Element © Copyright 2010. SAP AG. All rights reserved

9.3.9 Correlations

Previously, we mentioned that integration processes can continue to receive messages long after they have been created. However, from a runtime perspective, this raises an important question: how does the system know which message goes with which process instance? This dilemma is solved using *correlations*.

According to SAP, a correlation "...joins messages that have the same value for one or more XML elements. A correlation is therefore a loose coupling of messages: at design time, it enables you to define which message a receive step must wait for, without you having to know the message ID" (SAP AG). To put all this into perspective, consider a situation in which you are using an integration process to broker the exchange of a purchase order message between a pair of business systems. Here, let's imagine that the business requirements state that you should send a functional acknowledgment to the sending system as soon as the PO has been confirmed by the receiver system. The UML activity diagram contained in Figure 9.26 illustrates this message flow.

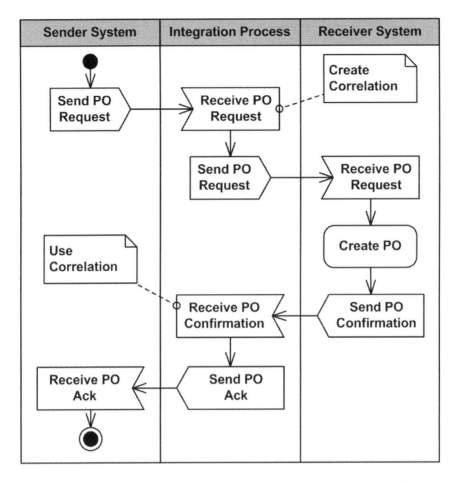

Figure 9.26: UML Activity Diagram Depicting Correlation Flow

Looking closely at the actions contained within the swim lane for the integration process shown in Figure 9.26, you can see that the order of operations is as follows:

1. The process is initiated by the receipt of a PO request message from the sender system. During this handshake, the system will create a new correlation to keep track of the PO and its related messages.

2. After the PO create message is received, it is forwarded on to the target receiver system.

3. In the target system, the PO request message is processed and a new PO is created.

4. Once the PO is created, a confirmation message is forwarded to the sender system via PI.

5. During the receipt of that confirmation message, the BPE will inspect the contents of the message to determine which process instance to forward the message on to.

6. Ultimately, the confirmation message is correlated and forwarded on to the sender system.

In the upcoming sections, we'll show you how to implement these kinds of relationships in your own integration processes.

9.3.9.1 Creating Correlations

Before you can utilize correlations in step definitions, you must first create a correlation in the process editor. This can be achieved via the following steps:

1. First, each of the messages used in the correlation must be defined as container elements.

2. Then, in the object area on the bottom right-hand corner of the process editor, select the *Correlation List* view. This view contains a table in which you can add one or more correlations to your process definition. Here, you can create a new correlation definition by typing in a name in the *Correlation Name* field (see Figure 9.27).

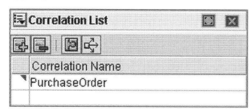

Figure 9.27: Creating a Correlation in the Correlation List
© Copyright 2010. SAP AG. All rights reserved

3. Once the correlation is created, select it in the *Correlation List* and click on the *Details* button (▣) to open the correlation up in the *Correlation Editor* view.

4. Within the *Correlation Editor* view shown in Figure 9.28, there are three sets of attributes that you must configure:

a. In the *Correlation Container* view, you must define a series of variables that represent the different elements used to identify a set of related messages.

b. In the *Involved Messages* view, you assign the messages that will be correlated with one another.

c. Finally, on the *Properties* view, you must define expressions that link elements from the related messages with elements defined within the *Correlation Container* view. These expressions are defined using the popup value help which guides you in constructing an XPath query[65].

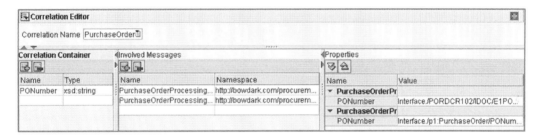

Figure 9.28: Editing a Correlation in the Correlation Editor View © Copyright 2010. SAP AG. All rights reserved

9.3.9.2 Activating a Correlation

In order to utilize correlations in your process definitions, you must first *activate* them in a send or receive step. For a given step definition, this can be achieved by filling in the *Activate Correlations* property as shown in Figure 9.29. At runtime, this will cause the BPE to create a new correlation based upon the values of the message that is being received by a receive step or sent by a send step.

---

[65] You can also plug in a type of pre-compiled XPath query called a *context object* here. We'll learn more about context objects in Chapter 12.

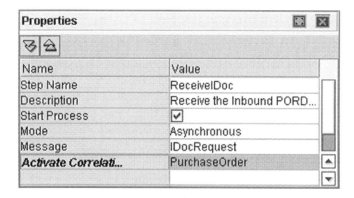

Figure 9.29: Activating Correlations in a Step Definition © Copyright 2010. SAP AG. All rights reserved

9.3.9.3 Using a Correlation in a Receive Step

Once a correlation has been activated in a previous step, you can utilize it in a corresponding receive step by filling in the *Use Correlations* property shown in Figure 9.30. This assignment is the glue that the system uses to determine which process instance an inbound message should be routed to.

Properties	
Name	Value
Step Name	ReceiveConfirmation
Description	Receive the PO Confirmation
Message	POConfirmation
Use Correlations	PurchaseOrder
Activate Correlati...	

Figure 9.30: Using Correlations in a Receive Step Definition © Copyright 2010. SAP AG. All rights reserved

9.4 Example Usage Scenarios

One of the best ways to get started with integration processes is to look at working examples. Fortunately, SAP has provided a slew of exemplary integration processes in the default `SAP BASIS` software component. You can locate these integration processes underneath the `http://sap.com/xi/XI/System/Patterns` namespace. These samples are intended to be used as patterns for adapting your own integration processes. Table 9.5 briefly describes each of the processes in turn.

Integration Process	Description
BpmPatternCollectMessage	This integration process demonstrates how you can collect a series of messages, bundle them together using a multi-mapping, and then forward the resultant message on to a target system.
BpmPatternCollectMultiIf	This process is similar to the BpmPatternCollectMessage. The primary difference in this case is that the process is collecting different types of messages from the sender(s).
BpmPatternCollectMultiIfCondition	This process extends the BpmPatternCollectMultiIf process to be more selective about the messages it is collecting.
BpmPatternCollectPayload	This process collects a series of messages in much the same way that the BpmPatternCollectMessage process does. However, rather than waiting for some terminating message to determine when to stop listening for messages, this process uses a loop to compare the number of received messages with a defined threshold. Once this threshold is met, the messages are combined and forwarded as per usual.
BpmPatternCollectTime	This process collects messages within an infinite loop. This loop is encapsulated within a block that has been configured to use deadline monitoring. In this case, the deadline has been set to an arbitrary value of 24 hours. Once the deadline is met, an exception is raised and the process then proceeds with forwarding the accumulated messages as per usual.

Integration Process	Description
BpmPatternMulticastParallel	This process receives a message and then processes it as follows: 1. First, it uses the receiver determination step to dynamically create a list of receivers to forward the message to. 2. Then, it uses the block step to define a "For Each" loop that sends the message on to each receiver in the receiver list in parallel.
BpmPatternMulticastSequential	This process is similar to the BpmPatternMulticastParallel process in that it multicasts a message on to multiple receivers. However, in this case, the messages are forwarded sequentially.

Integration Process	Description
BpmPatternReqRespAlert	This process brokers an asynchronous request/reply scenario between two systems. Here, the order of operations is as follows: 1. The process receives an asynchronous request message from the sender system. 2. It then forwards the request on to the receiver system. 3. At some point later, the receiver system will respond to the forwarded request with its response. 4. This response is then passed back to the sender. In order to handle situations where the receiver system never responds to the request from step 2, steps 3 and 4 above are wrapped up in a block that is configured to use deadline monitoring. In this case, if a response has not been received within 24 hours, an alert is triggered to notify interested parties of the delay.
BpmPatternReqRespTimeOut	This process expands on the BpmPatternReqRespAlert process by implementing an exception handler block that forwards an error message back to the sending system in the event of a timeout.
BpmPatternSerializeMultipleTrigger	This process receives a series of messages that can be sent in any order and then forwards them on to the receiver system in serialized fashion.

Integration Process	Description
BpmPatternSerializeOneTrigger	This process is similar to the BpmPatternSerializeMultipleTrigger process. However, in this case, only one of the source messages triggers the creation of the integration process.
BpmPatternSyncAsyncBridge	This pattern demonstrates how to implement a "synchronous-to-asynchronous" bridge using an integration process. Here, the integration process fulfills a synchronous message request using a pair of asynchronous request/reply interfaces hosted on the target system.

Table 9.5: Example Usage Scenarios Provided by SAP

9.5 Summary

In this chapter, you learned how integration processes can be used to orchestrate message processing within the Integration Server. When utilized properly, these processes can take your business process modeling to a whole other level. The key is knowing where and when to use them.

This chapter concludes our study of design time development tasks within the ESR. Now that you understand how to work with these various artifacts, you are ready to begin assembling them into real live integration scenarios. Therefore, in the next chapter, we will begin to explore the configuration options that you have at your disposal within the Integration Directory.

References

SAP AG. (n.d.). *Checklist: Making Correct Use of Integration Processes.* Retrieved December 20, 2010, from SAP Help Library: http://help.sap.com/saphelp_nwpi711/helpdata/en/43/d92e428819da2ce100 00000a1550b0/frameset.htm

SAP AG. (n.d.). *Correlation: Defining Assignment of Msgs to Process Instances.* Retrieved December 23, 2010, from SAP Help Library: http://help.sap.com/saphelp_nwpi711/helpdata/en/a5/64373f7853494fe100 00000a114084/frameset.htm

SAP AG. (n.d.). *Define a Condition.* Retrieved December 22, 2010, from SAP Help Library: http://help.sap.com/saphelp_nwpi711/helpdata/en/ae/fd773f12f14a18e1000 0000a114084/frameset.htm

SAP AG. (n.d.). *Defining an Integration Process.* Retrieved December 22, 2010, from SAP Help Library: http://help.sap.com/saphelp_nwpi711/helpdata/en/ae/fd773f12f14a18e1000 0000a114084/frameset.htm

SAP AG. (n.d.). *Defining and Managing Integration Processes.* Retrieved December 20, 2010, from SAP Help Library: http://help.sap.com/saphelp_nwpi711/helpdata/en/3c/831620a4f1044dba38 b370f77835cc/frameset.htm

Working with the Integration Builder

The Integration Builder is the central tool used to develop configuration objects within the Integration Directory. Therefore, in order to configure integration scenarios in PI, you must first understand how to work with this tool. In this chapter, we'll provide you with an introduction to the Integration Builder and show you how it is used to configure collaborative business processes.

After completing this chapter, you will be able to:

- ❖ Log on and navigate within the Integration Builder tool.

- ❖ Understand the concept of configuration objects and the different roles they play within the Integration Directory.

- ❖ Organize configuration objects using configuration scenarios.

- ❖ Understand software logistics concepts within the Integration Directory.

10.1   Getting Started

In Part 2 of this book, you learned how to develop repository objects in the ESR using the Java Web Start-based ES Builder tool. At configuration time, you'll work with another Java Web Start-based tool: the *Integration Builder*. This tool is used to develop configuration objects within the Integration Directory.

To access the Integration Builder, log onto the AS ABAP stack and execute transaction SXMB_IFR. This will open up the *Process Integration Tools* screen shown in Figure 10.1. From here, click on the *Integration Builder* link to load the Java Web Start application.

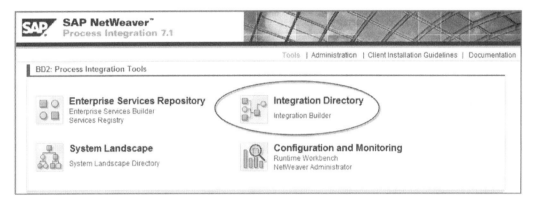

Figure 10.1: Logging onto the Integration Builder Tool © Copyright 2010. SAP AG. All rights reserved

Figure 10.2 depicts the user interface provided with the Integration Builder. As you can see, it has a similar look-and-feel to the ES Builder. Not surprisingly, this is by design as SAP wanted to provide a uniform development environment for PI developers. This implies that the functions provided in the menus/toolbars serve the same purpose in both tools, etc. Of course, if you have questions about specific functions, you can consult the online help documentation underneath the section entitled *Working with the Integration Builder* (SAP AG).

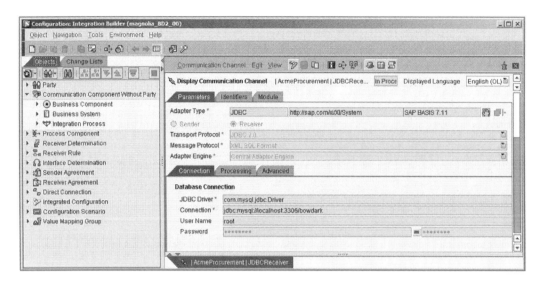

Figure 10.2: Getting Started with the Integration Builder © Copyright 2010. SAP AG. All rights reserved

10.2   Introduction to Configuration Objects

Within the Integration Directory, you configure integration scenarios by creating a series of *configuration objects*. In many respects, configuration objects are analogous to repository objects in the ESR. However, unlike repository objects, configuration objects are not defined within the context of a SWCV in the SLD. Instead, they are standalone objects defined exclusively within the Integration Directory.

Generally speaking, configuration objects can be classified according to the following categories:

> **Collaboration Profiles**
> Collaboration profile objects are used to model the endpoint systems that participate in integration scenarios.

> **Logical Routing Objects**
> Logical routing objects are used to configure the rules that the Integration Server uses to direct incoming messages on to their intended recipients.

➢ **Collaboration Agreements**
Collaboration agreements are used to define the technical details for the processing of a specific type of message that is either sent to or received from the PI Integration Server.

We'll get a chance to get hands on with each of these configuration object types beginning with Chapter 11.

10.2.1 Object Keys in Configuration Objects

Each configuration object within the Integration Directory is uniquely identified by an *object key* that is assigned whenever a configuration object is created. The structure of this object key varies depending on the selected object type, and cannot be changed after the configuration object is saved. However, in certain cases, you can specify the object key generically to cover a wider array of configuration scenarios. We'll see how all this works when we start looking at specific configuration objects in Chapter 11.

10.2.2 Change Lists and Version Management

Like repository objects in the ES Builder, changes to configuration objects in the Integration Builder are also tracked through *change lists*. As was the case in the ES Builder, you can access these change lists on the *Change Lists* tab shown in Figure 10.3. However, in this case, instead of having a separate change list per SWCV, you generally have one change list per user account.

Figure 10.3: Managing Change Lists © Copyright 2010. SAP AG. All rights reserved

You can view and manage the contents of a change list by double-clicking on it. This will open up the change list editor shown in Figure 10.4. From here, you can perform the following operations:

> To activate the entire change list, select the menu option *Change List → Activate*.

> To activate individual configuration objects in the change list, select the configuration object in the *Objects in Change List* table and click on the *Activate Changes...* toolbar button (▨).

> To remove individual configuration objects from the change list, select the configuration object and click on the *Remove Object from Change List* toolbar button (▨).

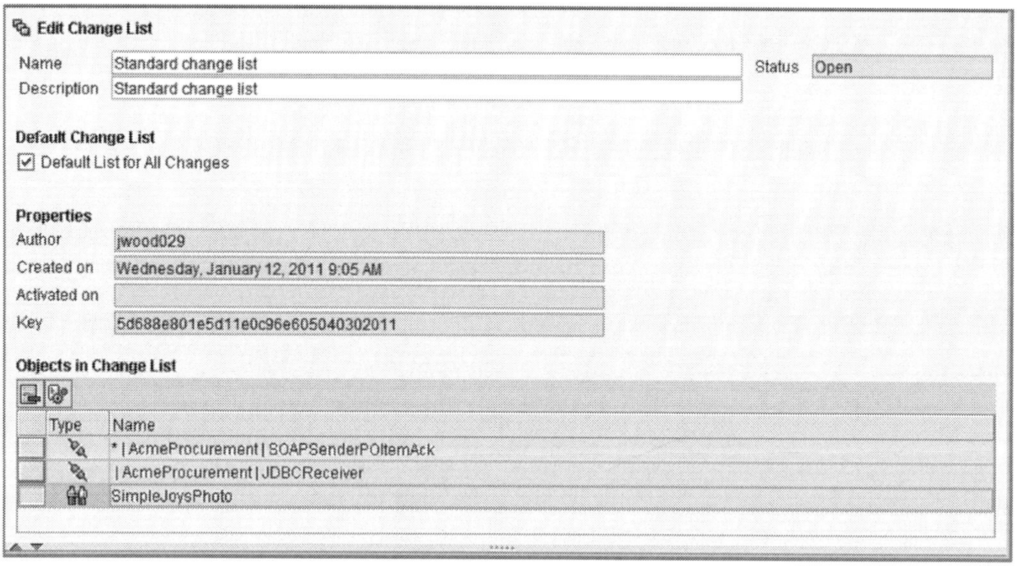

Figure 10.4: Editing Change Lists in the Integration Builder © Copyright 2010. SAP AG. All rights reserved

Each time you activate changes to a configuration object, a new *version* of the configuration object is created in the Integration Directory. If necessary, you can go back and retrieve prior versions of a configuration object by opening it up and selecting the *History* option in the object menu. This will open up the dialog box shown in Figure 10.5.

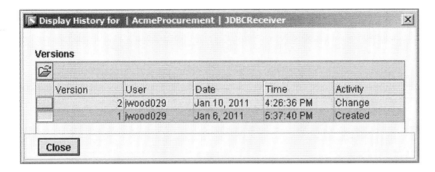

Figure 10.5: Viewing the Version History for a Configuration Object

To view a prior version of a configuration object, select it in the *Versions* table shown in Figure 10.5 and click on the *Open Version* toolbar button. If you wish to revert back to this version, simply add it to your change list by opening it up in edit mode. Then, save the configuration object version and activate your change list.

10.3   Configuration Scenarios

Though each configuration object within the Integration Directory is technically a standalone object, it is often helpful to be able to group together related objects used to implement a particular collaborative business process. Such groupings can be achieved in the Integration Directory by creating *configuration scenarios*.

For the most part, you'll find that configuration scenarios are analogous to folders in that they simply group together related configuration objects. As such, they're relatively easy to maintain. To create a new configuration scenario, perform the following steps:

1. To begin, select the *Object → New* menu option in the top level toolbar.

2. In the ensuing *Create Object* dialog box, expand the Administration submenu and choose the *Configuration Scenario* menu option.

3. Next, enter a name[66] and optional description for the configuration scenario and click on the *Create* button.

---

[66] Consult the SAP NetWeaver How-To Guide entitled *PI Best Practices: Naming Conventions* (SAP AG) for naming conventions.

4. This will open up the new configuration scenario in the editor screen shown in Figure 10.6. Click the *Save* button to save your changes.

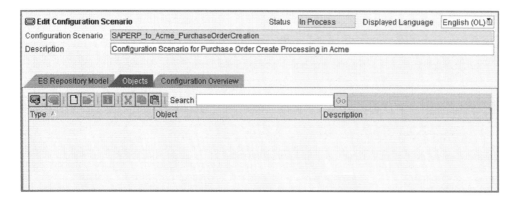

Figure 10.6: Editing Configuration Scenarios in the Integration Builder

Once a configuration scenario is created, you can begin adding configuration objects to them in several different ways:

➢   You can assign new objects to a configuration scenario by populating the *Add to Scenario* input field shown in Figure 10.7.

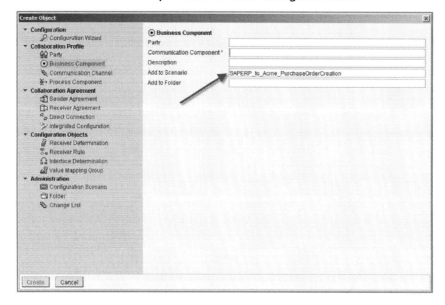

Figure 10.7: Adding an Object to a Configuration Scenario

> ➢ On the *Objects* tab within the configuration scenario editor, you can click on the *Add Objects to Scenario* (⬚) button to add existing objects to the scenario (see Figure 10.6).

> ➢ By right-clicking on a configuration object and selecting the *Assign Configuration Scenarios...* menu option.

After all of the relevant configuration objects have been assigned to a configuration scenario, you can see an overview of the configuration on the *Configuration Overview* tab (see Figure 10.8).

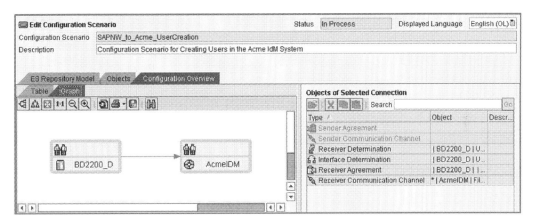

Figure 10.8: Overview for a Configuration Scenario © Copyright 2010. SAP AG. All rights reserved

10.3.1 Changing the View in the Navigation Area

One of the nice things about configuration scenarios is that they allow you to see the relationships between configuration objects at a glance. In release 7.1 of SAP NetWeaver PI, you also have the option of grouping related objects together in *folders*. Collectively, these options allow you to observe configuration objects at different levels of granularity. You can toggle between these different views using the drop-down list shown in Figure 10.9.

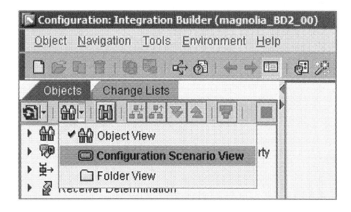

Figure 10.9: Changing the View in the Integration Builder © Copyright 2010. SAP AG. All rights reserved

Figure 10.10 shows how the navigation area changes whenever you select the *Configuration Scenario* view. In this case, you can see that related configuration objects are grouped together within their assigned configuration scenario (compare this with the *Object View* shown in Figure 10.2). You can drill in even further by selecting a configuration scenario and clicking on the *Only Display Selected Subtree* toolbar button shown in Figure 10.10.

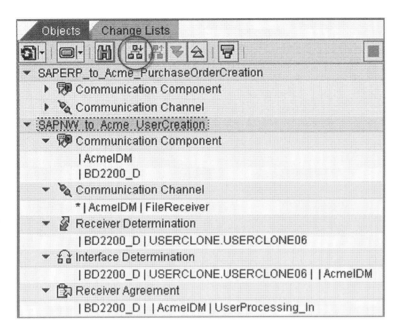

Figure 10.10: Working in the Configuration Scenario View © Copyright 2010. SAP AG. All rights reserved

10.3.2 Creating References to ESR Models

Another handy feature provided with configuration scenarios is the so-called *model configurator* tool. This tool can utilize models[67] defined in the ESR to automate the creation of configuration objects within a configuration scenario.

To access the model configurator tool for a configuration scenario, click on the *ES Repository Model* tab shown in Figure 10.11. As you can see, this function is initially disabled. To enable it, you must choose the type of ESR model you wish to reference from in the *Type of ES Repository Model* radio button group at the bottom of the page (see Figure 10.11). Then, once this is selected, you can click on the *Model Configurator* button to launch the model configuration wizard that will guide you in configuring your collaborative business process.

---

[67] Both the SAP Process Component Interaction Model and Process Integration Scenario model types are covered in Chapter 5. For more information about the SAP Process Variant Type model, consult the online help documentation.

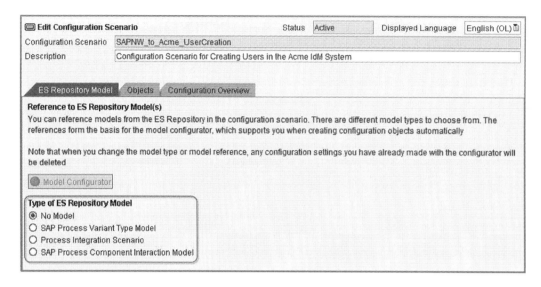

Figure 10.11: Creating References to ESR Models © Copyright 2010. SAP AG. All rights reserved

10.4   Transporting Directory Content

For the most part, you'll find that configuration objects can be transported using the same techniques described for repository objects in Chapter 4 (e.g., via the file system, CMS, or CTS+)[68]. However, in the case of configuration objects, there are some additional landscape-related issues to take into account.

At a high level, each of the configuration objects that you create within the Integration Directory are intended to help you map a collaborative business process to a given technical landscape. Most of the time, this process begins with the configuration of a process in the development system landscape. As configuration objects are transported, the endpoint systems referenced by these processes must be adjusted to coincide with the target landscape (e.g. QA, Production, etc.).

To demonstrate this concept, imagine an integration scenario in which an SAP ECC system is sending a message to some 3rd-party system. When you initially model this scenario in the PI development system, you will refer to the relevant SAP ECC and 3rd-party development systems in your

---

[68] See the online help documentation underneath the section entitled *Transporting Configuration Objects of the Integration Directory* (SAP AG) for further details

configuration. If you were to then transport this scenario to the PI quality assurance instance, the references to the SAP ECC and 3rd-party systems would need to be updated to point at the corresponding systems in the quality assurance landscape. Similarly, the same kind of transformation would have to happen again when the scenario is promoted on to the production landscape (see Figure 10.12).

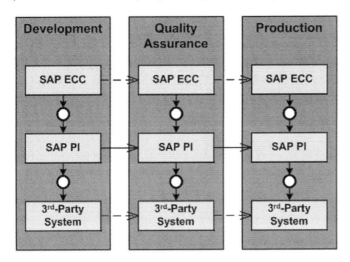

Figure 10.12: Defining Transport Groups

In Chapter 11, we'll show you how you can define relationships between certain types of endpoint systems in order to simplify the process of transporting directory content. However, as you cannot depend on this functionality across the board, it is always a good idea to get into the habit of double-checking your configuration objects in the target system to make sure that they're configured correctly for that landscape.

10.4.1 Working with the Integration Directory API

Recognizing the complexity involved in re-pointing configuration objects in the Integration Directory, SAP decided to publish a Web service-based API to allow you to automate this maintenance process. For more information about this API, check out the online help documentation underneath the section entitled *Integration Directory Programming Interface* (SAP AG).

10.5   Summary

In this chapter, you learned how to work with the Integration Builder tool that is used to configure collaborative business processes. In particular, you learned the ins-and-outs of configuration objects and their general maintenance. In the upcoming chapters, we'll expand on these concepts as we explore the creation of specific configuration objects within the Integration Directory.

References

SAP AG. (n.d.). *Integration Directory Programming Interface.* Retrieved January 12, 2011, from SAP Help Library: http://help.sap.com/saphelp_nwpi711/helpdata/en/48/d127e1e1c60783e10 000000a42189d/frameset.htm

SAP AG. (n.d.). *Transporting Configuration Objects of the Integration Directory.* Retrieved March 23, 2011, from SAP Help Library: http://help.sap.com/saphelp_nwpi711/helpdata/en/44/2c38d8afdf4674ae1a dc1364f4d454/frameset.htm

SAP AG. (n.d.). *Working with the Integration Builder.* Retrieved January 10, 2011, from SAP Help Library: http://help.sap.com/saphelp_nwpi711/helpdata/en/48/ceba4ce206035be100 00000a42189b/frameset.htm

Collaboration Profiles

11

Before you can begin configuring an integration scenario, you must first model the endpoint systems that will be involved in the message exchange. In SAP NetWeaver PI, you describe these entities using *collaboration profiles*.

After completing this chapter, you will be able to:

❖ Understand what collaboration profiles are and appreciate the role they play in configuring business processes in the Integration Directory.

❖ Define communication components that enable you to address various types of endpoint systems.

❖ Realize how communication channels are used to configure the use of a particular type of adapter to send or receive messages from an endpoint system.

11.1   What are Collaboration Profiles?

In Chapter 1, you learned how integration brokers like SAP NetWeaver PI abstract communication with endpoint systems through the use of various lightweight protocol adapters. This distributed approach to messaging creates a loose coupling between PI and the endpoint systems it exchanges messages with. Here, the only requirements for establishing connectivity are the selection of a messaging protocol and the specification of the relevant connection parameters (e.g. target host, port, and so on). In the Integration Directory, these details are captured in the form of a *communication channel*.

Technically speaking, communication channels provide the PI runtime environment with everything it needs to communicate with external systems. However, at configuration time, communication channels by themselves are insufficient for properly addressing endpoint systems. To maximize flexibility, a further layer of abstraction is needed to describe the parties/components involved in the message exchange. Collectively, these parties/components and their underlying communication channels combine to form what is known as a *collaboration profile* within the Integration Directory.

Why Logical Addressing is Important

Many developers new to SAP NetWeaver PI often wonder why this additional layer of abstraction is needed. To put this into perspective, consider the relationship between DNS host names and IP addresses: while you could use the physical IP address `66.96.146.86` to access this book's companion site, it is much more convenient to use the logical host name `www.bowdark.com`. Not only is this addressing scheme easier to use, it also provides a certain amount of location transparency as clients are shielded from changes to IP addresses, etc.

Similarly, the additional layers of a collaboration profile make it much easier to address the various entities that can communicate with SAP NetWeaver PI. This is particularly the case when dealing with multi-tier system landscapes. You'll see evidence of this as we progress through this section of the book.

Figure 11.1 illustrates the relationships between the objects that make up a collaboration profile. Starting from the bottom up, you can see that communication channels are defined within the context of *communication components* which are used to address the systems involved in the message exchange. Furthermore, you can see that communication components can be further classified through the specification of *communication parties* that represent the companies involved in a business-to-business (B2B) scenario. In the upcoming sections, we'll explore each of these objects and their relationships in further detail.

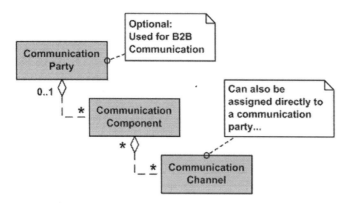

Figure 11.1: Understanding the Relationship between Objects in Collaboration Profiles

Overall, collaboration profiles are used to comprehensively describe the functions of the communication parties that exchange messages with SAP NetWeaver PI. As such, they represent the basis of just about every configuration object defined within the Integration Directory. In this chapter, we'll explore the various options you have for modeling endpoint systems using collaboration profiles.

11.2 Communication Parties

Looking back at the diagram shown in Figure 11.1, you can see that communication parties exist as an optional top layer within the collaboration profile hierarchy. Communication parties are used to represent the companies involved in a B2B process. For example, if you were developing a B2B scenario to purchase goods or services from an external vendor, then you would want to model that vendor as a communication party.

For the most part, you'll find the definition of communication parties to be very straightforward. To create a new communication party, log onto the Integration Directory and perform the following steps:

1. To begin, select the menu option *Object → New...* in the top-level menu bar.

2. In the ensuing *Create Object* dialog box, expand the *Collaboration Profile* submenu and then click on the *Party* node.

3. Next, you must enter a name[69] and optional description for the communication party (see Figure 11.2).

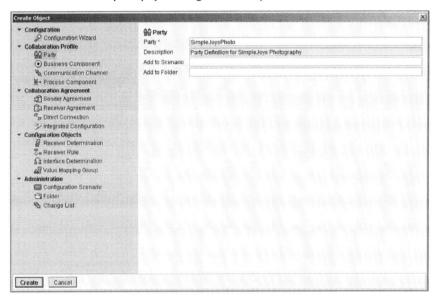

Figure 11.2: Creating a Communication Party
© Copyright 2010. SAP AG. All rights reserved

4. Finally, click on the *Create* button to open up the communication party in the editor screen shown in Figure 11.3.

As you can see in Figure 11.3, a communication party definition is split into three parts:

➢ On the *Identifiers* tab, you can specify various alternate identifiers that can be used as aliases for the party definition at runtime – more on this in Section 11.2.1.

➢ On the *Communication Components* tab, you can define the various communication components that will be used to communicate with

---

[69] Consult the SAP NetWeaver How-To Guide entitled *PI Best Practices: Naming Conventions* (SAP AG) for naming conventions.

the external party. We'll learn more about communication components in Section 11.3.

> ➤ On the *Communication Channels* tab, you can define party-specific communication channels. We'll learn more about communication channels in Section 11.3.4.

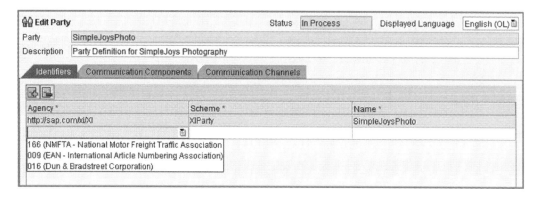

Figure 11.3: Editing a Party Definition in the Integration Directory

11.2.1 Defining Alternative Identifiers

From a functional point-of-view, communication parties provide you with a mechanism for addressing companies within the Integration Directory. However, in B2B processes, you'll find that companies are represented externally using a wide variety of identification schemes. You can define correlations between a communication party and these identification schemes by specifying alternate identifiers on the *Identifiers* tab shown in Figure 11.3.

As you can see in Figure 11.3, alternate identifiers are uniquely qualified by the specification of an *agency* and *scheme*. Though we originally learned about these concepts in Chapter 8 when we discussed value mapping groups, a brief refresher is in order here. In the context of communication parties, an agency is an entity that assigns globally-valid IDs to a company[70]. These IDs are encoded using various identification schemes.

To demonstrate how all this works, consider the relationship between your company and an external supplier. Internally, you would define a

---

[70] As was the case with value mapping groups, you can define your own custom agencies/schemes as necessary.

communication party to represent that supplier using some kind of meaningful name. However, depending upon the usage scenario, you might need to refer to that company externally using one of several different identification schemes. For example, one EDI standard might require that the company ID be defined in the message header using Dun and Bradstreet's D-U-N-S numbering scheme. In this case, you simply define an alternate identifier and plug in the D-U-N-S number as shown in Figure 11.4. You can create additional records as needed.

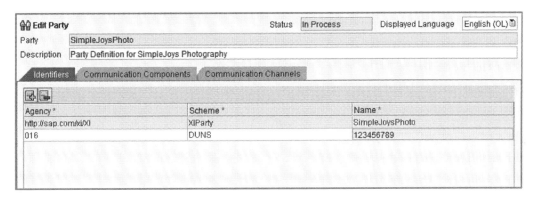

Figure 11.4: Specifying Alternate Identifiers for a Communication Party
© Copyright 2010. SAP AG. All rights reserved

In Section 11.4, we'll show you how these alternate identifiers are used in conjunction with communication channel definitions to enable translation between company identifiers at runtime.

11.3 Communication Components

According to SAP, a communication component "...represents an entity that can be used to address a sender or receiver of messages" (SAP AG). Within the Integration Directory, you can define three different types of communication components:

> **Business Systems**
> Business systems are used to address systems that are known within your system landscape. The details of these systems are captured within the System Landscape Directory (SLD) and then imported into the Integration Directory.

> **Business Components**
> In situations where you don't know much about the system you're communicating with, you can model the system as an abstract business component. This option comes in handy when you need to develop B2B integration scenarios or interface with systems that only publicize information about their interfaces.

> **Integration Processes**
> As you may recall from Chapter 9, it is possible to interject an integration process within an integration scenario to broker communication between two or more systems. From a configuration perspective, this implies that the integration process must be installed as a type of communication component within the Integration Directory.

Collectively, these communication component types provide you with the flexibility to model every kind of entity that could communicate with SAP NetWeaver PI. In the upcoming sections, we'll show you how to create all three types of communication components within the Integration Directory.

11.3.1 Defining Business Systems

As mentioned previously, business systems refer to application systems that are installed within your system landscape. For example, to address a local SAP ECC system in an integration scenario, you would want to define that system as a business system. Similarly, you can also describe various 3rd-party systems in your landscape using business systems.

In order to define a business system component in the Integration Directory, you must first create a business system within the SLD. Then, once the business system is created, you can import it as a communication component using a wizard provided with the Integration Builder tool. In the upcoming sections, we'll demonstrate how all this works. However, before we do, we first need to take a look at the relationship between business systems and technical systems in the SLD.

11.3.1.1 Technical Systems vs. Business Systems

Besides the software catalog described in Chapter 4, the SLD can also be used to store information about the various systems installed within your system landscape. Here, you can specify an assortment of technical attributes about an application system such as its host name, installed software components, and so on. Within the SLD, such details are captured in the form of *technical systems*.

From an integration point-of-view, a technical system may not be specific enough to properly model the senders and receivers of messages. For example, think about a technical system definition for an SAP ECC system. When you interface with this system, you are not addressing the system as a whole, but rather a specific client within the system. To fill in these gaps, the SLD allows you to associate a technical system with one or more *business systems*.

Conceptually, business systems in the SLD are "…logical systems, which function as senders or receivers within SAP NetWeaver PI" (SAP AG). Figure 11.5 illustrates the relationship between a technical system used to represent an SAP ECC development system and its associated business systems. In this case, the business systems represent each of the available clients within the SAP ECC system. Similarly, if you were to define a 3rd-party technical system, you could use business systems to represent different interfacing modules, and so on.

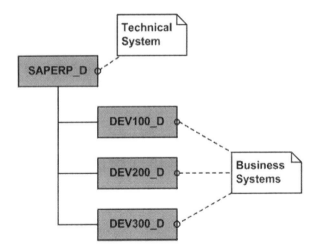

Figure 11.5: Understanding the Relationship between Technical Systems and Business Systems

11.3.1.2 Creating Technical Systems in the SLD

Now that you understand what technical systems are, let's briefly take a look at how they are maintained within the SLD. As you may recall from Chapter 4, you can access the SLD by opening up transaction SXMB_IFR and clicking on the *System Landscape Directory* link on the PI tools page. Then, from the main page, you can access the technical systems editor by clicking on the *Technical Systems* link in the *Landscape* area on the left-hand side of the page (see Figure 11.6).

By default, you'll find at least a couple of technical system definitions used to represent the AS ABAP and AS Java stacks of the SAP NetWeaver PI installation. In addition, it is likely that you may find other SAP-based technical systems representing the other SAP systems in your landscape. This is because SAP-based technical systems usually register themselves with the SLD using what is known as an *SLD data supplier*[71].

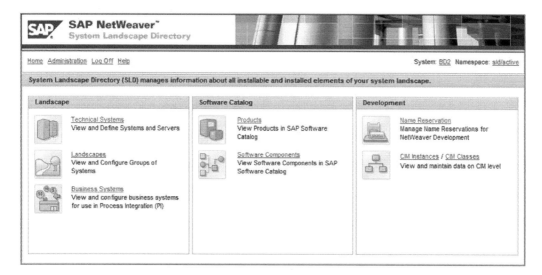

Figure 11.6: Maintaining the System Landscape in the SLD © Copyright 2010. SAP AG. All rights reserved

To demonstrate how technical systems are maintained within the SLD, let's consider the creation of a 3rd-party technical system used to represent the fictitious Acme application system originally described in Part 2 of this book. The steps required to create this system are as follows:

1. First, log onto the SLD and click on the *Technical Systems* link.

---

[71] These data suppliers are normally maintained by Basis personnel. For more information about this configuration, consult the online help documentation under the section entitled *Configuring Systems to Connect to the SLD* (SAP AG).

2. Then, in the technical systems editor, click on the *New Technical System...* button (see Figure 11.7).

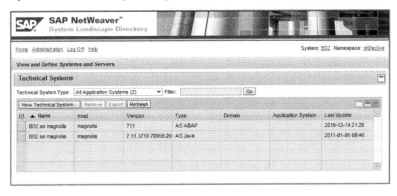

Figure 11.7: Creating a Technical System in the SLD (Part 1)

3. This will open up the Technical System Wizard shown in Figure 11.8. On the *System Type* step, you can choose between several different types of technical systems. In this case, we've chosen the *Third-Party* type. Click the *Next* button to continue.

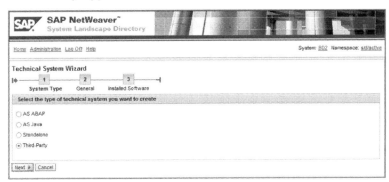

Figure 11.8: Creating a Technical System in the SLD (Part 2)

4. At the *General* step within the wizard, you must supply a name[72] for the technical system as well as the target system's host name (see Figure 11.9). Click the *Next* button to continue.

---

[72] Consult the SAP NetWeaver How-To Guide entitled *PI Best Practices: Naming Conventions* (SAP AG) for naming conventions.

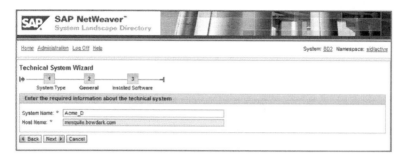

Figure 11.9: Creating a Technical System in the SLD (Part 3)

5. Finally, on the *Installed Software* step, you can select the products/software components that you wish to install on your technical system (see Figure 11.10). Click on the *Finish* button to confirm your changes.

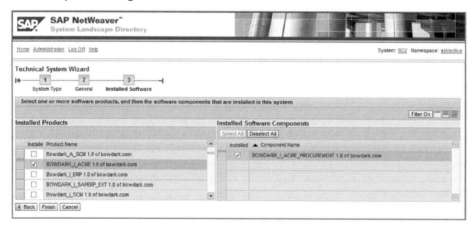

Figure 11.10: Creating a Technical System in the SLD (Part 4)

Looking over these steps, you might be wondering what it means to *install* products/software components on a technical system. These assignments will become clearer whenever we look at business system components in Section 11.3.1.4. For now, suffice it to say that this assignment is a virtual one; such selections will not spawn an installation wizard to physically install any software on the technical systems, etc.

11.3.1.3 Creating Business Systems in the SLD

As described in Section 11.3.1.1, business systems within the SLD are logical systems associated with a particular technical system. To demonstrate how these assignments work, let's see how to create a business system for the Acme_D technical system created in Section 11.3.1.2. These steps are outlined below:

1. First, log onto the SLD and click on the *Business Systems* link.

2. Then, in the business systems editor, click on the *New Business System...* button (see Figure 11.11).

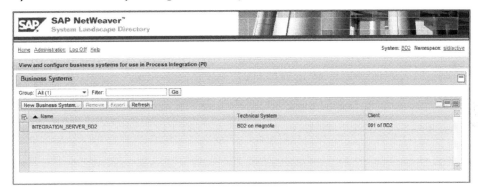

Figure 11.11: Creating a Business System in the SLD (Part 1)
© Copyright 2010. SAP AG. All rights reserved

3. This will open up the *Business System Wizard* shown in Figure 11.12. As you can see, the first step will prompt you to choose the type of technical system you wish to associate your business system with. In our particular case, we have selected the *Third-Party/Other* option (see Figure 11.12). Click the *Next* button to continue.

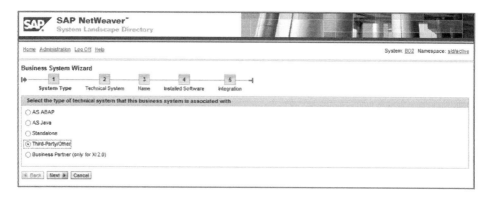

Figure 11.12: Creating a Business System in the SLD (Part 2)

4. At the *Technical System* step, you must select the actual technical
    system that you want to associate with in the *System* drop-down
    list shown in Figure 11.13. There, you also have the option of
    specifying a logical system name for the business system. This
    logical system name is used by the IDoc adapter to correlate a
    business system with a partner number in ALE/IDoc scenarios. Click
    the *Next* button to continue.

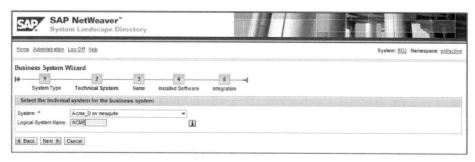

Figure 11.13: Creating a Business System in the SLD (Part 3)

5. On the *Name* step, you must specify a name[73] for the business
    system (see Figure 11.14). Click on the *Next* button to continue.

---

[73] Consult the SAP NetWeaver How-To Guide entitled *PI Best Practices:
Naming Conventions* (SAP AG) for naming conventions.

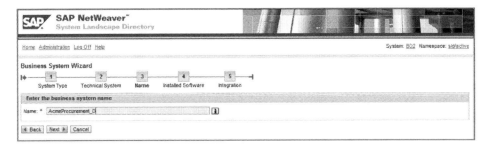

Figure 11.14: Creating a Business System in the SLD (Part 4)

6. On the *Installed Software* step, you have the option of adjusting the products that are to be installed on the business system. As you would expect, this list of installed products/software components is carried over from the technical system definition. Click on the *Next* button to continue.

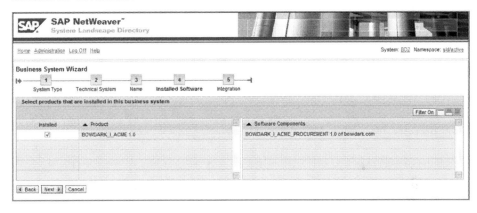

Figure 11.15: Creating a Business System in the SLD (Part 5)

7. Finally, on the *Integration* step, you must define the business system's *role*. For 3rd-party systems, this role is automatically populated with the value `Application System`. Furthermore, application systems must be assigned a related integration server which should be available in the *Related Integration Server* drop-down list (see Figure 11.16). Click on the *Finish* button to confirm your changes.

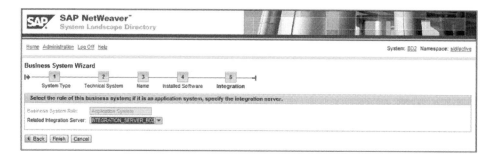

Figure 11.16: Creating a Business System in the SLD (Part 6)

Creating Business System Groups

In Chapter 10, we briefly touched on the concepts of transporting directory content and the relationships between application systems in different landscapes. Most of the time, such relationships have to be maintained manually. However, in the case of business systems, you can create groups of systems per landscape and then define a mapping between corresponding systems.

To define these relationships, you must first create a *business system group*. Business system groups define a logical relationship between business systems that utilize the same Integration Server for integration. To create a business system group, perform the following steps:

1. To begin, open up the SLD main page and click on the *Business Systems* link.

2. In the business systems editor, select the *Edit Groups...* menu option in the *Group* drop-down list (see Figure 11.17).

3. This will open up the *Business System Groups* editor screen shown in Figure 11.18. Click the *New Group...* button to continue.

4. Then, on the *Define Business System Group* screen shown in Figure 11.19, you can define a new group by providing a name, location, and associated Integration Server[74]. Click the *Create* button to save your changes.

---

[74] Note: These instructions assume that there is only one SLD defined within your PI landscape as per SAP's recommendations. If multiple SLDs are

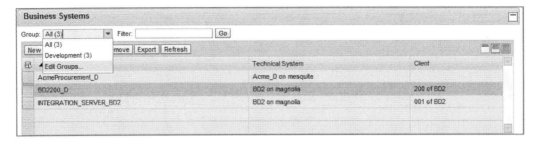

Figure 11.17: Creating Business System Groups (Part 1) © *Copyright 2010.*
SAP AG. All rights reserved

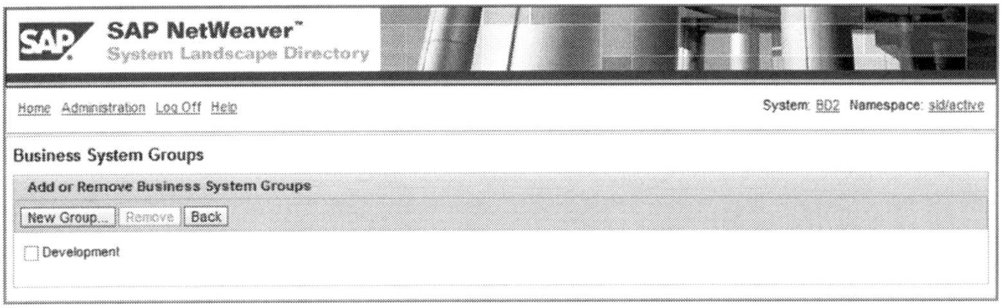

Figure 11.18: Creating Business System Groups (Part 2) © *Copyright 2010.*
SAP AG. All rights reserved

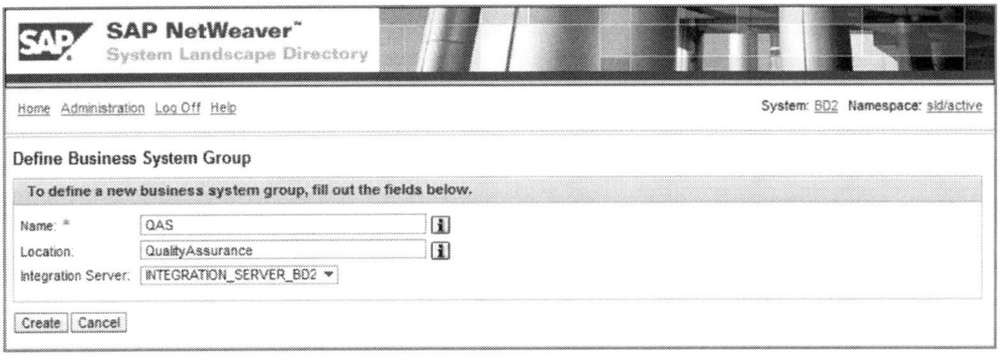

Figure 11.19: Creating Business System Groups (Part 3) © *Copyright 2010.*
SAP AG. All rights reserved

employed, then the landscape information for those SLDs will need to be
synchronized.

Assigning Transport Targets to a Business System

Once you have assigned your business systems to business system groups, you can define relationships between related business systems in these groups by opening up the business system in the SLD and selecting the *Transport* tab shown in Figure 11.20. There, you can click on the *Add/Change Target...* button to define a relationship between two business systems.

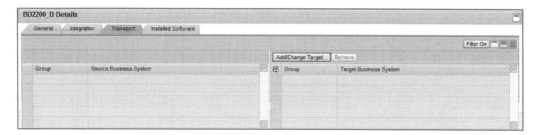

Figure 11.20: Defining Transport Targets between Business Systems

To understand how this works, imagine a 3-tier landscape consisting of development, quality assurance, and production systems. Furthermore, let's assume that you have modeled these systems as business systems. For a given development system in this scenario, you would want to define the corresponding quality assurance as the transport target. Similarly, you would define the production system as the transport target for the quality assurance system.

When these relationships are in place, the system will automagically convert between related systems as you transport Integration Directory content from system to system. As you can expect, this comes in very handy when dealing with large numbers of SAP application systems.

11.3.1.4 Importing Business System Components

Once a business system is defined within the SLD, the next step is to import it into the Integration Directory. This can be achieved via the following steps:

1. In the top-level menu bar, select the menu option *Tools → Assign Business System...*. This will open up the *Assign Business System* wizard. You can skip over the introduction by clicking on the *Continue* button.

2. On the *Assign Partner* step, you can choose whether or not you wish to assign the business system to a communication party (see Figure 11.21). Click on the *Continue* button to proceed.

Figure 11.21: Importing Business System Components (Part 1)

3. At the *Select Business Systems* step, you can select the business system you wish to import by clicking on its corresponding checkbox. As you can see in Figure 11.22, you also have the option to automatically create communication channels at this step by clicking on the *Create Communication Channels Automatically* checkbox.

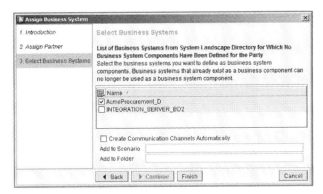

Figure 11.22: Importing Business System Components (Part 2)

4. Once you're satisfied with your selections, click on the *Finish* button to import the business system definition.

Figure 11.23 shows the imported business system component within the Integration Directory. As you can see, this definition carries over quite a bit of information from the SLD. Most notably, you can see that the product/software component assignments allowed the Integration Directory to automatically determine the sender/receiver interfaces that are *installed* on the business system component.

Over time, you may wish to go back and install other products/software components (and by extension, additional service interfaces) in your business system definition in the SLD. As these assignments are made, you can synchronize your business system component with the SLD[75] by selecting the *Other Attributes* tab and clicking on the *Compare with System Landscape Directory* button (see Figure 11.24).

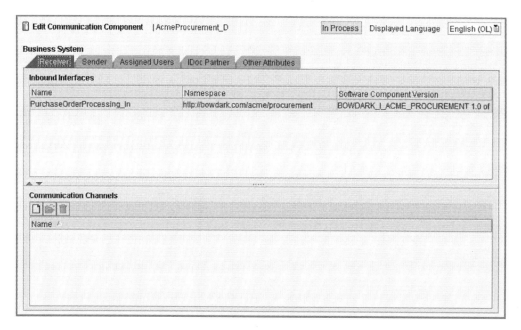

Figure 11.23: Business System Components in the Integration Directory
© Copyright 2010. SAP AG. All rights reserved

---

[75] If you find that your changes are not being synchronized properly, it could be because the local SLD cache in the Integration Builder tool needs to be updated. To clear this cache, select the *Environment → Clear SLD Data Cache* menu option in the top-level menu bar.

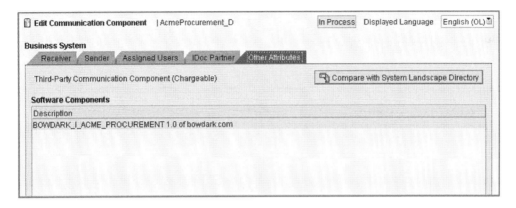

Figure 11.24: Synchronizing Business Systems with the SLD © Copyright 2010. SAP AG. All rights reserved

11.3.2 Defining Business Components

Oftentimes, you may not know very much about the systems you're interfacing with. For example, in most Web service scenarios, all you have to go on are a set of WSDL files that point to a particular provider host. Similarly, in B2B scenarios, business partners will likely go to great lengths to hide information about their system landscape for security reasons. Regardless of the circumstances, it makes little sense to try and model these types of systems in the SLD. Instead, you should model these abstract units as *business components* within the Integration Directory.

In some ways, you can think of a business component as a type of *modeling placebo*. Overall there's not much substance to them. They're simply a modeling construct used to address entities that communicate with SAP NetWeaver PI. As such, you'll find that they are relatively straightforward to work with.

To demonstrate how business components are defined, let's see how we would address our fictitious Acme system as a business component. The steps involved in the creation of this component are as follows:

1. To begin, open up the Integration Builder tool and select the *Object → New* menu option in the top-level menu bar.

2. In the ensuing *Create Object* dialog box, expand the *Collaboration Profile* submenu and choose the *Business Component* menu option.

3. On the right-hand side of the dialog window, you must provide a name[76] and optional description for the business component (see Figure 11.25). You also have the option of specifying a communication party in the *Party* field. If this field is left blank, then the business component is created as a standalone communication component.

4. Finally, click on the *Create* button to create the new business component object. This will open up the business component in the editor screen shown in Figure 11.26. Click on the *Save* button to save your business component.

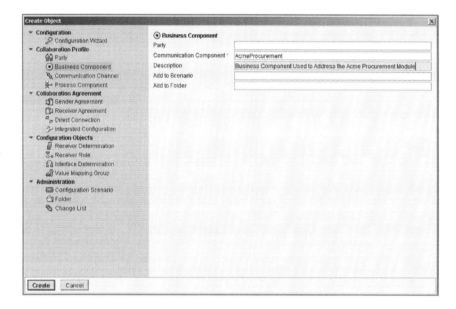

Figure 11.25: Creating a Business Component © Copyright 2010. SAP AG. All rights reserved

---

[76] Consult the SAP NetWeaver How-To Guide entitled *PI Best Practices: Naming Conventions* (SAP AG) for naming conventions.

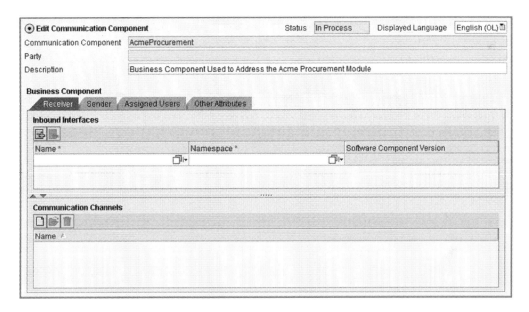

Figure 11.26: Maintaining Business Components in the Integration Directory

As you can see in Figure 11.26, the editor screen for business components has a very similar look-and-feel to the one used to maintain business systems. However, in the case of business components, the sender/receiver interface assignments are not automatically derived. Instead, you are provided with a table in which you can specify the various sender and receiver interfaces that you want to install on your business component. These assignments are made using the provided input helps on the *Sender* and *Receiver* tabs, respectively.

11.3.3 Defining Integration Process Components

In Chapter 9, you learned that integration processes can be used to send and receive messages. As such, they too play the role of communication component within the Integration Directory. This distinction makes it possible to address integration processes and senders and receivers of messages as per usual.

To define an integration process component, you must use a wizard provided in the Integration Builder tool. This wizard guides you through the process of importing an integration process definition from the ESR. To some extent, this process differs depending upon whether or not the integration process

component should be defined in terms of a communication party. The
following steps will guide you in either case:

1. To begin, open up the object view in the Integration Builder tool.
   Then, in the left-hand navigation area, you must locate the relevant
   Integration Process node. As you can see in Figure 11.27, you have
   the option of defining the integration process component in terms
   of a party or as a standalone communication component.

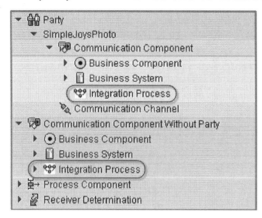

Figure 11.27: Defining the Context for Integration Processes

2. In either case, you will want to right-click on the *Integration
   Process* node and select the *New* context menu option. This will
   open up the aforementioned wizard that will guide you through the
   transfer process. You can skip the introductory notes by clicking on
   the *Continue* button.

3. At the *Select Process* step within the wizard, you can choose from a
   list of available integration processes defined within the ESR (see
   Figure 11.28). Once you locate the target integration process,
   select it by clicking on it and then click the *Continue* button to move
   to the next step.

4. Finally, on the *Select Name* step, you must assign a name[77] to the integration process component. Click on the *Finish* button to create the integration process component (see Figure 11.29).

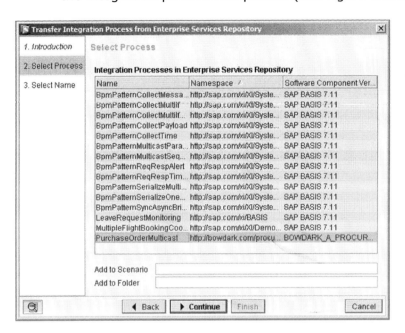

Figure 11.28: Selecting an Integration Process from the ESR © Copyright 2010. SAP AG. All rights reserved

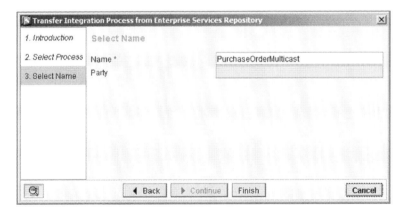

Figure 11.29: Defining an Integration Process Component in the Integration Directory © Copyright 2010. SAP AG. All rights reserved

---

[77] Consult the SAP NetWeaver How-To Guide entitled *PI Best Practices: Naming Conventions* (SAP AG) for naming conventions.

Figure 11.30 shows an imported integration process component in the Integration Builder. As you can see, the wizard derives the relevant sender and receiver interfaces via the integration process definition in the ESR. Consequently, you cannot change these assignments within the Integration Directory. Instead, you must update the integration process directly within the ESR.

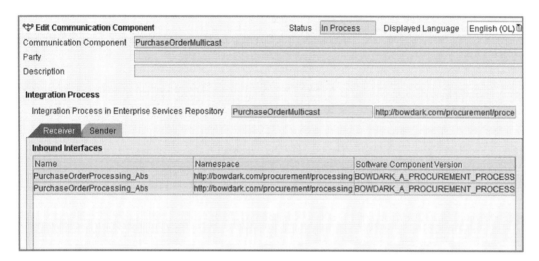

Figure 11.30: Editing an Integration Process in the Integration Builder

11.3.4 Adapter-Specific Identifiers

Conceptually speaking, communication components provide a mechanism for logically addressing the senders and receivers of messages within SAP NetWeaver PI. However, when addressing these components externally, a particular communication protocol might dictate the use of an entirely different identification scheme. For example, when communicating with an SAP system using ALE/IDoc technology, a business system corresponds with a logical system.

You can define a translation table for these identification schemes in your communication components by specifying *adapter-specific identifiers*. These identifiers are used by particular adapter types at runtime to translate between different identification schemes.

To define adapter-specific identifiers for a communication component, open it up and select the *Communication Component → Adapter-Specific Identifiers* menu option. This will open up the dialog box shown in Figure 11.31. Here, you can specify relevant identifiers for the different data types shown[78]. Once you are satisfied with your changes, click on the *Apply* button and save the communication component.

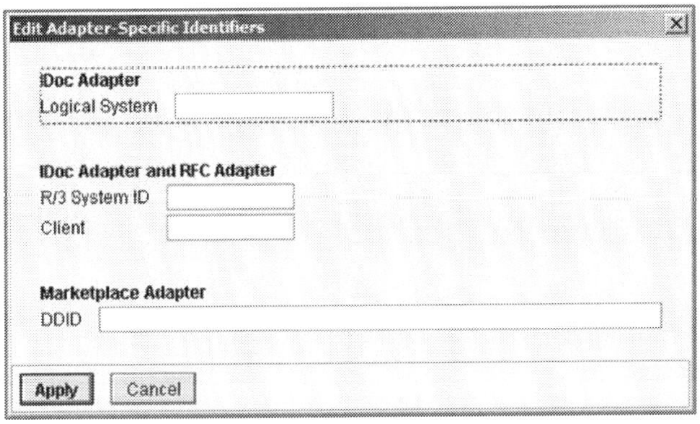

Figure 11.31: Editing Adapter-Specific Identifiers © Copyright 2010. SAP AG. All rights reserved

11.4   Communication Channels

As you have seen throughout this chapter, communication parties and communication components provide you with a convenient means for addressing endpoint systems. However, what they don't do is provide you with the technical details necessary to communicate with these systems. For this, you must configure *communication channels*.

According to SAP, a communication channel[79] is a configuration object that you can use to "...define the type and configuration of the adapter used during inbound or outbound processing" (SAP AG). For example, to communicate with an SAP system using IDocs, you would define a receiver channel using the IDoc adapter that is provided out-of-the-box by SAP. Similarly, to provide a Web service endpoint to a sender system, you would configure a sender channel using the standard SOAP adapter.

---

[78] In the case of SAP-based business systems imported from the SLD, the IDoc and RFC Adapter-based identifiers will be disabled as these values are maintained exclusively within the SLD.

[79] Communication channels are commonly referred to simply as *channels*. Going forward, we will also use this convention for describing communication channels.

In this section, we'll show you how to define and configure communication channels. However, given the plethora of options and adapters you have to work with, we cannot reasonably cover every possible setting[80]. Instead, our focus will be on basic concepts that will guide you in getting where you need to go. For more specific questions, your best bet is to consult the online help documentation and associated SAP notes.

11.4.1 Adapters

Up until now, we have referred to adapters in a very general sense. However, in order to work with communication channels, we first need to develop a better understanding of adapters and their functions. So, without further adieu, let's take a look at adapters and the environment that they run in.

To understand the function of an adapter, you can look no further than the root word *adapt*. According to Webster's dictionary, the word *adapt* is defined as a transitive verb that means "to make fit (as for a new use); often by modification" (Merriam-Webster). In the case of SAP NetWeaver PI, adapters are responsible for conversions between various technical protocols and the proprietary XI protocol used within the Integration Server. As such, adapters serve as a type of gateway that makes it possible for PI to communicate with a wide variety of application systems.

Figure 11.32 illustrates how adapters bridge the communication gaps between the PI Integration Server and the systems it exchanges messages with. To understand how this works, let's consider each side of the message exchange:

> ➢ On the sender side, an adapter presents a façade that allows sender systems to send messages to PI using a particular communication protocol. For example, to allow a sender system to send messages to PI using the SOAP protocol, you would configure the SOAP adapter to intercept those messages. Internally, the SOAP adapter's job is to convert the request into the proprietary XI protocol and forward it on to the Integration Server. All of this is completely transparent to the sender system.

---

[80] You can, however, find such details in the online help documentation underneath the section entitled *Defining Communication Channels* (SAP AG).

> ➤ On the receiver side, an adapter is used to translate between the internal XI protocol and the communication protocol used to send messages to the receiver system. Here, for example, you might use the File/FTP adapter to send a message to a receiver system via FTP.

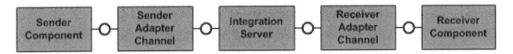

Figure 11.32: Understanding the Positioning of Communication Channels

One of the nice things about adapters is that you can mix and match them in all kinds of different ways. For example, imagine a legacy SAP system that needs to perform a real-time lookup via some external database. In this scenario, you could use the RFC and JDBC adapters to allow PI to proxy the database query on behalf of the SAP system. Similarly, you could use the IDoc and File/JMS adapters to allow an SAP ERP system and a mainframe system communicate with one another, and so on.

11.4.1.1   Understanding the Adapter Framework

As you learned in Chapter 1, most adapters provided with SAP NetWeaver PI are packaged as Java-based resource adapters[81] based on the *Java Connector Architecture* (JCA). These adapter modules are deployed on the Advanced Adapter Engine (AAE). There, they are supplemented by the core services provided with the AS Java application server.

In addition to the core J2EE services offered by the AS Java stack, adapters are also supported by an *Adapter Framework* within the AAE that provides common services to adapters such as reliable messaging, lifecycle management, logging, and so on. Figure 11.33 illustrates the structure of the Adapter Framework. As you can see, there are quite a few moving parts involved in an adapter implementation.

---

[81] The exceptions to this are the IDoc, HTTP, and XI adapters which are deployed on the AS ABAP stack.

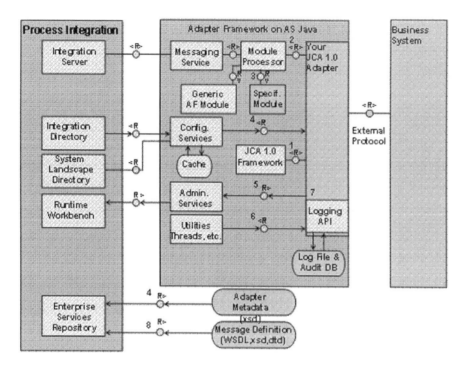

Figure 11.33: Structure of the Adapter Framework (SAP AG)
© *Copyright 2010. SAP AG. All rights reserved*

Part of the complexity you see in Figure 11.33 is due to the fact that the JCA 1.0 specification only describes communication in one direction (in this case, from the Integration Server to the endpoint system). Therefore, in order to support bi-directional communication in PI, each adapter must be enhanced to integrate with the *Module Processor* component shown in Figure 11.33. This component serves as the gateway for bringing in messages from external systems; how the messages get to this point in the first place is a detail left to the adapter provider.

The primary function of the Module Processor is to convert between the XI protocol and the native communication protocol supported by the adapter (and vice versa). This is achieved by chaining together a series of *adapter modules* that are implemented in the form of EJB 2.0 Session Beans. These modules can be mixed and matched to define the proper runtime behavior. Furthermore, SAP also allows you to develop your own custom adapter modules to supplement the functionality of an adapter. For a step-by-step overview of this development process, we highly recommend William Li's SAP

SDN article entitled *Developing Adapter User-Module to Encrypt XML Elements in Process Integration 7.1* (Li).

11.4.1.2   Adapter Types

By default, SAP provides you with quite a few standard adapter types that can be used to implement most common integration scenarios. Table 11.1 describes each of these standard adapters in turn.

Adapter Type	Deployment Type	Description
IDoc	AS ABAP	This adapter type is used to send and receive IDoc messages via the Integration Engine. Here, you'll find advanced support for acknowledgment processing, serialization, etc. For more information about the IDoc adapter, its functionality, and its integration with SAP's *Application Link Enabling* (ALE) framework, we highly recommend *Mastering IDoc Business Scenarios with SAP NetWeaver PI* (Krawczyk, 2010).
RFC	Java/JCA	This adapter type allows you to connect to SAP systems using the RFC protocol. Here, you can use the RFC adapter to call an RFC function or provide one.
Plain HTTP	AS ABAP	This adapter type is deployed as an ICF service within the AS ABAP stack. Here, you can send and receive messages using XML/HTTP.
SAP BC	Java/JCA	This adapter type provides backwards compatibility with the legacy SAP Business Connector software. Here, the adapter is used to transparently replace a Business Connector instance with SAP NetWeaver PI.

Adapter Type	Deployment Type	Description
File/FTP	Java/JCA	The File/FTP adapter can be used to exchange messages via the file interface or the FTP protocol: ❖ If the file interface is used, the adapter can read/write files from the local file system or via a file system that is mounted via the Network File System (NFS) protocol. ❖ If the File Transfer Protocol (FTP) is used, then the adapter can be used to get/put files on the remote host using the FTP protocol.
JDBC	Java/JCA	The JDBC adapter is used to connect to database systems using the vendor-agnostic Java JDBC API. Here, you can: ❖ Add, change, or remove records from the database using the SQL INSERT, UPDATE, and DELETE statements. ❖ Read database content by issuing SQL queries or calling stored procedures. ❖ Configure the adapter to periodically scan the database for changes and send those changes to the Integration Server (e.g., like database triggers).
JMS	Java/JCA	The JMS adapter is used to allow the Integration Server to send and receive messages from a JMS-based MOM provider. This provider could be IBM's WebSphere® MQ, the default JMS provider included with the SAP AS Java, or some other JMS-compliant provider.

Adapter Type	Deployment Type	Description
SOAP	Java/JCA	The SOAP adapter is used to send and receive messages using the SOAP protocol. As such, it is used extensively to develop Web service scenarios with SAP NetWeaver PI. For advanced scenarios, you can integrate custom handler modules defined within the Apache Axis framework to enhance the message processing capabilities of the SOAP adapter. See the online help documentation and SAP Note 856597 for more details.
Marketplace	Java/JCA	The Marketplace adapter is used to allow the Integration Server to connect to Internet marketplaces. Here, the adapter converts between the XI message format and the *MarketSet Markup Language* (MML).
Mail	Java/JCA	The Mail adapter is used to connect the Integration Server with e-mail servers: ❖ On the sender side, the Mail adapter will retrieve messages using the *Post Office Protocol* (POP) or *Internet Message Access Protocol* (IMAP) and then forward them to the Integration Server. ❖ On the receiver side, the Mail adapter forwards messages to a mail server using the *Simple Mail Transfer Protocol* (SMTP).
XI	AS ABAP[82]	The XI adapter is used to exchange messages between Integration Engines using the native XI protocol. As such, it is used when the sender or receiver systems utilize the ABAP or Java proxy runtimes.

---

[82] Beginning with release 7.11 of SAP NetWeaver PI, you can now use the SOAP adapter to communicate using the native XI protocol. See the SAP NetWeaver How-To Guide entitled: *How To Set Up the Communication between ABAP Backend and SOAP Adapter using XI Protocol* for more details.

Adapter Type	Deployment Type	Description
WS	AS ABAP	The WS adapter is used to communicate with Web service runtimes that utilize the WS-ReliableMessaging (WS-RM) protocol (e.g. backend SAP systems with a modern Web service runtime).

Table 11.1: Standard Adapter Types Provided with SAP NetWeaver PI

If none of the standard adapters meet your needs, you may be able to find a suitable alternative by browsing through the list of certified 3rd-party adapters that are provided by SAP's software partners. You can find an up-to-date list of these adapters on the SAP Developer Network which is available online at *http://www.sdn.sap.com/irj/sdn*. From the home page, select the menu path *SOA Middleware → Service Bus* in the detailed navigation area on the left-hand side of the page. There, you should see a *Third-Party Adapter* link that will take you to a list of available adapters.

A last-ditch alternative might be to create your own JCA resource adapter. However, such efforts are not for the faint of heart: you really have to know your way around the JCA and SAP APIs to do this right. SAP does at least provide you with a sample adapter implementation that you can use to get started. You can find detailed documentation about this adapter and its implementation in the online help underneath the section entitled *Developing Adapters and Modules* (SAP AG).

11.4.2 Creating Communication Channels

Now that you understand the basics of communication channels, let's turn our attention towards their creation in the Integration Directory. For the most part, you'll find that the required steps are basically the same regardless of the adapter type being used. However, one thing that you have to determine up front is where the channel definition should sit within the collaboration profile hierarchy. Here, you have several options to choose from. In particular, you can define a channel in the context of:

> ➢ Communication parties

> ➢ Communication components embedded within communication parties

> Standalone communication components[83]

Once you determine the proper context, you can define a communication channel by performing the following steps:

1. To begin, open up the object view in the Integration Builder tool. Then, in the left-hand navigation area, you must locate the relevant *Communication Channel* node, right-click on it, and select the *New* menu option (see Figure 11.34).

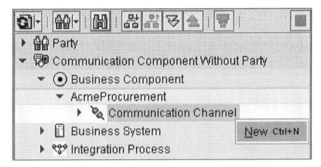

Figure 11.34: Creating a Communication Channel (Part 1)
© Copyright 2010. SAP AG. All rights reserved

2. This will open up the *Create Object* dialog box shown in Figure 11.35. As you can see, the party/communication component assignment are automatically populated based upon the selected context. Therefore, you need only to enter a name[84] and an optional description for the channel definition. Click the *Create* button to proceed.

---

[83] The lone exception to this rule is that you cannot define communication components within an integration process component (for obvious reasons).
[84] Consult the SAP NetWeaver How-To Guide entitled *PI Best Practices: Naming Conventions* (SAP AG) for naming conventions.

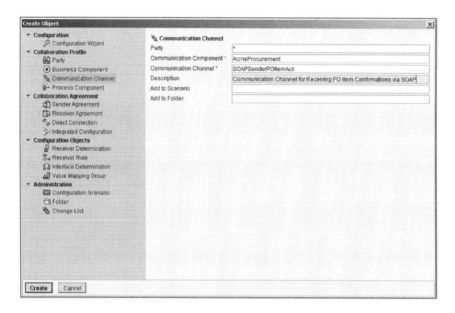

Figure 11.35: Creating a Communication Channel (Part 2)

3. As you can see in Figure 11.36, the communication channel editor
   initially starts you off with a clean slate. To proceed with the
   configuration, you must first select the appropriate adapter type.
   For this task, you must utilize the value help provided in the
   Adapter Type field. This will open up the *Choose Adapter Metadata*
   dialog box shown in Figure 11.37. There, you can select the
   appropriate adapter type and then click on the *Apply* button to
   confirm your selection.

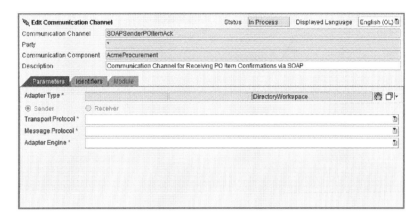

Figure 11.36: Editing a Communication Channel Definition

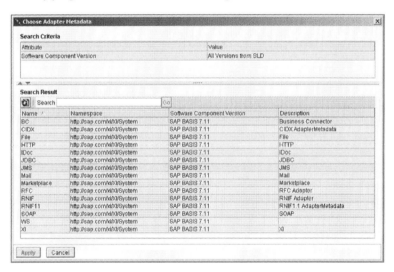

Figure 11.37: Selecting an Adapter Type for a Channel Definition

4. Before you can proceed with the configuration of the various technical attributes, you must determine the *direction* of the message processing. For messages sent from a sender system to PI, you'll select the *Sender* radio button shown in Figure 11.36. Similarly, for messages sent from PI to a receiver system, you'll choose the *Receiver* radio button.

5. Finally, you can fill in the relevant attributes for the channel definition and save your changes. Note that these changes will not

take effect until you activate[85] the channel definition in your change list.

As mentioned previously, the parameters that you must specify for a given channel definition will vary greatly depending upon the adapter type selection and the direction of the message processing. For example, Figure 11.38 shows an example of a JDBC receiver channel. Here, you can see how we have provided the parameters needed to create a connection to a MySQL® database. Naturally, if we were to adjust the adapter type to JMS, the parameters would change accordingly.

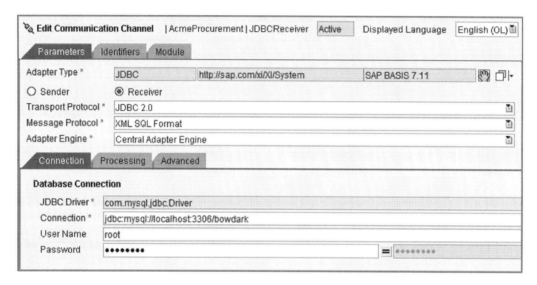

Figure 11.38: Maintaining Communication Channel Definitions © Copyright 2010. SAP AG. All rights reserved

For information about the parameters defined for a specific adapter type, consult the online help documentation underneath the section entitled *Defining Communication Channels* (SAP AG). There, you will find detailed documentation for each adapter type as well as a reference to an accompanying SAP Note that posts up-to-date information about the adapter, FAQs, and so on.

---

[85] Whenever you activate a communication channel definition, the relevant connection details are copied over into a special cache area in the AAE called the *Collaboration Profile Agreement* (CPA) cache.

11.4.2.1 Specifying Identification Schemes

In Section 11.2.1, you learned how to define alternate identifiers for communication parties. As you may recall, these alternate identifiers are used in B2B scenarios to address companies by the appropriate identification scheme.

At runtime, the translation between a communication party and an external identifier is executed at the adapter layer. Of course, in order for this to work, the adapter needs to know which identification schemes to translate between. Therefore, within a communication channel definition, you have the option of defining *identifiers* for communication parties.

As you can see in Figure 11.39, identifiers for communication parties are defined on the *Identifiers* tab within the channel editor. There, you can select an identification scheme for senders and receivers of messages. At runtime, this information is used as an index for searching in the identifiers table of the overarching communication party definition to locate the proper party to address during message routing.

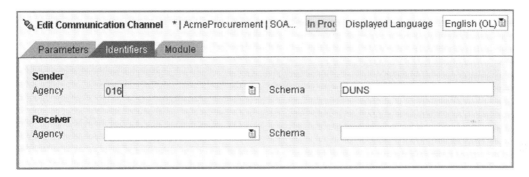

Figure 11.39: Specifying Identifiers in a Communication Channel
© Copyright 2010. SAP AG. All rights reserved

11.4.2.2 Customizing the Sequence of Adapter Modules

In Section 11.4.1.1, you learned how adapters interact with the Module Processor component to perform translations between the native XI protocol and an external communication protocol. One of the advantages of this architectural approach to adapter development is that the fact that you can mix and match adapter modules within the Module Processor to implement the desired runtime behavior. For example, if you need to adjust the payload of an incoming or outgoing message, you can do so by inserting a custom adapter module into the processing sequence.

You can adjust the processing sequence for adapter modules within your channel definition by clicking on the *Module* tab in the channel editor. Here, you'll find that the processing sequence for the standard adapter types is pre-populated by default. For example, in Figure 11.40, you can see the processing sequence for a JMS receiver channel. In this case, there are two adapters modules involved in the message processing:

1. First, the ConvertMessageToBinary module is called to convert the XI message payload into a binary format.

2. Then, the SendBinaryToXIJMSService module forwards the binary payload on to the JMS provider via the Java JMS API.

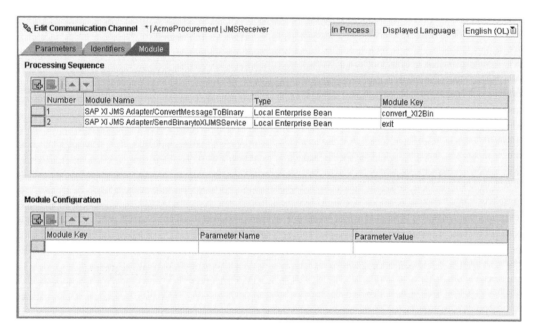

Figure 11.40: Adjusting the Module Processing Sequence © Copyright 2010. SAP AG. All rights reserved

For each module included in the processing sequence, you must specify three basic properties:

> **Module Name**
> This property assigns a name to an adapter module instance. In this case, since adapter modules are implemented as EJB 2.0 Session Beans, the name value refers to the *Java Naming & Directory Interface* (JNDI) path used to reference the adapter module.

> **Type**
> This property is used to determine the type of module that you're
> interjecting into the sequence. In almost all cases, you'll want to keep
> the default value here as it is the one prescribed by SAP. The other
> options are a carry-over from prior releases of PI.

> **Module Key**
> With this property, you can specify a key that is used to reference the
> module in the *Module Configuration* section of the module editor
> shown in Figure 11.40.

The behavior of each module within the process sequence can be further
influenced via the specification of parameters within the *Module
Configuration* section on the bottom portion of the module editor screen (see
Figure 11.40). There, you can add parameters for specific module instances
by selecting the appropriate module key in the *Module Key* column. The
parameters themselves are configured using name/value semantics (e.g., via
the *Parameter Name* and *Parameter Value* fields, respectively).

Working with SAP Standard Modules

In addition to the default modules configured for adapter types, SAP also
provides a series of standalone modules that you can use to enhance
message processing. You can find information about these standard modules
in the online help documentation underneath the section entitled *Adding
Modules to the Module Processor* (SAP AG). There, you'll find adapter
modules that enable you to build sync/async or async/sync bridges using the
JMS adapter, as well as other generic modules that can enhance the
message payload, etc.

11.5   Summary

In this chapter, we considered the ins-and-outs of collaboration profiles. As
you learned, collaboration profiles model the endpoint systems involved in
integration scenarios. Therefore, they are part of the basis of most every
configuration object within the Integration Directory. In the next two
chapters, we'll see evidence of this as we turn our attention towards the
configuration of various types of integration scenarios.

References

Krawczyk, M. K. (2010). *Mastering IDoc Business Scenarios with SAP NetWeaver PI, 2nd Edition.* Boston: SAP PRESS.

Li, W. (n.d.). *Developing Adapter User-Module to Encrypt XML Elements in Process Integration 7.1.* Retrieved April 7, 2011, from SAP Developer Network (SDN): http://www.sdn.sap.com/irj/sdn/soa-servicebus?rid=/library/uuid/f0ac06cf-6ee2-2c10-df98-e17430ca5949

Merriam-Webster. (n.d.). *Adapt: Definition.* Retrieved January 7, 2011, from Merriam-Webster Online: Dictionary and Thesaurus: http://www.merriam-webster.com/dictionary/adapt

SAP AG. (n.d.). *Adding Modules to the Module Processor.* Retrieved January 10, 2011, from SAP Help Library:
http://help.sap.com/saphelp_nwpi711/helpdata/en/cd/5af7c0c994e24fb0d0088443513de2/frameset.htm

SAP AG. (n.d.). *Business Systems.* Retrieved January 5, 2011, from SAP Help Library:
http://help.sap.com/saphelp_nwpi711/helpdata/en/48/b6813496655295e10000000a42189b/frameset.htm

SAP AG. (n.d.). *Communication Channels.* Retrieved January 7, 2011, from SAP Help Library:
http://help.sap.com/saphelp_nwpi711/helpdata/en/48/d0067005ae154ee10000000a421937/frameset.htm

SAP AG. (n.d.). *Communication Components.* Retrieved January 4, 2011, from SAP Help Library:
http://help.sap.com/saphelp_nwpi711/helpdata/en/48/ced1d618d3424be10000000a421937/frameset.htm

SAP AG. (n.d.). *Configuring Systems to Connect to the SLD.* Retrieved January 5, 2011, from SAP Help Library:
http://help.sap.com/saphelp_nwpi711/helpdata/en/48/b6812896655295e10000000a42189b/frameset.htm

SAP AG. (n.d.). *Defining Communication Channels.* Retrieved January 7, 2011, from SAP Help Library:

http://help.sap.com/saphelp_nwpi711/helpdata/en/48/d0066d05ae154ee10
000000a421937/frameset.htm

SAP AG. (n.d.). *Developing Adapters and Modules.* Retrieved January 7,
2011, from SAP Help Library:
http://help.sap.com/saphelp_nwpi711/helpdata/en/8b/895e407aa4c44ce100
00000a1550b0/frameset.htm

SAP AG. (n.d.). *Structure of the Adapter Framework.* Retrieved April 7, 2011,
from SAP Help Library:
http://help.sap.com/saphelp_nwpi711/helpdata/en/fd/16e140a786702ae100
00000a155106/frameset.htm

Integration Server Configuration

12

In the previous chapter, you learned how to model the endpoint systems that participate in collaborative business processes. Now that you understand these concepts, you're ready to learn how to define the rules that determine how incoming messages are forwarded on to their intended recipients. In this chapter, we'll see how all this works in the context of Integration Server-based communication.

After completing this chapter, you will be able to:

- ❖ Understand the core functions and features of the Integration Engine.

- ❖ Configure logical routing rules that determine how incoming messages are forwarded on to their intended recipients.

- ❖ Define collaboration agreements that specify the technical details for message processing.

12.1   Basic Concepts

In order to leverage all of the features of the SAP NetWeaver PI runtime environment, you must configure *Integration Server-based communication*. This communication variant delegates the majority of the heavy lifting for message processing to the AS ABAP-based Integration Engine (IE). Internally, the IE utilizes configuration settings specified within the Integration Directory to direct the flow of incoming messages.

In this chapter, we will explore the configuration objects that are used to implement Integration Server-based communication. However, before we start down this path, we first need to take a closer look at the architecture and functionality of the IE itself. Having an understanding of these concepts will give you a better feel for how these configuration objects are used from a runtime perspective.

12.1.1   Integration Engine Overview

From an architectural point-of-view, the IE plays the role of integration broker within SAP NetWeaver PI. As such, its job is to coordinate message processing between the various application systems that communicate with PI. Of course, those systems don't communicate directly with the IE; rather, they communicate with various protocol adapters which broker communications to and from the IE.

Figure 12.1 illustrates the positioning of the IE within the overall Integration Server architecture. As you can see, the IE is deployed on the AS ABAP. Underneath the hood, the functionality provided by the IE is realized in the form of Internet Communication Framework (ICF) services, a series of ABAP Objects classes, and various other development objects included in the SXMSF package.

Internally, the IE processes messages using the SAP proprietary XI protocol, which is an extension of the industry standard *SOAP with Attachments* (SwA) protocol. While most of these details are shielded from developers, the important thing to take note of here is that all messages processed within the IE are encoded using XML[86]. This commonality makes it possible to

---

[86] That's not to say they start out or end up that way. One of the primary tasks of adapters is to perform conversions between an external communication protocol and the XI protocol. As such, adapters (and, more

implement sophisticated message routing rules, etc. using industry-standard technology such as XPath. We'll learn more about this beginning in Section 12.2.

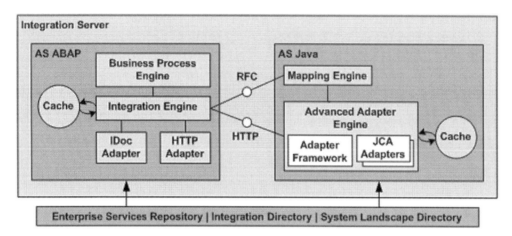

Figure 12.1: The SAP NetWeaver PI Integration Server

Note
While most people typically associate the IE with SAP NetWeaver PI, it is important to note that the IE is a component that can be used in *any* AS ABAP-based application system. In the latter case, the IE provides a runtime environment for executing *ABAP proxies*. We'll explore these concepts in further detail in Appendix A.

12.1.1.1   Caching Concepts

Looking closely at Figure 12.1, you might be wondering about the cache area attached to the IE. This cache area serves as a *runtime cache*, supplying the IE with the rules it must use to process a given message. As you might have guessed, these rules originate from configuration objects maintained within the Integration Directory. Here, whenever configuration objects are activated, the corresponding data is replicated over to the IE runtime cache to improve performance. You can view and maintain the contents of this cache via transaction SXI_CACHE.

---

specifically, adapter modules) can be used to translate proprietary message formats into XML and vice versa.

12.1.1.2 The Integration Engine Pipeline

In general, messages are passed to the IE in one of two ways:

> ➢ As an HTTP request message[87] forwarded from an adapter in the AAE.

> ➢ Via a direct call from the adapter types installed on the AS ABAP (i.e. the IDoc adapter, etc.).

In either case, once the message has been received, it is handed over to the *Integration Engine pipeline* for further processing. As the term "pipeline" connotes, the IE pipeline defines a channel in which messages are processed via a series of services that are logically chained together. To understand how all this works, let's take a look at the central pipeline definition utilized for message processing in PI.

To view the default pipeline definition used by the IE, execute transaction SXMB_ADM and double-click on the *Display Pipeline Definition* link shown in Figure 12.2. This will open up the *Pipeline Definition Display* screen shown in Figure 12.3. Here, you must select the SAP_CENTRAL pipeline ID and hit the *Enter* key. Then, if you click on the *Pipeline Element* tab, the selected pipeline definition will be displayed on the screen shown in Figure 12.4.

As you can see in Figure 12.4, a pipeline definition consists of a series of pipeline elements that are arranged in logical order for message processing. Each of these pipeline elements refers to a *pipeline service* which implements a particular aspect of the message processing. For example, the Receiver Determination element shown in Figure 12.4 refers to a pipeline service called PLSRV_RECEIVER_DETERMINATION. As the name suggests, this service helps the IE determine the receiver(s) of a given message.

---

[87] The URL used to forward the request is of the form *http(s)://{AS ABAP Host}:{AS ABAP Port}/sap/xi/engine*. If you are interested to learn how this ICF service is implemented, check out method IF_HTTP_EXTENSION~HANDLE_REQUEST() of class CL_XMS_HTTP_HANDLER in the ABAP Workbench.

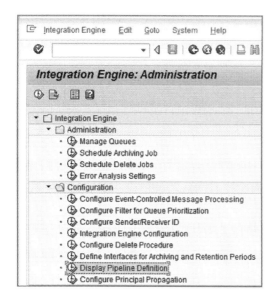

Figure 12.2: Displaying the IE Pipeline Definition in SXMB_ADM

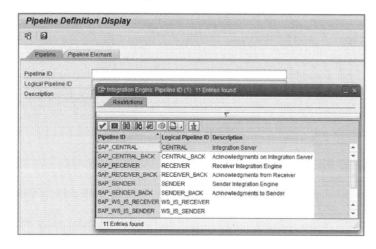

Figure 12.3: Selecting the Proper Pipeline Definition

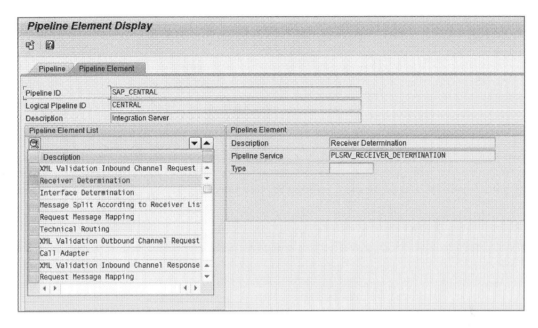

Figure 12.4: Displaying a Pipeline Definition © Copyright 2010. SAP AG. All rights reserved

Table 12.1 describes the services[88] provided by each of the pipeline elements contained within the SAP_CENTRAL pipeline definition.

Pipeline Element	Description
XML Validation Inbound Channel Request	This pipeline element is used to validate an incoming message according to a specified XML Schema type.
Receiver Determination	This element is used to determine the receiver(s) of a given message.
Interface Determination	Once the receiver(s) are determined in the previous step, this pipeline element is used to determine the interface(s) that should be called on the receiver system(s).

---

[88] To see how these services are implemented, have a look at the contents of the ABAP Dictionary table SXMSPLSRV. There, you can discover which ABAP Objects classes/methods are used to implement a particular pipeline service.

Pipeline Element	Description
Message Split According to Receiver List	If the Receiver Determination step determined that a given incoming message should be routed to multiple receivers, then this element is used to multicast the message based upon the derived receiver list.
Request Message Mapping	If an XML transformation needs to take place before the target interface is called, this pipeline element will be used to call the specified operation mapping. If the mapping program is implemented in the ABAP Workbench, then the mapping program is executed via a local call. For mapping programs developed in the ESR (i.e. graphical message mappings, Java mappings, or XSLT mappings), an RFC call is made to execute the mapping program in the mapping environment of the AS Java.
Technical Routing	This pipeline element is used to lookup the communication channel used to forward a message on to its intended recipients.
XML Validation Outbound Channel Request	This element can be used to validate an outgoing XML message before it is sent to the receiver. Normally, this element is used to validate the message generated by the previous message mapping step.
Call Adapter	This element uses the channel definition derived at the Technical Routing step to call the adapter used to send a message to a given application system. For adapters deployed on the AAE, this implies an intermediate HTTP hop to forward the message on to the AAE's Adapter Framework.
XML Validation Inbound Channel Request	If the service operation was called synchronously, then you have the option of performing an XML Schema validation using this pipeline element.

Pipeline Element	Description
Request Message Mapping	If the service operation was called synchronously, then this element can be used to call an XML mapping program to transform the synchronous response into a format the sender expects.
XML Validation Outbound Channel Response	After the previous transformation step, you have the option of performing another XML validation using this pipeline step.

Table 12.1: Pipeline Elements within the IE Pipeline

12.1.2   Configuration Overview

In the previous section, you learned how messages are processed within the IE pipeline. There, we hinted that the behavior of this message processing was influenced by a series of configuration objects defined within the Integration Directory. In this section, we will highlight the configuration objects used to implement Integration Server-based communication.

To understand the positioning of these objects, let's consider a simple integration scenario between a sender and receiver system. The UML sequence diagram contained in Figure 12.5 illustrates this scenario in terms of the technical components involved in the message exchange. As you can see, there are four main configuration objects that influence the behavior of these components at runtime:

> **Sender Agreement**
> Sender agreements define the technical details for the inbound processing of a given message.

> **Receiver Determination**
> Receiver determinations are used to determine which receiver system(s) should receive a message.

> **Interface Determination**
> Once the list of receivers has been determined, an interface determination specifies which interfaces should be called on those systems.

> **Receiver Agreement**
> Receiver agreements define the technical details for the outbound processing of a message.

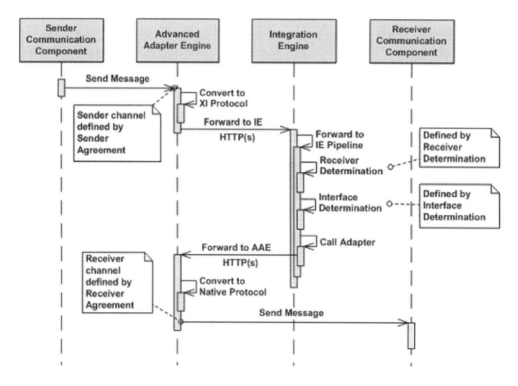

Figure 12.5: Configuration Objects Used for Integration Server-Based Processing

Over the course of the next few sections, we'll show you how these configuration objects work in conjunction with collaboration profiles to specify the configuration of a given collaborative business process.

12.2   Receiver Determinations

Put simply, receiver determinations are used to determine the receivers of a given inbound message. While this sounds straightforward enough on paper, the actual implementation details can become much more complicated that you might expect. Fortunately, you'll find the definition of receiver determinations to be quite flexible. In the next few sections, we'll show you how to work with receiver determinations.

12.2.1   Defining Standard Receiver Determinations

One of the best ways to illustrate the concept of receiver determinations is to see how they are maintained within the Integration Directory. Therefore, before we delve into an explanation about specific attributes, etc., let's briefly explore the creation of a receiver determination using the Integration Builder. The steps required to achieve this are as follows:

1. Log onto the Integration Builder and select the *Object → New* menu option from the top level menu bar. This will open up the *Create Object* dialog box shown in Figure 12.6. Here, you'll want to expand the *Configuration Objects* submenu on the left-hand side of the screen and select the *Receiver Determination* menu option.

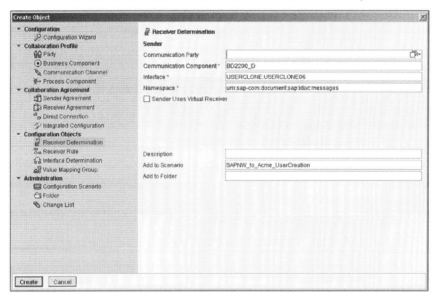

Figure 12.6: Creating a Receiver Determination

2. As you can see in Figure 12.6, the object key for a receiver determination consists of several key fields that are used to uniquely identify the sender of a message. Here, you must specify:

   ❖ The sender's communication party in the case of B2B scenarios.

   ❖ The communication component used to address the sender.

   ❖ The sender service interface and its corresponding namespace as defined within the ESR.

3. Finally, once you determine the object key for the receiver determination, click the *Create* button to open up the receiver determination editor tool shown in Figure 12.7.

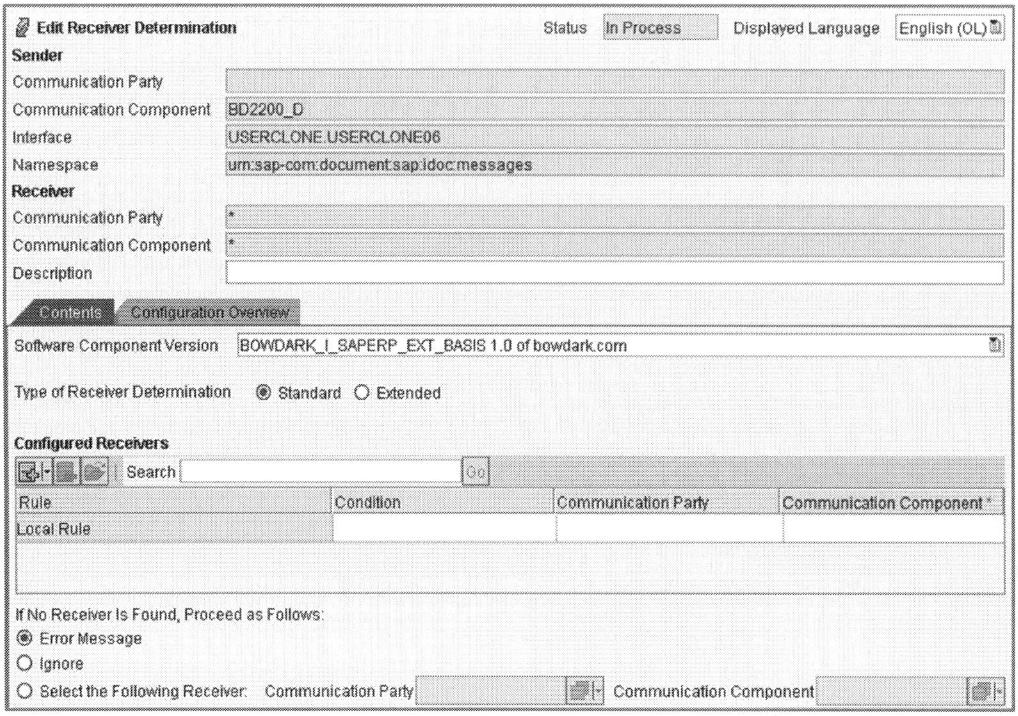

📝 Edit Receiver Determination		Status	In Process	Displayed Language	English (OL) 🔽
Sender					
Communication Party					
Communication Component	BD2200_D				
Interface	USERCLONE.USERCLONE06				
Namespace	urn:sap-com:document:sap:idoc:messages				
Receiver					
Communication Party	*				
Communication Component	*				
Description					

Contents | Configuration Overview

Software Component Version   BOWDARK_I_SAPERP_EXT_BASIS 1.0 of bowdark.com 🔽

Type of Receiver Determination   ⦿ Standard   ○ Extended

Configured Receivers

📇 | 📇 | ■ | 📁 | Search [   ] Go

Rule	Condition	Communication Party	Communication Component *
Local Rule			

If No Receiver Is Found, Proceed as Follows:
⦿ Error Message
○ Ignore
○ Select the Following Receiver: Communication Party [   ] 📇 Communication Component [   ] 📇

Figure 12.7: Editing Receiver Determinations in the Integration Builder

As you can see in Figure 12.7, the receiver determination editor is basically like a rules editor in which you can configure the set of receivers for a given incoming message. To define a receiver for a message, you simply add a row to the *Configured Receivers* table and plug in the target communication component (and its corresponding communication party in the case of B2B communication). Here, you also have the option of defining *conditions* that qualify these assignments based upon logical expressions. We'll explore this concept in further detail in Section 12.2.1.1.

Besides the selection of the receivers themselves, you also need to specify how the receiver determination service should react in situations where no receiver(s) are found. Here, you have three options to choose from:

> ➢ If you select the *Error Message* option, then the IE will output an error message to the message log – we'll learn how to navigate through these logs in Chapter 14.

> ➢ If you choose the *Ignore* option, then the system will simply discard the incoming message without logging an error.

> ➢ The *Select the Following Receiver* option allows you to plug in a default receiver in the event that no receivers are found. This option can come in handy if you want to route "junk mail" to a dead letter queue of some kind, etc.

In most cases, that's about all there is to a receiver determination. However, in the next few sections, we'll take a look at some advanced features that you can use to handle more complex receiver selection use cases.

12.2.1.1 Working with the Condition Editor

In basic receiver determination scenarios, you probably know which receivers you want to route a message to ahead of time. However, occasionally, you may wish to derive such assignments dynamically. For example, for purchase order messages, you might want to route a message to different receivers based upon the PO's document type. Within a receiver determination, you can express such logic using *conditions*.

You can specify conditions in the *Condition* field contained within the *Configured Receivers* table shown in Figure 12.7. There, you can select the value help button ( ) to open up the *Condition Editor* screen shown in Figure 12.8. As you can see, this editor enables you to build complex expressions using familiar Boolean operators such as EQUALS (=), NOT EQUALS (≠), AND, OR, and so on. These expressions compare the values of elements (or attributes) selected from the source document in the *Left Operand* field with constant values specified in the *Right Operand* field[89].

In order to compare values from the source document, we need a way to easily address elements and attributes. For this task, SAP employs the industry-standard *XML Path Language* (XPath[90]). Fortunately, rather than forcing you to hack your own XPath queries, SAP provides you with a value

---

[89] You can find detailed documentation on the functions and operators of the Condition Editor in the online help documentation underneath the section entitled *Using the Condition Editor* (SAP AG).

[90] As you may recall from Chapter 7, XPath allows you to define queries to locate XML components using a similar syntax to the one used in file systems. You can read more about XPath online at *http://www.w3.org/TR/xpath/*.

help in the *Left Operand* field that opens up the *Expression Editor* shown in Figure 12.9. Here, you can navigate through the components defined in the source message's XML Schema to build the proper expression.

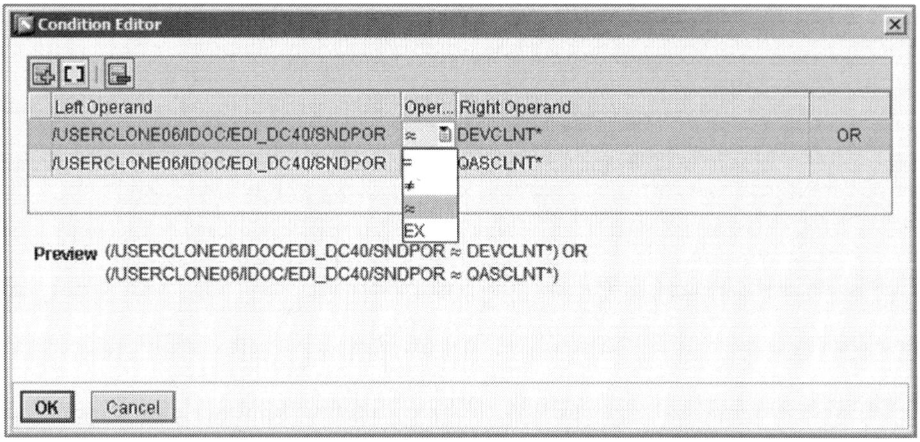

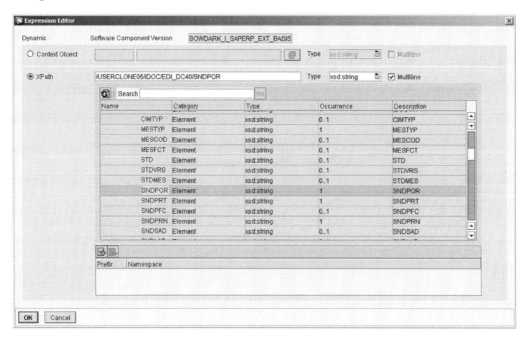

Figure 12.8: Working with the Condition Editor © Copyright 2010. SAP AG. All rights reserved

Figure 12.9: Defining Conditional Expressions Using the Expression Editor © Copyright 2010. SAP AG. All rights reserved

Once you define your expression(s), the receiver determination service will evaluate them at runtime to conditionally forward incoming messages on to the selected receiver components. Of course, such evaluations are not provided gratis – there is some processing overhead associated with scanning through a source document to determine if it meets the requisite criteria. So, if you find yourself constructing highly complex expressions, you might want to take another look at the business process logic. Alternatively, you can consider using *extended receiver determinations* which are described in Section 12.2.2.

Context Objects

Looking back at the *Expression Editor* screen shown in Figure 12.9, you might have noticed another option for selecting values from the source document: *context objects*. For the most part, you can think of a context object as a type of reusable, pre-compiled XPath query. As such, they can be easier to work with when building conditional expressions and the like.

Context objects are defined within the ESR using the ES Builder tool. To create a context object, perform the following steps:

1. Log onto the ES Builder tool and select the *Object → New* menu option from the top-level menu bar.

2. Then, in the ensuing *Create Object* dialog box, expand *the Interface Objects* submenu and select the *Context Object* menu option.

3. Finally, provide a name[91] and optional description for the context object and click on the *Create* button. This will open up the context object in the editor screen shown in Figure 12.10. Be sure to save your changes.

As you can see in Figure 12.10, there's not a whole lot to context objects. Indeed, the only thing you need to configure is the *Reference Type* field. Here, you can choose between several built-in XML Schema data types to define the *type* of the context object. In this case, you will want to select the built-in type that matches the data type you wish to index. In the example shown in Figure 12.10, we are defining a context object for indexing user names, so therefore the reference type will be xsd:string.

---

[91] Consult the SAP NetWeaver How-To Guide entitled *PI Best Practices: Naming Conventions* (SAP AG) for naming conventions.

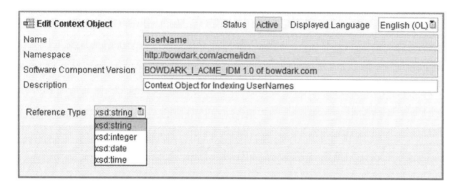

Figure 12.10: Editing Context Objects in the ES Builder © Copyright 2010. SAP AG. All rights reserved

Conceptually speaking, context objects are similar to *typed pointers* or *aliases* that are used in programming languages to reference other variables. In this instance, context objects are used to reference elements or attributes within an XML message. These reference assignments are made at design time whenever you define a service interface in the ESR.

To see how this works, take a look at the service interface editor screen shown in Figure 12.11. Here, you'll notice that there's a *Context Objects* toolbar button contained within the *Messages* table in the bottom right-hand portion of the screen. If you click this button, you will open up the *Context Object Assignment* dialog box shown in Figure 12.12. There, you can drill into a request message's XML Schema components to locate the proper location path. Then, once you find the right path, you can plug in your context object in the *Context Object* field.

After context object assignments have been made (and activated) in the ESR, you can use them in place of XPath queries when defining conditions in a receiver determination, etc. Here, you simply choose the *Context Object* radio button in the Expression Editor shown in Figure 12.9 and navigate to your context object definition. As you can imagine, this shorthand convention can be quite useful in complex expressions – especially if you use the same expression in multiple rule definitions.

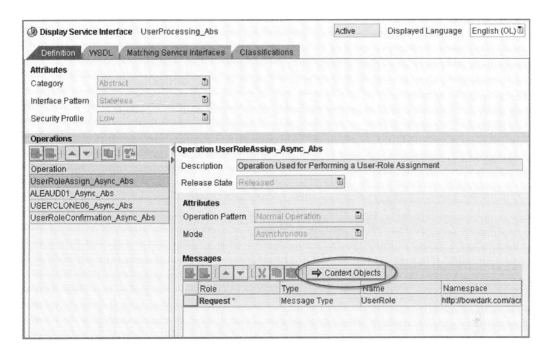

Figure 12.11: Defining Context Objects within a Service Operation (Part 1)

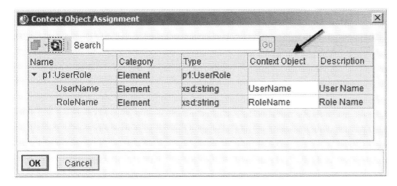

Figure 12.12: Defining Context Objects within a Service Operation (Part 2)

12.2.1.2 Defining Virtual Receivers

Sometimes, in B2B scenarios, you may want to mask the particulars of your system landscape by defining *virtual receivers*. To put this into perspective, let's consider an example. Imagine a scenario in which an external business partner is sending a message that will ultimately be processed by an SAP ERP system within your system landscape. From a configuration perspective, this implies that you define a receiver determination to route the incoming message from the external business partner to the backend SAP ERP system. However, such a definition results in a fairly tight coupling between the external business partner and your internal system landscape.

To provide a looser coupling between these two entities, you can interject a *virtual receiver*. In this case, the external business partner sends the message to this virtual receiver and is otherwise unaware of what happens to the message thereafter. Internally, you can then redirect the message from the virtual receiver on to the target backend SAP ERP system.

To configure virtual receivers, you must select the *Sender Uses Virtual Receiver* checkbox upfront in the *Create Object* dialog box when you create a receiver determination (see Figure 12.13). Once this checkbox is selected, you will then have the option of filling in the virtual receiver details in the *Communication Party* and *Communication Component* fields that pop up below. From here, you configure the receiver determination as per usual. The only difference the fact that you're actually routing the incoming message from the virtual receiver on to the target backend components.

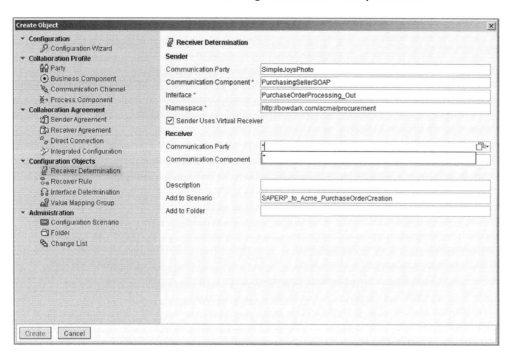

Figure 12.13: Specifying Virtual Receivers in a Receiver Determination

12.2.1.3 Specifying Receiver Determinations Generically

Besides the configuration of virtual receivers, you also have the option of generically specifying receiver determinations. Here, rather than selecting a specific sender communication party/component, you can simply plug in a wildcard ($*$) as shown in Figure 12.14[92]. In this example, we are defining a generic receiver determination that can be used to process an incoming USERCLONE.USERCLONE06 IDoc message from *any* sender system.

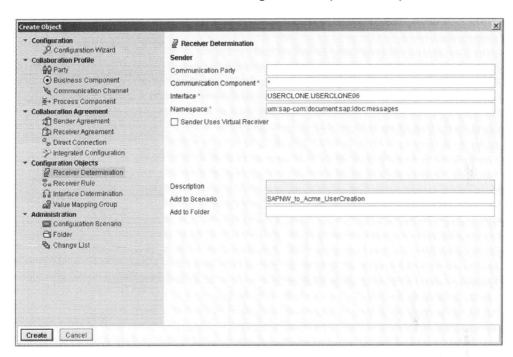

Figure 12.14: Specifying Generic Receiver Determinations © Copyright 2010. SAP AG. All rights reserved

The introduction of generic receiver determinations can bring up an interesting dilemma at runtime: what happens if there are multiple receiver determinations that could be used to process an incoming message? In these situations, the receiver determination service will select the most specific receiver determination as this takes precedence over more generically-defined receiver determinations. In general, we recommend that you strive

---

[92] For more information about the syntax options here, consult the online help documentation underneath the section entitled *Defining Configuration Objects Generically/Specifically* (SAP AG).

to define receiver determinations as fully as you can to avoid any such ambiguities.

12.2.2 Defining Extended Receiver Determinations

Up until now, our discussion on receiver determinations has been focused on the configuration options included with *standard* receiver determinations. However, in addition to these standard features, you also have the option of creating *extended receiver determinations*.

For the most part, extended receiver determinations are created in the same way that standard receiver determinations are. The primary difference is the selection of the *Extended* radio button from the *Type of Receiver Determination* radio button group (see Figure 12.15). This will cause the bottom portion of the editor screen to switch from the familiar *Configured Receivers* editor view to the view shown in Figure 12.15. As you can see, the revised editor view allows you to specify an operation mapping that is used to perform the receiver determination.

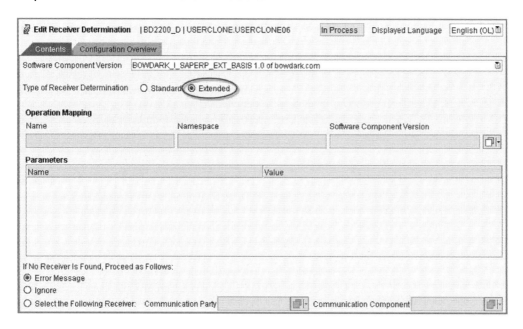

Figure 12.15: Defining Extended Receiver Determinations © Copyright 2010. SAP AG. All rights reserved

At this point, you might be wondering what operation mappings have to do with receiver determinations. To put all this into perspective, let's take a look at what is going on with extended receiver determinations at runtime. Figure 12.16 illustrates this process.

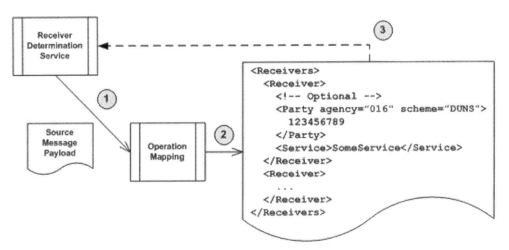

Figure 12.16: Behavior of Operation Mappings for Extended Receiver Determinations

Looking at the process depicted in Figure 12.16, let's consider each of these processing steps in turn:

1. Whenever the receiver determination service selects an extended receiver determination, it will evaluate its configuration attributes to determine which operation mapping to call. Here, the contents of the source message payload will be passed in to that operation mapping for evaluation.

2. Internally, the operation mapping (and its underlying message mapping) uses the contents of the source message's payload to build a list of receivers.

3. Then, the receiver determination service uses the generated XML to process the receiver list just as it would in a standard receiver determination.

When you look at extended receiver determinations in this light, you can see that they basically delegate all of the heavy lifting for receiver determination to an operation mapping. Beyond that, and the optional specification of some parameters that get passed to the operation mapping, that's about all there is to it.

12.2.2.1 Creating the Operation Mapping

Generally speaking, you maintain the operation mappings for extended receiver determinations just as you would any normal operation mapping. The primary difference in this case is the static assignment of the target `ReceiverDetermination` service operation which is included in the standard `ReceiverDetermination` service interface provided by SAP[93].

Figure 12.17 illustrates the structure of the target message that will be generated by the operation mapping. As you can see, the root `Receivers` element of this structure contains a series of child `Receiver` elements that can be used to specify one or more receivers for a given message. Here, you also have the option of qualifying each receiver with a communication party.

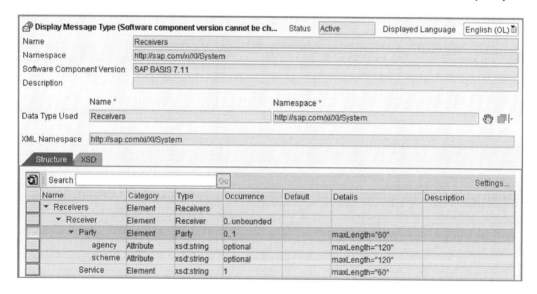

Figure 12.17: Viewing the Receivers Message Type in the ESR © Copyright 2010. SAP AG. All rights reserved

Besides the hard requirement for specifying the target operation, you are free to implement the operation mapping in pretty much any way you desire (e.g. as a graphical message mapping, XSLT mapping, and so on).

---

[93] The `ReceiverDetermination` service interface definition is provided in the `SAP BASIS` software component that is installed by default with every SAP NetWeaver PI installation. You can find the service interface and its underlying message/data types underneath the `http://sap.com/xi/XI/System` namespace.

Internally, you can build complex algorithms to scan the source document to determine the corresponding receivers.

12.2.3   Defining Reusable Receiver Rules

By default, each of the rules that you specify within a standard receiver determination are defined *locally*. This is to say that you cannot reuse the logic encoded in one receiver determination in another receiver determination. However, beginning with release 7.1 of SAP NetWeaver PI, you now have the option of specifying such rules *globally* using *receiver rules*. These configuration objects can be used to encapsulate receiver selection logic that is applicable for multiple receiver determination definitions.

To create a receiver rule, perform the following steps:

1. To begin, select the *Object → New* menu option in the top-level menu bar.

2. This will open up the familiar *Create Object* dialog box. Here, expand the *Configuration Objects* submenu and select the *Receiver Rule* menu option.

3. Finally, provide a name and an optional description for the receiver rule and click on the *Create* button. This will open up the receiver rule in the editor screen shown in Figure 12.18. Click the *Save* button to save your changes.

As you can see in Figure 12.18, the receiver rule editor contains a *Configured Receivers* table that can be used to specify the receiver rules just like the one used to configure local rules in a receiver determination. Across the board, you'll find the behavior here to be identical to that of the receiver determination editor. Here, as before, you'll work with the Condition Editor to define the conditions in which a particular receiver component should receive a message. However, in this case, notice that the receiver rule is not defined in terms of any particular sender component/interface. Instead, such details are determined whenever a receiver rule is added to a receiver determination. Naturally, this generic approach increases the opportunity for reuse.

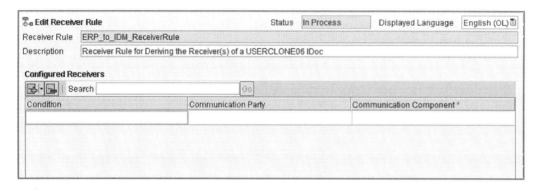

Figure 12.18: Maintaining Receiver Rules in the Integration Builder

Once a receiver rule is created, you can add it to a receiver determination by expanding the *Insert Receiver* (⬛⁛) button list and selecting the *Insert Receiver Rule* menu option. Then, you can plug in the receiver rule in the *Rule* column shown in Figure 12.20.

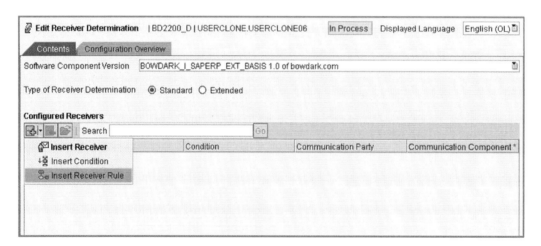

Figure 12.19: Adding a Receiver Rule to a Standard Receiver Determination

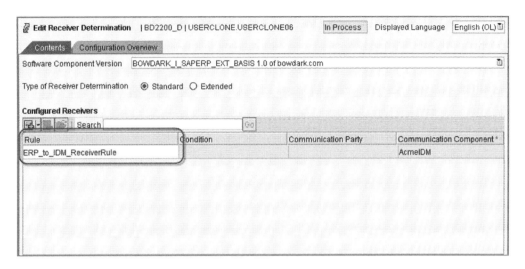

Figure 12.20: Adding a Receiver Rule to a Standard Receiver Determination

12.3   Interface Determinations

During Integration Server-based message processing, the logical routing of an inbound message takes place in two steps:

1. First, the receiver determination service is used to determine the application systems that should receive the message.

2. Then, the interface determination service is used to determine which interface to call on the selected systems in order to forward on the message.

Having learned how to perform receiver determinations in the previous section, let's now turn our attention towards the specification of *interface determinations*. We'll begin our discussion by looking at how interface determinations are maintained in the Integration Builder. From there, we'll then explore the various configuration options you have when defining interface determinations. Finally, we'll conclude our analysis by showing you how to assign operation mappings to interface determinations.

12.3.1   Creating an Interface Determination

Before we investigate the ins-and-outs of interface determinations, let's first take a look at how they are maintained within the Integration Builder. To create a new interface determination object, perform the following steps:

1. To begin, select the *Object → New* menu option from the top-level menu bar.

2. Then, in the ensuing *Create Object* dialog box, expand the *Configuration Objects* submenu and choose the *Interface Determination* menu option.

3. Next, you must define the object key for the interface determination by filling in the sender/receiver information shown in Figure 12.21. Here, note that you have the option of specifying the sender/receiver details generically using the wildcard syntax described in the online help documentation underneath the section entitled *Defining Configuration Objects Generically/Specifically* (SAP AG).

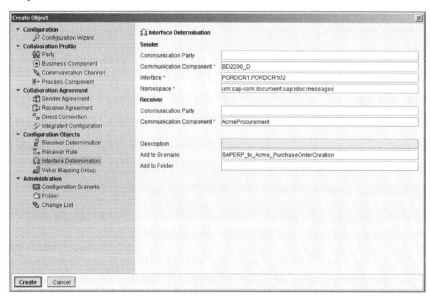

Figure 12.21: Creating an Interface Determination
© *Copyright 2010. SAP AG. All rights reserved*

4. Finally, once you determine the object key for the interface determination, click the *Create* button. This will open up the editor screen shown in Figure 12.22. Be sure to save your changes.

12.3.2   Specifying Receiver Interfaces

Once you have created an interface determination, the next step is to identify the interface(s) that should be used to forward the incoming message on to the selected receiver component. These details are captured in the *Receiver Interfaces* table located at the bottom portion of the editor screen shown in Figure 12.22. As you can see, each selected interface record contains multiple attributes. These attributes are described in further detail in Table 12.2.

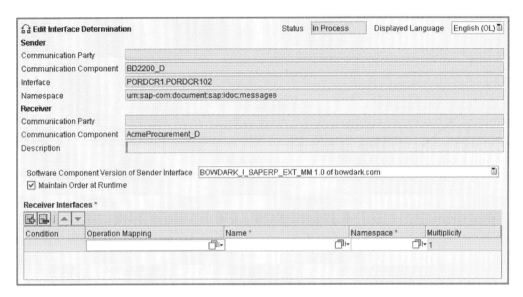

Figure 12.22: Editing Interface Determinations in the Integration Builder

Interface Attribute	Description
Condition	This field is used to specify the conditions in which a receiver interface is invoked. These conditions are defined using the familiar Conditions Editor introduced in Section 12.2.1.1. Here, you can build logical expressions based upon elements/attributes from the source message in order to determine whether or not a particular receiver interface should be called.
Operation Mapping	Since the sender/receiver interface pair being linked often has different XML Schema types, you can use this field to plug in an operation mapping that is used to define an XML transformation at runtime. We'll explore this concept further in Section 12.3.3.

Interface Attribute	Description
Name	In this field, you select the operation of the service interface that is to be invoked on the receiver component. Here, if the service interface defines multiple service operations, you have the option of specifying each operation separately.
Namespace	This field refers to the namespace of the service interface from the ESR.
Multiplicity	This field is derived from selected operation mapping assignment. We'll look at this in further detail in Section 12.3.3.

Table 12.2: Attributes of Receiver Interfaces in Interface Determinations

In situations where you forward an incoming message on to multiple receiver interfaces, there are a couple of runtime implications that you should be aware of. Looking back at the editor screen shown in Figure 12.22, you'll notice a checkbox with the label *Maintain Order at Runtime*. This checkbox determines the sequence of interface calls at runtime: when checked, the receiver interfaces will be called in the order they are specified; otherwise there are no guarantees about the order of the service calls.

12.3.3   Operation Mapping Assignments

More often than not, the underlying message schemas of the source and target interfaces will not match up. To address these incompatibilities in an interface determination, you must assign an operation mapping for each incompatible sender/receiver combination. In essence, this assignment informs the IE pipeline of the fact that it needs to call an XML mapping program before it forwards an incoming message on to the designated receiver component/interface.

As you can see in Figure 12.23, you can make operation mapping assignments by plugging an existing operation mapping from the ESR in the *Operation Mapping* column of the *Receiver Interfaces* table. Furthermore, you can also provide arguments[94] for importing parameters in the bottom portion of the screen (see Figure 12.23).

---

[94] You can use the corresponding value helps to guide you in selecting the appropriate values.

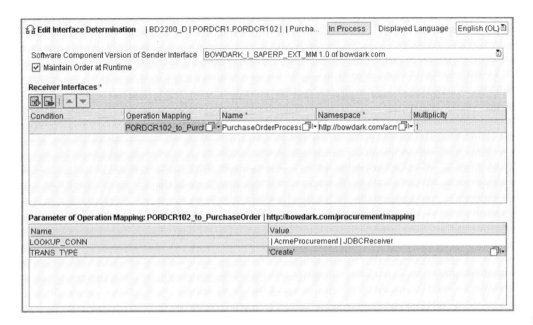

Figure 12.23: Specifying an Operation Mapping for a Receiver Interface

12.3.3.1   Configuring Mapping-Based Message Splits

In Chapter 8, you learned how multi-mappings can be used to split a message up into multiple sub-messages. Then, in Chapter 9, you saw how these multi-mappings could be used within an Integration Process definition to convert an incoming message into multiple interface calls at runtime. While this feature is powerful, it does introduce some extra overhead to the process through the addition of the intermediate integration process. Fortunately, you can achieve the same results without having to use an integration process by configuring *mapping-based message splits*.

From a configuration perspective, the only thing required to configure a mapping-based message split is to plug in an operation mapping that has a target operation with an occurrence value of $0..\texttt{unbounded}$ (see Figure 12.24). At runtime, the IE pipeline will utilize these settings to split the incoming message up and multicast the generated messages on to their intended recipients. The messages will be transmitted based upon the order defined within the generated multi-mapping message package.

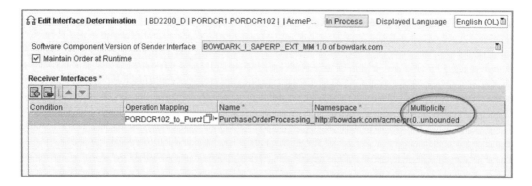

Figure 12.24: Configuring Mapping-Based Message Splits © Copyright 2010. SAP AG. All rights reserved

12.4 Collaboration Agreements

So far, you've learned how to configure the who, what, when, and where of Integration Server-based message processing. Therefore, at this point, the only thing missing is the *how*. In other words, we know which communication components are going to be participating in a collaborative business process, but we need to nail down the specific technical details of the message processing. Here, we're looking for answers to questions such as:

> ➤ Which communication protocol is a given sender system going to use to send a message to PI?

> ➤ Which communication protocol should PI use to forward a message on to a receiver system?

> ➤ What technical parameters are needed to establish the lines of communication?

You can provide the answers to all these questions and more by defining *collaboration agreements*.

Conceptually speaking, you can think of collaboration agreements as a configuration object that binds a given sender or receiver system/interface combination with a communication channel. As such, collaboration agreements come in two forms: *sender agreements* and *receiver agreements*. We'll look at each of these object types in the upcoming sections.

12.4.1 Defining Sender Agreements

According to SAP, a sender agreement "...defines the technical details for inbound processing of a message for a particular sender/receiver pair, that is, how the Integration Server behaves towards the sender of a message." (SAP AG). Naturally, these technical details are expressed using a sender communication channel definition.

To see how these pieces fit together, let's see how a sender agreement is maintained within the Integration Directory. You can create a new sender agreement by performing the following steps:

1. In the top-level menu bar, select the *Object* → *New* menu option.

2. This will open up the *Create Object* dialog box shown in Figure 12.25. Here, you can create a new sender agreement expand the *Collaboration Agreement* submenu and select the *Sender Agreement* menu option.

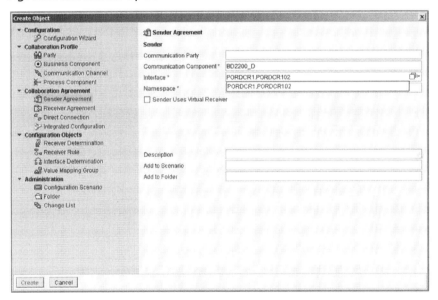

Figure 12.25: Creating a Sender Agreement Definition
© Copyright 2010. SAP AG. All rights reserved

3. Next, you must provide an object key for the sender agreement. Here, you must select the sender component (as well as its overarching party definition in B2B scenarios) and the sender interface that you want to define the collaboration agreement for.

4. If you want to define receiver-dependent sender agreements, you can select the *Sender Uses Virtual Receiver* checkbox. See section 12.2.1.2 for more details about this feature.

5. Finally, you can enter an optional description for the sender agreement and then click the *Create* button to confirm your entries. This will open up the sender agreement in the editor screen shown in Figure 12.26. Be sure to click the *Save* button to save your changes.

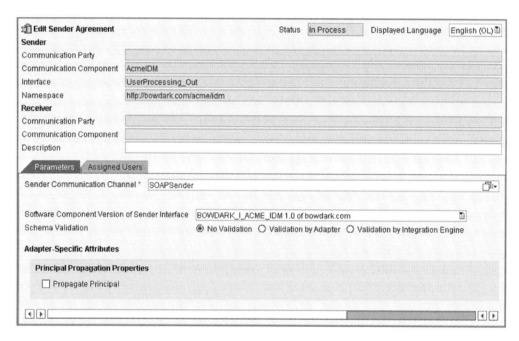

Figure 12.26: Editing a Sender Agreement in the Integration Builder

As you can see in Figure 12.26, there are four basic attributes that you can configure for a sender agreement:

> **Sender Communication Channel**
> Here, you must specify the sender communication channel definition that defines the technical attributes for the inbound connection.

> **Schema Validation**
> This attribute allows you to specify whether or not the contents of the incoming XML message should be validated against an XML Schema definition. For more details on this capability, check out the SAP

NetWeaver How-To Guide entitled *How To Perform XML Validations in SAP NetWeaver Process Integration 7.1* (SAP AG).

➢ **Adapter-Specific Attributes**
Depending upon the adapter type used in the sender channel definition, you may have the option of specifying various adapter-specific attributes. See the documentation for a particular adapter type for further details.

➢ **Assigned Users**
In some cases, you may wish to lock down incoming messages to a select handful of users. One way to achieve this is to click on the *Assigned Users* tab and plug in the user accounts you wish to grant access to. For more information about this feature, check out the online help documentation in the section entitled *Access Control Using Assigned Users* (SAP AG).

In some scenarios, the specification of a sender agreement is an optional step during the configuration process. Table 12.3 provides you with a guideline for determining when and where sender agreements are required.

Adapter Type	Sender Agreement Required?	Notes
File/FTP	Yes	Each of these adapter types receives inbound messages using pull-based semantics. For example, a JDBC sender channel is not notified by the database if a record changes. Rather, it polls the database periodically looking for relevant updates.
JMS	Yes	
JDBC	Yes	
		Therefore, since a sender component is not driving the message exchange, the address fields of the incoming message are provided by the sender agreement definition. To avoid ambiguity, these sender channels must be assigned to only one sender agreement definition.
RFC	Yes	N/A
IDoc	No	Due to their close proximity to the IE, these

Adapter Type	Sender Agreement Required?	Notes
HTTP	No	adapter types are generally able to figure out how to handle an incoming message without a sender agreement definition.
XI	No	
SOAP	No	N/A
Mail	No	N/A
Marketplace	Yes	N/A
BC	Yes	N/A

Table 12.3: Sender Agreement Requirements for Specific Adapter Types

12.4.2   Defining Receiver Agreements

To define the technical details of outbound message processing, you must specify a *receiver agreement*. Much like sender agreements, receiver agreements register a receiver communication channel with a specific sender/receiver pair. At runtime, this information is used to establish a connection for sending a message on to its intended recipient(s).

In general, you'll find the process for defining receiver agreements to be the same as the one used to define sender agreements. Here, you must perform the following steps:

1. In the top-level menu bar, select the *Object → New menu* option.

2. This will open up the *Create Object* dialog box shown in Figure 12.27. Here, you'll want to expand the *Collaboration Agreement* submenu and then select the *Receiver Agreement* menu option.

3. As you can see in Figure 12.27, in addition to the selection of the receiver interface, the object key for receiver agreements also includes attributes that match up a pair of sender and receiver components. However, you are permitted to mask the sender party/component and the receiver interface as necessary – see the online help documentation underneath the section entitled *Object Key in Configuration Objects* for more details (SAP AG).

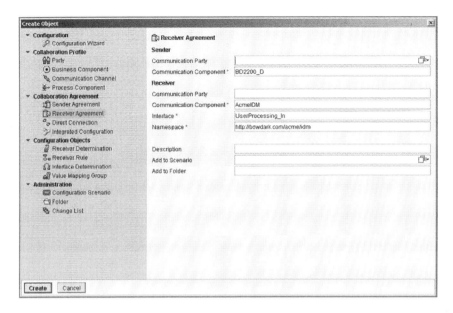

Figure 12.27: Creating a Receiver Agreement

4. After you specify the object key, you may provide an optional description for the receiver agreement and click on the *Create* button to confirm your selections. This will open up the receiver agreement in the editor screen shown in Figure 12.28. Be sure to click on the *Save* button to save your changes.

As you can see in Figure 12.28, there are three basic attributes that you must configure when defining a receiver agreement:

➤ **Receiver Communication Channel**
Here, you select the receiver communication channel which defines the technical details for outbound message processing.

➤ **Schema Validation**
If desired, you can select the *Schema Validation* checkbox in order to validate the outgoing XML message against its associated XML Schema. For more information about this option, check out the SAP NetWeaver How-To Guide entitled *How To Perform XML Validations in SAP NetWeaver Process Integration 7.1* (SAP AG).

> ➤ **Header Mapping**
> In certain cases, you may wish to override the derived sender or
> receiver communication party/component with different values at
> runtime. For example, in a B2B scenario, you might want to mask
> internal landscape component with generic placeholder components.
> Whatever the reason might be, you can achieve these overrides using
> the checkboxes provided in the *Header Mapping* area at the bottom of
> the receiver agreement editor screen (see Figure 12.28). For more
> details about this option, check out the online help documentation
> underneath the section entitled *Define Header Mappings* (SAP AG).

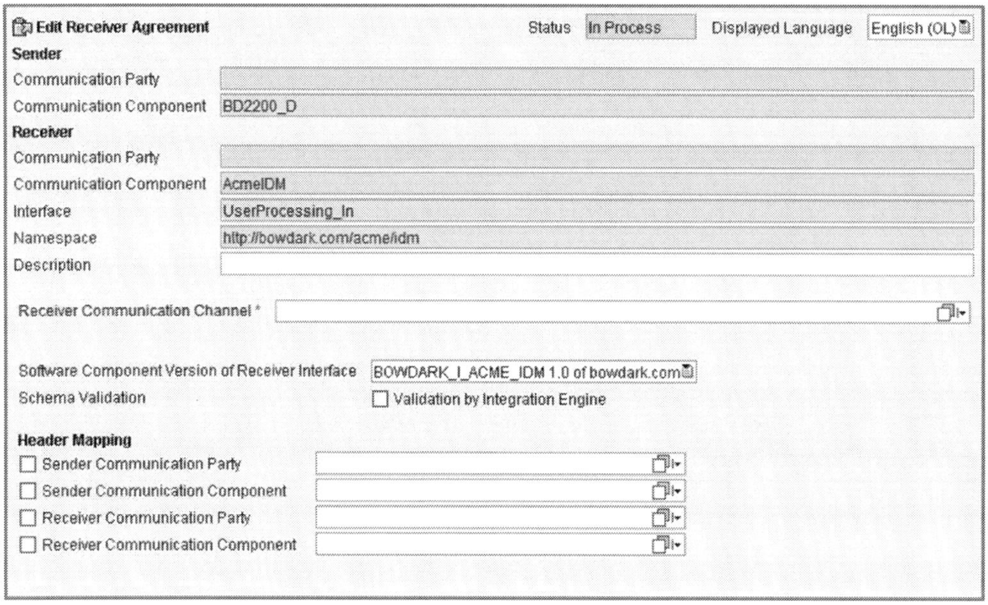

Figure 12.28: Editing a Receiver Agreement in the Integration Builder
© Copyright 2010. SAP AG. All rights reserved

Depending upon the adapter type used in the receiver communication
channel definition, you may also have the opportunity to configure certain
adapter-specific attributes within a receiver agreement. Typically, these
attributes allow you to specify additional security settings for the outbound
processing, etc.

12.5 Working with the Configuration Wizard

At this point, you should have a pretty good feel for the types of
configuration objects used to configure Integration Server-based

communication. While these objects are fairly straightforward to work with in and of themselves, they can be somewhat tedious to work with on a large scale. Recognizing this, SAP has provided you with a configuration wizard that can greatly simplify this process.

To access this wizard, click on the *Configuration Wizard* button in the top-level toolbar (see Figure 12.29). This will open up the *Configuration Wizard* dialog box shown in Figure 12.30. As you can see, you have two options for Integration Server-based communication: *Internal Communication* and *Party Communication*. These options are used to configure A2A and B2B scenarios, respectively. Once you choose your option, you can get things going by clicking on the *Continue* button (see Figure 12.30).

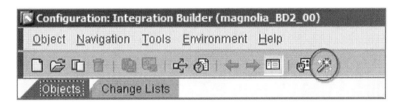

Figure 12.29: Accessing the Configuration Wizard © Copyright 2010. SAP AG. All rights reserved

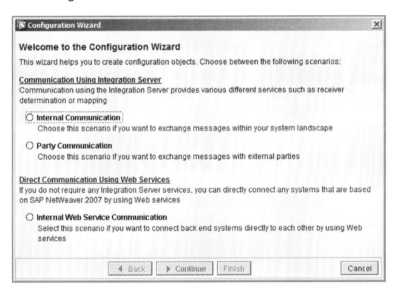

Figure 12.30: Working with the Configuration Wizard (Part 1) © Copyright 2010. SAP AG. All rights reserved

Over the course of the next several steps, you will be asked to provide details for specific aspects of the communication. For example, in the *Inbound Message: Specify the Sender* step shown in Figure 12.31, you must select the sender component/interface that initiates the integration scenario. Along the way, the wizard will guide you in leveraging existing configuration objects, determining if specific configuration objects are required, and so on.

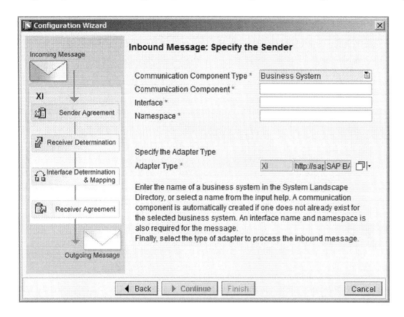

Figure 12.31: Working with the Configuration Wizard (Part 2) © Copyright 2010. SAP AG. All rights reserved

Finally, after you proceed through all the intermediate steps, you will arrive at the *Generate Objects* step shown in Figure 12.32. Here, before the various configuration objects are generated, you have the option of selecting a configuration scenario in which to group them together. Once you're satisfied with your changes, click the *Finish* button to start the generation process.

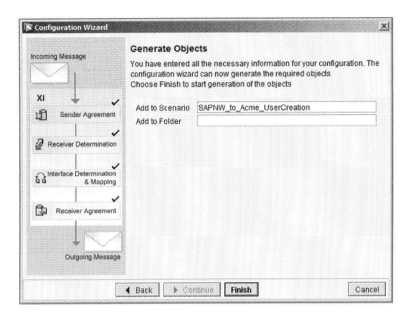

Figure 12.32: Working with the Configuration Wizard (Part 3) © Copyright 2010. SAP AG. All rights reserved

Assuming all goes well, you should arrive at the generation overview log screen shown in Figure 12.33. This informational screen simply shows you which configuration objects were created/leveraged to implement the configuration scenario.

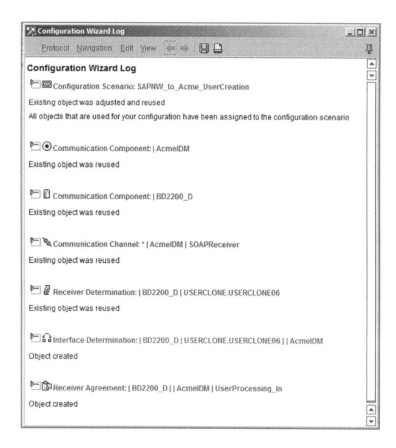

Figure 12.33: Working with the Configuration Wizard (Part 4) © Copyright 2010. SAP AG. All rights reserved

12.6   Summary

In this chapter, you learned how to configure collaborative business processes for execution on the Integration Server. Now that you understand these concepts, you should be ready to design and configure all kinds of collaborative business processes. However, as the saying goes, there's more than one way to skin a cat. Therefore, in the next chapter, we'll explore some of the new and advanced configuration options you have to work with in SAP NetWeaver PI 7.1.

References

SAP AG. (n.d.). *Access Control Using Assigned Users.* Retrieved January 27, 2011, from SAP Help Library:
http://help.sap.com/saphelp_nwpi711/helpdata/en/48/cea362e206035be100 00000a42189b/frameset.htm

SAP AG. (n.d.). *Define Header Mappings.* Retrieved January 27, 2011, from SAP Help Library:
http://help.sap.com/saphelp_nwpi711/helpdata/en/48/cf9ea79bf23e49e100 00000a421937/frameset.htm

SAP AG. (n.d.). *Defining Configuration Objects Generically/Specifically.* Retrieved January 25, 2011, from SAP Help Library:
http://help.sap.com/saphelp_nwpi711/helpdata/en/48/c7a379da5e31ebe100 00000a42189b/frameset.htm

SAP AG. (n.d.). *Defining Sender Agreements.* Retrieved January 27, 2011, from SAP Help Library:
http://help.sap.com/saphelp_nwpi711/helpdata/en/48/ce4bd3a0d7154ee100 00000a421937/frameset.htm

SAP AG. (n.d.). *How To Perform XML Validations in SAP NetWeaver Process Integration 7.1.* Retrieved January 27, 2011, from SAP Developer Network (SDN): http://www.sdn.sap.com/irj/scn/index?rid=/library/uuid/d06dff94-9913-2b10-6f82-9717d9f83df1

SAP AG. (n.d.). *How to Set Up the Communication between ABAP Backend and SOAP Adapter using XI Protocol.* Retrieved January 27, 2011, from SAP Developer Network (SDN):
http://www.sdn.sap.com/irj/scn/go/portal/prtroot/docs/library/uuid/70066f7 8-7794-2c10-2e8c-cb967cef407b?QuickLink=index&overridelayout=true

SAP AG. (n.d.). *Object Key in Configuration Objects.* Retrieved January 27, 2011, from SAP Help Library:
http://help.sap.com/saphelp_nwpi711/helpdata/en/48/c7a08ada5e31ebe100 00000a42189b/frameset.htm

SAP AG. (n.d.). *Using the Condition Editor.* Retrieved January 25, 2011, from SAP Help Library:
http://help.sap.com/saphelp_nwpi711/helpdata/en/48/d1d23790d75430e10 000000a42189b/frameset.htm

Advanced Configuration Concepts

One of the downsides to having a distributed architecture like the one utilized in SAP NetWeaver PI is the fact that there is some overhead associated with shuffling messages between the different components. While this additional processing time goes unnoticed in many cases, there are occasions when a more direct approach is warranted.

In this chapter, we'll explore some new communication variants that you can use to improve the performance of message processing. After completing this chapter, you will be able to:

❖ Configure collaborative business processes that are processed locally within the AAE.

❖ Define direct communication scenarios which enable a pair of SAP-based Web service runtimes to communicate with each other directly without having to go through PI.

13.1 Overview

Prior to release 7.1 of SAP NetWeaver PI, every message processed by PI was routed through the central Integration Engine. Nowadays, with the advent of the AAE and some new features provided in release 7.11, this is no longer the case. Now, you have the option of implementing local message processing within the AAE or, in some cases, bypassing PI altogether.

Over the course of the next couple of sections, we'll explore these new communication variants and see when and where they should be used. Furthermore, since these technologies are new and evolving, we'll point you in the direction of relevant documentation sources so that you can keep track of the latest changes and feature additions.

13.2 Configuring AAE-Based Communication

In Chapter 1, we compared and contrasted the hub-and-spoke integration broker-based middleware architecture with the more modern enterprise service bus (ESB) architecture. There, we highlighted some of the characteristics that set the ESB architecture apart:

> Adaptability for a wide variety of integration requirements

> A flexible and distributed architecture

> Selective deployment and usage of integration components on an as-needed basis

Over time, the architecture of PI has evolved to incorporate more and more of these ESB-style characteristics. Perhaps nowhere is this more prevalent than in the metamorphosis of the adapter engine. In this section, we'll explore these changes and show you how the AAE can be used to broker communication without having to involve the AS ABAP-based Integration Engine.

13.2.1 The Adapter Engine: Reloaded

In many ways, SAP NetWeaver PI's dual-stack architecture is unique within the industry. For the most part, the majority of competing products in the marketplace are installed exclusively on a particular application server platform (which is often J2EE-based). Though there are many benefits to the distributed approach adopted by SAP, there are also some drawbacks – particularly as they relate to performance.

Recognizing these limitations, SAP began to look at ways of streamlining the processing of messages that didn't require all the sophisticated features offered by the AS ABAP-based IE. Naturally, the existing J2EE-based Adapter Engine and its underlying Adapter Framework provided a fertile ground from which to start. Over time, the innovation in this area gave rise to what is now known as the Advanced Adapter Engine (AAE).

In addition to its continued support for JCA-based protocol adapters, the AAE now offers the capability of *local message processing*. This implies that, instead of simply handing a message off the IE, the AAE now takes on the additional responsibilities of logical message routing, etc. By eliminating the additional stack hops, message processing performance can improve up to fourfold[95].

13.2.2   When Can I Use Local Processing?

Because AAE-based communication does not involve the AS ABAP-based components of the Integration Server, there are certain functions/features that are not available for local message processing. Here, you are restricted from using:

> Adapter types that are deployed on the AS ABAP. This list of adapters includes:

  o   IDoc Adapter

  o   Plain HTTP Adapter

  o   XI Adapter

  o   WS Adapter

> Any ABAP-based mapping programs provided in the ABAP Workbench

> Mapping-based message splits

> Integration processes and the BPE

Assuming you don't need to use any of these types of features, then you should be all set to configure local message processing in the AAE.

---

[95] This metric was published by SAP in the SAP NetWeaver How-To Guide entitled *How-to Configure Integration Configurations in the Advanced Adapter Engine* (SAP AG).

Including Support for Proxy Objects

When the AAE-based communication variant was first released, you could not configure scenarios that utilized ABAP or Java-based proxy objects since the XI adapter is located on the AS ABAP stack. To address this limitation, SAP elected to enhance the Java-based SOAP adapter to include support for the native XI protocol. For more details about how this works, check out the SAP NetWeaver How-to Guide entitled *How-To Set Up the Communication between ABAP Backend and SOAP Adapter using XI Protocol* (SAP AG).

13.2.3 Defining Integrated Configurations

Unlike Integration Server-based configuration that distributes configuration elements across multiple configuration objects, local message processing in the AAE only requires a single configuration object: the so-called *integrated configuration* object. This compact object collects the same kind of information specified in the other objects; it just does so a little bit more concisely.

To see how this works, let's see how to create an integrated configuration. The steps required to implement this scenario are as follows:

1. In the top-level menu bar of the Integration Builder, select the *Object → New* menu option.

2. Then, in the ensuing *Create Object* dialog box, expand the *Collaboration Agreement* submenu and select the *Integrated Configuration* menu option. As you can see in Figure 13.1, the object key for integrated configurations consists of:

   a. An optional sender communication party

   b. A sender communication component

   c. A sender interface/namespace from the ESR

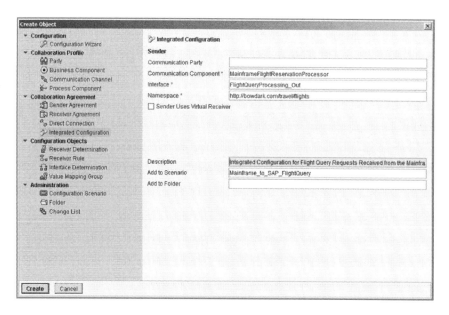

Figure 13.1: Creating an Integrated Configuration

3. Once you are satisfied with your selections, click on the *Create* button to open the integrated configuration up in the editor screen shown in Figure 13.2. Be sure to save your changes.

As you can see in Figure 13.2, the configuration attributes for an integrated configuration are scattered across a series of tabbed editor panes. Naturally, these tabs are arranged in logical order based upon the way you would specify the flow of an incoming message. Table 13.1 describes the purpose of each of these tab editor screens in further detail.

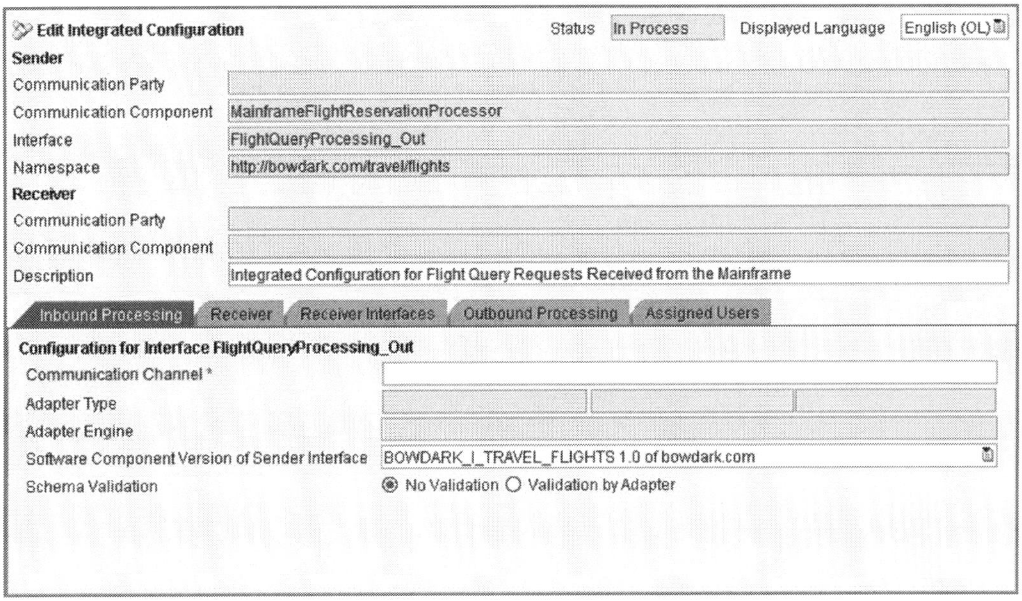

Figure 13.2: Maintaining an Integrated Configuration © Copyright 2010. SAP AG. All rights reserved

Tab Label	Analogous To	Usage
Inbound Processing	Sender Agreements	On this tab, you specify the sender communication channel used to initiate the integration process. Naturally, this channel must be defined using a JCA adapter deployed on the AAE. Besides the specification of the sender channel, you can also choose the target adapter engine[96] that the scenario will run on as well as whether or not you wish to validate the incoming message against an XML Schema type.

---

[96] Here, keep in mind that it is possible to have *many* adapter engines installed within a PI system. These adapter engines might be added to improve performance, open up communication outside of the corporate firewall, etc.

Tab Label	Analogous To	Usage
Receiver	Receiver Determinations	This tab allows you to select the receiver(s) of an incoming message. As such, its look-and-feel is almost identical to that of a standard receiver determination. Here, you specify conditions to implement content-based routing[97], and so on.
Receiver Interfaces	Interface Determinations	Once the receiver(s) are selected on the Receiver tab, you can use this tab editor to select the interface/operations to call on the receiver systems. Here, you also have the option of plugging in an operation mapping to translate between different message schema types.
Outbound Processing	Receiver Agreements	This tab allows you to specify the communication channel(s) used to communicate with the selected receiver system(s). These channels must be defined using JCA adapter types deployed on the AAE. In addition to the receiver channel selection, you can also define translations between header fields in the same way that you learned how to define these fields for receiver agreements in Chapter 12.
Assigned Users	N/A	On this tab, you can plug in a set of service users that make up an access control list that restricts access to the runtime environment.

Table 13.1: Tab Editor Screens for Integrated Configurations

13.2.4 Runtime Considerations

Whenever you activate an integrated configuration, the relevant attributes are replicated over to the runtime cache of the selected AAE. This allows the AAE to function autonomously at runtime. In Chapter 14, we'll show you how

---

[97] Note: Content-based routing was a feature added in Enhancement Pack 1 of SAP NetWeaver PI 7.1. Prior to this, you could only define static assignments.

to monitor components of the AAE and trace the messages it processes locally.

13.3   Configuring Direct Communication

Throughout the course of this book, we have demonstrated the many benefits of *mediated communication* with SAP NetWeaver PI. However, there are times when such functionality is overkill. For example, if an SAP CRM system needs to consume a Web service hosted on an SAP ECC system, it makes sense from a runtime perspective to simply hook the two Web service runtimes together directly without putting PI in the middle.

However, as you learned in Chapter 1, one of the major downsides to the direct point-to-point communication approach is the fact that it introduces a *tight coupling* between the two systems involved in the exchange. This implies that a change to the technical landscape on the provider side necessitates maintenance on the consumer side, and so on. Over time, if you accumulate multiple occurrences of these types of connections, the maintenance costs can increase exponentially.

Ideally, there would be a way to achieve the best of both worlds when it comes to these kinds of Web service-based scenarios. In other words, we want to enjoy the benefits of shared collaboration knowledge within PI without having to actually route the messages through the PI Integration Server at runtime. Beginning in release 7.1 of SAP NetWeaver PI, this very thing can be achieved by configuring *direct communication*.

SAP defines direct communication as a scenario in which "...two (business) systems use the Web service runtime to communicate with each other directly without using a central Integration Server or the Advanced Adapter Engine" (SAP AG). In particular, we're talking about two business systems based upon the AS ABAP and the ABAP Web service runtime[98]. In the upcoming sections, we'll explore how such interactions are achieved.

13.3.1   Conceptual Overview

Before we delve into a discussion about direct communication on a nuts-and-bolts level, it is helpful to take a look at how direct communication works from a conceptual point of view. Figure 13.3 provides an overview of this

---

[98] As of the time of this writing, only the AS ABAP version 7.10+ is supported.

process in terms of the participating components. As you can see, the steps involved here are as follows:

1. The process begins with the specification of a service interface in the ESR. The service interface can be developed using the inside-out or outside-in approach.

2. Once the service interface is specified, the next step is to define a *direct connection* object within the Integration Directory. As the name suggests, this configuration object defines the point-to-point connection details between the selected sender/receiver systems.

3. Whenever the direct connection is activated, the connection details are replicated down to the sender/receiver systems and stored in the IE runtime cache.

4. At runtime, whenever the sender interface is invoked on the sender business system, the cached metadata is utilized to facilitate a direct connection to the receiver system.

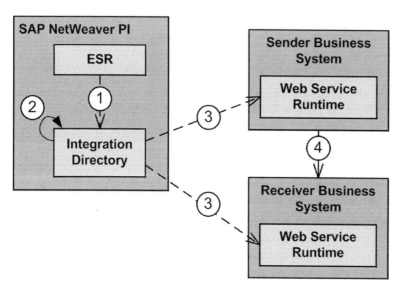

Figure 13.3: Conceptual Overview of Direct Communication

In the next few sections, we'll explore these interactions in further detail. You can also find a more detailed investigation of what is happening behind the scenes in the SDN article entitled *Point-to-Point Direct Connection Design and Configuration in SAP using NetWeaver Process Integration 7.1* (Li).

13.3.2 System Setup Requirements

As you learned in the previous section, the configuration details specified within a direct connection are propagated down to the sender/receiver systems whenever the direct connection object is activated. In order for this to work, the Integration Builder needs to know how to communicate with the backend systems. In particular, it needs to know:

> The URL it should use to communicate with a backend system

> The user account that should be used to establish that connection

The URL used to connect to the backend business system is defined whenever the business system is created in the SLD. Here, the URL is specified in the *Configuration URL* field on the *Integration* tab (see Figure 13.4).

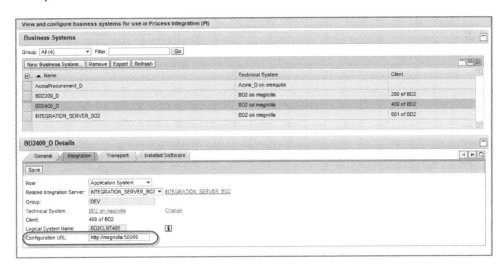

Figure 13.4: Defining the Configuration URL for a Business System

Once the business system is imported into the Integration Directory, you can specify the logon account data on the *Logon Data* tab within the business system editor shown in Figure 13.5.

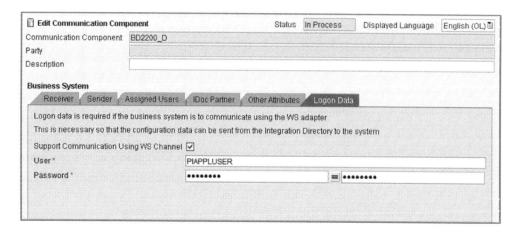

Figure 13.5: Configuring Logon Data for a Business System in the Integration Directory © Copyright 2010. SAP AG. All rights reserved

13.3.3   Defining a Direct Connection

In Section 13.3.1, you learned that the primary configuration object that drives direct communication is the so-called *direct connection* object. Much like integrated configurations described in Section 13.2, this streamlined object combines all of the relevant connection details in a single package.

Perhaps the easiest way to explain direct connections is to look at an example. Therefore, let's see how direct connections are maintained within the Integration Directory. Here, you must perform the following steps:

1. In the top-level menu bar, select the menu option *Object → New*.

2. Then, in the ensuing *Create Object* dialog box, expand the *Collaboration Agreement* submenu and then select the *Direct Connection* menu option.

3. As you can see in Figure 13.6, the object key for a direct communication includes:

    a. An optional sender communication party

    b. The sender communication component

    c. The sender interface/namespace from the ESR

    d. An optional receiver communication party

    e. The receiver communication component

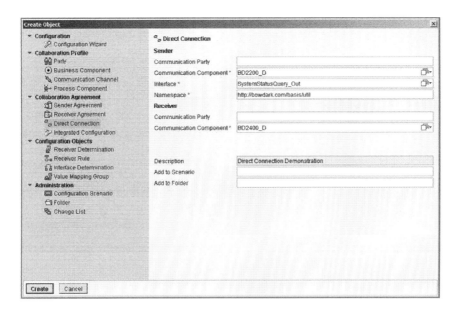

Figure 13.6: Creating a Direct Connection in the Integration Builder
© Copyright 2010. SAP AG. All rights reserved

4. Once the object key is defined, you can click on the *Create* button
    to create the new direct connection object. This will open up the
    direct connection in the editor screen shown in Figure 13.7.

As you can see in Figure 13.7, there are two basic attributes that you must
define for a direct connection:

> **Receiver Communication Channel**
> This attribute refers to a receiver channel definition based upon the
> WS adapter type. The channel definition provides all of the connection
> details needed to access a Web service provided by the receiver
> system. We'll learn more about the WS adapter type in Section
> 13.3.4.

> **Receiver Interface**
> This attribute refers to the receiver interface/namespace that
> specifies the Web service provided by the receiver system.

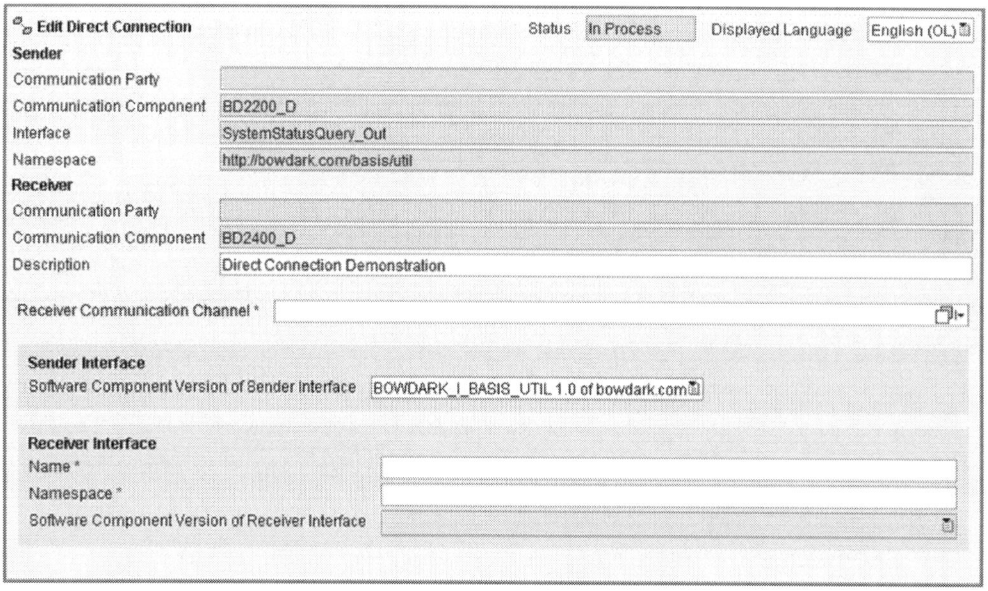

Figure 13.7: Maintaining a Direct Connection in the Integration Builder
© Copyright 2010. SAP AG. All rights reserved

Besides the selection of the receiver channel/interface, you also have the option of specifying some adapter-specific attributes within a direct connection. These attributes are define communication aspects such as messaging security, HTTP proxy setup, and so on.

Once the relevant configuration settings are in place, you can save your changes and activate the direct connection object to propagate the configuration details to the satellite systems. Section 13.3.5 describes the steps that you can take to verify that the configuration changes are replicated to the backend systems.

13.3.4 Working with the WS Adapter

Among the many new features included with release 7.1 of SAP NetWeaver PI was the introduction of a new adapter type: the *WS adapter*. As you may have guessed by now, this adapter type is used in Web service scenarios. In particular, it is well suited to integrating with Web service runtime environments that support modern protocol extensions to SOAP such as WS-ReliableMessaging, and so on.

While a complete overview of the features provided with WS adapter is beyond the scope of this book[99], we should point out its usage within the context of direct communication. Here, as you learned in Section 13.3.3, you are required to specify a receiver channel based upon the WS adapter type.

Figure 13.8 depicts a WS receiver channel within the Integration Builder tool. As you can see, the attributes here are mostly focused on technical communication settings, etc. The key takeaway from all this is that these configuration settings represent the basis from which a direct connection between a sender and receiver system can be established at runtime. Behind the scenes, the backend runtime environments are able to fill in the gaps in terms of target URL, and so on.

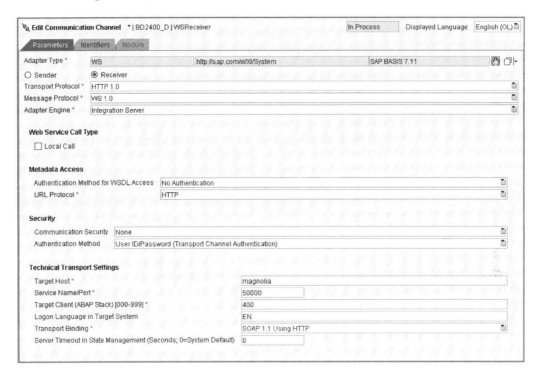

Figure 13.8: Defining a WS Receiver Channel © Copyright 2010. SAP AG. All rights reserved

---

[99] Such details can be found in the online help documentation underneath the section entitled *Configuring the Communication Channel with Adapter Type WS* (SAP AG)

13.3.5 Verifying the Replication of Configuration Data

In a perfect world, all of the communication settings defined within a direct connection would be successfully replicated over to the backend systems. Unfortunately, we don't live in a perfect world, and oftentimes this process can break down somewhere along the way. Therefore, it is important that you understand how to troubleshoot replication errors.

In general, there are two places that you need to look whenever you are troubleshooting replication errors:

> ➢ First, you want to check the cache status overview within the Integration Builder tool.

> ➢ Then, if everything looks good in the Integration Builder, you can log onto the backend systems and validate the runtime cache in transaction SXI_CACHE.

You can access the cache status overview in the Integration Builder tool by selecting the menu option *Environment → Cache Status Overview*. This will open up the *Cache Status Overview* dialog box shown in Figure 13.9. Here, you can view the status of individual cache updates using the traffic light icons displayed within the *Cache Updated* and *Perform Notification* columns shown on the *Change List View* tab. If necessary, you can repeat an update by selecting a cache instance and clicking on the Repeat Cache Update for Instance (🖳) toolbar button. Furthermore, you can find a detailed error report for failed cache updates on the *Problems* tab.

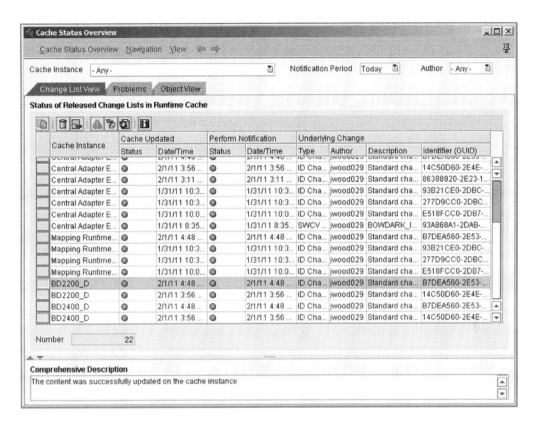

Figure 13.9: Accessing the Cache Status Overview Screen © Copyright 2010. SAP AG. All rights reserved

Once you validate a cache update in the Integration Builder tool, you can verify the update in the backend systems by executing the familiar SXI_CACHE transaction. As you can see in Figure 13.10, the IE runtime cache for application systems contains a *Direct Connection* node that you can use to verify that direct connection data is properly synchronized. If necessary, you can force a cache update using the relevant menu options in the *Runtime Cache* menu.

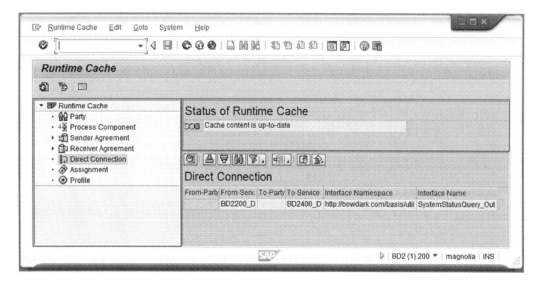

Figure 13.10: Verifying the Runtime Cache in the Backend Systems

13.3.6   Reliable Messaging and WS-RM

Whenever you enter into a point-to-point communication scenario, you start to appreciate all of the little things that PI takes care of on your behalf. For example, with mediated communication, you don't care if the receiver of a message is available or not whenever you send a request. This is because you can depend on PI to store the message and reliably forward it on whenever the receiver comes back online. Similarly, if you have a sequential processing requirement, you simply click on a few checkboxes at configuration time and PI will ensure that messages are delivered in order.

Unfortunately, in a direct communication scenario, you don't have those luxuries. Nevertheless, you still require a mechanism for reliably delivering messages to their receivers. Fortunately, this functionality is provided with the WS-ReliableMessaging (WS-RM) extensions added to the ABAP Web service runtime in SAP NetWeaver 7.0, SP 14.

While a detailed overview of WS-RM and the corresponding API provided for ABAP developers is beyond the scope of this book, we thought it worth mentioning in the context of direct communication. Rather than reinventing the wheel in client applications, you should take a look at the services this framework has to offer to ensure that messages are processed reliably. You can find a detailed overview of WS-RM and its integration into the ABAP Web service runtime in the SAP NetWeaver How-To Guide entitled *How-to Develop, Monitor and Debug WS Consumer and Provider* (SAP AG).

13.4   Summary

In this chapter, you learned about some of the new and advanced message processing functions available in release 7.1 of SAP NetWeaver PI. When used correctly, these features can be used to greatly improve the performance of message processing. Over time, SAP has made it known that they will continue to grow these functions to offer you even more flexibility in the configuration of collaborative business processes.

This chapter concludes our investigation of configuration objects within the Integration Directory. Combined with the knowledge gained in the design portion of this book, you are now ready to take on just about any set of business process requirements that come your way. Of course, it helps if you can re-trace your steps at runtime. Therefore, in the next chapter, we'll look at some of the functions you have for monitoring and troubleshooting integration scenarios in SAP NetWeaver PI.

References

Li, W. (n.d.). *Point-to-Point Direct Connection Design and Configuration in SAP using NetWeaver Process Integration 7.1.* Retrieved February 1, 2011, from SAP Developer Network:
http://www.sdn.sap.com/irj/sdn/go/portal/prtroot/docs/library/uuid/b00bbb 77-75bc-2a10-6b9a-a6f8161515a6

SAP AG. (n.d.). *Configuring Direct Communication.* Retrieved February 1, 2011, from SAP Help Library:
http://help.sap.com/saphelp_nwpi711/helpdata/en/48/ce5bf1a0d7154ee100 00000a421937/frameset.htm

SAP AG. (n.d.). *Configuring the Communication Channel with Adapter Type WS.* Retrieved February 1, 2011, from SAP Help Library:
http://help.sap.com/saphelp_nwpi711/helpdata/en/48/ce285e3a8e5430e100 00000a42189b/frameset.htm

SAP AG. (n.d.). *How-to Configure Integrated Configurations in the Advanced Adapter Engine.* Retrieved January 27, 2011, from SAP Developer Network (SDN):
http://www.sdn.sap.com/irj/scn/go/portal/prtroot/docs/library/uuid/700058f 0-b1a1-2a10-39a8-ab2627b87cfa?QuickLink=index&overridelayout=true

SAP AG. (n.d.). *How-to Develop, Monitor and Debug WS Consumer and Provider.* Retrieved February 1, 2011, from SAP Developer Network:
http://www.sdn.sap.com/irj/scn/go/portal/prtroot/docs/library/uuid/d06b639 2-cde7-2c10-8f8b-bdea5d781dd9?QuickLink=index&overridelayout=true

SAP AG. (n.d.). *How-to Set Up the Communication between ABAP Backend and SOAP Adapter using XI Protocol.* Retrieved January 27, 2011, from SAP Developer Network (SDN):
http://www.sdn.sap.com/irj/scn/go/portal/prtroot/docs/library/uuid/70066f7 8-7794-2c10-2e8c-cb967cef407b?QuickLink=index&overridelayout=true

Process Integration Monitoring 14

From a developer's perspective, the final phase in the interface development lifecycle is the *maintenance phase*. During this phase, you are responsible for monitoring message traffic and making sure that everything is running smoothly.

In order to carry out this task, you must have adequate monitoring tools to help you dig in and investigate whenever things go wrong. In this chapter, we'll explore the toolset that SAP provides to monitor PI components. After completing this chapter, you will be able to:

- ❖ Work with the core monitoring tools provided out of the box with SAP NetWeaver PI.

- ❖ Trace the flow of messages from system to system.

- ❖ Reprocess messages that contain errors.

14.1 Monitoring Tool Overview

During the course of message processing, there are many potential obstacles that can prevent a message from reaching its final destination. Such obstructions could be caused by a poorly formatted message, a failure in a backend system, and so on. Whenever these errors occur, you need to be able to pinpoint the problems quickly so that you can correct the problem(s) and restore connectivity.

Troubleshooting the various kinds of errors that could occur while a message is being processed requires several different types of monitoring tools. Here, you need tools to monitor the PI messaging components as well as lower-level components such as queues, system services, and so on. Table 14.1 highlights the PI monitoring tools provided by SAP. Throughout the remainder of this chapter, we'll introduce each of these tools and show you how they can be used to perform routine monitoring tasks.

Monitoring Tool	Description
Integration Engine Monitoring (Transaction SXMB_MONI)	An ABAP-based tool provided on the SAP NetWeaver PI system that can be used to display a detailed audit trail of messages processed within the Integration Engine.
Runtime Workbench (RWB)	A Web-based tool hosted on the PI AS Java stack that supports monitoring of the following types of components: ❖ Adapter Engines/Communication Channels ❖ Message Monitoring ❖ End-to-End/Performance Monitoring ❖ Cache Monitoring In addition, the RWB also enables you to configure alerting based upon various business rules, etc.

Monitoring Tool	Description
SAP NetWeaver Administrator (NWA)	An SAP standard Web-based monitoring tool that allows you to view system/application logs as well as the overall health of the underlying application servers. In release 7.1 of SAP NetWeaver, the NWA also allows you to monitor PI-based components in much the same way that you would monitor these components in the RWB.
Computing Center Management System (CCMS)	An SAP standard ABAP-based monitoring tool that can be used to monitor technical aspects of the system such as disk space, database health, queue blockages, and so on. CCMS can be configured to implement auto-reaction methods that respond to certain conditions within the system. For example, if a queue gets blocked, you can set up a method to alert key stakeholders of the problem.
PI Monitoring with SAP® Solution Manager	In addition to the PI-centric tools, you can also monitor certain aspects of message processing centrally using dashboards provided with SAP Solution Manager.

Table 14.1: Process Integration Monitoring Tools

14.2   Working with the Runtime Workbench

The primary monitoring tool that is provided out of the box with SAP NetWeaver PI is the *Runtime Workbench* (RWB). This Web-based tool enables you to monitor message processing/throughput as well as individual communication components such as adapter engines, etc.

To access the RWB, log onto the AS ABAP stack and execute transaction SXMB_IFR. Then, from the *Process Integration Tools* screen, click on the *Runtime Workbench* link underneath the *Configuration and Monitoring* section on the bottom right-hand corner of the screen. After you authenticate, you will arrive at the overview screen shown in Figure 14.1.

Figure 14.1: Accessing the Runtime Workbench © Copyright 2010. SAP AG. All rights reserved

As you can see in Figure 14.1, the functions of the RWB are scattered across a series of tab pages which group together related functions. In the following sections, we'll explore some of these functions and demonstrate how they can be used to perform typical monitoring tasks. For a more thorough treatment of these functions, we recommend that you read over the RWB documentation provided in the online help underneath the section entitled *Process Integration Monitoring* (SAP AG).

14.2.1   Component Monitoring

Whenever you initially open up the RWB, you are routed to the *Component Monitoring* tab. This tab provides functions that allow you to monitor the technical components that are included (or integrated) with SAP NetWeaver PI. From the main screen, you can use the *Components with Status* drop-down list to view all components, or just components that are in error (i.e. the *Red* status), etc. (see Figure 14.2). Once you make your selection, you can click on the *Display* button to open up the overview screen shown in Figure 14.3.

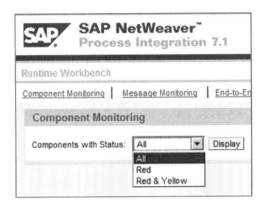

Figure 14.2: Selecting the Status Level for Component Monitoring © Copyright 2010. SAP AG. All rights reserved

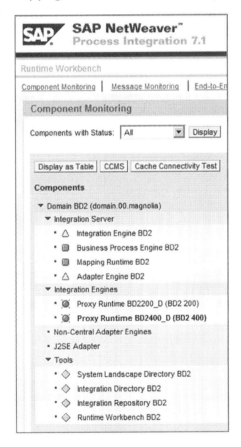

Figure 14.3: Monitoring PI Components within the RWB © Copyright 2010. SAP AG. All rights reserved

To monitor individual components from the component overview screen shown in Figure 14.3, simply click on the corresponding component node in the tree. This will open up a status overview pane within the bottom of the screen. For example, Figure 14.4 shows the status overview for the central adapter engine (i.e. the *Adapter Engine BD2* node from Figure 14.3). Here, you are provided with a report of the current status of the AAE as well as functions to monitor individual communication channels, etc. Naturally, the types of functions provided will vary from component to component.

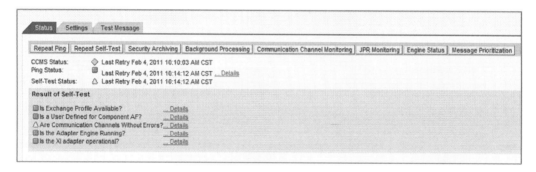

Figure 14.4: Monitoring the Status of the Central AAE © Copyright 2010. SAP AG. All rights reserved

While a complete survey of the component monitoring functions available is beyond the scope of this book, there are several useful features that bear mentioning. We'll explore these features in the upcoming sections.

14.2.1.1 Monitoring Communication Channels

You can monitor the health of individual communication channels by selecting the corresponding adapter engine node and clicking on the *Communication Channel Monitoring* button in the status overview pane (see Figure 14.4). This will open up the *Communication Channel Monitoring* screen shown in Figure 14.5. Here, you can (optionally) provide some filter parameters and then click on the *Use Filter* button to display a list of channel definitions. Within this list, you can view the status of individual channel definitions, start or stop the channels, and so on.

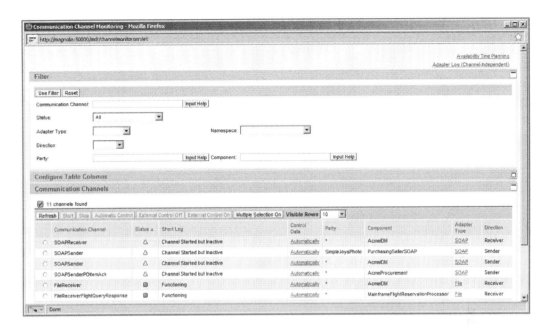

Figure 14.5: Monitoring Communication Channels in the RWB © Copyright 2010. SAP AG. All rights reserved

14.2.1.2 Sending Test Messages to Components

Besides monitoring the overall health of messaging components such as the IE or AAE, you also have the option of sending a *test message* to these components. Here, you simply click on the *Test Message* tab within the component overview pane (see Figure 14.6). This will allow you to fill in header/payload information in much the same way that you might draft an e-mail message. To send the message, simply click on the *Send Message* button.

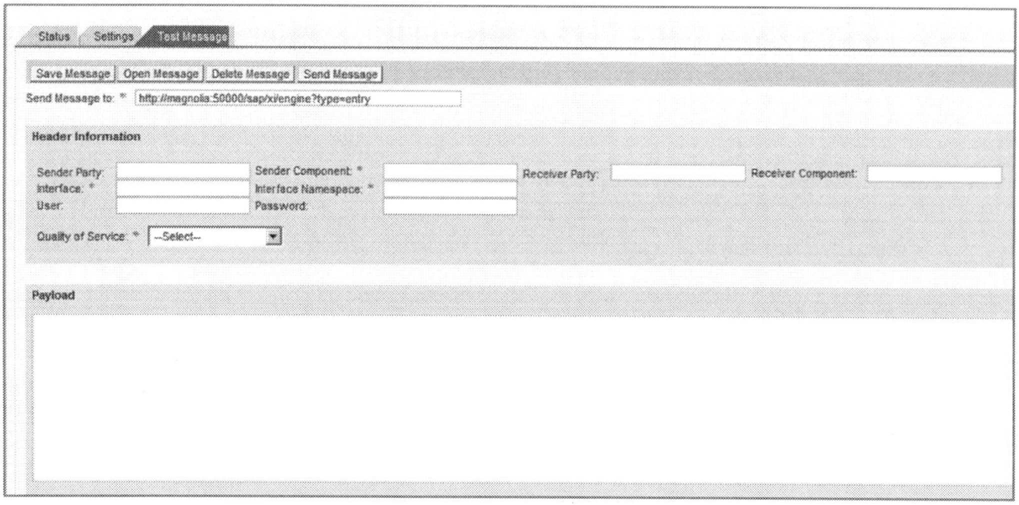

Figure 14.6: Sending a Test Message to the IE © Copyright 2010. SAP AG. All rights reserved

14.2.1.3   Scheduling Background Jobs in the AAE

Another handy feature included with the AAE monitoring component is the job scheduler function. You can use this function to schedule periodic jobs that restart failed messages, archive completed messages, or remove messages that do not need to be archived. To access this feature, open up the AAE component monitor and click on the *Background Processing* button (see Figure 14.4). This will open up the *Job Configuration* dialog window shown in Figure 14.7.

To create a new job, click on the *Create* button and fill in the job details in the *Job Details* tab pane at the bottom of the page (see Figure 14.7). Here, you must specify the following:

> **Active**
> This checkbox determines whether or not the job is active whenever you save it.

> **Job Name**
> This attribute is used to provide a name for the job.

> **Job Type**
> With this attribute, you can choose between several standard job types. The names of these job types are fairly intuitive:
> • Delete

- Restart
- Archive
- Recover

➤ **Start Date/Time**
This attribute is used to determine the start date/time for the job.

➤ **Frequency**
You can use this attribute determine the frequency of the job in terms of hours or days.

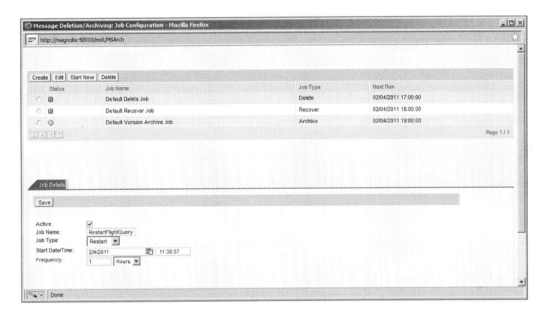

Figure 14.7: Scheduling a Background Job within the AAE (Part 1)
© Copyright 2010. SAP AG. All rights reserved

Once you're satisfied with your selections, you can click on the *Save* button to save the job definition. At this point, depending upon the job type selection, you can configure additional rules that dictate how and when the job should run. For example, in Figure 14.8, we are using the *Rules* tab to define the rules that determine the types of messages that should be reprocessed when the `RestartFlightQuery` job from Figure 14.7 is run. As you can see, the rules editor allows you to build complex expressions that can allow you to configure restart jobs for particular interface scenarios.

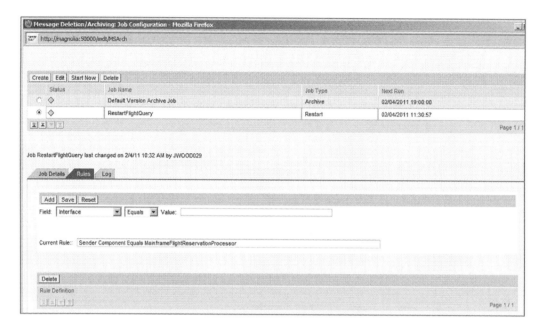

Figure 14.8: Scheduling a Background Job within the AAE (Part 2)

14.2.2   Message Monitoring

As a PI developer, you'll probably spend the majority of your time in the RWB on the *Message Monitoring* tab. On this tab, you can perform the following types of functions:

> Trace a message as it flows through the various PI messaging components.

> View the contents of messages before/after XML transformations.

> Troubleshoot errors that occur during message processing.

> Reprocess and/or cancel messages in error.

Figure 14.9 shows the initial screen you will see when you select the *Message Monitoring* tab. Before you can begin building your query, you first need to narrow down the selection range. Here, there are two basic selection parameters that you must configure:

> **Messages from Component**
In this drop-down list, you must select the messaging component that processed the message(s) you wish to search for.

> **From**
> In this drop-down list, you must select the *data source* from which to search from. Typically, you'll choose between one of three different data source types (which are intuitively named):
>
> ○ Database
>
> ○ Database (Overview)
>
> ○ Archive

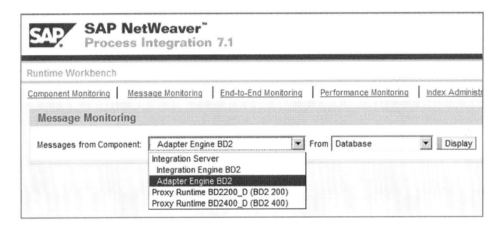

Figure 14.9: Selecting the Target Messaging Component © Copyright 2010. SAP AG. All rights reserved

After you determine the proper selection range, you can begin building your message query by clicking on the *Display* button (see Figure 14.9). This will cause the monitoring tab to refresh and reveal the *Filter* view shown in Figure 14.10. By default, this view contains some basic selection parameters that can be used to perform message queries. If necessary, you can expand on these parameters by clicking on the *Show Additional Criteria* button. This will reveal a series of extended query parameters as shown in Figure 14.11. Once you have constructed your query, you can initiate your search by clicking on the *Start* button.

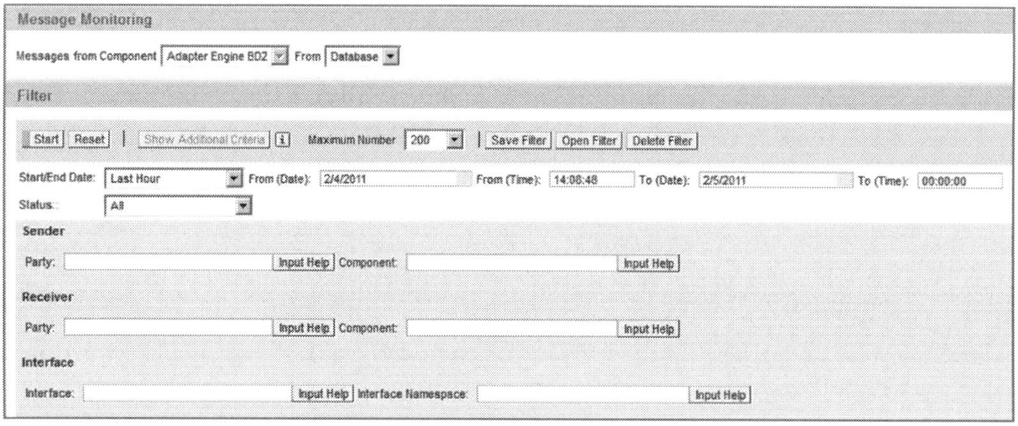

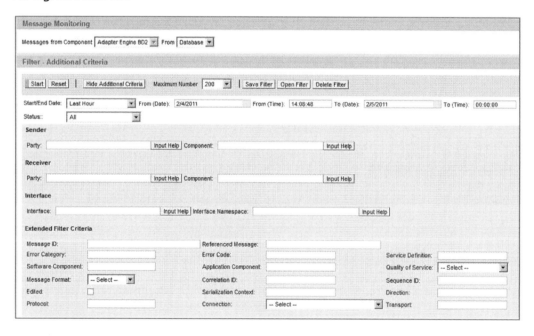

Figure 14.10: Building a Message Query (Part 1) © Copyright 2010. SAP AG. All rights reserved

Figure 14.11: Building a Message Query (Part 2) © Copyright 2010. SAP AG. All rights reserved

Figure 14.12 shows the result list that will appear whenever you perform a message search. As you can see, this list contains an overview of some of the basic attributes of a message (e.g. its status, start/end time, sender/receiver, etc.). Furthermore, you can drill in and examine a given message in further detail by selecting its corresponding checkbox and clicking on the various buttons provided in the toolbar. Table 14.2 describes each of these functions in further detail.

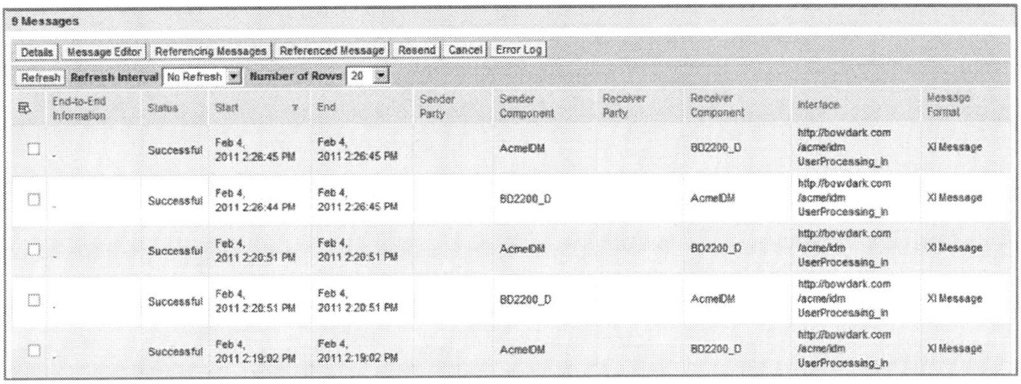

Figure 14.12: Viewing the Search Results of a Message Query © Copyright 2010. SAP AG. All rights reserved

Message Function	Description
Details	This function will open up the message in the *Message Display Tool*. This tool provides you with a detailed audit log of the message. We'll learn more about this tool in Section 14.2.2.1.
Message Editor	If an asynchronous message fails to process, you can use this function to edit the contents of the message payload in order to correct the error(s).
Referencing Messages / Referenced Message	These functions can be used to view the set of messages related to the selected message in the log.
Resend	This function can be used to re-transmit a message in the event of an error (e.g. backend system outage, etc.).
Cancel	This function is used to cancel messages that contain errors. Once a message has been canceled, it can no longer be reprocessed.
Error Log	This function can be used to view an error log for messages with errors.

Table 14.2: Message Functions within the Message Monitor

14.2.2.1   Working with the Message Display Tool

In the previous section, you learned how to view the details for a particular message by opening it up in the Message Display Tool. This tool provides quite a bit of information about a particular message. Depending upon the selected messaging component, you'll find this information scattered across different tab panes. The following sections highlight some of the more common tab panes you will encounter during message monitoring.

Message Data Tab

On the *Message Data* tab, you can view a message's metadata. Here, for example, you can determine the message's ID number (GUID), status, sender/receiver components, and so on (see Figure 14.13). You can also view processing statistics such as when the message processing started/ended, etc.

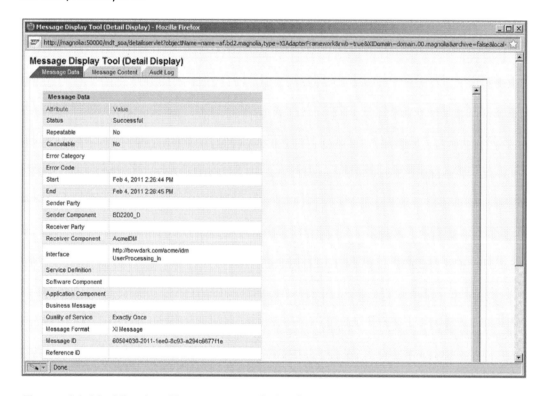

Figure 14.13: Viewing Message Details in the Message Display Tool

Message Content Tab

On the *Message Content* tab, you can view the contents of the message. As you can see in Figure 14.14, the message contents can be split into two parts: the overarching *SOAP document* and the embedded *attachment payloads*. The *SOAP Document* message part contains the XI-SOAP message constructed by the PI runtime environment during message processing. Here, you'll see all of the proprietary SAP header and body elements that annotate the message with processing details/statistics. If you select the payload message part, you'll see the actual XML payload of the message being processed (see Figure 14.15).

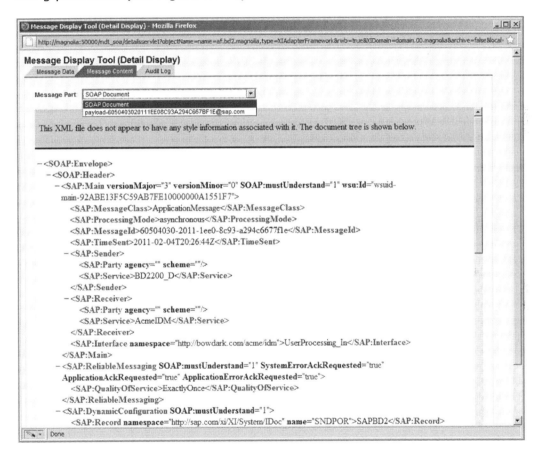

Figure 14.14: Viewing the Contents of a Message in the MDT (Part 1)

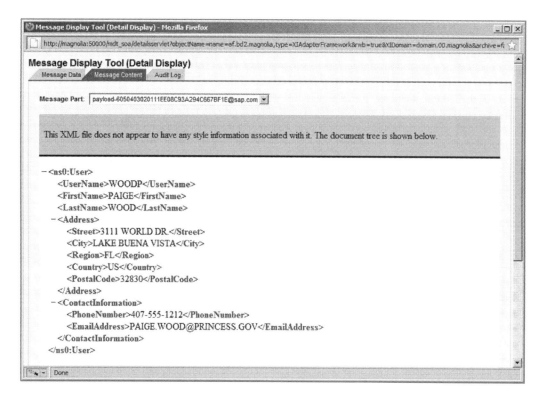

Figure 14.15: Viewing the Contents of a Message in the MDT (Part 2)

Audit Log Tab

If you're monitoring message processing within the Adapter Engine, you can view an audit trail of the message processing on the *Audit Log* tab. As you can see in Figure 14.16, this view provides a detailed audit log from each of the Adapter Framework components that participate in message processing.

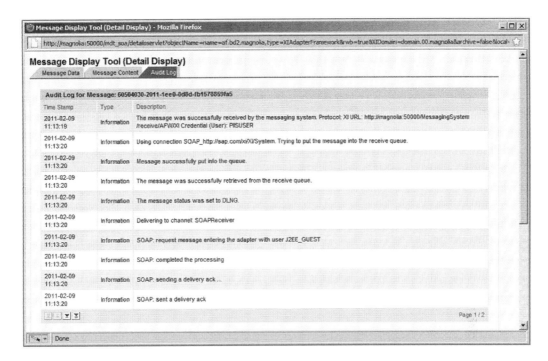

Figure 14.16: Viewing the Audit Log for a Message in the MDT © Copyright 2010. SAP AG. All rights reserved

14.2.3 End-to-End Monitoring

If you want to monitor message processing at a higher level, then you can utilize the functions provided on the *End-to-End Monitoring* tab. As you can see in Figure 14.17, this tab provides you with a graphical view of a particular business process in terms of the participating communication components. Within the graphical display, you can view processing statistics and also drill in to look at errors that might have occurred, etc.

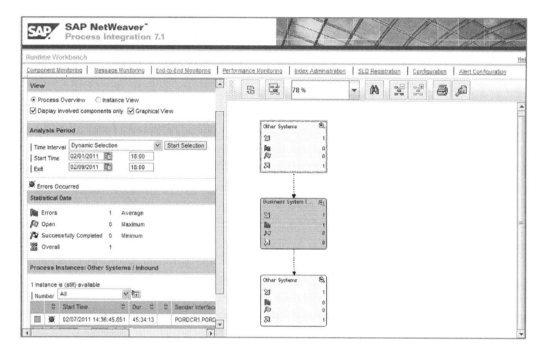

Figure 14.17: Performing End-to-End Monitoring in the RWB © Copyright 2010. SAP AG. All rights reserved

The data depicted in the *End-to-End Monitoring* tab is provided by a separate monitoring component called the *Process Monitoring Infrastructure* (PMI). This tool can be configured to monitor various PI messaging components as well as messaging components from backend SAP systems. For further information about the PMI and its configuration, check out the online help documentation underneath the section entitled *Process Monitoring with PMI* (SAP AG).

14.2.4   Performance Monitoring

Occasionally, you may be asked to produce metrics that provide insight into the overall performance of message processing within PI. One way to gather these statistics is to use the functions provided on the *Performance Monitoring* tab. Here, you can extract performance data directly from the Integration Server or via the PMI described in Section 14.2.3.

Figure 14.18 depicts an overview of the *Performance Monitoring* tab. As you can see, you are provided with a series of selection criteria that allows you to pull performance metrics for a particular period/data source. The results are loaded into the *Performance Data* table shown at the bottom of Figure 14.18.

Here, you can see the number of messages processed within the selected time interval, average throughput, and so on. If desired, you can download these metrics by clicking on the *Download* button provided in the toolbar.

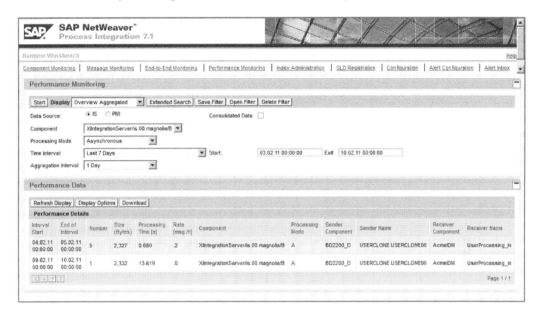

Figure 14.18: Performance Monitoring in the RWB © Copyright 2010. SAP AG. All rights reserved

14.2.5 Index Administration

Each of the message monitoring functions considered thus far requires you to perform structured searches based upon *static* search criteria. While these features are useful, there are times when more dynamic search capabilities are called for. For example, instead of asking for a list of messages created within a specific time window, you might want to search for sales order messages containing a particular sales order number. Here, you need to have the capability to scan through message payloads to locate the message you're looking for.

Given the number of messages that flow through PI on a daily basis, it is unrealistic to perform real-time scans through message payloads. However, such searches are possible if the payloads are *indexed* beforehand. This is analogous to the way that search engines like Google crawl through the myriad of pages within the World Wide Web to identify content relationships, build search indices, and so on. With SAP NetWeaver PI, such indices can be built using *TREX[100]*, which is SAP's search and classification engine. As soon as the indices are built, they can be used as a data source for message monitoring using the functions provided on the *Message Monitoring* tab in the RWB. See the online help documentation underneath the section entitled *Message Search Using Index* (SAP AG) for more details about this feature.

As you may have guessed, the configuration of the message indexing takes place on the *Index Administration* tab within the RWB. Normally, the configuration tasks on this tab are performed by Basis personnel. However, if you're interested in learning more about this feature, consult the online help documentation underneath the section entitled *Index Administration* (SAP AG).

14.2.6   Alert Configuration and the Alert Inbox

While it is useful to be able to perform interactive analysis using the tools provided by the RWB, there are times when you may wish to be notified of an error directly rather than having to keep a watchful eye on the message logs. In this case, you can configure *alerts* so that the system will notify you of runtime errors, etc. In the upcoming sections, we'll show you how to configure alerts in the RWB.

14.2.6.1   Creating Alert Categories in ALRTCATDEF

Before you can begin configuring alerts within the RWB, you must first define the details of the individual alerts by creating one or more *alert categories*. These categories are maintained on the PI AS ABAP stack using transaction ALRTCATDEF. Within this transaction, you can organize alert categories by assigning them to different *alert classifications*. To demonstrate how all these pieces fit together, let's see how to create an alert category in transaction ALRTCATDEF[101].

Figure 14.19 shows the initial screen of transaction ALRTCATDEF. On the left-hand side of the screen, you can see the list of alert classifications maintained within the system. To add your own classifications to this list, simply right-click on the desired classification level and choose the *Create*

---

[100] For a general overview on TREX, check out the presentation entitled *TREX - SAP NetWeaver's Search and Classification Engine* on the SDN (SAP AG).

[101] This task requires specific user authorizations which are described in the online help documentation underneath the section entitled *Alert Management* (SAP AG).

menu option. This will open up the *Edit Alert Classification* dialog box shown in Figure 14.19. Here, you'll simply provide a name for the classification as well as a short text description. Hit the *Enter* key to confirm your additions.

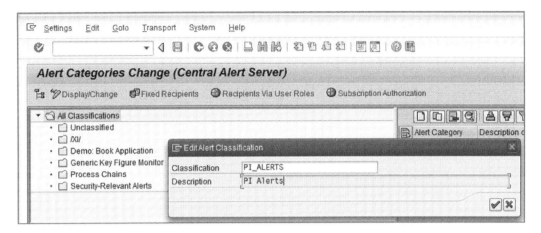

Figure 14.19: Defining Alert Classifications © Copyright 2010. SAP AG. All rights reserved

After you create/select the desired alert classification level, you can define a new alert category by clicking on the *Create Alert Category* (⬜) button shown in Figure 14.20. This will add a new entry that allows you to specify an alert category name[102] and description. Hit the *Enter* key to confirm your entry.

---

[102] See the SAP NetWeaver How-To Guide entitled *PI Best Practices: Naming Conventions* for naming conventions.

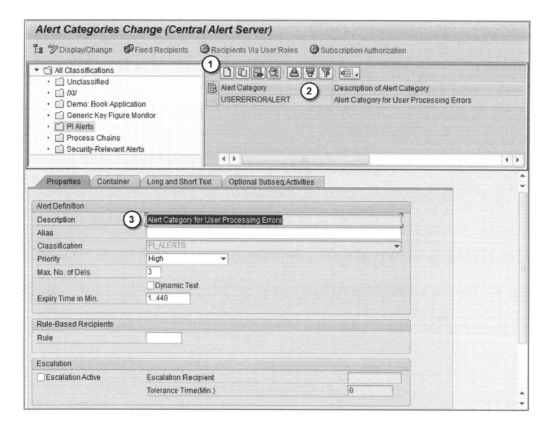

Figure 14.20: Creating an Alert Category in ALRTCATDEF © Copyright 2010. SAP AG. All rights reserved

Once the new alert category has been defined, you can specify various attributes in the alert definition such as the alert priority, expiration time, and so on. Furthermore, you can provide information about the alert and/or instructions by filling in attributes on the following tabs:

> **Long and Short Text**
> On this tab, you can specify the message text that will be displayed whenever the alert is sent out at runtime. As you can see in Figure 14.21, you can plug in various container variables that provide information about the alert condition (e.g. the message ID, sender/receiver components, etc.). You can find a comprehensive listing of the container variables available for selection in the online help documentation underneath the section entitled *Creating Alert Categories* (SAP AG).

> **Optional Subsequent Activities**
> On this tab, you can provide instructions that will guide users in reacting to the error conditions associated with the selected alert category. In addition to some narrative text, you can also include URL links to external tools, etc.

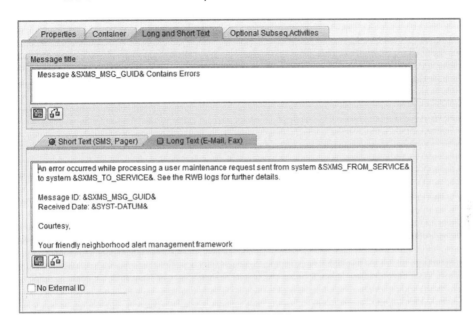

Figure 14.21: Specifying the Message Text for an Alert Category © Copyright 2010. SAP AG. All rights reserved

Defining the List of Recipients of an Alert Category

The last thing you need to determine when setting up an alert category is the list of intended recipients. Here, you can use the following toolbar buttons to define your selections (see Figure 14.20):

> **Fixed Recipients**
> With this option, you can define a fixed list of user accounts that should receive alerts from this category at runtime.

> **Recipients Via User Roles**
> With this option, you define the recipient list in terms of a series of user roles (e.g. ABAP roles defined in transaction PFCG). In this case, alerts from this category will be sent to users that are assigned to one or more of these user roles.

> ➢ **Subscription Authorization**
> This option is similar to the *Recipients Via User Roles* option in that you define the recipient list in terms of a series of user roles. However, in this case, the alerts are only delivered to users who deliberately *subscribe* to the alerts in their alert inbox.

14.2.6.2 Defining Alert Rules

Once you have defined the requisite alert categories, you can use them to create alert rules within the RWB by clicking on the *Alert Configuration* tab. As you can see in Figure 14.22, a rule definition is defined by specifying the *conditions* in which an alert from a particular alert category should be dispatched. For example, in the rule shown in Figure 14.22, we have specified that alerts from the category USERERRORALERT should be triggered if an error occurs during the processing of a message for a particular sender/receiver component combination.

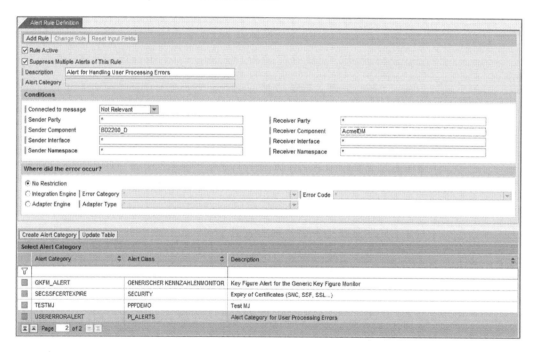

Figure 14.22: Defining an Alert Rule in the RWB © Copyright 2010. SAP AG. All rights reserved

After the rule definition is completed, you can save your changes by clicking on the *Add Rule* button. Whether or not the rule is active depends upon whether or not the *Rule Active* checkbox is checked (see Figure 14.22). You can choose to deactivate a rule at any time by deselecting this checkbox and clicking on the *Change Rule* button.

14.2.6.3 Viewing Alerts in the Alert Inbox

Once the relevant alert configuration settings are in place, you'll start to see alerts dispatched whenever errors occur at runtime. You can view these alerts by logging onto the RWB and clicking on the *Alert Inbox* tab[103]. As you can see in Figure 14.23, this inbox contains a list of alerts assigned to your user account. For a given alert message, you can:

> ➤ Acknowledge it by clicking on the *Complete* button.

> ➤ Forward it on to other users by clicking on the *Forward* button.

> ➤ Take ownership of the alert by clicking on the *Reserve* button. This kind of feature comes into play if there are multiple recipients for the alert. In this case, a reservation removes the alert from the other user's inboxes.

> ➤ Remove the message from your inbox by clicking on the *Reject* button.

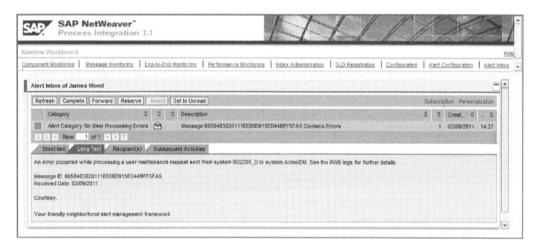

Figure 14.23: Viewing Alert Messages in the Alert Inbox © Copyright 2010. SAP AG. All rights reserved

---

[103] If desired, you can also integrate the alert inbox into the *Universal Work List* (UWL) of the SAP Enterprise Portal.

Besides the individual message functions, the alert inbox also provides the following links that allow you to customize the alert display:

> **Subscription**
> This link opens up the *Subscription of Alert Categories* screen shown in Figure 14.24. Here, you can determine whether or not you wish to subscribe to alert categories whose recipient lists are defined using the *Subscription Authorization* button described in Section 14.2.6.1. You can choose to subscribe or unsubscribe from alerts of a particular category by clicking on the *Subscribe* and *Unsubscribe* buttons, respectively.

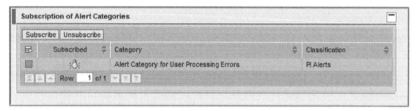

Figure 14.24: Subscribing to Alert Categories
© Copyright 2010. SAP AG. All rights reserved

> **Personalization**
> This link opens up the *Personalization of Alert Delivery* screen shown in Figure 14.25. Here, you can specify substitutes for alert processing, the desired communication method, and so on.

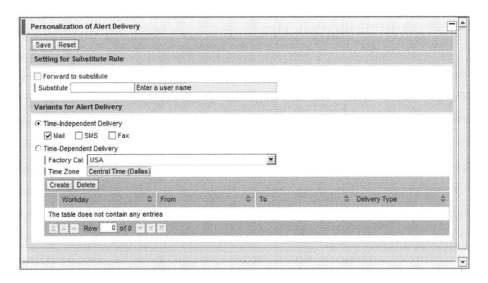

Figure 14.25: Personalizing the Alert Inbox

Receiving Alerts via External Communication Methods

Behind the scenes, alerts are processed using the *Alert Management* (ALM) framework provided as a Basis component within the AS ABAP. In addition to the features seen thus far, this framework also supports the transmission of alert messages using external communication methods such as e-mail, fax, or even SMS (for text messages). To configure these methods in your system, consult a member of your local Basis team.

14.2.7 Cache Monitoring

As you learned in Part 3 of this book, both the IE and AAE maintain a runtime cache that contains local copies of relevant configuration objects maintained within the Integration Directory. Normally, these objects are synchronized so reliably behind the scenes that you hardly even notice that they're there. However, in the rare case where synchronization errors do occur, they can be difficult to troubleshoot.

If you suspect an issue with a cache object, you can confirm your suspicions by reviewing the cache contents using the functions provided on the *Cache Monitoring* tab within the RWB. As you can see in Figure 14.26, this tool provides you with search criteria that allows you to select the target *cache instance* (e.g. the Integration Server cache, etc.) as well as the *cache object type* (e.g. receiver determination, channel, etc.). From there, you can drill in to look at the contents of the cache objects and compare them with the current values in the Integration Directory.

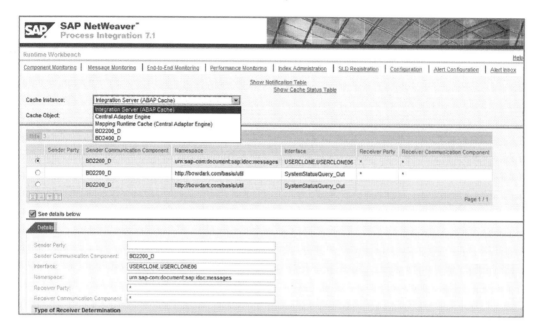

Figure 14.26: Viewing Cache Contents within the RWB © *Copyright 2010. SAP AG. All rights reserved*

14.3   Integration Server Monitoring

As you learned in Section 14.2, you can use the RWB to monitor all of the messaging components provided with SAP NetWeaver PI – including the Integration Engine. However, if you want to dig in further and really see what's going on inside the IE pipeline or BPE, you can utilize the monitoring tools provided on the AS ABAP stack. In the upcoming sections, we'll take a look at what these tools have to offer.

14.3.1   Integration Engine Monitoring

To monitor the flow of messages within the IE, you'll want to use transaction SXMB_MONI. As you can see in Figure 14.27, this tool provides you with a list of sub-transactions that you can use to monitor processed XML messages, perform persistence layer analysis, and so on. Also, you can use this tool to retrieve XML messages that might have been archived months or even years ago.

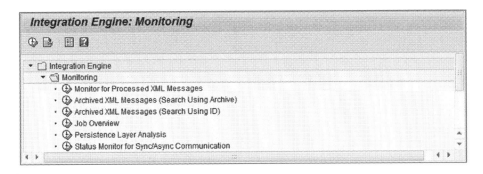

Figure 14.27: Performing IE Monitoring in Transaction SXMB_MONI

Most of the time, you'll perform your day-to-day monitoring operations by double-clicking on the *Monitor for Processed XML Messages* node (which can also be accessed directly by opening up transaction SXI_MONITOR). This will open up the *Monitor for Processed XML Messages* screen shown in Figure 14.28. Here, you can use the provided search criteria to search for messages processed within a specific date/time range, etc. You can also enter more advanced search criteria (e.g. message ID) by clicking on the *Advanced Selection Criteria* tab. Once you identify your target selection criteria, you can perform a message search by clicking on the *Execute* ( ) button in the toolbar.

Figure 14.29 shows what the results list looks like for messages matching the given selection criteria. Here, you have a number of options for displaying message details, reprocessing failed messages, etc. To access these features, simply select a message instance and click on the corresponding toolbar button. Table 14.3 describes each of these toolbar buttons in depth.

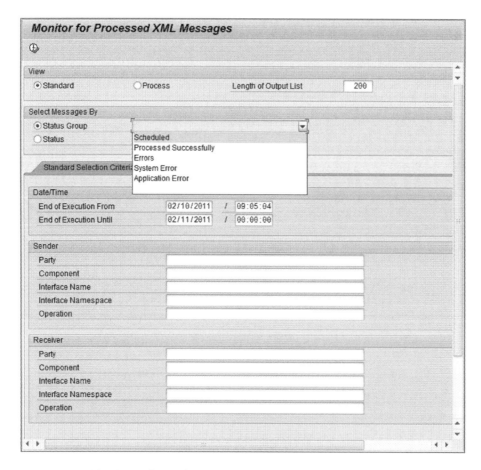

Figure 14.28: Searching for Messages in SXI_MONITOR © Copyright 2010. SAP AG. All rights reserved

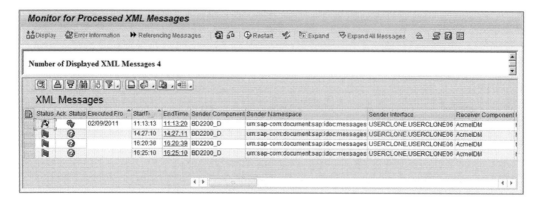

Figure 14.29: Viewing the Message List in SXI_MONITOR © Copyright 2010. SAP AG. All rights reserved

Toolbar Function	Usage
Display	This function opens the message up in an analysis window that allows you to trace through the message processing details, view the contents of the message payload, and so on. We'll explore this function further in Section 14.3.1.1.
Error Information	This function pops up a dialog box showing you a brief description of an error that occurred during message processing.
Referencing Messages	If the message contains references to other messages, then you can use this function to display those references.
Refresh (Display)	This function can be used to refresh the display as additional messages come in that meet the requisite criteria.
Refresh Status	You can use this function to refresh the status of the messages in the list. You might use this function to monitor messages that are being reprocessed after an error condition has been removed.
Restart	If a message fails, you can use this function to restart the message processing from the point of failure. You can automate this function on a wider scale by running SAP standard report `RSXMB_RESTART_MESSAGES` in the background.
Cancel Processing of Messages with Errors	If you determine that a message cannot be processed any further, you can use this function to *cancel* the message. Once you select this function, you will no longer be able to reprocess the message.
Expand/Hide Versions	These functions allow you to view (or hide) *versions* of a message. These versions only exist if a message is processing with logging turned on.
Message History	This function provides an overview of a message's history (e.g. when it was received, etc.).
Documentation	This function provides some basic documentation about the monitoring tools and their functions.

Toolbar Function	Usage
Legend	This function opens up a legend that helps you interpret all of the various icons displayed within the monitor.

Table 14.3: Toolbar Functions for Messages in SXI_MONITOR

14.3.1.1 Reviewing XML Messages in SXI_MONITOR

As a message is processed through the IE pipeline, each of the pipeline services will annotate the SOAP header with trace information, processing statistics, etc. To review this information, simply double-click on the message in the SXI_MONITOR list (see Figure 14.29). Alternatively, you can select the message in the list and click on the *Display* toolbar button. In either case, you will wind up on the *Display XML Message Versions* screen shown in Figure 14.30.

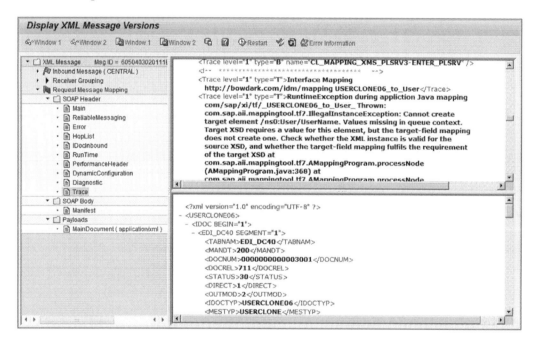

Figure 14.30: Viewing Message Details in SXI_MONITOR © Copyright 2010. SAP AG. All rights reserved

As you can see in Figure 14.30, the message display tool is split up into three panels:

➢ In the left-hand navigation area, you can see an overview of the XI SOAP message at different stages of the pipeline processing (e.g. *Receiver Grouping*, *Request Message Mapping*, and so on). Each node within the list is context-sensitive; you can view further details about the node by double-clicking on it.

➢ On the right-hand side of the screen, you have two windows that you can use to display different components within a given SOAP message. For example, in Figure 14.30, we are displaying the SOAP message trace for the *Request Message Mapping* node in window 1 and the message payload in window 2. You can download the contents of either one of these windows by clicking on the *Download Window 1* and *Download Window 2* buttons, respectively.

As you browse through the message details, you have the option of performing certain message-specific functions such as restart, etc. by clicking on the corresponding toolbar buttons. These toolbar buttons are identical to the ones described in Section 14.3.1 and won't be examined further here.

14.3.2 BPE Monitoring

Much like the SXMB_MONI transaction used to monitor the IE, the BPE also has its own monitoring transaction: SXMB_MONI_BPE. Figure 14.31 shows the initial screen of this transaction. From this main page, you can perform generic searches for integration processes, or directed searches based upon a particular message (type). Most of the time, you'll want to direct your searches using a particular message type. That way, you can trace a message from the point of receipt through the workflow and beyond.

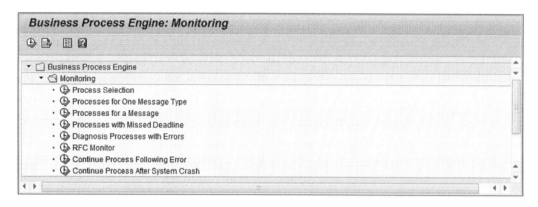

Figure 14.31: BPE Monitoring in Transaction SXMB_MONI_BPE © Copyright 2010. SAP AG. All rights reserved

Figure 14.32 shows the selection screen for the *Processes for One Message Type* selection option (see Figure 14.31). Here, you can enter the abstract interface name/namespace that triggers the process, as well as a selection variant, and selection period. If we selected the *Processes for a Message* selection option, we would have also had the option of specifying a message ID to narrow down the search even further. In either case, you can initiate the search by clicking on the *Execute* button.

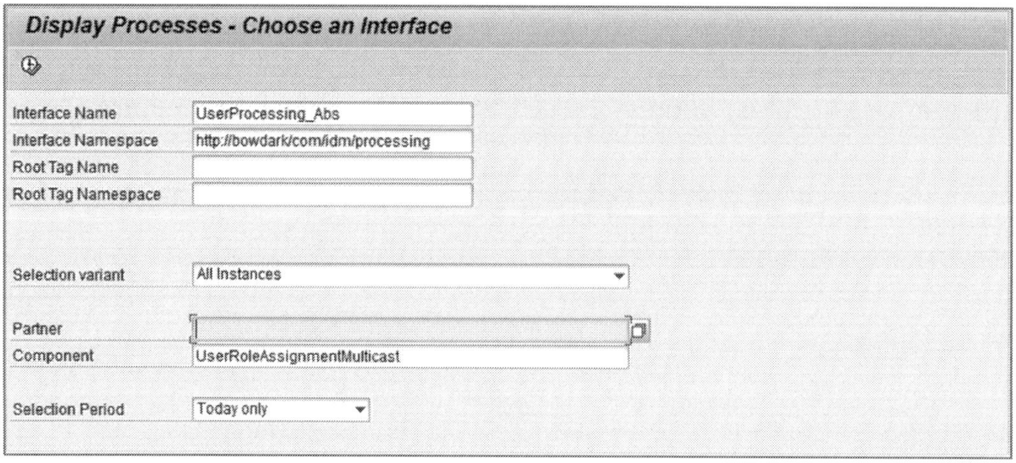

Figure 14.32: Searching for Integration Processes by Interface © Copyright 2010. SAP AG. All rights reserved

Figure 14.33 depicts the results list that is displayed if the system finds matching workflow instances. You can drill down further for a particular workflow instance by selecting it in the results list and clicking on the *Display*

Workflow Log (▓) toolbar button. This will open up the familiar *Workflow Log* screen shown in Figure 14.34[104].

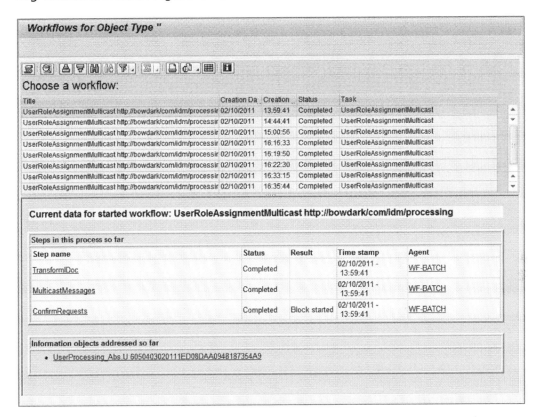

Figure 14.33: Searching for Integration Processes © Copyright 2010. SAP AG. All rights reserved

---

[104] Well, it's familiar if you happen to have experience developing workflows using SAP Business Workflow.

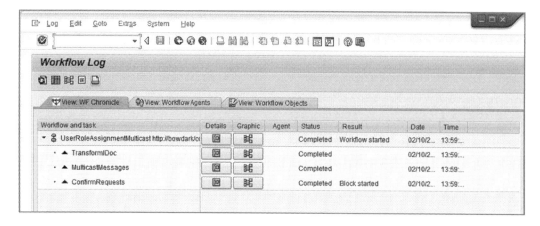

Figure 14.34: Viewing the Workflow Log (Part 1) © Copyright 2010. SAP AG. All rights reserved

From the *Workflow Log* screen shown in Figure 14.34, you can drill down even further to view log details by selecting the *List with Technical Details* (▦) and *Graphical Workflow Log* (▦) buttons in the toolbar, respectively. In the former case, you'll be routed to a detailed listing screen like the one shown in Figure 14.35. Otherwise, you'll end up on a graphical overview screen like the one shown in Figure 14.36. In either case, you can use the provided functions to see a step-by-step overview of the process flow, the values of various container elements, and so on. You can find more information about each of these functions in the online help documentation underneath the section entitled *Monitoring Integration Processes* (SAP AG).

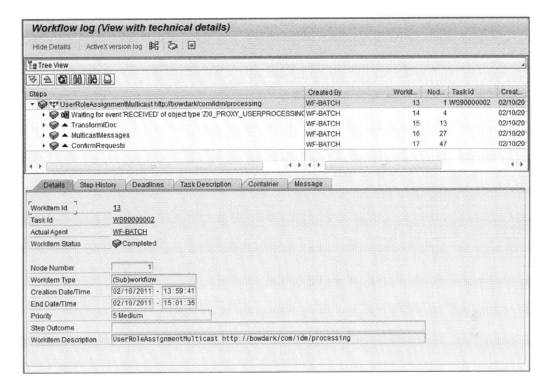

*Figure 14.35: Viewing the Workflow Log (Part 2) © Copyright 2010. SAP AG.
All rights reserved*

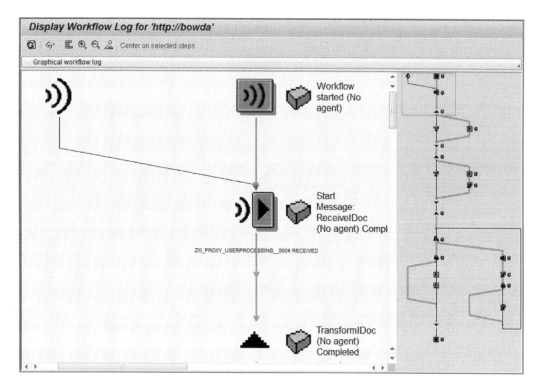

Figure 14.36: Viewing the Workflow Log (Part 3) © Copyright 2010. SAP AG. All rights reserved

14.3.3 IDoc Adapter Monitoring

Another useful monitoring tool included on the ABAP stack is the IDoc adapter monitor which is available in transaction IDX5. If you are familiar with ALE monitoring transactions such as WE05, then you should feel right at home with this transaction as it has a similar look-and-feel (see Figure 14.37). Figure 14.38 shows the results screen that is displayed whenever the IDoc adapter monitor finds IDocs that match the given selection criteria. From this screen, you can double-click on a message to be taken directly to the message entry in transaction SXI_MONITOR. You can also use the extended toolbar functions to trace the IDoc to/from the backend ALE system.

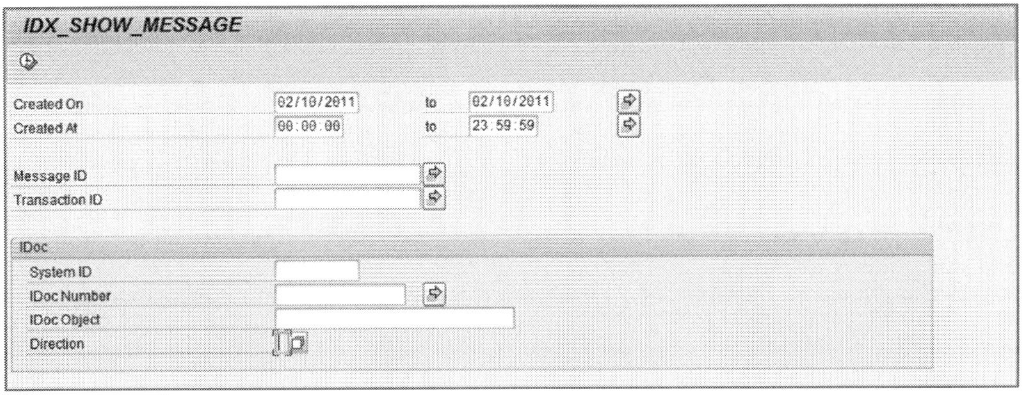

Figure 14.37: Searching for IDocs in Transaction IDX5 (Part 1) © Copyright 2010. SAP AG. All rights reserved

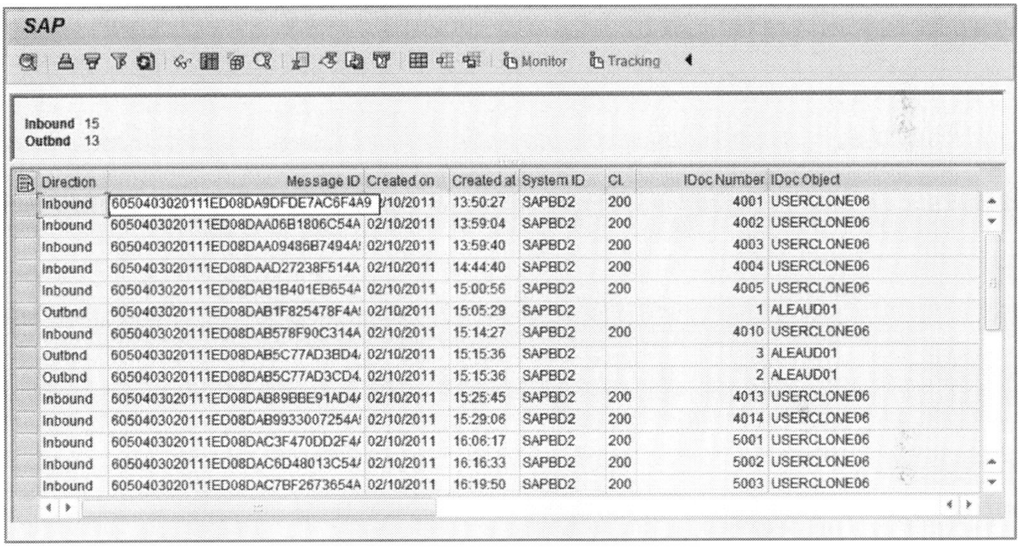

Figure 14.38: Searching for IDocs in Transaction IDX5 (Part 2) © Copyright 2010. SAP AG. All rights reserved

14.4 RFC Monitoring

Underneath the hood, PI utilizes various flavors of remote function call (RFC) technology to enable system-to-system connectivity, queue-based processing, and more. While such technical plumbing issues are usually managed by Basis personnel, it is useful to at least be aware of some of the monitoring tools available so that you can identify messages that get stuck along the way. In the upcoming sections, we'll briefly consider these tools.

14.4.1 Verifying Connections

In order to execute an RFC call within an ABAP context, you must reference an *RFC destination*. This destination provides the ABAP runtime environment with the connection details it needs to be able to connect to a remote service provider. Internally, PI maintains several RFC destinations to enable connectivity between distributed messaging components. Furthermore, the IDoc adapter also uses RFC destinations to send IDoc messages to backend systems.

If you encounter or suspect a connectivity problem with any of these RFC destinations, you can perform connectivity tests using transaction SM59. Here, you simply locate the target destination in the list of available connections and double-click on it (see Figure 14.39). This will bring you to the destination maintenance screen shown in Figure 14.40. From here, you can perform a connectivity test by clicking on the *Connection Test* button. You can also verify security settings by selecting the menu option *Utilities* → *Test* → *Authorization Test*.

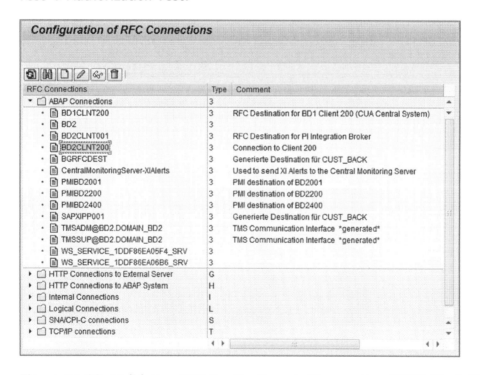

Figure 14.39: Validating RFC Destinations in Transaction SM59 (Part 1)

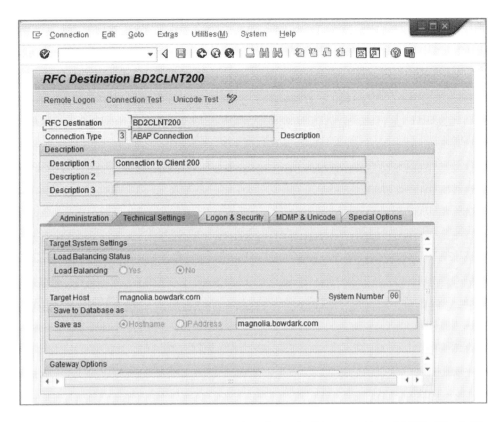

Figure 14.40: Validating RFC Destinations in Transaction SM59 (Part 2)
© Copyright 2010. SAP AG. All rights reserved

14.4.2   tRFC Monitoring

Conceptually speaking, the RFC protocol comes in several different flavors. Besides the default synchronous RFC (sRFC) protocol, you also have the option of implementing transactional asynchronous calls using the transactional RFC (tRFC) protocol. In this case, the system will ensure that a message is delivered exactly once to its final destination. Thus, if that backend system is unavailable, the system will queue up the request until such a time as it can be delivered successfully.

One of the more prominent use cases for the tRFC protocol is in ALE IDoc processing. Here, the ALE processing layer (and, by extension, the PI IDoc adapter) utilizes the tRFC protocol to ensure reliable delivery of IDoc messages. Most of the time, the RFC communication layer within the AS ABAP is so robust that you hardly even realize any of this is going on behind the scenes. However, if you experience an outage in a backend system that you are communicating with using IDocs, then tRFC monitoring becomes something of a concern.

For the most part, you'll find all the tools you need to monitor tRFC processing inside transaction SM58. Figure 14.41 shows the selection screen that you can use to look for tRFC transactions. Once you specify your desired selection criteria, you can perform the lookup by clicking on the *Execute* button. This will bring you to the transaction entry screen shown in Figure 14.42. From here, you can access the functions in the *Edit* menu to view, execute[105], debug, and delete individual tRFC transactions.

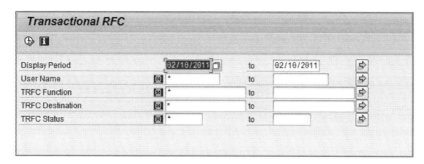

Figure 14.41: Searching for tRFC LUWs in Transaction SM58 © Copyright 2010. SAP AG. All rights reserved

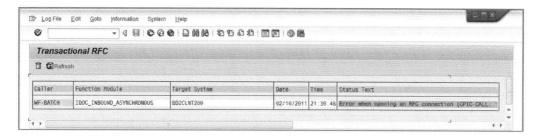

Figure 14.42: Performing tRFC Monitoring in Transaction SM58 © Copyright 2010. SAP AG. All rights reserved

14.4.3   qRFC Monitoring

The tRFC protocol is useful in situations where you need to ensure the delivery of a message. However, one thing the tRFC protocol doesn't do is guarantee that a series of transactions are processed in a particular order. In terms of quality of service, we're talking about *exactly once in order* (EOIO)

---

[105] You can automate the reprocessing of multiple tRFC transactions using SAP standard report program RSARFCEX.

delivery. Within an ABAP context, such functionality is realized using queued RFC (qRFC) protocol.

In order to implement EOIO processing, the qRFC protocol serializes messages through a series of qRFC queues which come in two distinct varieties:

> **Outbound Queues**
> Outbound queues are used to serialize messages that are being sent to an external RFC provider.

> **Inbound Queues**
> Inbound queues are used for internal queue-based processing within the AS ABAP.

Internally, PI uses both types of queues to process messages[106]. You can monitor these queues using transactions SMQ1 and SMQ2, respectively. For more information about these monitoring tools, consult the online help documentation underneath the section entitled *qRFC Administration* (SAP AG).

14.5   System Monitoring with NWA and CCMS

So far, our evaluation of monitoring tools has been limited to those tools which monitor various messaging components. However, in order to implement a holistic monitoring infrastructure, you also require tools that monitor the health of the PI system as a whole. For example, you need tools to monitor disk space, database connectivity, etc. For these tasks, you can enlist the help of the *SAP NetWeaver Administrator* (NWA) and the *Computing Center Management System* (CCMS).

Both the NWA and CCMS provide you with a series of functions for monitoring various technical and application-level components within the AS ABAP and AS Java application servers. While an in-depth discussion on these tools is beyond the scope of this book, you can find detailed information in the online help documentation underneath the sections entitled *SAP NetWeaver Administrator* (SAP AG) and *Monitoring in the CCMS* (SAP AG),

---

[106] You can see a list of standard queues utilized by PI by opening up transaction SXMB_ADM and double-clicking on the *Manage Queues* node within the *Administration* submenu. Here, you'll see the queue prefix names for the various queue types used for processing messages.

respectively. Also, you can find out about some newer PI-centric monitoring features in the NWA in the section entitled *PI Monitoring Using the SAP NetWeaver Administrator* (SAP AG).

14.6   PI Monitoring with SAP Solution Manager

A common complaint among PI practitioners is that the provided monitoring functions are scattered across too many tools. Rather than having to go search for errors in each of these tools, their preference is to have a centralized dashboard that can provide them with an overview of the system at a glance. As it turns out, these kinds of dashboards are readily available in the SAP Solution Manager tool.

Within Solution Manager, not only can you monitor the health of individual technical components, you also have the option of performing *business process monitoring*. Here, you can monitor individual interface scenarios and drill in to investigate errors as needed. While an in-depth coverage of these functions is beyond the scope of this book, you can find some useful information to get you started in the SDN presentation entitled *Monitoring in Enhancement Package 1 for SAP NetWeaver PI 7.1* (Dinev).

14.7   Summary

In this chapter, you learned about some of the core monitoring tools that you can use to monitor the operations of an SAP NetWeaver PI system. Not only do these tools allow you to interactively search for and troubleshoot errors, they also provide sophisticated alert notification capabilities that can be used to deliver alert messages in a timely manner. Collectively, these tools provide you with everything you need to keep your PI system up and running smoothly.

References

Dinev, V. (n.d.). *Monitoring in Enhancement Package 1 for SAP NetWeaver PI 7.1.* Retrieved February 15, 2011, from SAP Developer Network (SDN): http://www.sdn.sap.com/irj/scn/go/portal/prtroot/docs/library/uuid/d05c14c3-34af-2b10-a1b1-fa2a39e0d2ae

SAP AG. (n.d.). *Alert Management.* Retrieved February 9, 2011, from SAP Help Library: http://help.sap.com/saphelp_nwpi711/helpdata/en/49/4782b737042221e10000000a42189d/frameset.htm

SAP AG. (n.d.). *Creating Alert Categories.* Retrieved February 9, 2011, from SAP Help Library: http://help.sap.com/saphelp_nwpi711/helpdata/en/d0/d4b54020c6792ae10000000a155106/frameset.htm

SAP AG. (n.d.). *Index Administration.* Retrieved February 10, 2011, from SAP Help Library: http://help.sap.com/saphelp_nwpi711/helpdata/en/43/6031cee92f5f87e10000000a1553f6/frameset.htm

SAP AG. (n.d.). *Message Search Using Index.* Retrieved February 10, 2011, from SAP Help Library: http://help.sap.com/saphelp_nwpi711/helpdata/en/43/60359ae92f5f87e10000000a1553f6/frameset.htm

SAP AG. (n.d.). *Monitoring in the CCMS.* Retrieved February 10, 2011, from SAP Help Library: http://help.sap.com/saphelp_nwpi711/helpdata/en/49/6272376d3bfa2be10000009b38f8cf/frameset.htm

SAP AG. (n.d.). *Monitoring Integration Processes.* Retrieved February 10, 2011, from SAP Help Library: http://help.sap.com/saphelp_nwpi711/helpdata/en/96/0a2441509fa831e10000000a1550b0/frameset.htm

SAP AG. (n.d.). *PI Monitoring Using the SAP NetWeaver Administrator.* Retrieved February 10, 2011, from SAP Help Library: http://help.sap.com/saphelp_nwpi711/helpdata/en/48/b2b52d7895307be10000000a42189b/frameset.htm

SAP AG. (n.d.). *Process Integration Monitoring.* Retrieved February 4, 2011, from SAP Help Library:
http://help.sap.com/saphelp_nwpi711/helpdata/en/7c/14b5765255e345a9e3f044f1e9bbbf/frameset.htm

SAP AG. (n.d.). *Process Monitoring with PMI (Process Monitoring Infrastructure).* Retrieved February 9, 2011, from SAP Help Library:
http://help.sap.com/saphelp_nwpi711/helpdata/en/a8/a81b0b6473cb49bc34effad6eab13b/frameset.htm

SAP AG. (n.d.). *qRFC Administration.* Retrieved Feburary 10, 2011, from SAP Help Library:
http://help.sap.com/saphelp_nwpi711/helpdata/en/48/9c43f42ab0062fe10000000a42189d/frameset.htm

SAP AG. (n.d.). *SAP NetWeaver Administrator.* Retrieved February 10, 2011, from SAP Help Library:
http://help.sap.com/saphelp_nwpi711/helpdata/en/45/2bdafff14003c3e10000000a1553f6/frameset.htm

SAP AG. (n.d.). *TREX - SAP NetWeaver's Search and Classification Engine.* Retrieved February 10, 2011, from SAP Developer Network (SDN):
http://www.sdn.sap.com/irj/sdn/go/portal/prtroot/docs/library/uuid/00de20e1-6160-2b10-b6ab-dedb9d10b8e8

Proxy Programming Concepts

In Chapter 6, you learned about the outside-in approach to service development in which service interfaces defined in the ESR are used as the basis for generating proxy objects in backend SAP systems. These proxy objects provide an abstraction that simplifies the way that services are accessed within application programs. Here, the complexities of XML message parsing, HTTP communications, etc. are handed off to a proxy runtime environment that assumes the responsibility for message delivery.

For the most part, proxy calls are processed within SAP NetWeaver PI just like any other interface. Of course, there are several steps that must be taken on the backend systems to make all this happen. In this appendix, we'll look at these steps from a developer's perspective.

After reading this appendix, you will be able to:

- ❖ Understand basic proxy programming concepts.
- ❖ Generate and implement proxy objects in ABAP.
- ❖ Execute proxy calls within ABAP programs.

A.1   Conceptual Overview

When you get right down to it, interface programming is not particularly hard; it's just tedious. From parsing messages in XML to navigating between various layers of communication protocols, there's a lot of moving parts for programmers to keep track of. Fortunately, much of this tedium can be avoided by introducing a layer of abstraction between the application program layer and the communications layer. Programmers can then access this intermediate layer using a specialized object called a *proxy object*.

From a programmer's perspective, proxy objects behave just like any normal programming object. Indeed, in terms of the call semantics, the call to a proxy object looks like a typical method call. However, behind the scenes, it's a different story. Internally, proxy objects transparently take care of serializing a method call, calling the remote service, and so on. Similarly, going in the other direction, the proxy layer will take care of converting an external server call into a local method call for server-side processing.

Through the years, the proxy approach to interface processing has emerged over and over again as a means for implementing distributed method calls. And, beginning with the SAP NetWeaver 2004 release, a new flavor of proxy objects was introduced to enable direct communications between backend SAP systems and PI using the native XI protocol. In the upcoming sections, we'll show you how to program with proxies in SAP NetWeaver.

A.2   Proxy Programming with SAP NetWeaver

As mentioned in the previous section, support for proxy-based programming was added in the SAP NetWeaver 2004 release. Here, both the AS ABAP and AS Java were enhanced with a proxy runtime environment that can communicate directly with the PI Integration Server using the native XI protocol. This makes it possible for backend systems based upon these server types (most notably SAP Business Suite systems such as SAP ECC, SAP CRM, and so on) to communicate directly with PI.

Figure A.1 illustrates the positioning of this proxy runtime environment on both the AS ABAP and AS Java application server types. As you can see, there are several layers involved in the process of a proxy call in ABAP or Java. The process begins with a proxy object call within an application program (e.g. an ABAP report program, Web Dynpro for Java application, and so on). From there, the proxy objects work in conjunction with the corresponding proxy runtime environment to convert the proxy method call into an interface call. At the bottom of the stack, you can see that the low-level messaging operations are handled exclusively by the runtime environment which communicates directly with the PI Integration Server using the native XI protocol.

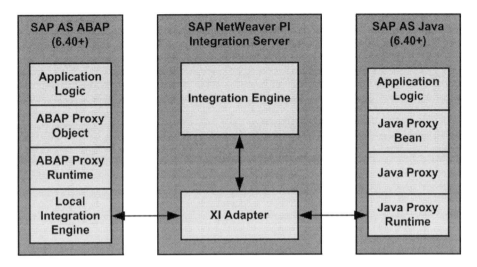

Figure A.1: Understanding the Proxy Runtime Environment

From a developer's perspective, proxy objects are *generated objects* that are created using specialized proxy generation tools included with the ABAP Workbench and SAP NetWeaver Developer Studio. These tools utilize the metadata from service interface definitions in the ESR as the basis for constructing proxy classes that contain methods whose signatures mirror the format of the request/response messages defined within the service operations.

If you're confused by all this, don't worry. In the next section, we'll show you how all these pieces fit together in the context of a real-live integration scenario based upon ABAP proxy objects.

A.3 Case Study: Proxy Programming in ABAP

In order to understand how proxy programming works a little better, let's take a look at an example of the proxy development process from start to finish. Since most proxy development takes place on the AS ABAP, we'll base our example off of a pair of ABAP-based proxies: one on the client side and one on the server side. In this contrived example, the server proxy will report the current system time back to the client proxy. Of course, in the real-world, you will rarely encounter proxy-to-proxy scenarios like this. Instead, you may see a client proxy paired up with a JDBC update, a flat file converted into a server proxy call, and so on.

A.3.1   Developing the Client Proxy

Since proxy objects are generated off of a service interface description, the first step in the proxy development process is the specification of an outbound service interface in the ESR. Here, you can define the structure of the messages being exchanged using message types in the ESR, or you can use external definitions based on XML Schema, etc. For the purposes of our example, we have laid out the service interface as shown in Figure A.2, Figure A.3, and Figure A.4, respectively.

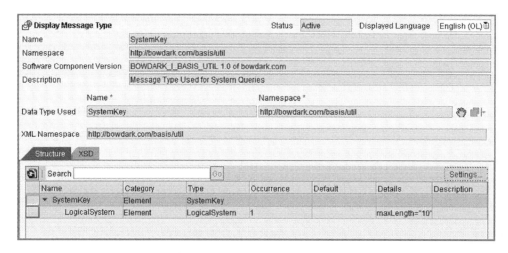

Figure A.2: Defining the Request Message Type in the ESR © Copyright 2010. SAP AG. All rights reserved

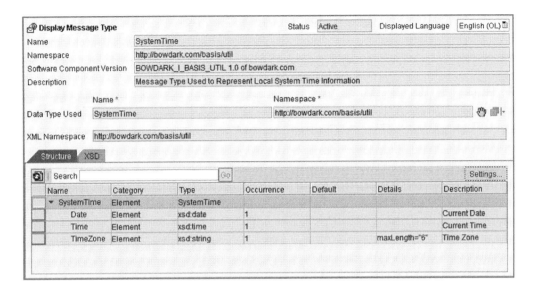

Figure A.3: Defining the Response Message Type in the ESR © Copyright 2010. SAP AG. All rights reserved

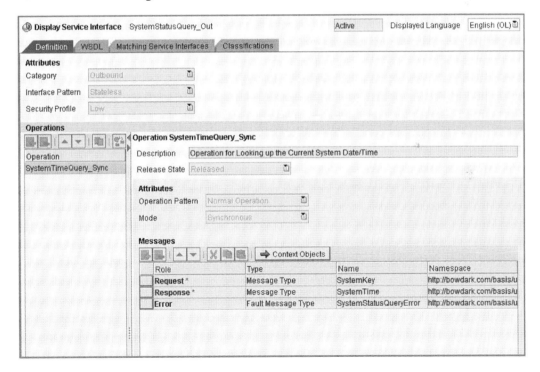

Figure A.4: Defining the Outbound Service Interface for the Client Proxy © Copyright 2010. SAP AG. All rights reserved

Once the outbound service interface is activated in the ESR, you can use it as the basis for generating a client proxy in a backend AS ABAP system using transaction SPROXY[107]. As you can see in Figure A.5, this transaction provides you with a view of repository objects defined within the ESR. To create a client proxy, you must locate your outbound service interface and perform the following steps:

1. To begin, right-click on the target outbound service interface and select the *Create Proxy* menu option (see Figure A.5).

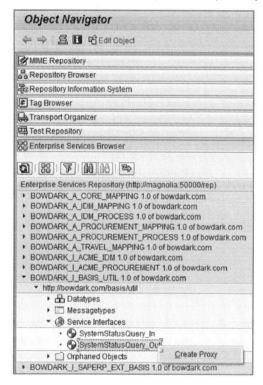

Figure A.5: Creating a Client Proxy in Transaction SPROXY (Part 1)
© *Copyright 2010. SAP AG. All rights reserved*

---

[107] Of course, this backend system must be hooked up to communicate with the ESR in which the service interface is defined. You can verify the settings for your backend system by clicking on the *Connection Test* ( ) button in transaction SPROXY and following the instructions in the *Connection Test* dialog box. Or, better yet, get your local Basis staff to take a look at it!

2. This will open up the proxy generation wizard shown in Figure A.6. Here, you must select an ABAP development package and CTS request to keep track of the ABAP development objects created during the generation process. You also have the option of specify a naming prefix for the generated development objects in the *Prefix* input field (see Figure A.6).

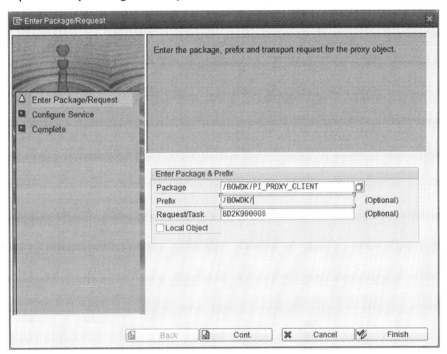

Figure A.6: Creating a Client Proxy in Transaction SPROXY (Part 2)

3. After you have specified the target package/CTS request, you can kick off the proxy generation process by clicking on the *Finish* button (see Figure A.6).

4. Assuming all goes well, you will end up on the service consumer screen shown in Figure A.7. You can activate the client proxy by clicking on the *Activate* button in the toolbar (see Figure A.8).

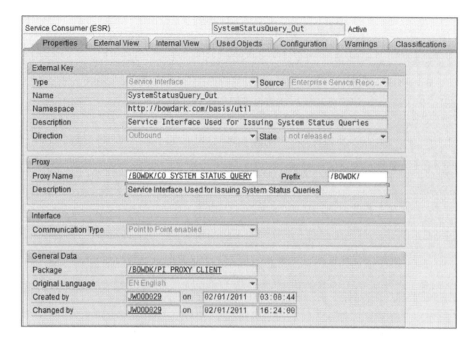

Figure A.7: Viewing a Client Proxy in Transaction SPROXY © Copyright 2010. SAP AG. All rights reserved

Figure A.8: Activating a Client Proxy in Transaction SPROXY © Copyright 2010. SAP AG. All rights reserved

During the proxy generation process, the system used the WSDL metadata in the outbound service interface to create an ABAP Objects class. You can locate this class in the service consumer screen shown in Figure A.7 by double-clicking on the value in the *Proxy Name* field. As you can see in Figure A.9, this generated class defines methods that emulate the service operations defined in the basis service interface. Naturally, these are the methods that you will use to invoke the client proxy at runtime. We'll see how that part works in Section 0.

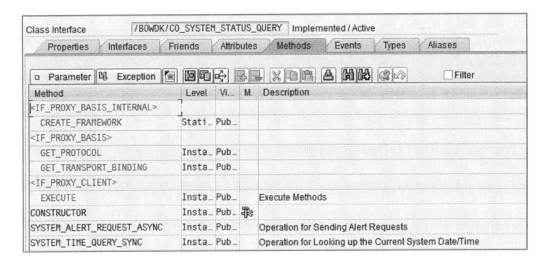

Figure A.9: Viewing a Client Proxy Class in the Class Builder © Copyright 2010. SAP AG. All rights reserved

A.3.2   Developing the Server Proxy

For the most part, you'll find that the process for defining server proxies is almost the same as the one used to define client proxies. The primary difference in this case is that the generated ABAP Objects class defines methods whose implementations are *undefined*. Here, it is up to you as the developer to provide this implementation in whatever way you see fit.

The first step for defining a server proxy is to create an inbound service interface. Here, you can define the format of the request/response messages using data types defined in the ESR or via external definitions based on XML Schema, etc. In our contrived proxy example, we have chosen to define this service interface using the same message types used to define the client proxy (see Figure A.10).

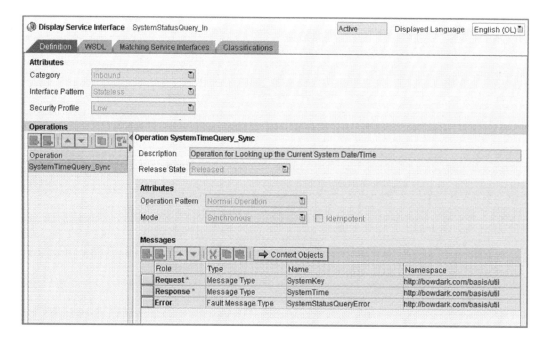

Figure A.10: Defining an Inbound Service Interface for a Server Proxy

After the inbound service interface is defined and activated in the ESR, you can log onto the target backend system and generate the server proxy in transaction SPROXY. Since this process is the same for both client and server proxies, we won't describe it again here. Once the generation process is complete, you will arrive at the service interface screen shown in Figure A.11. Then, after you activate the server proxy, you can navigate to the generated proxy class by double-clicking on the value in the *Provider Class* field (see Figure A.11). This will take you to the Class Builder screen shown in Figure A.12.

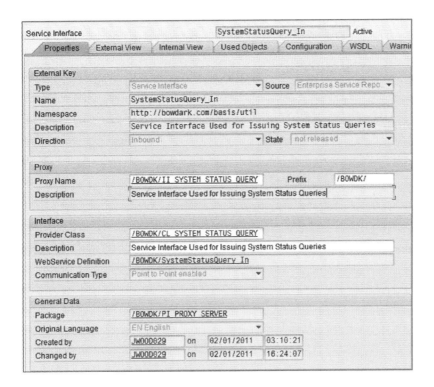

Figure A.11: Viewing a Server Proxy in Transaction SPROXY © Copyright 2010. SAP AG. All rights reserved

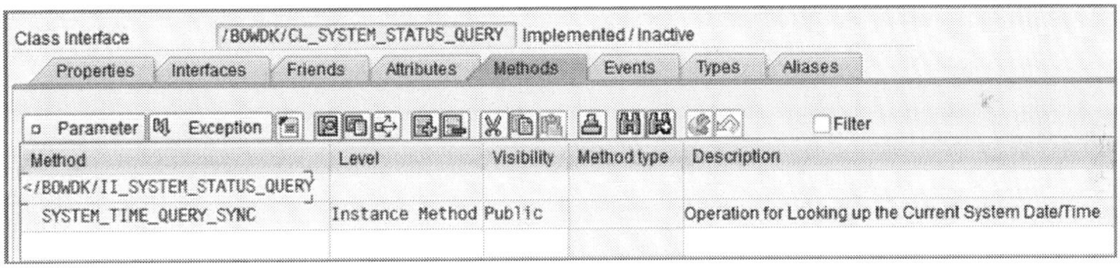

Figure A.12: Editing the Server Proxy Class in the Class Builder © Copyright 2010. SAP AG. All rights reserved

As mentioned earlier, no default implementation is provided for the server proxy methods. Instead, it is up to you as the developer to fill in these blanks. For the purposes of our contrived example, we are simply copying over the current system time stamp into the `OUTPUT` parameter (see Figure A.13). As you can see, the structure the `OUTPUT` parameter mirrors the response message type illustrated in Figure A.3.

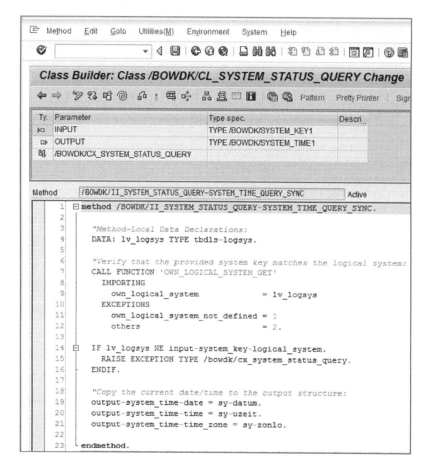

Figure A.13: Implementing a Server Proxy Method in the Class Builder
© Copyright 2010. SAP AG. All rights reserved

A.3.3 Executing the Proxy Call

Now that you have a feel for how to implement proxy objects both on the client side and on the server side, let's take a closer look at how proxy calls are made within an ABAP program. Listing A.1 contains a sample program called /BOWDK/SYNC_PROXY_DEMO that demonstrates how these calls are made. As you can see, the proxy call is basically carried out in two steps:

1. First, the client proxy class (/BOWDK/CO_SYSTEM_STATUS_QUERY), is instantiated using the CREATE OBJECT statement.

2. Then, the proxy method SYSTEM_TIME_QUERY_SYNC() is invoked using the familiar CALL METHOD statement.

```abap
REPORT /bowdk/sync_proxy_demo.

CLASS lcl_main DEFINITION.
  PUBLIC SECTION.
    CLASS-METHODS:
      execute IMPORTING im_logsys TYPE logsys.
ENDCLASS.

CLASS lcl_main IMPLEMENTATION.
  METHOD execute.
    "Method-Local Data Declarations:
    DATA: lo_proxy   TYPE REF TO /bowdk/co_system_status_query,
          ls_output  TYPE /bowdk/system_key1,
          ls_input   TYPE /bowdk/system_time1,
          lo_cust_ex TYPE REF TO /bowdk/cx_system_status_query,
          lo_appl_ex TYPE REF TO cx_ai_application_fault,
          lo_syst_ex TYPE REF TO cx_ai_system_fault,
          lv_message TYPE string.

    TRY.
      "Instantiate the client proxy object:
      CREATE OBJECT lo_proxy.

      "Call the system time lookup method:
      ls_output-system_key-logical_system = im_logsys.

      CALL METHOD lo_proxy->system_time_query_sync
        EXPORTING
          output = ls_output
        IMPORTING
          input  = ls_input.

      "Output the results:
      WRITE: / 'System Time for:',
               ls_output-system_key-logical_system.
      WRITE: / 'Current Date:',
               ls_input-system_time-date MM/DD/YYYY.
      WRITE: /(60) ls_input-system_time-time
               USING EDIT MASK 'Current Time: __:__:__'.
      WRITE: / 'Time Zone:', ls_input-system_time-time_zone.
    CATCH cx_ai_system_fault INTO lo_syst_ex.
      lv_message = lo_syst_ex->get_text( ).
```

```
      MESSAGE lv_message TYPE 'I'.
    CATCH /bowdk/cx_system_status_query INTO lo_cust_ex.
      lv_message = lo_cust_ex->get_text( ).
      MESSAGE lv_message TYPE 'I'.
    CATCH cx_ai_application_fault INTO lo_appl_ex.
      lv_message = lo_appl_ex->get_text( ).
      MESSAGE lv_message TYPE 'I'.
    ENDTRY.
  ENDMETHOD.
ENDCLASS.

PARAMETERS:
  p_logsys TYPE logsys.

START-OF-SELECTION.
  "Defer processing to the main method:
  CALL METHOD lcl_main=>execute( p_logsys ).
```

Listing A.1: Executing a Proxy Call from ABAP

As you can see in Listing A.1, the INPUT and OUTPUT parameters for the proxy method are defined in terms of the request/response message types shown in Figure A.2 and Figure A.3, respectively. Depending upon the format of the XML schema types in the ESR, these generated structure types may be nested arbitrarily deep with complex child components (e.g. complex structures, table types, and so on). Similarly, if the service interface defines fault messages, then the proxy method will be declared to throw class-based exceptions based upon generated ABAP Objects exception classes.

> **Note**
>
> In the case of our contrived example, the proxy methods in question are executed synchronously. Of course, it is also possible to define these methods using the asynchronous mode. For the most part, all this is transparent to you as the developer. However, we should point out that you must execute a COMMIT WORK statement after you call the asynchronous proxy method in order to release the message for outbound processing.

A.3.4   Runtime Considerations

At runtime, proxy calls in ABAP are processed internally by the ABAP proxy runtime, which in turn delegates processing to a local instance of the Integration Engine that gets installed on all AS ABAP systems (version

6.40+). Figure A.14 illustrates the processing of a client proxy call in ABAP. As you can see, most of the heavy lifting is performed by the ABAP proxy runtime and the local IE.

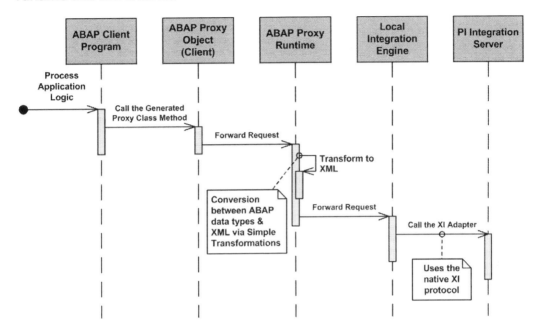

Figure A.14: Understanding the Message Flow for an ABAP Proxy Call

In addition to abstracting the low-level communication details for an interface call, the ABAP proxy runtime also provides you with another valuable feature at runtime: *reliable messaging*. As proxy calls are processed through a local IE, the IE assumes the responsibility for reliably delivering messages on to the PI Integration Server. Thus, if the target PI system is down, you can locate the message in transaction SXMB_MONI and reprocess it just as you would for messages processed within the central PI Integration Engine (see Figure A.15). You can also view the results of inbound proxy calls in the receiver system using this transaction.

Figure A.15: Viewing Proxy Calls in the SXMB_MONITOR Transaction

A.3.5   Configuring Proxy Calls in PI

For the most part, proxy calls are processed just like any other interface. Here, the messages are received and/or sent via the XI adapter deployed on the AS ABAP stack. From there, incoming messages are processed via the Integration Engine as per usual.

New in Enhancement Pack 1

Alternatively, beginning with version 7.11 of SAP NetWeaver PI, you have the option of processing proxy calls directly within the AAE using the SOAP adapter. Among other things, this feature allows you to include proxy calls in integrated configurations which execute exclusively on the AAE. For more information about how this works, check out the SDN article entitled *How-To Set Up the Communication Between ABAP Backend and SOAP Adapter Using XI Protocol* (SAP AG).

A.4   Java Proxy Development Concepts

In prior releases of SAP NetWeaver PI, Java proxies were generated in much the same way that ABAP proxies were; albeit using Java-based development tools. However, with release 7.1 of SAP NetWeaver PI, SAP decided to introduce a new model for Java proxy development based upon the *Java API for XML Web Services* (JAX-WS) API included with Java EE5. For more information about this new model and some insight into the old one, check out the SDN article entitled *Migration Guide for Java Proxies* (Kiefer & Zubev). You can also find a step-by-step development guide in *Developing Enterprise Services for SAP* (Pohl & Peter, 2010).

References

Kiefer, A., & Zubev, A. (n.d.). *Java Proxy Migration Guide.* Retrieved February 18, 2011, from SAP Developer Network (SDN): http://www.sdn.sap.com/irj/scn/index?rid=/library/uuid/508bb504-87cf-2c10-2aaf-f3a5df75e651

Pohl, T., & Peter, M. (2010). *Developing Enterprise Services for SAP.* Boston: SAP PRESS.

SAP AG. (n.d.). *How-To Set Up the Communication Between ABAP Backend and SOAP Adapter Using XI Protocol.* Retrieved February 19, 2011, from SAP Developer Network (SDN): http://www.sdn.sap.com/irj/scn/index?rid=/library/uuid/70066f78-7794-2c10-2e8c-cb967cef407b

Enhancing Enterprise Services Provided by SAP

For the most part, this book has been focused primarily on custom service development using SAP NetWeaver PI. However, in many cases, you may find that you're able to leverage pre-existing services provided by SAP rather than having to create a new interface from scratch.

Oftentimes, the tricky part about leveraging standard interfaces is figuring out how to *enhance* them. For example, an interface might provide 90-95% of what you need, but you may need to tweak a thing or two. In this appendix, we'll show you the proper way to enhance enterprise services delivered by SAP.

After reading this appendix, you will be able to:

❖ Understand the proper way for enhancing enterprise services delivered by SAP.

❖ Enhance data types in the ESR by creating *data type enhancements*.

B.1   Introduction

As part of their on-going SOA initiative, SAP has been working furiously over the course of the past several years to deliver a comprehensive set of enterprise services that can be used to leverage core functionality and services provided with the SAP Business Suite[108]. These services were developed from the ground up using the best practices for enterprise service development described in Chapter 5. As such, they represent a superior choice for developing new integration solutions on top of the SAP Business Suite than legacy technologies such as IDocs and RFCs.

SAP models their enterprise services using the SAP Enterprise Services Metamodel. Among other things, this implies that the service interfaces are well-conceived and thought out. Still, there are times whenever you might want to tweak a thing or two. For example, you might want to pass in a couple of customer-specific fields, etc.

Based upon what you know thus far, you can probably conceive of a couple of ways to implement such enhancements:

> ➢ You could modify the existing service provided by SAP in the ESR (sometimes referred to as a *core modification*).

> ➢ You could copy the service into a customer-based SWCV/namespace and enhance the newly-created duplicate service separately.

However, both of these options can introduce some problems from a maintenance perspective. In the former case, the modifications make it very difficult (if not impossible) to install upgrades provided by SAP. In the latter case, you have the difficult task of trying to figure out how to back port the updates provided by SAP to the service copies. Fortunately, there's a better way.

Within the ESR, you can enhance the structure of the messages passed in a service interface by creating *data type enhancements* (DTEs). DTEs allow you to enhance the data types that make up a message type by adding new elements or attributes. These components are added in such a way that there are not collisions with components added by SAP during an upgrade.

---

[108] You can find detailed, up-to-date information about the set of provided services by logging onto the SAP Enterprise Services Workplace at *http://esworkplace.sap.com*.

As you might expect, this guarantee is realized on a technical level by namespace-qualifying the newly created XML schema components using a customer-defined namespace.

From an implementation perspective, DTEs are used in conjunction with other common SAP enhancement technologies such as append structures and Business Add-Ins (BAdIs) to enable you to pass custom data elements back and forth using the standard SAP services. In the upcoming sections, we'll show you how all these pieces fit together.

B.2　Enhancement Process Overview

For the most part, you'll find that the process of enhancing an enterprise service is more or less the same each time. Here, you must perform the following steps[109]:

1. The first step is to create a customer SWCV in the SLD that will be used to implement the service enhancements. This SWCV must have a dependency created between it and the SWCV that defines the target service provided by SAP. If you can't recall how to create dependencies between SWCVs, refer back to Chapter 4.

2. Next, you must import the customer SWCV into the ESR and create the namespace you will use to perform your custom development. By default, this namespace will also be used as the namespace for the extended XML schema components. However, you can choose to override this default behavior as necessary.

3. Once the SWCV is set up, you can proceed with creating the DTEs that will enhance the data types used to define the signature of the service interface provided by SAP. We'll see how to achieve this in Section 0.

4. After the DTEs are activated, you can use them to enhance the ABAP proxy objects on the backend systems. This is achieved by *generating* the DTEs using transaction SPROXY. During this generation process, the generated ABAP structure types will be enhanced with append structures that contain the custom fields that were added in the DTE.

---

[109] These steps are described in further detail in the *Enterprise Services Enhancement Guide* (SAP AG) provided on the SDN.

5. Finally, you can access the enhanced fields within the enterprise service implementations by implementing BAdIs provided for inbound/outbound processing. These BAdIs are made available for each of the enterprise services supplied by SAP.

In the next section, we'll demonstrate how these steps are performed using a real-live enhancement scenario.

B.3   Case Study: Enhancing an SNC Service

In the previous section, you learned how to enhance an enterprise service from a conceptual perspective. In this section, we'll show you how these steps are implemented in a real-live enhancement scenario. Here, we'll demonstrate the enhancement of a service interface called `ProductActivityNotification_In` that is included as part of the ESR content provided with the SAP® Supplier Network Collaboration (SNC) product in the SAP Business Suite.

B.3.1   Step One: Creating the Custom SWCV

As you learned in Section 0, the first step in the service enhancement process is the creation of a custom SWCV in the SLD that has a dependency relationship to the SWCV that contains the service that is being enhanced. Figure B.16 shows how we have defined a custom SWCV for our SNC enhancement scenario. Here, we've created an installation-time dependency to the `SNC 7.0` SWCV (which coincides with the current release of SAP SNC at the time of this writing).

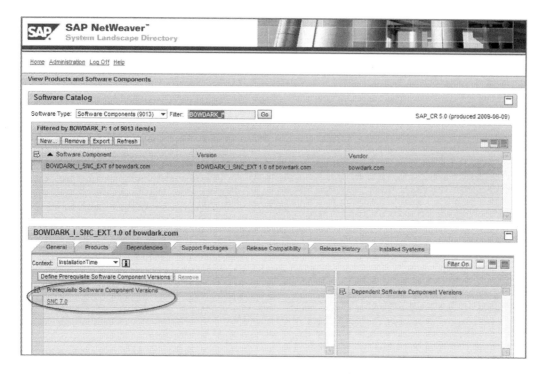

Figure B.16: Creating a Custom SWCV in the SLD © Copyright 2010. SAP AG. All rights reserved

B.3.2   Step Two: Importing the Custom SWCV

After the custom SWCV is created, the next step is to import it into the ESR just as you would any normal SWCV. Here, a custom namespace must be defined as per usual. Figure B.17 shows how we have structured the BOWDARK_I_SNC_EXT software component created for our SNC scenario.

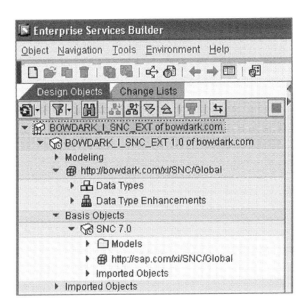

Figure B.17: Importing the Custom SWCV into the ESR © Copyright 2010. SAP AG. All rights reserved

B.3.3   Step Three: Creating the Data Type Enhancement

After the custom SWCV is in place, the next step is to create one or more DTEs to enhance the structure of the request message defined within the `ProductActivityNotification_In` service (message type `ProductActivityNotification` in this case). This can be achieved by right-clicking on the target namespace and selecting the *New* menu option. Then, in the *Create Object* dialog box shown in Figure B.18 provide a name[110] for the DTE and click on the *Create* button.

---

[110] See the SAP NetWeaver How-To Guide *PI Best Practices: Naming Conventions* (SAP AG) for naming conventions.

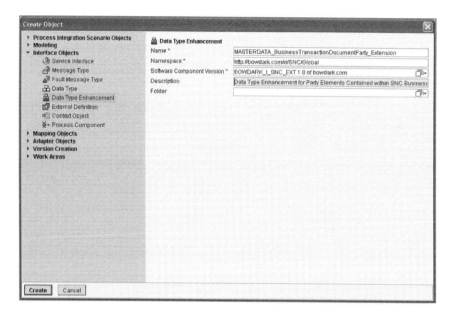

Figure B.18: Creating a DTE in the ESR (Part 2) © Copyright 2010. SAP AG.
All rights reserved

Figure B.19 shows the DTE editor screen within the ES Builder. For the purposes of this demonstration, let's assume that we're enhancing the `MASTERDATA_BusinessTransactionDocumentParty` data type[111] to include contact information (e.g. telephone number, e-mail, etc.) for business partners included in a product activity notification message. Of course, we could have enhanced *any* of the data types used within the `ProductActivityNotification` message type. In any case, besides the definition of the custom XML schema components, there are two additional attributes that we must configure:

> ➢ In the *Data Type Enhancement* field, you must reference the SAP standard data type that you wish to enhance. Here, you can only reference types that are defined in underlying SWCVs of the custom SWCV.

> ➢ In the *XML Namespace* field, you can define the namespace used to qualify the custom XML schema components. As mentioned earlier,

---

[111] Keep in mind that many of these data types may be reused in other enterprise services. You can click on the *Where-Used List* button ( ) in the toolbar to evaluate these dependencies.

this value is defaulted from the ESR namespace in which the DTE is defined.

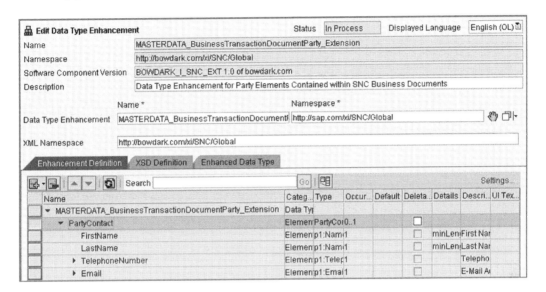

Figure B.19: Editing a DTE in the ES Builder Tool © Copyright 2010. SAP AG. All rights reserved

As you can see in Figure B.19, the actual XML schema components are added to the DTE using the same editor tools/functions provided in the normal data type editor. This implies that you can define the components in terms of core XML Schema types, or custom types defined within the ESR. Figure B.20 shows the completed enhanced data type whenever we have finished adding the custom components.

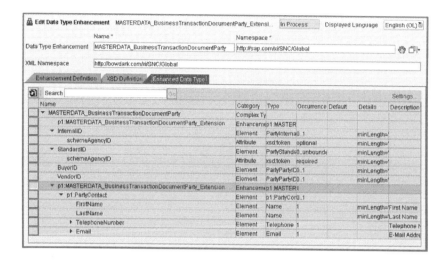

Figure B.20: Viewing the Enhanced Data Type in the DTE Editor © *Copyright 2010. SAP AG. All rights reserved*

B.3.4   Step Four: Generating the DTE in SNC

Once the DTE is saved and activated, we can use it to enhance the service implementation in the backend SNC system by executing transaction SPROXY. This will open up the *Object Navigator* screen shown in Figure B.21. From here, we can generate the DTE by right-clicking on it and selecting the *Create Proxy* menu option (see Figure B.21).

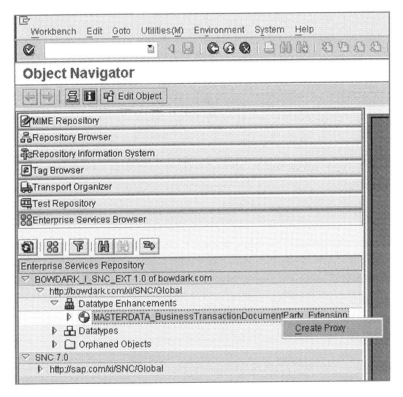

*Figure B.21: Enhancing the Proxy Object in the Backend SNC System ©
Copyright 2010. SAP AG. All rights reserved*

This will open up a proxy generation wizard that guides you through the
generation process. To navigate through this wizard, perform the following
steps:

1. At the *Enter Package/Request* step, you must select an ABAP
   development package and CTS transport request to keep track of
   the ABAP development objects created during the generation
   process (see Figure B.22). You also have the option of specifying a
   naming prefix for the generated objects in the *Prefix* input field.
   Click the *Continue* button to proceed.

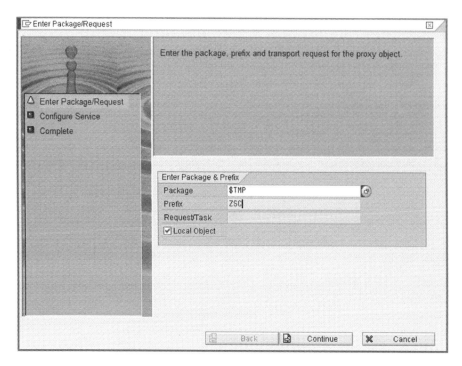

Figure B.22: Generating a DTE Using SPROXY (Part 1)

2. At the *Complete* step, simply click on the *Complete* button to kick off the proxy generation process (see Figure B.23).

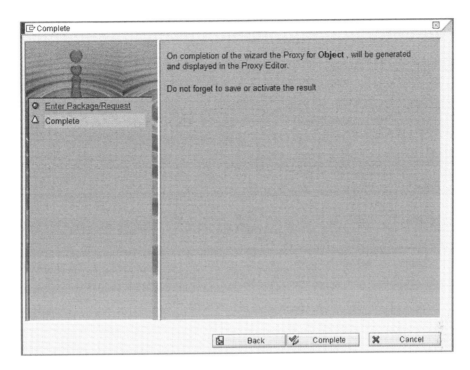

Figure B.23: Generating a DTE Using SPROXY (Part 2)
© Copyright 2010. SAP AG. All rights reserved

3. Assuming all goes well, the DTE will generate without errors and you will end up at the *Data Type Enhancement* screen shown in Figure B.24.

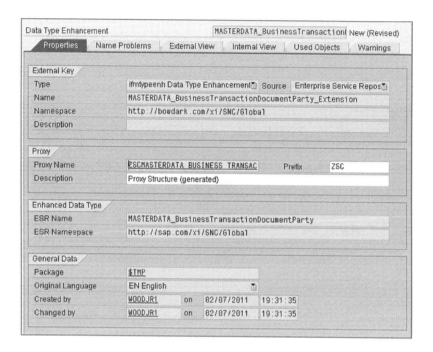

Figure B.24: Generating a DTE Using SPROXY (Part 3)

4. Finally, click on the *Activate* button ( ) in the toolbar to activate the DTE and apply the updates to the proxy object.

Behind the scenes, the proxy generator will evaluate the metadata contained within the selected DTE to determine how it should go and update the standard data type delivered by SAP. You can view the updates it has made by viewing the standard data type in transaction SPROXY. For example, in Figure B.25, you can see how the custom fields from the DTE were added to the MASTERDATA_BusinessTransactionDocumentParty data type. As you can see, the fields were added to the underlying structure type via an append structure[112] in the ABAP Dictionary – see Figure B.26. Ultimately, you'll see these changes reflected in the signature of provider method in the ABAP proxy class (method EXECUTE_ASYNCHRONOUS() of class /SCA/CL_BIF_PROACT_IN in this case).

---

[112] For more information about append structures, check out the online help documentation underneath the section entitled *Append Structures* (SAP AG).

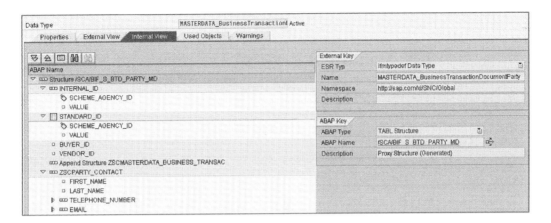

Figure B.25: Viewing the Enhanced Fields in the Standard Data Type © Copyright 2010. SAP AG. All rights reserved

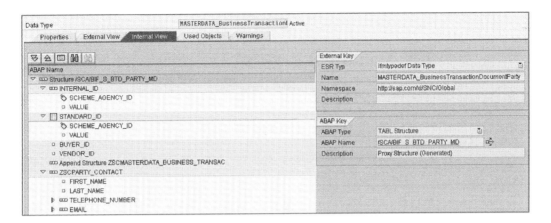

Figure B.26: Viewing the Append Structure in the ABAP Dictionary © Copyright 2010. SAP AG. All rights reserved

B.3.5   Step Five: Implementing the BAdI

The last step in the service enhancement process is the implementation of a BAdI that can be used to copy the enhancement fields from the XML into the native data structures used to post the update (or vice versa for outbound service interfaces). For example, in our SNC scenario, we can use the `/SCMB/BIF_I_PROACT` BAdI to copy over the data before it is processed internally. Here, the BAdI interface defines a method called `BEFORE_CONVERSION()` that can be used for this purpose.

In most cases, you should be able to locate the BAdI you're looking for very easily by digging around a little bit in the surrounding code. Alternatively, a quick search on the SAP SDN will usually help you find what you're looking for.

References

SAP AG. (n.d.). *Append Structures.* Retrieved February 17, 2011, from SAP Help Library:
http://help.sap.com/saphelp_nwpi71/helpdata/EN/cf/21eb61446011d189700
000e8322d00/frameset.htm

SAP AG. (n.d.). *Enterprise Services Enhancement Guide.* Retrieved February 17, 2011, from SAP Developer Network (SDN):
https://www.sdn.sap.com/irj/sdn/go/portal/prtroot/docs/library/uuid/c0bb56
87-00b2-2a10-ed8f-c9af69942e5d

SAP AG. (n.d.). *PI Best Practices: Naming Conventions.* Retrieved February 17, 2011, from SAP Developer Network (SDN):
http://www.sdn.sap.com/irj/scn/go/portal/prtroot/docs/library/uuid/40a66d0
e-fe5e-2c10-8a85-e418b59ab36a?QuickLink=index&overridelayout=true

Collecting Mapping Requirements

As a middleware developer, one of the more challenging tasks you will encounter is figuring out how to map between different message types. Here, you must work with business analysts and developers familiar with both systems to determine how to match up corresponding elements, etc.

While there are no shortcuts around this difficult task, there are steps you can take during the requirements gathering process that can help you avoid unforeseen complications during the implementation of mapping programs. In this appendix, we will show you some tips for collecting mapping requirements.

After reading this appendix, you will be able to:

- ❖ Adopt a consistent process for collecting mapping requirements.
- ❖ Capture mapping rules in a format that simplifies the mapping development process.

C.1   Introduction

As a middleware developer, you will typically find yourself in the middle of a lot of things. At design time, you may find yourself playing the role of mediator; helping analysts on both sides of an interface scenario communicate with one another by eliminating technical barriers. Normally, this is a two step process:

1. First, your expertise may be needed to help business analysts/developers understand which fields in a message correspond with screen and/or database fields in the backend system. This is especially the case whenever the message types are encoded using XML.

2. Then, once the messages on either side of the exchange are well understood, you will have to work with both teams to iron out rules for determining how to map fields from the source message to fields in the target message.

One way to initiate this dialog is to create a mapping spreadsheet that lays out the mapping rules in a visual manner. This document can then be edited collaboratively by business analysts and IT resources involved in the development of the interface. In the next section, we'll show you how these spreadsheets are organized.

C.2   Creating a Mapping Spreadsheet

In order to capture requirements on both sides of the message exchange, mapping spreadsheets need to be broken up into at least three sections:

➢ On the left-hand side of the spreadsheet, you want to identify all of the elements/attributes from the source message type that are used within the mapping scenario.

➢ On the right-hand side of the spreadsheet, you want to identify all of the elements/attributes that will be mapped in the target message type.

➢ In the middle, you can capture any non-standard transformation rules that bind source and target fields together.

Figure C.27 depicts a mapping spreadsheet that we use to capture mapping requirements[113].

	Source Message Type: PORDCR1.PORDCR102							Target Message Type: PurchaseOrder				
#	Source Element	Occurrences	Data Type	Size	Description	Default Value or Mapping	Rules	Target Element	Occurrences	Data Type	Size	Description
1	\PORDCR102\E1PORDCR1\E1BPMEPOHEADER	1						\PurchaseOrder	1			
2	\PORDCR102\E1PORDCR1\E1BPMEPOHEADER\PO_NUMBER	1	CHAR	10	PO Number			\PurchaseOrder\PONumber	1	xsd:token	35	
3						Current System Time		\PurchaseOrder\CreationDate	1	xsd:dateTime		
4	\PORDCR102\E1PORDCR1\E1BPMEPOHEADER\VENDOR	1	CHAR	10	Vendor Number			\PurchaseOrder\VendorID	1	xsd:token	10	
5								\PurchaseOrder\VendorName	0 or 1	xsd:string	60	
6	\PORDCR102\E1PORDCR1\E1BPMEPOTEXTHEADER[1]\TEXT_LINE	0...n	CHAR	132			1	\PurchaseOrder\Notes\Note	1	xsd:string	100	
7	\PORDCR102\E1PORDCR1\E1BPMEPOITEM	1...999999999						\PurchaseOrder\Item	0...n			
8	\PORDCR102\E1PORDCR1\E1BPMEPOHEADER\PO_NUMBER	1	CHAR	10				\PurchaseOrder\Item\PONumber	1	xsd:token	35	
9	\PORDCR102\E1PORDCR1\E1BPMEPOITEM\PO_ITEM	1	CHAR	5				\PurchaseOrder\Item\ItemNumber	1	xsd:positiveInteger		
10	\PORDCR102\E1PORDCR1\E1BPMEPOITEM\MATERIAL	1	CHAR	18				\PurchaseOrder\Item\Product	1	xsd:token	40	
11	\PORDCR102\E1PORDCR1\E1BPMEPOITEM\QUANTITY	1	QUAN	15				\PurchaseOrder\Item\Quantity	1	xsd:decimal	19,6	
12	\PORDCR102\E1PORDCR1\E1BPMEPOITEM\PO_UNIT	1	UNIT	3		EA		\PurchaseOrder\Item\Quantity\@unitCode	N/A	xsd:token	3	
13	\PORDCR102\E1PORDCR1\E1BPMEPOITEM\NET_PRICE	1	DEC	28,9				\PurchaseOrder\Item\NetValue	1	xsd:decimal	19,6	

Figure C.27: Sample Mapping Spreadsheet

Figure C.28 contains a more close-up view of the kinds of details captured for the source/target message types. As you can see, we are providing a complete path to the XML elements/attributes being used so that hierarchical relationships are understood. In addition, we have also provided the cardinalities of the elements (e.g. an element occurs *n* number of times, is optional, etc.) as well as the data types for each of the elements. Finally, we have included a column to provide a description of the field/notes.

Source Message Type: PORDCR1.PORDCR102				
Source Element	**Occurrences**	**Data Type**	**Size**	**Description**
\PORDCR102\E1PORDCR1\E1BPMEPOHEADER	1			
\PORDCR102\E1PORDCR1\E1BPMEPOHEADER\PO_NUMBER	1	CHAR	10	PO Number
\PORDCR102\E1PORDCR1\E1BPMEPOHEADER\VENDOR	1	CHAR	10	Vendor Number
\PORDCR102\E1PORDCR1\E1BPMEPOTEXTHEADER[1]\TEXT_LINE	0...n	CHAR	132	
\PORDCR102\E1PORDCR1\E1BPMEPOITEM	1...999999999			
\PORDCR102\E1PORDCR1\E1BPMEPOHEADER\PO_NUMBER	1	CHAR	10	
\PORDCR102\E1PORDCR1\E1BPMEPOITEM\PO_ITEM	1	CHAR	5	

Figure C.28: Capturing Important Details for Message Mapping

Between the source and target message types, we have included a couple of columns that can be used to define mapping rules (see Figure C.29). These rules could be as simple as a default mapping (e.g., map the current system time or a constant) or as complex as an algorithm. In the latter case, the rule is annotated with a number and a link to a *Rules* tab on the spreadsheet

---

[113] This sample template is available for download at the book's companion site.

that contains more sophisticated rule definitions. For example, if you were to follow the link for rule #1 illustrated in Figure C.29, you would find these instructions: *Copy the first 100 characters from the text segment.*

Description	Default Value or Mapping	Rules	Target Element
			\PurchaseOrder
PO Number			\PurchaseOrder\PONumber
Creation Date			\PurchaseOrder\CreationDate
Vendor Number			\PurchaseOrder\Vendor\ID
Name 1			\PurchaseOrder\Vendor\Name
		1	\PurchaseOrder\Notes\Note
			\PurchaseOrder\Item
			\PurchaseOrder\Item\PONumber
			\PurchaseOrder\Item\ItemNumber
			\PurchaseOrder\Item\Product
			\PurchaseOrder\Item\Quantity
	EA		\PurchaseOrder\Item\Quantity\@unitCode
			\PurchaseOrder\Item\NetValue
	USD		\PurchaseOrder\Item\NetValue\@unitCode

Figure C.29: Capturing Mapping Rules

Normally, the details of mapping documents are entered in reverse order. In other words, you start by filling in all of the required elements/attributes in the target message type. Then, you back track and determine which elements/attributes from the source message type are needed to populate the target fields. Finally, any special mapping rules are specified in the rules columns that are in between the source/target message types.

C.3 Why Requirements Gathering is Important

In some ways, you can think of this mapping spreadsheet as a type of survey that allows each of the key stakeholders to weigh in with their thoughts about mapping requirements. While this may seem tedious (and indeed, it usually is), it is important that you collect as much of this information up front as you can so that you can make informed decisions about mapping strategies at implementation time. For instance, if you know up front that there are a lot of complex rules for field mappings, you might think twice about trying to implement your map using graphical message mappings.

Another thing to keep in mind as you work through these requirements is the amount of data being mapped. If, for example, you notice that there are many repeating elements with multiple field mappings per occurrence, then you can probably guess that you may have performance issues on your hands.

In general, mapping programs are among the most difficult types of programs to maintain. Often, a mapping program contains hundreds or even thousands of rules that are interspersed among line after line of XML parsing code. When you put all that into perspective, you begin to understand how important it is to have as many of the facts as you can up front. Indeed, discovering unforeseen relationships between data elements midstream can prove disastrous for even the simplest of mappings.

Unlike other development efforts in which the only true documentation is the code, we cannot stress enough the importance of having a good design document to lean on for mapping programs. Not only do these requirements documents simplify the development process, they also make it easier to maintain and/or refactor mapping programs as new requirements crop up over time.

Index

S

T

About the Author

James Wood is the founder and principal consultant of Bowdark Consulting, Inc., an SAP NetWeaver consulting and training organization. With over 10 years of experience as a software engineer, James specializes in custom development in the areas of ABAP Objects, Java/J2EE, SAP NetWeaver Process Integration, and the SAP NetWeaver Enterprise Portal.

Before starting Bowdark Consulting, Inc. in 2006, James was an SAP NetWeaver consultant for SAP America, Inc. and IBM Corporation, where he was involved in multiple SAP implementations. He holds a master's degree in software engineering from Texas Tech University. He is also the author of *Object-Oriented Programming with ABAP Objects* (SAP PRESS, 2009) and *ABAP Cookbook* (SAP PRESS, 2010). To learn more about James and the book, please check out his Website at *http://www.bowdark.com*. You can also contact him directly via e-mail at *james.wood@bowdarkconsulting.com*.

Made in the USA
Lexington, KY
05 December 2014